W9-ACE-541

Dislocating Race & Nation

Dislocating Race & Nation

Episodes in
Nineteenth-Century
American Literary Nationalism

ROBERT S. LEVINE

The University of North Carolina Press
Chapel Hill

Set in Arno Pro by Keystone Typesetting, Inc.
Manufactured in the United States of America

The paper in this book meets the guidelines for permanence
and durability of the Committee on Production Guidelines for
Book Longevity of the Council on Library Resources.

The University of North Carolina Press
has been a member of the Green Press Initiative since 2003.

Library of Congress Cataloging-in-Publication Data
Dislocating race and nation : episodes in nineteenth-century
American literary nationalism / Robert S. Levine.
p. cm.
Includes bibliographical references and index.
ISBN 978-0-8078-3226-4 (cloth : alk. paper)
ISBN 978-0-8078-5903-2 (pbk. : alk. paper)
1. American literature—19th century—History and criticism. 2. National
characteristics, American, in literature. 3. Literature and history—United States—
History. 4. Nationalism and literature—United States—History. 5. American
literature—18th century—History and criticism. 6. Literature and society—
History. 7. Race relations in literature. 8. Black nationalism in literature.
I. Levine, Robert S. (Robert Steven), 1953–
PS217.N38D57 2008
810.9'3581—dc22   2008008445

cloth   12 11 10 09 08   5 4 3 2 1
paper   12 11 10 09 08   5 4 3 2 1

To my parents,
JOAN *and* HAROLD LEVINE,
and in memory of
JAY FLIEGELMAN

Contents

Acknowledgments ix

Prologue: Undoings 1

CHAPTER 1. Charles Brockden Brown,
Louisiana, and the Contingencies of Empire 17

CHAPTER 2. Circulating the Nation: David Walker, the Missouri
Compromise, and the Appeals of Black Literary Nationalism 67

CHAPTER 3. Genealogical Fictions:
Melville and Hannah Crafts in Hawthorne's *House* 119

CHAPTER 4. Frederick Douglass's
Hemispheric Nationalism, 1857–1893 179

Epilogue: Undoings Redux 237

Notes 245

Index 303

Acknowledgments

I am pleased to acknowledge the assistance I have received from a number of individuals and institutions. For their helpful responses to sections of the book, my thanks to Jana Argersinger, Philip Barnard, Christopher Castiglia, Russ Castronovo, Mark Kamrath, Caroline Levander, Lee Person, Hollis Robbins, Xiomara Santamarina, Brook Thomas, Stephen Shapiro, and Todd Vogel. My special thanks to Caroline Levander for pushing me to think more hemispherically. I am particularly indebted to Leonard Cassuto and Ivy Goodman for their meticulous readings of the entire manuscript. I am grateful as well to Gregg Crane and John Stauffer, the outside readers for the University of North Carolina Press, whose engaged commentary prompted a substantial final revision.

A fellowship from the Graduate Research Board at the University of Maryland provided much-appreciated time for the writing. I did the bulk of my research at the Library of Congress and University of Maryland's McKeldin Library, and I thank the expert librarians at both institutions.

My arguments in this book developed over time, and earlier versions of sections of some of the chapters were first published as essays. I would like to thank the editors of the following books and journals for the useful forums: *Revising Charles Brockden Brown: Culture, Politics, and Sexuality in the Early Republic* (2004), *In Search of Hannah Crafts: Critical Essays on "The Bondwoman's Narrative"* (2004), *The Black Press: Literary and Historical Essays on the "Other" Front Page* (2001), *African American Review* (2000), *Leviathan* (1999), and *Yearbook of Research in English and American Literature* (1998). I also delivered portions of this book as talks, and I did my best to take advantage of the many provocative questions and comments that came up during the discussions. In particular I would like to thank Robert Caserio at Pennsylvania State University, Christopher Castiglia at Loyola University (and now at Pennsylvania State University), Michael Drexler at Bucknell University, John Ernest at West Virginia University, J. Gerald Kennedy at Louisiana State University, Caroline

Levander at Rice University, Sarah Mesle at Northwestern University, Donald Pease at the Dartmouth College American Studies Institute, and Christina Zwarg at Haverford College.

My warm thanks to Sian Hunter, my wonderfully energetic, supportive, and knowledgeable editor at the University of North Carolina Press. For their editorial labors at the Press, I would also like to thank Nathan McCamic, Ellen Bush, Kathleen Ketterman, and, for his excellent copyediting, Jay Mazzocchi. My thanks as well to Mark Mastromarino for his fine work on the index.

My colleagues and friends at the University of Maryland—John Auchard, Jonathan Auerbach, Ralph Bauer, Vincent Carretta, Neil Fraistat, Theodore Leinwand, Marilee Lindemann, Elizabeth Loizeaux, Carla Peterson, Martha Nell Smith, Mary Helen Washington, and many others— continue to provide the ideal intellectual and collegial community. But none of my work would matter without the sustaining love and dislocating good humor of my wife, Ivy Goodman, and son, Aaron.

This book is dedicated to my parents and in memory of Jay Fliegelman. Jay was my mentor and friend for over thirty years. An inspiration to all who knew him, Jay died much too young at the age of fifty-eight. I like to think that he would have taken pleasure in certain Fliegelmanesque aspects of this work. Jay dedicated his first book to his parents, whom he described as "the two people who, by their example, showed me how to love." Following Jay's lead, I dedicated my own first book to my parents, and for their continuing love and support, I am happy to offer this second dedication.

Dislocating Race & Nation

Prologue

Undoings

Dislocating Race and Nation is about literary practice in a historical mode. It does not set forth a new theory of American literary nationalism; it does not "locate" race and nation or offer any other all-encompassing explanatory paradigm; it does not argue for unbroken connections between the works and periods that are examined in its four main chapters or "episodes." In crucial respects, this book is about undoing paradigms and rethinking historical connections; it seeks to disrupt rather than construct, even as it suggests the reconstructive potential of disruption. Proceeding chronologically, it moves from the late eighteenth century through the nineteenth century and turns to the works under consideration for guidance in thinking about issues currently central to Americanist literary debate, particularly the vexed connections (and disconnections) between race and nation. This book attempts to complicate our understanding of American literary nationalism by emphasizing the conflicted, multiracial, and contingent dimensions of its various articulations. In addition, it attempts to understand selected works in relation to debates of their contemporary moment in ways that, I hope, can help to complicate thinking about race and nation in our own moment. Because I am interested in recovering a sense of the provisional and contested nature of American literary nationalism, I could tendentiously say that this study does not impose an interpretive frame or paradigm upon selected texts but instead permits those texts to speak their truths across the centuries to our current critical moment. But the fact is that this book, like all critical books, is about the needs of the present and is thus shaped by the present, though it makes an effort to explore and to some extent recover aspects of the past. It is a book that is indebted to the historical turn in American literary studies, but, as elaborated below, it is also critical of recent historicist criticism that has too confidently imposed

{1}

fixed narratives on the past—a practice that risks diminishing the otherness or alterity of the past and thus closing off, rather than opening up, the complexities, problematics, and specifics of debates on race and nation both of an earlier age and our own.

According to historical theorist David Scott, the most valuable critical works display a "fidelity to a distinctive mode of historical criticism, one in which the nature of the question the past is called upon to answer is self-consciously shaped by the discontent in the present . . . in order to fashion a future without those sources of dissatisfaction."[1] Though I see great value in such utopian imaginings, I am concerned that Scott and other like-minded critics can be too quick to read the past entirely in terms of the demands and concerns of the present. Much recent historicist criticism emphasizes the implication of writers in the power structures of their culture. But as I will be emphasizing in the pages to follow, writers of the past can be just as knowing about their culture, and just as resistant, as the critics who seek to expose their blind spots, and thus they may make the best sort of allies for critical projects intended to fashion a better future.[2] Writers convey their knowingness in their writings, and *Dislocating Race and Nation* thus pays close attention to form and language, whether of novels, essays, newspaper articles, or diplomatic missives. But equally important to this study is the *unknowingness* that writers convey in their writings, an unknowingness that often takes expression as a resistance to cultural certainties and what I would term a wise bafflement about the meanings, trajectories, and plots of the unfolding narratives of history. In this brief prologue, I want to sketch out the implications of such unknowingness for a literary-historical investigation of race and nation in nineteenth-century U.S. literary and cultural studies. But first a few words about American literary nationalism.

As conventionally understood, American literary nationalism arose at the Revolutionary and post-Revolutionary moment as a crucial component of nation building. Desirous of a national literature that would display the emerging United States as different from and better than monarchical England, cultural leaders called for distinctively "American" writings that would draw on native materials (the landscape, Native Americans, colonial history, and so on), emphasize the nation's republican political culture, and bring a new sense of unity and pride to the postcolonial citizenry. As Eve Kornfeld remarks, American literary nationalists such as Philip Freneau, Noah Webster, Joel Barlow, and Timothy Dwight "hoped to create a vital national culture to unify a heterogenous society, to heal political divisions and quiet political contentiousness, to foster republican citizenship, and to achieve respect for the new state in the eyes of the world."[3] For these cultural nationalists, the emergence of a great national literature would help to ease Americans' anxieties about their cultural inferiority to Great Britain while signaling the new nation's republican values and potentially glorious future. In chapters 1 and 2, I will provide a fuller picture of developments in American literary nationalism, but suffice it to say here that much of what U.S. writers produced over the first several decades of the existence of the new nation struck many observers as imitative of the British tradition. As I will discuss in chapter 3, during the 1840s and 1850s, with the emergence of the writers we now associate with an "American Renaissance," a more confident note was struck by the American literary nationalists associated with New York's Young America literary circle. The story of American literary nationalism thus generally follows a triumphant arc in which we move from the allegedly imitative writings of Freneau and Dwight to the supposedly more authentic "American" writings of Emerson and Whitman (and Hawthorne, Melville, and others) who generally have been regarded, at least since the publication of F. O. Matthiessen's *American Renaissance* (1941), as having fulfilled the goals of the first generation of U.S. literary nationalists.

This story of national literary development and fulfillment has a measure of explanatory power, but as critics over the past several decades have noted, it is limited for a number of reasons. In a very basic way, the historical premises of such a story are invariably anachronistic, the result of the needs, interpretive models, and desires of a relatively small number of literary nationalists being imposed retrospectively and all too neatly on literary debates that were much messier at the time than subsequent literary critics have generally allowed. The story of the emergence of a distinctively American literature also assumes that nonimitative is best (and even possible), when the reality is that most American literary nationalists of the early period saw imitation as a form of literary talent, even genius. Benjamin Franklin was not alone in extolling the value of imitation; and imitation and convention were crucial to much popular writing of the early national and antebellum period, ranging from Susanna Rowson's *Charlotte Temple* (1791, 1794) to Washington Irving's *Sketch-Book* (1820–21) and Harriet Beecher Stowe's *Uncle Tom's Cabin* (1852). When the full array of U.S. writings is taken into account, especially texts by women, it quickly becomes clear that U.S. literature was in conversation with and indebted to a wide range of literatures from across the Atlantic.[4] For many readers, the idea of the "national" may have been of relatively little importance.

The traditional story of American literary nationalism also incorrectly assumes that those in the various sections and regions of the U.S. nation who did value the national had a shared understanding of the nation and its literature. Benjamin Spencer notes in his pioneering *The Quest for Nationality: An American Literary Campaign* (1957) that American literary nationalists "sought to define the nature of nationality in American literature by presenting the full play of conflicting doctrines and, indeed, of counternationalistic currents."[5] This observation implies dialogue and contest, which one can readily discern in various regional, sectional, and ethnic writings of the nineteenth century. But in his overall study, Spencer, as would most subsequent chroniclers, focuses on the "rise" of a consensually acclaimed American literature. True, there were moments of consensus in U.S. culture, particularly in the immediate wake of the Revolution, but for the most part conflict, rather than consensus, helped to define American literary nationalism from the 1790s through the nineteenth century. In chapter 2 in particular, I will be attending to conflicts between northerners and southerners in nationalist and literary-nationalist thinking, and I will consider these conflicts in relation to the debates on the Missouri Territory and to African American literary nationalism (which, like most literary nationalisms in the United States, engaged the nation's founding documents and political ideals). As I will be emphasizing in all of the chapters of this study, literary nationalism, like early formations of U.S. nationalism, remained a site of perpetual struggle in which, as David Waldstreicher underscores, "local, regional, and national identities existed simultaneously, complementing or contesting one another."[6]

Central to the analyses in *Dislocating Race and Nation*, then, will be considerations of the conflicts and debates that were integral to the sometimes competing nationalist ideologies in the developing United States. Conventional accounts of American literary nationalism generally focus on manifesto-like pronouncements that convey a shared national vision. But such pronouncements often emerged from intranational conflict and were calculated efforts to shape the terms of a seeming consensus through the elision of conflict. Arguably, our current understanding of American literary nationalism is indebted to the "victors," those who achieved the greatest rhetorical and material success in laying claim to the nation. Most critics writing in the literary-nationalist mode have ignored southern and minority perspectives, taking it as a given that the North would triumph in the Civil War (for the simple reason that it did). As a result, literary-nationalist imaginings from the South or West—or from African Americans, Native Americans, and other racial and ethnic minorities—have generally been looked at in subordinate relation to or apart from the literary-historical arc of the U.S. literary nationalism that runs, say, from the Connecticut Wits to Emerson and Whitman. In the four main chapters of this book, I consider such noncanonical literary figures as David Walker and Hannah Crafts, as well as noncanonical writings by canonical figures such as Brockden Brown and Frederick Douglass, but my main aspiration is to present not a wholly reconceived canon, in the manner of the multiculturalist revisionism of the past few decades, but a reconceived way of thinking about a wide range of texts in relation to provisional and contested notions of U.S. national identity.[7]

Working against paradigms of an unfolding or rising U.S. literature, I will sketch out a disjunctive history of American literary nationalism that emphasizes the constitutive role of conflict and debate in the development of U.S. historical identities and literary traditions. Rather than presenting an evolutionary history of American literary nationalism, I will be focusing on how writers mobilize or appropriate various discursive formations of the U.S. nation, often in opposition to competing formations. This approach will restore a sense of contingency to the literary history of the United States consistent with the contingency of the nation itself. Accordingly, this book will emphasize how the nation's literature, like the U.S. nation, is continually being reinterpreted, reinvented, and reimagined in response to internal and external pressures. Moreover, as an interracial literary history, it will argue for the importance of attending to the writings of white and black writers in the formation and revision of American literary nationalism, and it will work against the critical binary that typically presents whites as generally complicitous in, and blacks (and other minorities) as generally subversive of, dominant national formations. Inspired by the hemispheric turn in American literary studies, it will also emphasize the importance of geographical fluidity and uncertainty to expressions of American literary nationalism—the importance, that is to say, of the ever-changing borders and boundaries of the continental United States—and thus will consider those multiple and sometimes conflicting traditions of American literary nationalism that have regional, trans-American, and transnational dimensions.[8] Haiti, for instance, has an important place in three of the four chapters in this study, and the role of Haiti is obviously very different from the role of Great Britain in the construction of U.S. literary nationalism.

Traditional accounts of the rise of American literary nationalism have virtually nothing to say about race (or Haiti). Recent theoretical work on literary nationalism, however, has placed race at the center of analysis. Kwame Anthony Appiah has argued that literary nationalists during the eighteenth and nineteenth centuries regarded the nation itself as "the key middle term in understanding the relations between the concept of race and the concept of literature."[9] Inspired by the writings of Johann Gottfried Herder and other Enlightenment theorists, literary nationalists in Europe and the emerging United States looked to literature to express that which was ethnically or racially distinctive about the nation. Assumed as a given in much of the writings by the most culturally influential eighteenth- and nineteenth-century U.S. literary nationalists, race (that is to say, a belief in the white racial identity of the nation) generally remained submerged in their best-known pronouncements. By the mid-nineteenth century, however, as I will be exploring in detail in chapters 3 and 4, literary nationalists and political leaders spoke more explicitly about their desires for a distinctively American literature and nation grounded in an Anglo-Saxon whiteness. These calls had important sources in the political and literary debates of early national culture, when U.S. nationalists sought to differentiate themselves from the French, Spanish, blacks, and Native Americans by emphasizing their blood ties to whites descending from British or Germanic stock. Nationalism in the United States during these early decades thus had both a civic and racial basis. And because many literary nationalists no doubt shared in these sometimes unvoiced assumptions, there can appear to be unbroken trajectories running from the nationalism of the 1790s to the more explicitly racialized nationalism of the mid- to late nineteenth century.[10] But as I will be emphasizing in chapters 1 and 3 of this study, that does not necessarily mean that a "white" (literary) nationalism was uncritically accepted by all whites.

Dislocating Race and Nation brings race to the forefront of its revisionary account of U.S. literary nationalism, providing an interracial history of the construction and disruption of the privileging of whiteness. Disruptions will be central to my analyses, which will put me somewhat at odds with the readings of race and nation that have emerged in recent years under the influence of what has come to be termed "whiteness studies." Although whiteness theorists have usefully disclosed the hitherto barely acknowledged racial underpinnings of nationalist ideologies and cultural formations, they have developed interpretive models that tend to present race and nation as fixed categories. In a searching critique of the most influential critics in this field of inquiry, historian Peter Kolchin calls for "greater attention to historical and geographical context, more precision in delineating the multiple meanings of 'whiteness,' continued effort to move beyond a strictly binary approach to race even while emphasizing the distinctive ways African Americans experienced race and racism, continued exploration of the complex relationship between race and nation, closer consideration of the South's role in shaping American notions of race, more sustained treatment of actual lived relations, and more inclusive examination of the way nonwhites and whites-in-the-making have perceived whiteness (and nonwhiteness)."[11] I will be discussing some white writers who undermined hegemonic models and some black writers who found certain aspects of the national ideology inspiring. By focusing on specific texts and contexts through a case-study method, and by attending to questions of sectionalism and regionalism, I pose a challenge to broad generalizations about a single national logic of white supremacy, showing how white and black writers together participated in the sometimes uneven and not always coherent development of American literary nationalism, even as they experienced race in the United States in fundamentally different ways.

Ultimately, this study seeks to recover a sense of the tenuousness, provisionality, and even fictiveness of the connections between race and nation, which is not to say that these connections did not have a very real basis in various social formations, especially as enforced by law and custom. Etienne Balibar has influentially argued for the centrality of race to constructions of modern nationalisms, underscoring the ways in which the "broad structure of racism" contributes to the production of a "fictive ethnicity around which it [the nation] is organized." It is precisely what Balibar terms fictive or ambiguous identities that I will be exploring in this study, paying particular attention to the "relative indeterminacy" of that which appears to be fixed and settled: the racial or racialized nation. In chapter 3, I take up Balibar's notion that the racial identity of the nation is maintained through a fictional schema of genealogy in order to raise questions about the extent to which such a racial fiction was uncritically accepted in a multiracial culture. By looking at writers who in significant ways loosen the bonds between race and nation and expose what Balibar calls "the imaginary singularity of national formations," I attempt to identify not the few brave writers who posed a challenge to notions of national unity and purity but, in a larger sense, the representativeness of such skeptical and/or anxious thinking.[12] Whiteness may well have been a constitutive component of American literary and cultural nationalism, but its terms were precarious and dependent upon fictions of blood that, as I emphasize in chapter 3, sometimes were apprehended simply as fictions.

Fictive or not, historical trajectories suggesting the implication of literary nationalism in the development of a white U.S. empire (which in some ways U.S. literary nationalism may have helped to produce) cannot be discounted. As Reginald Horsman and many other historians have demonstrated, ideologies of white Anglo-Saxonism were absolutely crucial to the Mexican War and other expansionistic and imperialistic ventures undertaken by the United States during the nineteenth century; as I discuss in chapters 3 and 4, these ideologies had a place in U.S. literary nationalism as well.[13] Especially since the publication of Amy Kaplan and Donald E. Pease's landmark *Cultures of United States Imperialism* (1993), investigations of connections among race, nation, and imperial power in U.S. writings of the nineteenth century (with literature, in Appiah's formulation, as "the middle term" between race and nation) have become a major concern of Americanist literary study.

Although I will be contesting certain aspects of imperialism studies, I fully recognize that the most boosterish forms of American literary nationalism, at least from the time of Philip Freneau and Hugh Henry Brackenridge's "The Rising Glory of America" (1772, 1786), have linked the logic of *translatio imperii*, or the westward course of empire, to white imperial expansionism. In "The Rising Glory of America" itself, after all, which was read by Brackenridge at the December 1771 commencement ceremony of the College of New Jersey (later renamed Princeton) and then revised fifteen years later by Freneau in light of the successful outcome of the Revolutionary War, the poets imagine a glorious national future in which "the savages of America" give way to the avatars of liberty and art. "But *here*," the poets remark on the dire situation of the North American continent prior to the arrival of the white colonists,

amid this northern dark domain
No towns were seen to rise.—No arts were here;
The tribes unskill'd to raise the lofty mast.

The poets then hail the dawn of a new day brought forth by the enterprising white English colonists:

But what a change is here!—what arts arise!
What towns and capitals! how commerce waves
Her gaudy flags, where silence reign'd before!

These are the liberty-loving colonists who are in the process of ridding the continent of different sorts of savages: the British (the very people, of course, that many of the colonists had thought of themselves as part of just a few years earlier). "O cruel race, O unrelenting Britain, / Who bloody beasts will hire to cut our throats." In a poem about revolutionary aspirations to liberty and freedom, Freneau and Brackenridge racialize the British, linking them to the "savage" mercenaries they have enlisted to fight the patriots, thereby establishing the patriots' "legitimate" claims to the continent by underscoring their civilizing whiteness.[14]

Similar strategies of linking whiteness, nation, expansion, and conquest can be found in a number of texts that are generally thought of in relation to American literary nationalism (see, for example, some of the pronouncements by New York's Young America literary nationalists discussed in chapter 3 of this study, or the novels of James Fenimore Cooper). Given such linkages, it is not surprising that an extensive critical literature has emerged that to a certain extent responds to the question Norman Mailer asked back in 1967, *Why Are We in Vietnam?* (or, to update the question, Iraq, Central and South America, and many other parts of the globe), by pointing to the writings that the literary nationalists hailed as distinctively "American." Richard Slotkin, for example, argued both explicitly and implicitly in his influential *Regeneration through Violence* (1973) that the sources of U.S. involvement in the war in Vietnam could be located in the Puritans' accounts of their murderous assaults on Indians (never mind that the nonseparatist Puritans retained their British identity and that invasion and killing were the modus operandi of all of the colonial powers who came to the New World), and that the very tradition running from the Puritans to the literary-nationalist historical romances of the early nineteenth century was allied with the violent securing of white empire. In a representative recent effort to employ literary and other cultural sources to limn a similar imperial history that (in this case) can be seen as helping us understand why the United States is in Iraq, Andy Doolen, in *Fugitive Empire: Locating Early American Imperialism* (2005), "locates" the discourses emerging from the New York conspiracy trials of 1741, a murderous assault on the blacks of the city, as "an embryonic stage of U.S. imperialism" and literary nationalism (never mind that most New York elites in 1741 thought of themselves as British and that the emergence of the United States from British America was hardly inevitable in 1741). In his focus on the "historical trajectories of U.S. imperial culture," Doolen considers Charles Brockden Brown and James Fenimore Cooper as equally complicitous with New York's white racists of 1741 in emerging forms of U.S. imperialism and racism. Though he finds hope in Native American writer William Apess's critique of "white power," Doolen primarily draws on literary nationalistic writings of the first few decades of the new nation to develop a picture of how, "since its inception, the American state has consistently crafted, wielded, and justified imperial power in the name of freedom."[15]

In his ambitious *Literary Culture and U.S. Imperialism: From the Revolution to World War II* (2000), John Carlos Rowe makes similar claims about such continuities and draws even longer trajectories, as he seeks "to connect Manifest Destiny, antebellum slavery, and the economic racism and sexism in the industrialized Northeast . . . with our foreign ventures in the South Pacific, the Philippines, China, Japan, Korea, Southeast Asia, the Caribbean and Latin American, and Africa" and to understand these connections in large part through literature. Rowe's cultural narrative extends backward as well: "There are good reasons to extend the history of U.S. imperialism [back] beyond the Revolution to the colonial period, including thereby its narratives of Indian captivity, travel and natural description, as well as religious and historical writings." Though his study of what he terms "our 'internal colonialism' and more recognizably colonial ventures in foreign countries from the end of the eighteenth century to the 1940s" does not argue for a single connecting thread and offers complex readings of individual texts, the use of "our" implies a consensual understanding of culture that implicates all U.S. readers of the volume in the unbroken imperial histories Rowe traces. And yet there are limits to that implication, for we seem to know more and better than our predecessors. Rowe remarks that as part of his critical project he has "historicize[d] carefully the ideological limitations of each writer considered. None is free of intellectual limitations occasioned by the specific historical and political situation in which that intellectual worked."[16] But this phrasing begs the question of what sorts of moral measurements will be brought to bear on the various writers under consideration, how such measurements will be transported over time, and whether we are simply going to be judging writers by the terms of our own intellectual and moral limitations or, as implied by the tight connections drawn from the Puritans to "our" present moment, regarding the past as a version of the present.

My concern here is not with the linking of the rhetoric of republican freedom to imperial national power. Doolen, Rowe, and others who have addressed connections between U.S. literary-nationalist expression and imperialism are surely right about how such rhetoric can be deployed by those in power, whether in the United States or elsewhere, and they are no doubt right about how literature can participate in such moves. But I am troubled by the exceptionalism of their claims about the long precolonial history of U.S. imperialism, as if western European and other nations somehow stand apart from such a critique, and as if the national was always inherent in what some call the "prenational."[17] Slotkin's, Rowe's, Doolen's, and other literary and cultural studies that address U.S. expansionism and imperialism in relation to U.S. literary history tend to present clear and unbroken links and trajectories from the Puritans through the nineteenth century and beyond. One gets little sense of contestation or even uncertainty within the larger culture; white canonical writers in particular are often simply linked to the power structures of their times. The effort to "locate" a history of imperialism in the manner of a Global Positioning System (it is there and there and there, and you get from point A to point B to point C through a simple connecting of the dots) has an overdetermined feel in which contingencies go by the wayside and historical actors are subsumed to the history that has already happened and thus is conceived of as inevitable. In this mode of critical writing, entrapment and emplotment would appear to go hand in hand, and for this reason, I would suggest, such cultural critique implicates our own time in ways that current critics have failed to acknowledge. For if writers and other historical actors were locked into the inevitable trajectories leading to and from their own historical moments, why is the same not true for us? Does the simple act of claiming to "see" or locate a historical trajectory through a retrospective imposition of a fixed narrative history somehow free us to create better futures? Or might such a vision of writers locked into their respective historical moments simply confess to our own profound sense of futility and entrapment, a conviction that our own histories are in various ways overdetermined and that hopes for change at the current moment are grim? In short, to return to the critical imaginings of David Scott, I would maintain that if we wish to look to the past as a way of fashioning a better future, we need to recover a sense of possibility (and provisionality and contingency) in the past that will help

Gramley Library
Salem Academy and College
Winston-Salem, N.C. 27108

us to reconceive our own moment as a time of possibility (and provisionality and contingency).

Counterfactuals are a potentially useful heuristic tool for reimagining such possibilities, though I should say from the outset that, although counterfactual theory informs aspects of this book, I use it lightly and at times skeptically. After all, in historical studies counterfactuals, or contrary-to-fact speculations, have generally been employed to ask "What if?" questions about alternative outcomes in ways that can resemble mere gamesmanship. "What if the colonists had not rebelled against England?" "What if the South had won the Civil War?" These are the sorts of questions that have engaged the intellectual energies of counterfactually inclined historians who generate speculative new narratives of possible histories based on their understanding of the same political, material, and discursive conditions that we know produced other outcomes. Such alternative histories are meant to remind us of the uncertain, even chaotic workings of history, the idea that, as Jeremy Waldron puts it, "the historic record has a fragility that consists, for large part, in the sheer contingency of what happened in the past. What happened might have been otherwise."[18]

It is this idea of "sheer contingency" that I will be emphasizing in my approach to historical narrative. I am interested in counterfactual theory that, rather than encouraging the development of alternative narratives of histories that never happened, simply reminds us that alternative histories are always immanent in particular cultural moments. Such a reminder, as Stephen M. Best nicely puts it in his analysis of the value of counterfactuals, "performs a negative operation on the certitude of historicist conceit."[19] As readers of *Dislocating Race and Nation* will observe, the four main chapters of the study do not eschew narrative; in fact, I make use of narrative to tell stories about authors and texts in history. But I present those stories in relatively suppositional and conditional terms, and the chapters of this book are themselves linked suppositionally. Nevertheless, because of the chronological arrangement of the chapters, beginning with the Louisiana Purchase and ending with U.S. interventions in the Caribbean in the late nineteenth century, one could read this book as telling a coherent story of the linkage of American literary nationalism to a racially based imperialism and expansionism. Or, one could read these chapters as they are presented, as "episodes" in which the linkages between discrete moments are not overly insisted upon, in which outcomes remain vague and unpredictable, and in which the authors themselves have no clear sense of connections between their contemporary present moments and possible pasts and futures.

In the spirit of Best's call for a dislodging of historical certitude, *Dislocating Race and Nation* works with and against the interpretive narratives proposed by Rowe and Doolen, though with an emphasis on what Catherine Gallagher has termed narratives of "undoing," efforts to think apart from the received "truths" of our current critical moment. This book thus seeks to undo the certitude of an unbroken and untroubled imperialism narrative (I do not see 1898 as implicit or embryonic in Brockden Brown's 1799 *Edgar Huntly*). And there are other "undoings" as well: it works against the certitude of traditional arcs of American literary nationalism (and literature), against the certitude of moral assessments of figures such as Hawthorne and Douglass, and against the certitude of whiteness studies and the too tightly fused linkages of race and nation. The value of such "undoings" is to force us to ask fresh questions about the connections among race, nation, and literature and to proceed with greater caution about producing our own revisionary national narratives. Such an approach works against teleological narratives of American literary nationalism and helps to restore a fuller sense of agency to those writers trying to make sense of their own historical moment. Perhaps most importantly, it establishes a more vital sense of connection between past and present by making clear that what we share with the past is a chaotic, even anarchic, sense of possibility that demands responsible choices and action.

In the epilogue, I will return to Gallagher's notion of narrative and historical undoings, but I would note here my agreement with one of her primary contentions, that an "enlarged sense of temporal possibility correlates with a newly activist, even interventionist, relation to our collective past."[20] "Undoing" narratives emphasize that histories are always in the process of being made and unmade; potentially, then, they can help us to reframe writers so that we can see them in relation to possible alternative consequences and narratives and not simply as always already implicated in dire futures to come. To take the example with which this study begins: the Brockden Brown whom some critics have located within his historical era as an enabler of imperialism can be reimagined as a writer forcefully engaging the key terms of imperialism in the dynamic context of the various plausible outcomes that could have emerged from the Louisiana Purchase. This is a Brown who has more to teach us about race and nation than we usually allow.

Such an approach to Brown and the other writers in this study ultimately dislocates them, for it disrupts the disciplinary machinery in which we take as one of our critical tasks the illumination of a writer's "ideological limitations." I use "dislocating" broadly in this book to refer both to authorial narrative strategies and critical efforts to attend to those strategies. I regard virtually all of the texts under consideration in this study as "dislocating" narratives in the sense that they work in various ways to upset and disrupt conventional notions of the close linkages between race and nation, and I therefore approach them as texts that compel us to reexamine our own thinking about what we may have come to regard as fixed and settled. In an eloquent statement of the temporal reorientation of present and past enabled by counterfactual thinking, E. D. Hirsch Jr. writes: "Responsible interpretation exists in two worlds at once, the world of the past and the world of the present, the world of the writer and the world of the reader. The problematics of textual interpretation arise chiefly from this counterfactual yoking of historical moments that do not in reality exist. The only way we can bridge these two historical moments is through counterfactual thinking."[21] To put this somewhat differently, the past can speak to the present, and the present to the past, through an imagining and reimagining of plausible chronologies that allow for a kind of two-way critical ventriloquism that is respectful of difference while allowing for possibilities of exchange.

With the large, interrelated goals of undoing, disrupting, and reconstructing, *Dislocating Race and Nation* seeks to make a number of contributions to nineteenth-century U.S. literary and cultural studies. As an interracial literary history, it will explore the constitutive work of white and black writers in the formation and revision of American literary nationalism. (See especially the analysis of David Walker's construction of African American literary nationalism in chapter 2.) It will emphasize the centrality of intra-American conflict to the development of American literary nationalism, and it will consider multiple and sometimes conflicting traditions of American literary nationalism, including those that have regional, trans-American, transnational, and especially hemispheric dimensions. Focusing on specific historical and geographical contexts and locations, and eschewing the diagnostic interpretive method characteristic of much recent cultural criticism, it will examine the complex interlinking of race and nation in a number of literary texts, paying particular attention to the respective writers' own understandings of their participation in various modes of literary nationalism. This book seeks to broaden our conception of American literary nationalism itself, which is generally understood in terms of the polemics and manifestos appearing in the journals of the period and not, as I will also be presenting it, in terms of the works that responded to such literary nationalistic discourses. Consisting of "episodes" and case studies—Brockden Brown and the Louisiana Purchase; David Walker and the debates on the Missouri Compromise; Hawthorne, Melville, and Hannah Crafts and blood-based literary nationalism and expansionism; Frederick Douglass and his over thirty-year interest in Haiti—*Dislocating Race and Nation* develops a simultaneously disjunctive and (I hope) fairly coherent alternative "raced" history of American literary nationalism over a 100-year period. This provisional history is considerably different from the United States versus Great Britain model that continues to be the starting point for most discussions of American literary nationalism, even those revisionary studies that look at longer and wider imperial histories and take fuller account of race. Consistent with these newer approaches, but with the aim of undoing, I begin with a consideration of Brockden Brown in the context of debates on race, empire, and the U.S. nation with respect to the Louisiana Territory and Haiti. Rather than considering Brown as a "representative" figure in the embryonic stages of white imperial empire, I attempt to tell a different story about his apprehensions of the contingencies of empire.

1

Charles Brockden Brown,
Louisiana, and the Contingencies of Empire

It is generally acknowledged that Charles Brockden Brown was an American literary nationalist. In his oft-cited prefatory note to *Edgar Huntly* (1799), he called on American writers to address "the condition of our country," maintaining that "the field of investigation, opened to us by our own country, should differ essentially from those which exist in Europe." Among the "new views" open to the American writer, he stated somewhat self-servingly, were "incidents of Indian hostility, and the perils of the western wilderness," the very topics that he explored in his novel. Brown also published numerous essays on the need for a vital literary culture in the United States, remarking, for example, on the importance of demonstrating to "foreigners" that they are wrong about "the apathy and disregard apparently shown by Americans to literature." At the same time, he worried that Americans' "love of gain" and desire to "acquire property" threatened to make "THE LITERARY CHARACTER OF AMERICA . . . EXTREMELY SUPERFICIAL"; and he remained perpetually concerned that the availability of cheap British reprints would make it difficult for American writers to sell their own books, given that publishers could always say, "I have a choice of books from England, the popularity and sale of which is fixed and certain, and which will cost me nothing but the mere expenses and publication." Nevertheless, Brown clung to the hope that works by U.S. authors would one day "extend beyond the limits of our own country, and the whole learned world will recognize their value."[1]

Brown's comments resemble those of a number of other American literary nationalists of the time who also proclaimed that U.S. writers should draw on native materials in order to create a distinctively American literature; that Americans needed to rise to the challenge of literary production by putting the spiritual (or artistic) above mere gain; that Americans must refute the claims of European geographers such as the

Comte de Buffon, who maintained that the New World brought about the degeneracy of plant, animal, and human species; and that the ultimate challenge of American literary nationalism was to embrace the fabled promise of the westward migration of culture and knowledge (*translatio studii*) so as to produce works that were *different* from and ultimately better than those produced in Europe.[2] Because "Europe" often meant England, American literary nationalism, as articulated by these advocates, could therefore be understood as part of a decolonization effort to "complete" the American Revolution through the establishment of an independent national literature in the United States.

Typically, historians of American literary nationalism have celebrated the movement, thereby providing consensus on apparent consensus. Benjamin T. Spencer describes "the persistent yearning of the post-Revolutionary writers for an independent literature" as a quest "for literary integrity"; Robert E. Spiller hails the "political independence" and "literary independence" that helped to produce a "genuinely American literature"; John P. McWilliams finds rhetorical common cause with those American literary nationalists who believed that "an American epic would refute Buffon's galling claim that humanity and all its arts must degenerate in the western wilds"; and Gordon S. Wood exclaims over the cultural aspirations of the early Republic: "Never in American history have the country's leaders voiced such high expectations for the cultural achievements of the nation as did Americans in the 1790s. The arts and sciences were inevitably moving across the Atlantic to the New World and bringing America into a golden age."[3] The odd and perhaps unintended convergence of historical narrative and cultural cheerleading among these critics encapsulates the celebratory mode of American cultural nationalism, which has traditionally been displayed most prominently in reference-room literary histories, literary-nationalist readers, and classroom anthologies.

As discussed in the prologue, however, there is a very different, more skeptical approach to American literary nationalism that has become increasingly prevalent in recent writings on early national literary culture. For critics of what could be termed the demystifying school, Brown's American literary nationalistic preface to *Edgar Huntly*, with its invocation of "Indian hostility," speaks to whites' imperial project of removing and slaughtering Indians and other peoples of color, a project that is best understood not in the simple binary terms of the United States versus Great Britain but in the larger geopolitical field of U.S. whites' efforts to colonize the continent in the name of the nation. With a focus on *Edgar Huntly*, Jared Gardner, for example, has influentially argued that U.S. literary nationalism was ultimately an effort to develop "a national narrative that aimed to secure to white Americans an identity that was unique (not European) but not alien (not black or Indian)," and that American novelists played a crucial role in helping to create this narrative by "scripting stories of 'origins' that imagined white Americans as a race apart, both from the Europeans without and the blacks and Indians within the new nation." Along these same lines, John Carlos Rowe maintains that works such as Brown's *Edgar Huntly* simultaneously drew on and reinforced "the ideology of the new nation, especially as it would justify the violence against others required for its founding." Thus he indicts Brown for participating in "the shabby history of U.S. colonialism." David Kazanjian similarly asserts that "Brown's work—echoing U.S. Indian policy as well as the emerging fields of ethnography and archaeology—represents Native Americans as idealized, disembodied forms whose assimilation is the always incomplete precondition for the transformation of white settler colonials into national citizen-subjects."[4]

In traditional accounts of American literary nationalism, critics applaud early national writers' efforts to break away from the European (British) literary past and produce their own distinctive literature; in revisionary accounts, critics denounce such efforts as participating in imperialism, colonialism, slavery, racism, Indian removal and extermination, and other nefarious practices. These opposed readings of American literary nationalism, I would suggest, are two sides of the same consensual coin. Both fail to do justice to the instabilities, contradictions, conflicts, and confusions of the period; both work selectively with well-known statements on American literary nationalism to argue for something like unanimity among early nationals on matters of art, politics, and nation; and both work with overdetermined interpretive paradigms that fail to recognize individual authors' own efforts to understand and engage their historical moment (however conflicted, confused, and contradictory that engagement might be). Celebratory American literary nationalists view the period in Whiggish terms as the time when the first steps were taken towards the achievement of the telos: the emergence of the great writers of F. O. Matthiessen's "American Renaissance." For the demystifying critics, canonical writers such as Brown took the first steps toward a different sort of telos: the spread of white U.S. empire into Mexico, the Philippines, and elsewhere. Within this darker scheme in which, as Rowe puts it, writers offered "subtle endorsements of the imperial policies of the young republic as it expanded westward," there is little sense of the unpredictable and contingent, of ideologies in formation, working against themselves, or on the verge of collapse—in short, little sense of what Nancy Ruttenburg has termed early national culture's "ideological incoherence."[5] Instead, there is an insistence on the pervasive influence of something that Rowe calls "the ideology of the new nation."

But did the new nation have a coherent and shared national ideology? Historian David Waldstreicher warns against reading U.S. nationalism of the early national period as a "a realm of unthinking consensus," suggesting that to do so is to accept uncritically the claims of those who sought to control the consensus. According to Waldstreicher, conflicts among "several ideologies in a larger cultural field" were the order of the day, and those conflicts, even when they had international contexts, can best be discerned in the domestic or internal debates that helped to produce competing ideas of the U.S. nation.[6] From the debates of the mid-1780s on the Northwest Territories to the debates of the early 1800s on the Louisiana Territory, there were ongoing discussions about how to determine the boundaries of the nation in the larger context of the Americas, how peripheries should be constituted, how new states could be created, how national identities and citizenship would be defined both within the original states and the new states to come, and how best to address the presence of Native Americans, slaves, free blacks, and ethnic minorities. There were no easy and settled answers to these questions; much remained in contention; and precisely because so much remained in formation or simply unclear, there was an anxious but excited sense among those who contributed to these debates that their participation mattered.

Questions of national formation and identity were absolutely central to the debates on Louisiana. Though it is widely agreed that the Louisiana Purchase of 1803 had a decisive impact on the course of U.S. history, historians continue to argue about just what that impact was. Did the Purchase unleash the expansionist, imperialistic energies of U.S. empire, or did it keep those energies in check? Did it extend the realm of freedom or contribute to the spread of slavery? Did it unify or divide the country? Lacking the retrospective knowledge that has allowed historians to construct their often conflicting narratives, historical participants of the time would have had no idea of the "true" implications or possible outcomes of the Purchase. But as unsure as they may have been about the consequences, early nationals who took an interest in what Thomas Jefferson termed "the affairs of Louisiana" were aware that they were confronting monumental questions of nationality and empire. In a letter of 18 April 1802 to Robert R. Livingston, his minister to France, Jefferson conveyed his own awed sense of the uncertainties of the moment: "Every eye in the United States is now fixed on the affairs of Louisiana. Perhaps nothing since the revolutionary war, has produced more uneasy sensations through the body of the nation." Following the Purchase, Jefferson hailed the expansion of what he regularly called an "empire of liberty," though he never specified what he thought that empire might be.[7] The doubling of the size of the new nation at a time of intense geopolitical conflict gave material support to those who were committed to expansion, while prompting dissenters to raise questions about the wisdom of expansion. As it turned out, Americans sharing Jefferson's vision of an "empire of liberty" were increasingly committed to slavery, Indian removal, and territorial acquisition. For this reason, some cultural historians have argued that the Louisiana Purchase led directly to the debates on Missouri, the hardening of sectional rivalries, the war with Mexico, the further expansion of slavery into the South and West, the Civil War, and the imperialism that would come to define the United States' global presence by century's end.

But the fact is that Jefferson, James Madison, and many others of the time had only modest territorial ambitions, hoping to secure the Floridas and the mouth of the Mississippi in order to strengthen the nation's commercial economy. However tempting it is to locate the Louisiana Purchase as the starting point for post-Louisiana narratives of what historian Peter Kastor terms "a simple trajectory of geopolitical and cultural imperialism on the part of the United States," such narratives, Kastor insists, fail to take account of the "negotiation, contingency, and accommodation" that accompanied the ongoing debates on the territory. Precisely because of their retrospective knowingness, such narratives also fail to take account of the possibly different outcomes that could have developed as these debates (and indeed history itself) unfolded.[8]

Contingency and to some extent counterfactual analysis will be central to my discussion of Brown's writings on Louisiana and empire. "Contingency," of course, has multiple and somewhat conflicting connotations, referring to an event that is likely to happen as a result of various conditions that are in place, but referring as well to an event that, however possible, may *not* occur for various reasons, such as free choice, happenstance, and phenomena that are not completely under anyone's control or realm of knowledge. When I refer to the contingencies of empire with respect to Louisiana, I am calling attention to a variety of geopolitical and other factors that contributed to the contemporary sense of uncertainty regarding the possible consequences of the Louisiana Purchase. Counter-factual analysis puts an emphasis on just such uncertainty, the "what if?" of alternative possibilities, and thus attempts to unsettle the too-sure sense of emplotted meanings in history and narrative that often attends retrospective analysis. A clear understanding of the meanings and conse-quences of history, as Brown well knew, was not immanent in the Pur-chase or in anything else in the culture, including the meanings and consequences of a "tradition" of American literary nationalism.

This chapter will consider Brown in relation to the "affairs of Loui-siana," and it will point to the limits of traditional formulations of U.S. nationalism, and literary nationalism, when viewed exclusively in terms of the United States versus Great Britain. Imperial conflict by the Mis-sissippi and in the Caribbean, the ongoing slave trade, and the close connections among the American Revolution, French Revolution, and Haitian Revolution were crucial to U.S. nationalism, literary nationalism, and the debates on Louisiana. There was no single nationalism or literary nationalism that encompassed all such developments. What we can say is that American literary nationalism during this period had a range of perspectives and numerous advocates and practitioners, and that the debates on the Louisiana Purchase brought a renewed attention to the dynamics of race as a constituent of nation. Despite what can appear to be his conventional expressions of American literary nationalism, Charles Brockden Brown sought to understand racial and national identities in all of their complexity, and he challenged a number of the orthodoxies that we tend to associate with a traditionally optative U.S. literary nationalism.

The chapter's starting point and principal focus is an "episode" in American literary nationalism: Brown's authoring of a series of political pamphlets during the 1800s, two of which focused on Louisiana and all of which addressed matters of U.S. nationhood and empire. How should we read such pamphlets by a literary "romancer," the author of four wildly inventive gothic novels during the 1798–1800 period and the author of two epistolary novels in 1801? What are the connections between these pamphlets and the romances? To what extent are the pamphlets fictional performances and the novels political utterances? In addressing these questions, I will be exploring Brown's views on race, nation, and empire and making several broad claims: that a reading of the early U.S. nation as defined by ideological conflict, contradiction, and even incoherence is truer to the reality of the time than any sort of consensual reading, whether celebratory or damning; that attending to such conflict, contradiction, and incoherence helps to amplify in the particular context of early U.S. nationality what Etienne Balibar calls "the relative indeterminacy of the process of constitution and development of the nation form";[9] and that Brown himself probed these indeterminacies in his writings on race, nation, and empire. Though I will be challenging those readings of Brown that present him as some sort of dupe, apologist, or promoter of white imperialism or colonialism, I am not suggesting that he "transcended" the cultural discourses and logics of his period. Sean X. Goudie writes that Brown is "singularly capable of probing the contours and central concerns of discourses of race, nation, and empire," and that his writings "consistently register the manifold ambiguities and ambivalences attending those discourses, especially the nation's tangled investments in them, *without himself being wholly complicit with, ironically detached from, or unaffected by their appeal and suasion.*"[10] I would add that Brown's dislocating writings suggest the contingencies of these large terms—race, nation, and empire—and the provisionality of the unfolding cultural narratives that were underwritten by such terms. As I hope to show by attending to the close connections between Brown's political and fictional works, Brown's writings perform and capture the "uneasy sensations" that Jefferson so acutely identified as the national spirit of the time, even as they remain "uneasy" themselves. Working against chronology, I begin with Brown on Louisiana and the related rebellion in Saint Domingue, move back to the late 1790s to reconsider Brown's major fiction, especially *Edgar Huntly*, in the light of these writings, and conclude with a second look at Brown in the first decade of the nineteenth century as he anticipated the great debates on American (literary) nationalism of the 1820s.

Race and Nation in Brown's Louisiana Writings of 1803

In 1803 Charles Brockden Brown published two pamphlets on the Louisiana territories: *An Address to the Government of the United States, on the Cession of Louisiana to the French*, and *Monroe's Embassy; or, The Conduct of the Government, in Relation to Our Claims to the Navigation of the Mississippi*. The message of these interrelated texts would seem to be relatively clear: that the U.S. government should work to bring about "the

deliverance of America from every foreign intruder"; that there are currently a host of threatening "aliens and enemies" in the Americas (blacks,
Indians, French, Spanish); that given Americans' rights to "America," the
proper action for the government with respect to navigation rights on the
Mississippi is not negotiation with Spain or France but war; that the best
way to win a war against the French and/or the Spanish (and the blacks
and Indians, who, Brown's narrative persona warns in both pamphlets,
would be deployed by the Spanish and particularly by the French to wage
an insurrectionary war against Americans) is for the nation's citizenry to
unite behind a federal effort to commit significant funds and troops to the
project. If Americans do not act decisively to take control of the Mississippi, he states in *Monroe's Embassy*, then in all likelihood "the consum-
mate arts of the French shall diffuse among our people . . . all the panic,
tumult and havock, which the insurrection of our slaves, the dissension of
our states, may occasion," and eventually "French power should cover the
globe." Given this threat, Brown concludes *Address* with an unequivocal
call to Congress: "FROM YOU, assembled Representatives, do we demand
that you would seize the happy moment for securing the possession of
America to our posterity: for ensuring the harmony and union of these
States: for removing all obstacles to the future progress of our settlements; for excluding from our vitals the most active and dangerous enemy
that ever before threatened us. . . . *The iron is now hot*: command us to rise
as one man, and STRIKE!"[11]

It has been traditional among Brown critics to separate Brown's three
years as a writer of "ambiguous" or "radical" novels (1798–1800) from the
rest of his career. Yet in his 1803 writings on Louisiana and in the major
fiction of the late 1790s, Brown addresses very similar questions: What is
the character of the U.S. nation? What are its boundaries, and how are
those boundaries to be defined and monitored? What is a citizen, and
how does one make distinctions between citizens and "aliens"? What
sorts of plots are in the air against the vulnerable new nation, and how
does one read and interpret them? Gardner links the pamphlets to the
novels, arguing that Brown's *Address* in particular "borrows much from his
earlier novelistic career in its depiction of a powerful villain, a 'discovered'
document, and a gothic tale of rape and conquest," and in its suggestion
(along the lines of *Edgar Huntly*) that nation building requires "constructing and exorcizing the alien." Race is pivotal to that construction, Gardner
asserts, for in Brown's writings, as in early national culture, "anxieties
about aliens were conflated with anxieties about race," and ultimately it

was race that enabled "[white] Americans to recognize common interests in each other, to recognize each other as Americans."[12] But I will be arguing that Brown's political message in his Louisiana tracts may not be so clear after all, for the pamphlets are troubled by (and trouble) some of the key terms and issues that inform the fictions he had written a few years earlier. These are novels, it is worth emphasizing, in which identities —national, gender, and even racial—seem anything but stable, and in which stability (or the ability to "recognize" identity) can appear to be the biggest fiction of all.[13]

Although I will be developing an analysis of Brown's Louisiana writings that departs from Gardner's, I share his wariness of critical accounts that insist on vast differences between Brown's pre-1800 and post-1800 political and aesthetic perspectives. Brown's career as a novelist, after all, spans only four years, and his significant writing and editorial career, from *Alcuin* (1798) to shortly before his death in 1810, spans little more than ten years. Nevertheless, a number of critics have argued that Brown's vision and practice changed dramatically at key moments during this short period of time. For example, on the evidence of Brown's letter of 1798 to Jefferson on the value of fiction, Jane Tompkins reads *Wieland* (1798) as an anxious Federalist meditation on the dangers of unconstrained individualism; yet she reads the subsequent *Arthur Mervyn* (1799–1800) as a celebration of liberal individualism in a Jeffersonian mode. Steven Watts, in his provocative critical biography of Brown, maintains that the significant transformation in Brown's politics and aesthetics occurred a year after that, "[o]n or about April 1800," at which time, Watts says, "Charles Brockden Brown changed," abandoning his putatively radical fictions to become a "bourgeois moralist" and advocate of "manifest destiny."[14] This notion of Brown's dramatic shift from radical to conservative, Republican to Federalist, bookish litterateur to militant nationalist has emerged as a generally accepted "truism" in Brown studies, and the truth of such a claim would seem to be evident in obvious ways: Brown's move to a more "conservative" epistolary fiction and then his virtual abandonment of novel writing in favor of what can appear to be a more pronounced Federalist political writing and journalism. And yet politics, journalism, and epistolary modes were also important to his writing career of the 1790s, and fictional experimentation and epistemological uncertainty would remain important to his post-1800 career as well.

In the critical accounts of Watts, Tompkins, and many others, interpreting Brown hinges on the matter of determining whether to read him as a Republican or Federalist, with the suggestion being that these political distinctions have crucial implications for understanding the thematic emphases and alleged shifts in his thinking and aesthetics, such as his supposed embrace of a reactionary, bourgeois conservatism and even militarism "[o]n or about April 1800." But we need to be wary of simple allegorizations of "Federalist" as "bad reactionary" and "Republican" as "good democratic progressive." After all, by the early nineteenth century it was the Republicans who were committed to Indian removal and western expansionism. Moreover, many of the supposedly reactionary and elitist Federalists were actually in the antislavery vanguard, even as they were vanishing into history. Brown scholars who talk of the author's "fall" into Federalism may want to reconsider their laments.[15]

I will be returning to the matter of Brown's Federalism. What needs to be emphasized here is that there are perhaps better ways of thinking about political and national identity during this period than through the simple binary of Federalist/Republican. In his magisterial book on the first 200 years of slavery in the Americas, Ira Berlin suggests a periodization of the 1790s and early 1800s in relation to transnational and trans-American revolutions and their aftermaths—specifically, the emergence from revolutions of the United States, the French Republic, and the Republic of Haiti.[16] Within this larger hemispheric frame, circa 1791–1804, Louisiana assumes particular significance as a site of contention not only between Federalists and Republicans but also, and more importantly, between the United States and France, France and Saint Domingue, France and England, and the United States and Spain. As I will be elaborating below, Brown in his Louisiana writings of 1803 attempts to articulate a coherent notion of American national identity amidst such contention, while at the same time taking account of geopolitical and racial conflict in order to pose an ethical challenge to forms of nationalist exceptionalism. Writing from what I would term a Federalist-nationalist post-Revolutionary perspective, Brown sought to use his Louisiana pamphlets not only to bring parts of the Louisiana Territory under the control of the United States but also to prompt U.S. citizens toward respect for peoples of color, particularly the black rebels of Saint Domingue. I will be exploring these desires and conflicts in Brown by looking closely at his magazine work in relation to his Louisiana writings. But first it would be useful to contextualize more fully the debates on Louisiana in the late 1790s and early 1800s.

To rehearse what is fairly well known: Louisiana was a Spanish colony from 1773 to 1803, though it was retroceded to France by the Treaty of San Ildefonso (1 October 1800), and France took possession of the territory on December 1, 1803. Even before the retrocession, many Federalists during the late 1790s Quasi-War with France were concerned that the French would attempt to take the Floridas and Louisiana from the Spanish. Thus Alexander Hamilton asserted to Harrison Gray Otis in a letter of 26 January 1799 that the United States should consider using military force to gain control of those territories because they were "essential to the permanency of the Union."[17] Like the Federalists, Thomas Jefferson thought of Louisiana as critical to U.S. trade and economic development. When he heard rumors shortly after assuming the presidency that the Spanish had indeed transferred Louisiana to the French, he wrote the U.S. minister in France, Robert Livingston, that he feared the French would now be able to control the lower Mississippi and thereby pose a threat to western farmers. Jefferson's fears seemed to have been borne out when the Spanish intendant closed New Orleans's ports in 1802. Convinced that France was behind this action, Jefferson ordered the marshaling of U.S. forces along the Mississippi and began the process of negotiating with France for the purchase of the Louisiana Territory. James Monroe joined Livingston in France to conduct those negotiations, and because the French were financially and militarily drained by their ongoing battles in Saint Domingue, Monroe and Livingston were able to purchase the territory for approximately $11 million. The Louisiana Territory came into U.S. possession in late December 1803. Although some Federalists and Republicans believed Jefferson overstepped his constitutional authority in negotiating the Purchase, he was willing to compromise his antifederal principles because he believed that the West had near-mystical powers of national regeneration. As he famously remarked after the Purchase: "By enlarging the empire of liberty, we multiply its auxiliaries, and provide new sources of renovation, should its principles, at any time, degenerate, in those portions of our country which gave them birth."[18]

Both before and after the Louisiana Purchase, Jefferson claimed that among the benefits of national territorial expansion was the possibility that the additional land would lead to the "diffusion" and eventual disappearance of slavery from the United States. But it is crucial to emphasize that Jefferson's desire for the end of slavery had much to do with his fear and loathing of blacks, and that for all his talk of "diffusion," he was well aware that in the short term western expansion would contribute to the spread of slavery into the newly acquired territories.[19] Arguably, it was his fear of blacks, his conviction that the United States would function best as an all-white nation, and his close connections to southern slave planters that informed much of his policy on Louisiana from the 1790s to the time of the Purchase and beyond.

As numerous historians have documented, Jefferson, like other southern planters, was particularly worried about the black uprisings in Saint Domingue, which he feared could result in a hemispheric slave revolution. Inspired by the American and French Revolutions, the blacks of Saint Domingue rose up against the French planters in the early 1790s in a violent revolution that lasted over a decade and claimed over 60,000 black and white lives. By the end of 1793, approximately 10,000 Saint Domingan masters, slaves, and free people of color had made an exodus to the United States, arriving in large numbers in New York, Philadelphia, and New Orleans; by the end of 1795, upwards of 12,000 Domingan blacks alone had entered the United States. Thus southern authorities began to worry about the potential for revolt among those of their slaves who, as Douglas R. Egerton puts it, "had been infected with the malady of insurrection."[20] Anxieties about black revolutionism were exacerbated by the Gabriel conspiracy of 1800, and that foiled but extensive conspiracy among Richmond's free and enslaved blacks had a crucial role in determining Jefferson's policy toward the French and Louisiana. During 1801 and most of 1802, Jefferson encouraged Napoleon's efforts to secure Saint Domingue from the black rebels, and he maintained policies favorable to France until late 1802, when he became concerned about the French taking control of the lower Mississippi. But even during the negotiations that led to the Louisiana Purchase, Jefferson calculated that French troops could quell the black insurrection in Saint Domingue if they had an operational base in Louisiana. Accordingly, he instructed Monroe in a letter of March 1803 to "admit the French to Louisiana without condition," urging him simply to negotiate some form of U.S. jurisdiction over New Orleans. Following the Purchase, which, ironically, was enabled by the very successes of the Saint Domingan revolutionaries, Jefferson refused to recognize Haiti when it became an independent republic in 1804. By implementing trade embargos against Haiti, he hoped in effect to quarantine Louisiana, particularly New Orleans, which remained a frightening place in his imagination, a locale wherein free-black militia units and free men of color demanded their rights and threatened to spread their antiracist politics of human freedom eastward toward Virginia.[21]

Jefferson's anxieties about the slave revolutions in Saint Domingue were shared by many Americans, northern and southern, Republican and Federalist. But some northern merchants and politicians, predominately Federalist, voiced their opposition to what they regarded as Jefferson's proslavery expansionism and assault on free trade, and that opposition no doubt had an impact on the Philadelphia merchant and importer Brockden Brown. In part because of their suspicion of the French (and southern enslavers), and their desire to continue trade relations with black Domingans, the supposedly conservative Federalists offered significant support for the nation-building efforts of the black revolutionaries of Saint Domingue. During the late 1790s, John Adams and other Federalist political leaders actually championed Toussaint L'Ouverture's struggles against French colonizers. They provided him with supplies and generally regarded him, as one historian puts it, as "the Haitian Washington leading his people out of domination." In 1798 President Adams dined with Toussaint's advisor, Joseph Bunel, a black man, displaying in his statecraft what Egerton describes as an "utter lack of racial animosity." That same year Adams's secretary of state, Timothy Pickering, remarked that Toussaint was "a prudent and judicious man possessing the general confidence of the people of all colours." After Jefferson became president, Federalists attempted to pressure him to modify his views in the direction of John Adams's. Motivated in part by economic self-interest, northern merchants regularly defied Jefferson's trade embargos on Haiti, while Federalist leaders urged diplomatic recognition first of Toussaint and then of his successor Dessalines and the newly independent black republic. Ironically, then, as Michael Zuckerman remarks, with respect to "St. Domingue it was the Federalists who held far more closely to the faith of the founders and the Jeffersonian Republicans who tried far more tenaciously to tether and traduce the will of the people. . . . It was the Federalists who fostered freedom and the Republicans who attempted the restoration of a colonial regime, and, indeed, the reimposition of slavery itself." Such were the contingencies of the moment—northerners' sentiments against slavery, the Federalists' resistance to the spread of plantation slavery into the Louisiana territories, and Adams's willingness to work with blacks as trading and political partners—that Egerton has speculated that had Adams not lost the presidency, "a second Adams term might have resulted not merely in a greater Spanish-American understanding but even in a possible Federalist acquisition of the Louisiana Territory from Spain under free-soil conditions."[22]

Given northern Federalists' resistance to Jefferson's politics of race and nation, we should be wary of critical accounts that seek to fit Brown's writings of the early 1800s into a supposed national consensus on whites' fearful response to black revolutionism in the Caribbean.[23] In his magazine writings circa 1799–1805, Brown clearly dissents from the anxious racism informing Jefferson's hemispheric vision. The magazines that Brown edited (and mostly wrote) during this period evince a bold antislavery politics and a rejection of the emerging "scientific" discourse of racial difference (limned in such texts as Jefferson's *Notes on the State of Virginia* [1785]) in favor of a vision of human oneness. Brown shared this antislavery and antiracist perspective with a number of literary Federalists of the time, most notably the poets known as the Connecticut Wits, whose nationalistic epics regularly deplored the existence of slavery in the Americas. In his 1794 *Greenfield Hill*, for example, Timothy Dwight laments that the black slave is "[c]ondion'd as a brute, tho' formed a man"; and he terms the institution of slavery itself: "Thou spot of hell, deep smirch'd on human kind, / The uncur'd gangrene of the reasoning mind."[24] It is significant in this regard that two of Brown's closest friends, the physician and poetry anthologist Elihu Hubbard Smith and the dramatist (and future biographer of Brown) William Dunlap, were antislavery Federalists who had been influenced by Dwight. In the early 1790s, both joined the New York City Manumission Society, which helped to establish schools for black children, and later in the decade they brought Brown to meetings.[25] From the antislavery persuasion of Federalist New York and Philadelphia, Brown came to regard the black Domingans' revolution against their French enslavers as compelling evidence of their humanity.

Assertions of blacks' humanity and the evils of slavery appeared in the first volume of Brown's *Monthly Magazine and American Review* (1799), wherein he printed an extensive selection from Johann Friedrich Blumenbach's *Observations on the Conformation and Capacity of the Negroes*. Against the grain of emerging scientific racism, Blumenbach proclaimed that "the negroes, in their mental faculties, are not inferior to the rest of the human race." In the same volume, Brown reviewed Robert Southey's "Sonnets on the Slave Trade," sharing his regrets that "there should be so much cause for virtuous indignation" at the practice of slavery in the United States. In the second volume of *Monthly Magazine*, Brown printed a letter from one H. L., almost certainly a fictional persona, who reports that "[i]n America, the current of opinion sits strongly against negro servitude," while confessing to his embarrassment as an American nationalist that "the *serfs* enjoy higher privileges than the *negroes*." Antislavery and antiracist writings also appeared extensively in Brown's subsequent magazine, the *Literary Magazine, and American Register,* the original contributions of which, as he confided to his friend John Blair Linn, were just about all authored by Brown himself.[26] In 1804 he printed a celebratory account of "Abolition of Slavery in New Jersey," the proceedings from a January 1804 antislavery meeting ("Address of the American Convention to the People of the United States"), and a polemic against the slave trade ("Extracts from a Speech on the Slave Trade"). The most pointed attack on slavery in *Literary Magazine* came in 1805 in an article titled "On the Consequences of Abolishing the Slave Trade to the West Indian Colonies." In that piece, the anonymous author, probably Brown, terms slavery "the most cruel experiment that ever was tried on human nature," and he elaborates an environmentalist argument that the "bad qualities ascribed to the negroes" have everything to do with their condition. These "qualities," he states, "belong rather to their habits than to their nature, and are derived either from the low state of civilization in which the whole race at present is placed, or from the manifold hardships of their situation." To support this claim, the writer reports that in "interior Africa," blacks are "far from wanting [in] ingenuity, they have made no contemptible progress in the arts; and have united into political societies of great extent and complicated structure." Extolling blacks' intelligence and humanity, he asserts that slave revolts have to be regarded as the result of whites' "short-sighted and wicked policy," and thus he warns that unless slavery is abolished in the United States, "the fate of St. Domingo will suddenly become the fate of all the negro settlements." This remarkable essay concludes by assailing "that arrogance, which would confine to one race, the characteristics of the species," and by honoring the "fidelity, courage, and other good qualities, remarkable in freed negroes."[27]

That "courage" and humanity, according to editor Brown, has been most dramatically on display in blacks' revolutionary uprisings against the French. In celebrating the revolution in Saint Domingue in his periodicals, Brown radically departs from the politics of fear and loathing of the Jeffersonians and aligns himself with the more humane and progressive politics of some northern Federalists, and even such black reformers as African American Freemason Prince Hall, who in his 1797 "A Charge, Delivered to the African Lodge" hailed the rebellion in "the French West-Indies" as a "blessed" response to the French masters' "pride, wantonness, and cruelty."[28] In an anonymous essay in the 1804 *Literary Magazine* titled

"Picture of St. Domingo," dated 3 October 1803 and supposedly penned by a reporter based in Havre-de-Grace, the writer (again most likely Brown) provides a trenchant account not of black but of French barbarism. According to this putative observer of the revolutionary scene, it is the French who "deal out death and destruction" and adopt a "plan of butchery" and "premeditated barbarity," while it is the blacks who are the "peaceful citizens." The reporter details the brutal policies of the French leaders Rochambeau and D'Arbois, such as their ordering of mass drownings of Saint Domingans, which he says "provoke[d] a general insurrection in the south of the island" and ultimately fostered desires among blacks for a "vengeance that called for the reddened blasts of an avenging hand." Brown printed several other pieces in *Literary Magazine* that further defended the nationalist aims of the black revolutionaries of Saint Domingue. In the 1804 essay "St. Domingo," for example, the anonymous writer (possibly Brown) states that Haiti has evinced "superiority to all other black nations," and that this nation is capable of "a similitude in manners, religion, arts, and language with the most potent and refined of the christian or European nations." In his 1807 *American Register*, Brown looks back on the Saint Domingan rebellion as an unqualified success, remarking that "it is now three or four years since the island [Haiti] has been in full possession of the negroes, and since they have maintained their claim to the dignity and privileges of an independent state."[29] Rather than stigmatizing black Haiti, or invoking the specter of Saint Domingue in the manner of the Jeffersonians, Brown makes clear in his magazine articles that the "enemy" that should most concern the United States in the early 1800s is imperialistic France. Using the ironic and indirect narrative methods of his novels of the late 1790s, he takes a similar position on France in *An Address to the Government of the United States, on the Cession of Louisiana to the French.*

Published anonymously in 1803, several months before the Louisiana Purchase, the widely read *Address* was something of a hoax, consisting in large part of a letter from a French consul urging Napoleon to turn his attention from the uprisings in Saint Domingue in order to consolidate his possession of the Louisiana Territory and conquer the United States. The letter is framed by the voice of the patriotic editor/narrator, who claims to have discovered the letter and now wishes to disseminate the threat of the French plot as it comes from "the *mouth* of an enemy."[30] Christopher Looby terms Brown's Louisiana pamphlet "crudely reductive" and "paranoid," but there were good reasons for Americans to be concerned about Napoleonic France at this particular historical moment. The prospect of the emergence of a powerful French colony on the borders of the new nation, historian Peter S. Onuf explains, "revived the founders' anxieties about the loyalty of the western settlers, the durability of the union, and the future of republican government in America."[31] Though there was hardly a consensus about how to address the situation, leaders of both political parties were concerned about the possibility of French aggression. Much more vitriolically than Brown, Alexander Hamilton declared in the *New York Evening Post* of 8 February 1803 that Spain's retrocession of Louisiana to France presents a *"manifest and great danger to the nation,"* and that "the right to resort at once to WAR . . . cannot be doubted." Despite the Francophilia of Jefferson and his Republican associates, their private correspondence suggests a similar concern about French imperial designs. In a letter of 18 April 1802 to Robert Livingston, Jefferson remarked that the "day that France takes possession of N. Orleans fixes the sentence which is to restrain her forever within her low water mark. . . . From that moment we must marry ourselves to the British fleet and nation. We must turn all our attention to a maritime force." Later that year, Livingston warned James Madison that should the French subdue Saint Domingue, they might next attack Natchez, and that there was therefore an urgent "necessity *of strengthening ourselves* as soon as possible both *by forces and ships at home and by alliance abroad.*"[32] Hardly a lone "paranoiac," Brown in his tracts of 1803 was speaking the language of his time—and more temperately than many.[33]

In *Address* in particular, Brown, like a number of national leaders, attempts to create unity among Americans by demonizing the French as aliens who exist apart from the nation while at the same time threaten to undermine the nation from within. "The French are alien to me," Brown declares in *Monroe's Embassy*;[34] and in *Address* there are repeated references to the "aliens and enemies within [U.S.] borders" (74). The national project, as Brown propounds it in the Louisiana tracts, should be for the "rightful" U.S. citizenry to rid itself of the "foreign race" in its "bosom" (73). What remains somewhat problematic in *Address* is how to distinguish the subversives from the countersubversives, the "alien" from the "American," imperialists from their prey. As Alan Axelrod and others have observed, *Address*, with its competing first-person narrators, ventriloquial motifs, and emphasis on secrecy, has the feel of a Brown romance, akin, say, to *Wieland, Edgar Huntly,* and "Memoirs of Carwin" (1803–5). Accordingly, there is every reason to be suspicious of both the subversive French consul and the countersubversive U.S. patriot, even as we recognize that *Address*, unlike the romances, does appear to have a specific political purpose: to push the United States toward war with France or any other imperial power that would contest the new nation's right to what the editor/narrator terms "the empire of the Mississippi" (91).[35]

Central to the French consul's plot to establish that empire, as elaborated in his letter in *Address*, is a plan to use blacks and Indians to undermine the U.S. nation. Just as the blacks of Saint Domingue rebelled against the French, the consul argues, so might they rebel against their U.S. enslavers. He thus urges Napoleon to work secretly on inciting slave insurrections in the United States, to "raise, at any moment, a . . . L'Ouverture to distract the counsels, and employ the force which might otherwise annoy himself [Napoleon]; whose own sad experience has informed him of the power of this weapon against the public peace" (73). Similarly, he urges Napoleon to "befriend and use" the Indians, whom he refers to as "aliens and enemies within their borders," claiming that the Indians, "whose delight is war" (74), could be "armed and impelled with far less trouble and expense than an equal number of our own troops" (74–75). Imagining the destruction that would inevitably result from the deployment of insurrectionary blacks and Indians, the consul exults in the manner of a gothic (or satanic) villain: "We shall find, in the bowels of the States, a mischief that only wants the well-directed spark to involve in its explosion, the utter ruin of half their nation. *Such will be the powers we shall derive from a military station and a growing colony on the Mississippi*" (75–76).

By linking the French with the native Americans and slaves (the red and the black), and by diametrically opposing the United States to the French, Brown appears to be implying that white national identity can come into being through the very act of resisting the call of the wild: the supposedly savage otherness of blackness and redness that the French consul wishes to exploit.[36] Viewing the pamphlet from this perspective, Gardner thus links Brown to those countersubversive Federalists who supported the 1798 Alien and Sedition Acts, portraying him as similarly intent in 1803 on exorcizing the alien, in this case the savage "racial" other. Recent evaluations of Brown as white-settler colonialist and imperialist have emerged quickly and seamlessly from this influential analysis.

But once again it is important to note that the Federalists were not as conservative on matters of race as the stereotype of the reactionary

Federalist might suggest. Not only were there debates between Jeffersonian Republicans and some Federalists on the proper response to the Saint Domingan rebels and the emergence of an independent Haiti, but there were also debates between the Federalists and Republicans about whether the Indians should be assimilated into the national culture, expelled, or exterminated. In the 1790s, Federalist philanthropists argued for the possibilities of cultural and even racial "assimilation." Jefferson initially shared the Federalists' philanthropic (albeit racially chauvinistic) mission of absorbing Indians into the new republic. But when he assumed the presidency, he became increasingly committed to Indian removal, writing James Monroe in 1801, for example, that he envisioned white settlers "cover[ing] the whole northern, if not southern continent, with a people speaking the same language, governed in similar forms, and by similar laws; nor can we contemplate with satisfaction either blot or mixture on that surface."[37] With the formal acquisition of the Louisiana Territory, Jefferson and his fellow Republicans sought to remove the Indians to the far reaches of the territory where, he believed, they would eventually die out. It was the Federalists who continued to champion the rights of Native Americans, calling for a slowing of the removal process. Their position was the more humane one, but it lost them votes.[38]

On the evidence of his magazine writings, Brown resisted the notion that "blot and mixture" should be expelled from the "white" nation. His championing of antislavery was never tied to a concomitant championing of African colonization. Similarly, though Brown does not comment directly on the issue of Indian citizenship, his writings on North American Indians suggest an equally capacious sense of human possibility that had important sources in his Enlightenment humanism and Quaker heritage. In the notes to his 1804 translation of C. F. Volney's *A View of the Soil and Climate of the United States of America*, for example, he rejects Volney's description of the Indians as "savages," ironically remarking that "an Indian can abjure his habits, and adopt all the modes of the whites which are worthy of adoption." And in an essay titled "An Account of the Late Proceedings of the Society of Friends (or Quakers) for the Civilization of Indian Tribes," which appeared in the 1805 *Literary Magazine, and American Register*, Brown extols his fellow Quakers for regarding Indians as capable of becoming part of the national community. Rather than seeking to convert the Indians, the Quakers he describes accept them on their own terms and wish simply to improve "their private and domestic condition." The Quakers' successful philanthropic efforts between 1795 and 1805,

Brown says, reveal the Indians' "disposition to improvement."[39] There is nothing in this essay about the Indians as warlike, un-American, or deserving of banishment or extermination; instead, the essay, even with its emphasis on a civilizationist agenda, shows the possibility of whites and Indians living together peacefully and productively while retaining some of their cultural differences.

All of which is to say that, given Brown's attacks on French colonial brutality in Saint Domingue and his essays on the capabilities of blacks and Indians alike, it would be a mistake to read the fictional French consul's comments in *Address* on the savage otherness of blacks and Indians as expressing anything other than the French consul's (not Brown's) views—that is, as the opinions of a character invented by Brown.[40] From the beginning of his letter to Napoleon, the consul approaches the issue of Saint Domingue altogether differently from the way Brown approaches Saint Domingue in his contemporaneous magazine writings. Whereas Brown applauds the Domingan rebels for bringing a worthy black republic into being, the consul lambastes the rebels for converting "those beautiful plantations into an African wilderness" (5). The consul is honest enough to concede that French troops have lost the battle in Saint Domingue, but instead of advising Napoleon to cut his losses in the Americas, he argues that the time is ripe to invade the United States and add to the French empire "not an island, indeed, but a *world*" (14). He asserts that the debacle in Saint Domingue actually provides an opportunity "of beginning a fresh career in the continent of North America" (32), for French troops are currently on the ready in the Americas and have learned much from the rebellious blacks of Saint Domingue. White Americans stand in relation to their slaves, the consul states, as the French did to theirs in Saint Domingue. Envisioning the whites and blacks of the United States killing each other in an apocalyptic war of extermination, the consul remarks that to set the slaves against their masters, all the French have to do is "fan at pleasure, the discontents of this intestine enemy" (75). And he asserts that the French would be best positioned to wreak such havoc on the United States from within the Louisiana Territory.

Although the consul's bloodthirsty, imperialistic plot to create a "Saint Domingue" moment in the United States works with racist notions that are antithetical to the sentiments expressed in Brown's magazine articles, it could be argued that Brown nonetheless is pushing for U.S. expansionism (and war with France) by tapping into whites' anxieties of rebellious blacks. Thus Bill Christophersen remarks of Brown's strategies in *Address*:

"Brown aims his appeal toward America's fear of her blacks—a fear that, he suggests, is well-founded."[41] That fear may have been well-founded (though it is by no means clear that such fears were harbored by all Americans), but Brown makes plain both in *Address* and in his periodical writings on slavery and Saint Domingue that those fears should be founded not on stereotypical notions of black savagery but on the fact of black humanity. Even the French consul recognizes that blacks' anger at U.S. whites has everything to do with their all-too-human hatred of slavery. Declaring that "a cruel servitude" has engendered in the slaves "all the passions of demons; whose injuries have been so great that the law of self-preservation obliges the State to deny to the citizen the power of making his slave free" (73), the consul hopes to spark a massive slave rebellion within the United States. Through the "mouth" of the racist consul, who shows a surprising sympathy for the slaves, Brown thus alerts his white readers to the dangers that the persistence of slavery (as opposed to the presence of blacks) poses to the new nation. In this regard, it is worth underscoring that right around the time of the publication of *Address*, numerous northern states were emancipating their slaves. The evidence suggests that Brown supported that movement. In his 1804 essay "St. Domingo," for instance, he presents the emergence of free "communities of negroes" in the United States as the logical outcome of black rebellion in the Americas, ironically holding out the hope that, despite their history of despotic and racist practices, "whites will be tolerated" within these new communities.[42]

Viewed in relation to his contemporaneous magazine writings, Brown's *Address* is hardly intent on ridding the nation of blacks. Rather, *Address* seeks to warn the nation of the dangers of regionalism and sectionalism, particularly as exacerbated by the immoral and divisive practice of southern slavery. Indeed, one of the large themes of *Address* is that the United States remains vulnerable precisely because regional and sectional politics threaten to fracture national unity. The French consul refers to the current states as "motley," spread out, and characterized by "many clashing jurisdictions and jarring interests" (62). The United States is "vulnerable at every point" (69), he writes, because of these clashing interests, and he similarly asserts that the U.S. government must make extraordinary efforts to "[keep] the hostile parts together" (70). When the patriotic narrator reemerges at the end of the tract to comment on the consul's secret letter, he elaborates arguments about the nation's regional and sectional conflicts consistent with the consul's assessment. As he remarks rhetorically:

"Do the people of the coast regard as aliens and enemies, those beyond the mountains? Those of the northern states, however distant in place and dissimilar in manners, do they regard with no paternal emotions, the happiness or misery of their southern countrymen? . . . Has a national government, and twelve years of its benign influence, done *nothing* towards the union and coherence of the states?" (77–78). In this expression of concern about a lack of national unity, it should be noted, the "aliens and enemies" are not blacks and Indians but fellow U.S. citizens. In order to bring those citizens together into a cohesive national whole, in order to revitalize and regenerate the nation, the narrator asserts in postheroic fashion that what is truly needed is a second Revolutionary War against colonial powers (in this case France) that would ensure both the "deliverance of America from every foreign intruder" (79) and "the union and coherence of the states" (78). Inspired by their "common interests" in preserving the nation's "liberty" (77), the nation's citizenry must rise to the challenge of expelling the French by immediately taking control of the Mississippi before "it is lost to us forever" (91).

As bellicose and expansionistic as Brown's narrator sounds at the conclusion of *Address*, there are good reasons to resist a reading of Brown as an uncritical avatar of Manifest Destiny. Watts writes that Brown's "boisterous rhetoric of manifest destiny barely covered a stinging critique of American factionalism, unrestrained passions, and money grubbing."[43] I would add that Brown's boisterous rhetoric also barely covered a critique of the boisterous rhetoric of Manifest Destiny. From beginning to end in *Address*, the French consul champions his own version of Manifest Destiny in plotting to spread French military power and culture throughout the western territories of North America. As he writes to Napoleon, he wants to conquer America and "people it with our own children, language, religion, and laws" (26). With his ethno-imperial desire to "people" the North American continent with "our own children," the consul reveals himself as a nationalist ideologue who accepts as a given the "natural" link between race (or biology) and nation.

When Brown's patriotic narrator speaks of his own desires to colonize the western territories, he expresses a vision of national destiny that seems similar to that of the French consul. But the narrator also develops his argument in terms of a realpolitik of self-defense against European enemies; and it is here that the narrator and Brown would appear to be speaking in the same voice. "Far be it from me to sanctify the claim to conquest" (86), the narrator writes of Louisiana, now distinguishing himself both from the French consul and millennialist U.S. nationalists as he asserts the primacy of self-defense.[44] In *Monroe's Embassy*, written the same year as his Louisiana pamphlet, Brown, in anticipation of the Monroe Doctrine of 1823, also places matters of national defense above what Jacksonians would come to call Manifest Destiny. On the one hand he maintains that Americans, by virtue of their situation in North America, should think of themselves as the "natural owners" of Louisiana. But rather than invoking providential destiny, he underscores issues of national self-preservation, arguing that the French would "disturb the peace, and endanger the concord and the safety of the brotherhood of which I am one." Perhaps the most interesting argument that he develops in *Monroe's Embassy*, though, is that the French are doing in North America precisely what U.S. leaders would do if they had a footing in France: attempting to advance their own national ends. Instead of presenting continental conflict in terms of good versus evil, Brown therefore relativizes and universalizes nations' geopolitical ambitions to "cover the globe," suggesting that such ambitions tend not to be the province of a single country. "I hate not the French," he remarks. "What I fear, is the French *patriotism*: and the ruin and confusion of my country I expect from their hands, because if they were in my place, and I in theirs, they would have reason to dread it from me, inasmuch as my country is the object of my chief love." That imperial love of power, he makes clear, has nothing to do with goodness or some inherent truth of national exceptionalism; instead, he portrays the quest for power as but one of what he calls the "human infirmities."[45]

Viewed from this perspective, expansionism is something that nations do, not because such activity is sanctioned by God (though some may believe it is), but because power fuels the geopolitics of nationhood. At the core of Brown's writings on Louisiana and imperialism during this time, then, especially when considered in relation to his attacks on French imperial ambitions in Saint Domingue and Louisiana, is a critique (or unmasking) of nationalist exceptionalism—a critique that is developed *not* through explicit statement but through the ironies of narrative performance, specifically through Brown's creation of a countersubversive nationalist narrator who champions exceptionalism in terms very similar to those of the subversive French nationalist. Somewhat paradoxically, Brown, by deploying the opposed but often overlapping personae of *Address*, pursues his nationalist agenda of gaining control of the mouth of the Mississippi by calling for an antiexceptionalist strategic expansionism that aspires to bring about national unity, coherence, purpose, and self-defense. *Address* and *Monroe's Embassy* are simultaneously anxious and reflective texts that, through their collapsing of the distance and differences between subversive and countersubversive, at once critique and sustain the nation. And they are hardly insistent on connections between whiteness and the nation. In *Address*, after all, Brown depicts U.S. citizens in analogous relation to the blacks of Saint Domingue: as freedom-loving peoples who aspire to liberate themselves from the dominion of France. Brown's suggestion that enslaved blacks might attempt a similar liberation from their U.S. enslavers could therefore be taken as a clear-eyed antislavery argument intended to advance the claims of black citizenship.

That said, there are suggestions in some of Brown's nonfictional writings that he imagines the United States as a white nation. In his 1804 "Thoughts on the Probable Duration of the American Republic," for example, the probable author Brown sounds very much like Crèvecoeur in the way that he leaves Africans and Indians (indeed all non-European and non-English peoples) out of his picture of the united nation. Americans, the writer claims, are a people "arising from the same stock, emigrating from the same country, possessing the same language." And yet even as Brown (or a particular Brown persona) now and again makes such assertions, or works with binaries suggestive of large differences between "Americans" and "aliens," he just as often collapses those differences into dualisms. Crucially, in his magazine writings on Saint Domingue, and in the interstices of his Louisiana pamphlets, Brown, despite the proto–Manifest Destiny braggadocio of his expansionism, presents an affirmative vision of a black nationality in the Americas. Moreover, though whiteness may be an important trope of some of Brown's writings on the U.S. nation, his main (and less ironically presented) desideratum, as enunciated in "How Far Do Slaves Influence Political Representation in America," is that the United States should aspire to be a land of "free people."[46] The achievement of that freedom, Brown suggests in a number of his essays and tracts of the early 1800s, is dependent upon abolition, sectional unity, and a strategic expansionism that creates "a complete barrier" not between white and red, or white and black, but between a still vulnerable nation and those European nations that are willing to exploit racial and ethnic conflicts for their own colonizing ends.

Brown's concerns about aliens, revolution, social instability, nationhood, and empire span the five-year period from *Wieland* to the Louisiana pamphlets, but his politics of the "alien" seem to me deliberately unclear.

If Brown wished to link the French and blacks as threatening aliens, then why did he insist in his magazine articles on the *differences* between the two? And if he was concerned in his pre-1800 writings with "exorcizing the alien," then why did he choose to create formally challenging and complex narratives that fail to convey readily discernible meanings or agendas about such a political project? As I will be arguing in the next section, Brown's novels, like the Louisiana pamphlets, are exceptionally *knowing* texts, novels that can be read both as expressions of anxiety about the "alien" and as social critiques that point to the cultural pathology of such anxieties. The novels can also be read in terms of the performative rhetorical strategies and contingencies that I have been tracing in this section. My focus will be on *Edgar Huntly*, currently regarded as Brown's colonialist/imperialist novel par excellence, which I will read through the lens of the Louisiana pamphlets as a text that blurs national and racial identities and obscures (and unfixes) historical trajectories. Before turning to *Edgar Huntly*, though, it would be useful to resituate Brown in the early 1800s—this time not as a pamphleteer but as a writer of fiction.

The Brownian Moment: Ed[gar] [Hu]n[tl]y

The same year that Brown published his Louisiana tracts, and several months after the announcement of the Louisiana Purchase, Brown founded a new journal, the *Literary Magazine, and American Register*, which he edited through 1807. In the "Editors' [sic] Address to the Public," printed in the inaugural October 1803 issue, Brown asserted that "I should enjoy a larger share of my own respect, at the present moment, if nothing had ever flowed from my pen, the production of which could be traced to me." Having "renounced" his earlier writings, he went on to declare that as editor of the journal he will pay "supreme regard . . . to the interests of religion and morality."[47] There is no reason not to regard the "Editors' Address" as a sincere expression of what was on Brown's mind "at the present moment." But we need to be wary of taking these remarks as conclusive evidence of a dramatic change in Brown's literary and political perspectives. Most of his not-so-earlier novels begin or conclude on moralistic notes and address broad questions of religion, and thus his statement of embarrassment about those novels could be read as a show of false modesty or, at the very least, as an artist's self-conscious assessment of his own limitations. More to the point, if Brown truly wished to renounce his earlier work, then how to explain his decision one month later to publish in his journal what would turn out to be a ten-issue serialization of "Memoirs of Carwin," a "prequel" to his 1798 *Wieland* that was clearly intended to entice readers to take another look at his first novel?

Brown never entirely renounced fiction. Though he did not publish any novels after 1801, he continued to publish his own fiction in his journals. In addition to "Memoirs of Carwin," he published "Somnambulism" and "The Romance of Real Life" in 1805 issues of the *Literary Magazine*, "Omar and Fatima" in an 1807 issue, and other fragments and tales, including a fictional piece, in the Federalist journal the *Port Folio*. He also regularly commented on fiction in his magazines, listed recently published novels, printed a wide range of European writers, and all the while continued to encourage an American literary nationalism.[48]

In 1801 Brown published two epistolary novels, *Clara Howard* and *Jane Talbot*, which, on the surface, can be read in relation to the editor's "Address" of 1803 as literary efforts to uplift the nation by teaching relatively orthodox lessons about the importance of religion and morality. Addressing the limits of a Godwinian rationalism, both novels attempt to instruct through their marriage plots that, as Clara puts it in *Clara Howard*, "the welfare of another may demand self-denial from us, and that in bestowing benefits on others, there is purer delight than in gratification merely selfish and exclusive." And yet a striking aspect of these novels, especially when compared to Brown's political pamphlets of 1803, is their relative lack of concern about articulating the distinct contours of the U.S. nation. When the nation is brought to the fore in these works, Brown emphasizes the fluidity of national identity, showing how the new nation is receptive to emigrants and can exist relatively comfortably in relation to other nations, even France and Spain. Indeed, the characters' complicated histories of migrations and emigrations raise all kinds of questions about the difficulties of defining national citizenship. As Mary Wilmot declares to Hartley in *Clara Howard*: "Alas! . . . I should be puzzled to say to what country I belong. I am a German by my father; English by my mother. I was born at a hotel in Paris, I was nursed by a woman of Nice, where I passed my infancy; and my youth and womanhood, and probably my whole life, belong to America. Now, what is the country, Germany, England, France, Italy or America, which I have a right to call my own." Mary is an unthreatening version of the transnational (even postnational) travelers described in Brown's novels of the late 1790s, such as the Syrian-born Martinette in *Ormond* (1799), who fights in the American and French Revolutions and eventually makes her way to Saint Domingue for reasons that remain obscure but seem to reflect her enthusiasm for bloody revolutionary conflict. In *Jane Talbot*, Jane's brother, like Martinette, journeys to France and joins the "republican troops." Yet there is nothing devious or threatening about him; he has simply chosen to be, "for the remainder of his life, a Frenchman." The only effort to limn a distinctive sense of an American nationality in either novel of 1801 occurs when Hartley, thwarted by his seeming inability to marry his beloved Clara, confesses to an obsessive interest in studying a map of the American West. For Hartley, the West is the essential United States, and he therefore announces his intention to embrace westward migration: "Tomorrow I go hence, in company with a person who holds an high rank in the Spanish districts westward of the Mississippi."[49] As it turns out, Hartley's western fantasies signal that he is on the verge of a mental breakdown, though it is worth noting that even in the midst of such fantasies, his reference to the Spanish suggests that he does not regard the Louisiana territories as manifestly destined for an exclusively U.S. nationality. Perhaps he was not so mad after all.

With his portrayal in his epistolary novels of 1801 of a porous, vulnerable, and still-developing nation, Brown looks forward to his vision of the nation in the Louisiana writings of 1803, while remaining fairly consistent to the vision of such late 1790s novels as *Wieland* and *Edgar Huntly*. Most critics, however, emphasize difference over similarity, seeing the slightly earlier novels as considerably more radical and aesthetically challenging, and thus lamenting Brown's fall into what are regularly termed conservative bourgeois fictions. Taking a very different perspective, Gardner celebrates the epistolary fictions over the slightly earlier fictions as moral and (to a certain extent) aesthetic advances. Arguing that Brown as an epistolary author of 1801 assumes the posture of an "editor" analogous to his work as an editor on his various magazines and journals during this same period, Gardner suggests that this more multivocal Brown came to recognize the sheer cultural nastiness of the early American novel that "he himself had helped bring to life: the novel of the autonomous individual, the story told through one voice, one psychology, and bound by the requirements of chronology, unity, and totalizing conclusion." As an editor and epistolary novelist, Gardner contends, Brown in this final phase of his career (beginning around 1801) tried his best "to rise above the poor choices the novel and the nation had to offer," specifically coming to rethink, and recoil from, the novel's participation in a univocal (white) American literary nationalism.[50]

There are reasons to resist such an analysis. Brown wrote virtually all of the anonymous material in his magazines, and so one wonders about the extent of his apparent catholicity. More to the point, when turning from Brown's epistolary fictions of 1801 back to his and other novels of the early republic, circa 1789–1801, we have to ask: Where is that totalized novel that should leave us shaking our heads in ethical dismay? And was early national writing so homogeneous? Epistolary modes are central to numerous novels of the period, and even in those novels where there is a seemingly monological voice of a single narrator, it takes little effort to discern, in Bakhtinian fashion, a play of competing voices and perspectives. The most popular novels of the period are characterized by a multivocality and, I would suggest, a basic uncertainty about the nation as it is coming into being, and uncertainty as well about its possible future. As one might expect during the postconstitutional moment, the popular novels of the time address, in varied and ultimately conflicted ways, questions of virtue, women's role in the republic, slavery and region, nationality, class conflict, transatlanticism, democracy versus republicanism, and the problem of interpretation.

Consider, for example, William Hill Brown's *The Power of Sympathy* (1789), generally regarded as the first novel published in the United States. While the novel clearly argues for the importance of republican virtue and family to the new nation, it also depicts a history of genealogical entanglement that makes it nearly impossible for individuals to tell the difference between a potential spouse and a sibling (the racial dimensions of such genealogical entanglements, which are not addressed directly in this novel, will be the main subject of chapter 3). Moreover, the novel points to a dangerously divided nation that hasn't yet figured out the place of slavery and race in its polity. When the hero Harrington travels to South Carolina, for instance, he reports on a virtuous female slave who bears a scar on her neck from protecting her young son from a whipping. Harrington celebrates her for possessing "a fire that the damps of slavery had not extinguished";[51] and in presenting her in this way, the novel suggests that such nobility would only add to the moral health of the republic. At a time when many northern states were abolishing slavery, *The Power of Sympathy* extends its sympathies across the boundaries of race without ever suggesting that the nation would be better off by removing virtuous blacks from within its borders. Royall Tyler's *The Algerine Captive* (1797) affirms that the nation *would* be better off by abolishing slavery from within its borders, and though its emphasis is on white slavery, the insistence on the suffering of the slave (whatever his or her race) works to break down barriers between whites and blacks.[52] In Tabitha Gilman Tenney's *Female Quixotism* (1801), the author goes even further in dissolving barriers between white and black, depicting the "sweet satisfaction" that a white woman experiences when, unbeknownst to her, she embraces a black man as her lover.[53]

Although popular works like Susanna Rowson's *Charlotte Temple* (1791, 1794) and Hannah W. Foster's *The Coquette* (1797) do not explicitly address race and can seem quite conservative in warning of the dangers of seduction facing vulnerable young women, they offer less-than-clear political messages about national vulnerability and ultimately advance agendas of female empowerment. After all, Rowson's heroine is British (thus making it difficult to sustain a U.S. nationalist allegorical reading of the novel), and in both works there is a feminist emphasis on encouraging women to become active agents within patriarchal culture. Even a seemingly conservative novel like Hugh Henry Brackenridge's multivolume *Modern Chivalry* (1792–1815) depicts a variety of social and political perspectives in what Looby has termed "a nearly anarchic textual field." The fact that Brackenridge worked on the novel for more than twenty years suggests an author who was trying to understand social and political tensions in a nation that, to the very end, he could not quite figure out. Concerned about the breakdown of class hierarchies, he nonetheless creates in the Irishman Teague O'Regan the most energetic and attractive character of the overall novel—a character who at one point speaks as "the orator of the human race" while dressed as "an Esquimaux Indian, and pass[ing] his aboriginal Irish, for the native dialect of that people." Concerned about the "foreign" in the midst of the domestic, Brackenridge nonetheless writes of foreigners in the novel's 1805 part 2, volume 2: "What right have we to exclude them? We are not born for ourselves; nor did we achieve the revolution for ourselves only. We fought the cause of all mankind."[54] Such Paine-like sentiments, whether espoused by Teague or the narrator, speak to a willingness to extend citizenship across the lines of class, ethnicity, and race, even as Brackenridge continues to worry over the implications of such democratic leveling.

As a group, then, early American novels participate in cultural debates, eschew easy nationalist allegories, and ultimately frame the difficulties of interpreting a confusing and changing world as one of their central subjects and problems. As Julia Granby of *The Coquette* concisely puts it: "How prone to error is the human mind!"[55] If, as we see in *The Power of Sympathy*, *Charlotte Temple*, *The Coquette*, and many other novels of the period, the mind is prone to error, then perhaps the implicit "Federalist" argument of these works is the need for strong institutions of social control.[56] But if the human mind is prone to error, then who is to say that the institutions and national formations created by such minds would not themselves be prone to error? Such are the epistemological quandaries, in small, of the early American novel, and such are the quandaries, on a much larger scale, of Brockden Brown's major novels of the 1790s.

Whatever their views on Brown's politics of the 1790s and beyond, most critics would agree that, as Michael T. Gilmore puts it, Brown's "writing destabilizes the epistemological certainties of republican culture."[57] Those certainties hinged in part on an Enlightenment confidence in the powers of the human mind—a confidence that is regularly brought into question in Brown's novels. As Clara acutely remarks in *Wieland* on the rationalist Pleyel's misreading of her actions: "What is man, that knowledge is so sparingly conferred upon him? . . . What are the bounds of human imbecility!"[58] During the 1790s and early 1800s, these "certainties" of republican culture also hinged on a series of binaries—virtue/immorality, self/other, civilized/savage, and so on—that Brown, both in his novels and his political pamphlets, regularly collapses into dualisms or oneness. J. G. A. Pocock famously coined the phrase "the Machiavellian moment" to describe those moments in republican culture when there is a loss of confidence in the terms of that culture and a concomitant intimation of the republic's "temporal finitude . . . in a stream of irrational events."[59] In a similar vein, I am coining the phrase "the Brownian moment" to describe those moments in Brown's fiction when there is a destabilization or collapse of the binaries that uphold the identity and coherence of self and republican nation—a destabilization or collapse that typically has everything to do with human frailty (and stupidity). Those dislocating moments, such as the merging of countersubversive and subversive in the Louisiana *Address*, ultimately raise questions about national ideologies and dominant cultural assumptions, and precisely because of the challenge they pose to the basic terms of early national culture, they disclose the contingencies of that culture as well.

In the Louisiana-inflected reading of *Edgar Huntly* that follows, I will be focusing on the collapse between American and foreigner, white and red, civilized and savage; and, unlike most recent readers of the novel, I will be arguing that what collapses stays collapsed and is not reconstituted into some sort of coherent nationalist allegory. In this respect, the novel is consistent with Brown's other major novels of 1798–1800. *Wieland* may well provide a lesson on the "evils of credulity on the one hand, and of imposture on the other," but it offers no clear guideposts as to how one might confidently read the world correctly, or how one might maintain one's difference from homicidal maniacs. As Clara declares after learning that her brother is a killer and that insanity runs in her family: "Now was I stupefied with ten-fold wonder in contemplating myself. Was I not likewise transformed from rational and human into a creature of nameless and fearful attributes. . . . Ere a new day should come, my hands might be embrued in blood, and my remaining life be consigned to a dungeon and chains."[60] Similar such Brownian moments of breakdown between self and other punctuate *Ormond* and *Arthur Mervyn*. One thinks, for example, of the close resemblances between the subversive Ormond and the countersubversive Sophia Courtland/Westwyn in *Ormond*, and between Arthur Mervyn and Welbeck in *Arthur Mervyn*. As in his journalistic writings on Saint Domingue of the late 1790s and early 1800s, moments of collapse and reversal are also pivotal to Brown's exploration of race in these novels. In both *Ormond* and *Arthur Mervyn*, Brown takes pains to depict blacks at the time of the yellow fever crisis as benevolent and humane, even as he shows selfish whites falling into the sort of barbarism that whites regularly projected onto blacks. In *Arthur Mervyn* in particular, he pointedly challenges racial differences, as Carroll Smith-Rosenberg observes, through two key mirror scenes that show black and white identities merging into one. If Mervyn near the end of the novel takes pride in his superiority to "two female blacks," whom he links to "an ape," the fact is that he ends up marrying a Jewish woman whose complexion is "dark and almost sallow."[61]

Motifs of racial destabilization, inversion, and collapse are central to *Edgar Huntly* as well. To be sure, the first-person narrator Edgar Huntly aspires to give coherent shape to the startling events he describes by developing a chronological narrative that has a beginning, middle, and end. As he states at the outset: "Let me place in order the incidents that are to compose my tale." But as he tells his tale, he refers again and again to the unpredictability and contingency of the various "incidents" that he both experienced (he claims) and now attempts to make sense of in his extended account to his betrothed. As he confides over the course of the narrative, these incidents, or what he terms "[a]ccidents . . . over which I had no control," unfolded "in a kind of chaos" that was "impossible to be computed or foreseen," leaving him with a heightened sense of the "instability of life and happiness . . . as well as the perniciousness of error."[62]

Deploying a narrator who attempts to tell a history that he professes not to understand, Brown presses his readers to regard Huntly's story as a rhetorical performance that, precisely because of its performative nature, should be distrusted, or at the very least (as with the voices in *Address*) regarded as partial and self-interested. Again and again the novel unsettles fixed narratives, suggesting alternative possibilities and competing angles of vision. Precisely for that reason, the novel lends itself to an analysis that goes against the grain of current historicists' impositions on the text and its historical moment of an irrevocably fixed narrative of emergent white American empire from the 1780s (the historical setting of the novel) to the late 1790s (the historical moment of the novel's composition), the imperial expansionism of the nineteenth century, and beyond. Geoffrey Hawthorne writes that a principal goal of counterfactual analysis is "understanding more and knowing less."[63] My reading of *Edgar Huntly* will be attending to the greater understanding that Brown attempts to develop in his readers by implicating them in the narrator's unknowingness. Central to the narrator's uncertainties are the difficulties of making distinctions between an (American) self and (non-American) other—the uncertainties, that is to say, that are also central to Brown's Louisiana pamphlet and much of his fiction.

LIKE BROWN'S OTHER MAJOR NOVELS of the late 1790s, *Edgar Huntly* has a complex, sometimes confusing plot, an oddly unreliable narrator, and gripping events that pull the reader into a story that initially (and deceptively) seems fairly simple. Edgar, who wishes to marry his friend Waldegrave's sister Mary, writes her an extended first-person narrative about the recent murder of her brother and his efforts to determine the killer. Edgar's chief suspect is a local "stranger" (14), the Irish immigrant Clithero Edny, the novel's initial non-American "other" and a sleepwalker whom Edgar obsessively spies on while Clithero obsessively digs around the nearby elm tree where Waldegrave had been shot. When Edgar confronts Clithero and demands "a confession of crimes" (32), the Irish immigrant has his own story to tell, not about the murder of Waldegrave but his own tragic past. In the lengthy autobiographical account, which Edgar includes in his larger narrative, Clithero, like Edgar, emphasizes the unpredictable and contingent in his dramatic storytelling, and it quickly becomes clear that the two young men have even more in common than their mutually obsessive behaviors and performative narratives might suggest. Clithero, the son of an Irish peasant, tells of how he had been informally adopted in Ireland by the wealthy Mrs. Lorimer, who eventually even provides him with a possible future wife, Clarice, the illegitimate daughter of Mrs. Lorimer's evil twin brother, Arthur Wiatte. But as becomes apparent in the telling, Clithero harbors a resentment towards Mrs. Lorimer precisely because he feels so beholden to her. That resentment manifests itself in a series of increasingly bizarre and unpredictable incidents that Clithero now describes to Edgar as part of his larger story. He tells of killing a stranger who assaulted him, only to find that that stranger was Wiatte himself, the father of his intended bride. Because Mrs. Lorimer had repeatedly said that the death of her brother would lead to her own death, Clithero, upon returning to Lorimer's, resolves to stab the woman sleeping there, with the hope of sparing her great unhappiness, only to be stopped by Mrs. Lorimer herself when she grabs him and reveals that he is about to kill Clarice. In an effort to explain the "philanthropic" basis of his actions, Clithero abruptly announces to Mrs. Lorimer that her brother is dead, and she keels over apparently dead herself. At a loss as to what to do next, Clithero leaves the estate, "assume[s] a beggar's attire," and eventually boards a ship to the "new world" (88) of Philadelphia.

What Edgar and Clithero have in common is this: like Arthur Mervyn, both are dependent on benefactors. Whereas Clithero depends upon Mrs. Lorimer, the hard-up Edgar depends upon his uncle, who offers him lodgings and may possibly bequeath him an inheritance. Edgar and Mary had also been depending on Waldegrave, who does bequeath his sister $8,000. But even with this inheritance, Edgar is in many respects as dependent upon the good will of others as Clithero, and equally resentful. Clithero and Edgar also share a connection to the surgeon Sarsefield, whom Mrs. Lorimer had loved before being forced by her family to marry Lorimer and who acted as a surrogate father to Edgar after his parents had been killed by Indians.

It is not surprising, then, that the Brownian moment, the paradigm that I've noted in other Brown novels as well, occurs relatively early in *Edgar Huntly*, as the distance between Edgar Huntly and Clithero Edny quickly collapses.[64] (Brown anticipates that collapse right from the start by planting Edny's name in Ed[gar] [Hu]n[tl]y.) Edgar describes himself after listening to Clithero's story as "sunk into imbecility and confusion" (91), declaring about Clithero what he could also declare about himself: "How imperfect are the grounds of all our decisions!" (92). He then begins to act precisely in the manner of the man he obsessively monitors, trailing him to a cave in the nearby wilderness area of Norwalk while exhibiting somnambulistic behavior similar to Clithero's. Edgar's interpretation of Clithero's sleepwalking as testimony to his guilt and anger with respect to Waldegrave turns out to be a compelling way of interpreting Edgar's own sleepwalking. Significantly, following two scenes in which Edgar pursues Clithero to the cave, Edgar reveals that he may have to postpone his marriage to Waldegrave's sister because the Waldegrave inheritance is threatened by a newcomer claiming the money as his own. Waldegrave, who seemed to have provided Edgar with financial freedom, becomes just another person who has let him down.

At this point in the novel there is a second Brownian moment, an apparent collapse of the significant differences not only between the "American" Edgar and the foreigner Clithero, but also between Edgar and the Indians just beyond the white settlements. In a key scene following the revelation of the possibly tainted inheritance, Edgar awakens in the wilderness, confused and disoriented in the manner of Clithero. He carries "an Indian tom-hawk" (161),[65] and he experiences a new ferocity that initially exhibits itself in a "savage" appetite. He writes (to his fiancée!) that he wanted to "bite the flesh from my arm" (164); and as Clara Wieland would declare that "I thirsted for his [Carwin's] blood,"[66] Edgar states: "My heart overflowed with cruelty, and I pondered on the delight I should experience in rending some living animal to pieces and drinking its blood and grinding its quivering fibres between my teeth" (164). Whereupon he kills a panther with his tom-hawk and devours it raw, drinking down its blood. Immediately thereafter, despite his "religious scruples" (179), he kills an Indian and drinks again: "To quench my thirst was a consideration by which all others were supplanted. I approached the torrent, and not only drank copiously, but laved my head, neck, and arms, in this delicious element" (179). Though it seems as if he is drinking the blood of the Indian in the same way that he drank the blood of the panther, on closer reading it is apparent that he walks past the dead Indian in order to reach a stream. But Brown deliberately blends blood and water to emphasize the extent to which Edgar has gone "savage." The "ferocious" (192) and savage Edgar then shoots additional Indians, ostensibly to help a young woman whom the Indians are holding for ransom.

Delirious at his killing of "[t]hree beings, full of energy and heroism, with minds strenuous and lofty" (194), he tumbles onto the body of one of the dead Indians, and their identities merge: "My head had reposed upon the breast of him who I had shot in this part of his body. The blood had ceased to ooze from the wound, but my dishevelled locks were matted and steeped in that gore which had overflowed and choked up the orifice" (197). Not surprisingly, when white settlers, including the young woman's father, come upon the scene of "carnage and blood" (194), they see Edgar as a red man. This will not be the only occasion of such a misperception.

As Edgar explains in the midst of narrating his savage killings, his ferocity is fueled in part by his desire for vengeance and not simply by his frustration at losing Waldegrave's money. And it is here, more than half-way through the novel, that Edgar reveals a crucial and heretofore re-pressed fact: his parents and a sibling had been killed by Indians when he was a boy. Though that event had occurred in the distant past, he now blames the Indians for his descent into savagery. Historian Bernard Sheehan describes such projection as typical of whites' rationalizations of their frontier violence against the Indians: "By striking out with indis-criminate rage at his savage enemy, the frontiersman demonstrated that the Indian in his desperate struggle for survival was yet capable of making the white man abandon his claims to cultural superiority." Or, to put this another way, "the white man interpreted his own atrocities as imitations of Indian savagery."[67] Such a conceptualization of cross-racial violence helped whites to distinguish themselves from the Indians as they sought to match savagery with savagery, and helped as well to justify the removal policies that Jefferson began to put into force after the acquisition of Louisiana. The view that Indian "savagery" created white savagery also worked to occlude the specifics of white colonial history, making white-red conflict into a simple matter of civilization versus savagery, rather than a part of a violent process of colonization and removal.

So the question that comes to the fore is this: what is Brown's perspec-tive on Edgar's "savage" white colonial violence? Some critics see little distance between Brown and Edgar, claiming that Brown is fully impli-cated in Edgar's homicidal hatred of the Indians. As Myra Jehlen remarks, "*Edgar Huntly*'s gothic conventions come alive in an implacable hatred of Indians that the author shares with his characters."[68] That supposed con-gruence between Huntly's and Brown's Indian hating—despite the fact that in the overall novel, as one critic notes, "Edgar is wrong about almost everything," and despite the even more pressing fact that Brown's narrators are just about always ironically conceived and comically unreliable—has led a number of recent commentators to assert that the novel, in the words of Rowe, "rationalizes the colonial displacement of and violence toward native peoples."[69] And yet just as Brown in his 1799–1805 magazine writings on Saint Domingue imaginatively embraces the perspective of black revolutionaries, and just as in his Louisiana writings he exposes the will to power of both French and U.S. imperialists (however implicated he may be in the U.S. imperial vision), so in the second half of *Edgar Huntly* does he imaginatively embrace the perspective of rebellious Indians and expose the brutalities of frontier colonialism (however implicated he may be in the work of such colonialism). Again I would emphasize that Brown's novel is representing conflicts and tensions in the colonial project at a time when there would have remained a relative uncertainty about what would happen next; the novel itself, by accentuating uncertainty, both resists its emplotment in an unfolding national narrative and disrupts that narrative. A text of and about decolonization and colonialism, *Edgar Huntly* expresses in "the interstices of Edgar's 'official' history," as Janie Hinds nicely puts it, Brown's postcolonial desire to trouble the dominant languages of colonialism.[70] As I have been suggesting, he does this by linking his main character, already linked to a resentful (and perhaps even revolutionary) Irish immigrant,[71] to the Indians, whom he may not hate after all.

When Edgar describes the traumatic murder of his parents and sibling, he locates that event both in a contemporary and larger historical context of cross-racial violence in the Pennsylvania frontier, noting that, "at this time, some hostilities had been committed on the frontier; that a long course of injuries and encroachments had lately exasperated the Indian tribes" (173). Oddly, in this telling he seems more sympathetic to the Indians than to his dead family. The novel's most fully developed Indian character, Old Deb, also known as Queen Mab, periodically seeks vengeance for injuries done to her and her people by the white colonizers, and it is Edgar who provides background on white-Indian relations, based on historical fact, that reveals the sources of Deb's rage: "This woman originally belonged to the tribe of Delawares of Lennilennappe. All these districts were once comprised within the dominions of that nation. About thirty years ago, in consequence of perpetual encroachments of the English colonists, they abandoned their ancient seats and retired to the banks of the Wabash and Muskingum" (207).[72] According to Edgar, there was only one Indian who resisted this emigration, Deb, who "declared her resolution to remain behind, and maintain possession of the land which her countrymen should impiously abandon" (207). Not only does Deb refuse to leave the land, but she also demands food and clothing from neighboring whites, and she continually challenges the terms of their complacent colonizing narrative. Edgar explains, "She conceived that by remaining behind her countrymen she succeeded to the government, and retained the possession of all this region. The English were aliens and sojourners, who occupied the land merely by her connivance and permission, and whom she allowed to remain on no terms but those of supplying her wants" (208–9). Crucially, as Edgar recalls this history, he experiences a heightened implication in white colonialism, even a heightened sense of his own status as "alien," for the "village inhabited by this clan was built upon ground which now constitutes my uncle's barn yard and orchard" (207).[73]

Edgar's land-grabbing uncle, of course, is the same uncle whom he fears will disinherit him; and it quickly becomes clear that his emphasis on the injuries and violations experienced by the Indians speaks to his own resentments about his marginal relation to the white community. It is therefore not all that surprising that he should come to empathize with Deb's anger (and seem relatively unmoved later in the narrative when he learns that his uncle has been killed by Indians). Edgar had also depended upon Waldegrave, whose death, we learn at the end of the novel, is also directly linked to Deb. Furious at having been forced to abandon her cottage and move twenty miles farther from the white settlements, Deb, after "enumerating the injuries which she had received from her neighbours" (280), urges the Indians to take violent revenge on the whites. Her rage inspires one Indian to execute the first white he meets after departing from Deb, and that unfortunate person, shot by "that fateful Elm" (7), turns out to be Waldegrave.[74] This Indian is but one of many Indians who, as Edgar explains, "were councelled and guided, in all their movement, by Queen Mab, who . . . boldly defied her oppressors" (281).

Kazanjian argues that Brown's romances are informed by "fears from white settler colonialism's unfinished business," and that his way of addressing those fears is to attempt "to close down any critical consideration of white settler colonialism."[75] But with his troubling of the binary of colonizing white and savage Indian, his sketches of the history of white settlers' dispossession of the Indians, and in particular his representation of Deb/Mab's turning of the linguistic tables to identify the white colonists as "aliens and sojourners" and "oppressors," Brown, as in his writings on Saint Domingue of just a few years later, scrutinizes the terms of white settler colonialism and displays the anger of its victims. He performs this cultural work in *Edgar Huntly* most dramatically through Edgar's sympathetic embrace of Deb. While most of the white townspeople of Solebury regard her as "a subject of mirth and good humour," Edgar takes to her as "an object of curiosity and speculation" (209). They even become friends. As he explains: "She frequently came to my uncle's house, and I sometimes visited her; insensibly she seemed to contract an affection for me" (209). That affection is clearly mutual, based in part, as the mention of her visits to his uncle suggest, on their shared resentment of the uncle. It is Edgar who had dubbed her Queen Mab, after the fairy in Shakespeare's *Romeo and Juliet*, presumably because as one of the possible murderers of his family she both haunts his dreams and enacts his desires.[76] It thus seems entirely appropriate that the sleepwalking Edgar should take refuge in Deb's hut before his climactic battles with the whites that she so despises.

Deb's denunciation of whites as "oppressors" is voiced but four paragraphs from the conclusion of Edgar's narrative and is nowhere contradicted; it is the knowledge that resonates throughout the final third or so of the novel. Reading *Edgar Huntly* in relation to Brown's slightly later writings on Louisiana and Haiti, we can discern striking similarities between his portrayal of the Saint Domingans' violent rebellions against the French and his portrayal of Queen Mab and her followers' violent rebellions against the Anglo-Americans on the western frontier of Pennsylvania. There is virtually nothing in *Edgar Huntly* that rationalizes the claims of the whites beyond the fact that the whites have more power than the Indians. If anything, considerations of the similarities between the resistant Saint Domingans and Indians suggest that what is most easily rationalized in *Edgar Huntly* is the anger of those who resist the encroachments of colonizing imperialists.

Where *is* Edgar at the end of the novel? And what does Brown suggest is the character of the nation itself? As I have been arguing, Brown's presentation of the dominant culture's binaries as dualisms that collapse back upon themselves creates all kinds of problems for any simple allegorization of the novel in relation to a politics of white nation or emergent empire. In this regard, it is worth noticing just how inconclusive and confusing the ending of the novel actually is. In a striking reversal, Edgar spends a good deal of time in the novel's final section doing battle not with Indians but with whites, who see him as an Indian, thereby further linking him with Deb. Among those who are shooting at him, and who conclude that he is dead, is Sarsefield, whom Edgar calls "the parent and fosterer of my mind, the companion and instructor of my youth, from whom I had been parted for years" (240). It is ironic that just as Sarsefield views Edgar as an Indian, so Edgar views Sarsefield and his compatriots as Indians, which is why they shoot at one another. It is additionally ironic that Edgar's final encounter with an actual Indian involves an exchange of glances in which Edgar simply watches him escape from the custody of whites. He remarks that the Indian's "flight might have been easily arrested by my shot, but surprize, added to my habitual antipathy to bloodshed, . . . made me hesitate" (266). In the context of the novel's collapsing of the distance between Edgar and the Indians, even to the point of blending their bloody bodies, there's a sense of a connection between Edgar and this particular Indian, as if they look at one another with a shared understanding of their positions as aliens.

In the novel's concluding chapters, there is also a reemphasis on the initial collapsing of identities of the "American" Edgar and the Irishman Clithero. In the sort of extraordinary coincidence that is the trademark of Brown's intricately contrived plotting, Sarsefield, who had been both Edgar's teacher and to a certain extent Clithero's rival for Mrs. Lorimer, now arrives in America with Mrs. Lorimer, who, it turns out, did not actually die when Clithero told her the news of her brother's death. Accompanying the couple is Mrs. Lorimer's niece Clarice, whom Sarsefield now hopes to marry off to Edgar, just as Mrs. Lorimer had initially hoped to marry her off to Clithero. Once again there are distinctive overlaps and similarities, which are underscored by Edgar's continued determination to help his double, this time by telling Sarsefield Clithero's story about how he killed Wiatte in self-defense and subsequently tried to spare Mrs. Lorimer the pain of learning about her brother's death by "philanthropically" killing her. One sleepwalker thus tells the story of the other sleepwalker to the man who increasingly resents them both. Of course both sleepwalkers have their own class resentments toward Sarsefield, and as it turns out, the two of them will be responsible for killing his heir. The question at the end of the novel, then, is the question that has been raised throughout and that informs much of Brown's writing from 1798 to 1810: How different are "Americans" from their various "others"?

And specifically with respect to *Edgar Huntly*, what sort of allegorical account of the emergence of the "American," if any, is this novel attempting to develop?[77]

Edgar's own statements at the end of the novel convey his utter confusion and suggest that if the future of the nation depends upon the emergence of this particular individual as an "American," then the nation is in a very sorry state indeed. "How little cognizance have men over the actions and motives of each other!" (278), Edgar declares in the manner of Clara Wieland upon realizing once again how similar he is to Clithero. Consistent with the linkages among Edgar, Clithero, and the Indians as rebels, the gravely wounded Clithero, whom the surgeon Sarsefield refuses to help, is eventually nursed back to health by women who use leeches as instructed by the Indians. The Indian-like rage toward Sarsefield of the recovered Clithero and Edgar then blurs and overlaps, as revealed in the novel's closing epistolary sequence. Over the course of two letters, Edgar warns Sarsefield that Clithero now knows about Mrs. Lorimer's existence and comes in pursuit of her. (Significantly, Edgar informs Clithero about Mrs. Lorimer while in Deb's hut.) In a final letter written from a ship off New York City, Sarsefield tells Edgar that his two letters of warning caused Mrs. Lorimer to go into labor and give birth to a stillborn child, and that Clithero then jumped into New York Bay and drowned. Sarsefield's final admonishing word to Edgar is "Farewell" (293). Edgar, it appears, is not just an Indian killer but also the killer of his white guardian's baby.

In short, there is no resolution in *Edgar Huntly*, no emergence in the historical moment chronicled by the novel (the 1780s) of a clearly defined white U.S. nation, but simply confusion, misunderstanding, chaos, and death. Rather than present readers with an allegory of nation creating through the heroic figure of an Indian killer, Brown breaks down distinctions among "Americans," Indians, and foreigners and provides virtually no clues as to how the nation might develop from the conflicts and confusions enacted in his novel. Moralistic assertions about the importance of early nationals learning "to read more justly than those whose reading has been schooled by newspapers or novels such as *Edgar Huntly*" simply make no sense; for if early nationals *had* taken an interest in *Edgar Huntly*, they would have encountered a fracturing narrative of frontier violence that, with its troubling of the conceptual categories of race and nation, could have helped them to read more justly. Ed White writes about frontier violence during the 1785 to 1815 period: "Given the deep challenges posed by these fundamentally internal conflicts, no easy sense of nation could develop, while the class and racial conflicts that these events expressed became entangled with the terminology of the nation."[78] With his portrayal of Edgar's and Clithero's class resentments and racial confusions, Brown is making a similar point in 1799, exploring rather than reifying identities. Or, to put this another way, rather than being a propagandist for the nation, he is trying to understand the nation, and he has anticipated many of the insights of his most critical postcolonial readers. As I have said, this is not to argue that Brown managed to "transcend" the conflicts, anxieties, racism, and discursive pressures of his period. Nonetheless, he had a vision of emerging U.S. empire that comprehended its contingency and in certain respects its incomprehensibility. Central to Brown's moral perspective in *Edgar Huntly*, then, is an unwillingness to suggest that he knows any more than he knows.[79]

Boundaries and Territories

Brown's anonymous 1800 essay "Thoughts on the Origin of the Claims of Europeans to North-America," which he published in his *Monthly Magazine and American Review*, can be read as a gloss on *Edgar Huntly*, and here Brown does seem more willing to present himself as knowing. In the essay Brown initially appears to be just another white American who accepts civilizationist notions of white ascent and Indian decline, along with traditional views that the English colonizers, when they came to the New World, encountered an essentially empty continent with just "a few scores of savages." But at the heart of the essay is a pointed challenge to the assumptions of those colonizers who believed they had the right to take lands from the Indians. Stating that the "claims of the Christian nations in general to America, were founded partly on the pre-eminence which their progress in refinement was supposed to confer," Brown puts a deliberately ironic pressure on the "supposed" to suggest, as in *Edgar Huntly* and his Louisiana writings, that the real issue in the contest for land between the colonists and the Indians was little more than power. Sympathetically writing of the Indians' efforts to resist the whites' taking of their lands, Brown points out what most white Americans failed to acknowledge: that "the claims of the Indians essentially resembled those by which every individual and every nation repel the encroachments of others." Ultimately, he says, frontier conflict can be blamed on whites, who have failed to work out equitable treaties with the Indians and have instead "quarrelled with each other about boundaries and territories."[80]

Questions of boundaries and territories would remain central to Brown's writings and U.S. culture during the early years of the nineteenth century, in large part because of the Louisiana Purchase. What exactly were the boundaries of the Purchase? Should new states be constructed from these territories, and, if so, should they be slave or free? What sort of policies should the federal government develop with respect to the Native Americans and slaves (and French Louisianans) within those new states or territories? Even with all of these questions and uncertainties, most Americans viewed the acquisition of the Louisiana Territory with excitement about the glorious possibilities for the ever-expanding nation. In an oration delivered at St. Michaels Church of Charleston nearly a year after the Purchase, the historian of Revolutionary America David Ramsay best captured that excitement when he proclaimed: "Louisiana is ours! If we rightly improve the heaven sent boon, we may be as great, and as happy a nation, as any on which the sun has ever shown." According to Ramsay, the Purchase would further stimulate commerce and thus bind the various regions of the country together in "one happy union." It would also help to make the United States independent of Europe by easing concerns that European nations would employ "untutored savages" to undermine "the peace of our frontier settlements." As Ramsay explained, "The Indians are now all our own—included within our limits, and so far dependent on us, that no other nation can interfere with them." He thus concluded his oration with a glorious vision of union, prosperity, and freedom: "Great God! All this country filled with freemen—with citizens of the United States!"[81]

From the time of the Louisiana Purchase to his death in 1810, Brown, despite his infinitely more complex perspective on questions of race and nation, shared Ramsay's desires for union and economic prosperity. Thus there is some truth to the claim that Brown during "the early 1800s ultimately envisioned an American imperial republic."[82] But there is also some truth to the opposed claim that during this same time, as Mark L. Kamrath says, Brown offered "a stinging indictment of the imperialist dimensions of American exceptionalism."[83] Unlike Ramsay in his millennial speech of 1804, Brown remained concerned about the possibly dire consequences of the acquisition of the new territories, continued to think about connections among race, writing, and nation, and produced texts, such as "Memoirs of Carwin the Biloquist," that made it difficult to discern what he thought those connections might be. Even at his most aggressively nationalistic, Brown conveyed a suspicion of nation, an un-certainty about race, and a cognizance of the limits of U.S. empire.

Around the time that Ramsay was extolling the possibilities of a new American empire that would incorporate the Indian, Brown was serializ-ing "Memoirs of Carwin the Biloquist" in his *Literary Magazine*, and the U.S. government was attempting to force Iroquois communities, includ-ing the Mohowks, to assume the role of Jeffersonian yeoman farmers or risk banishment to territories west of the Mississippi. Kazanjian con-cludes that Brown in the "national literary aesthetic" of his serialized sketch "articulated this assimilation and conversion policy in the cultural sphere" through a key scene in "Memoirs of Carwin": Carwin's ventrilo-quial echoing of the war cry of a Mohowk. Kazanjian instructs us on how we can do better than Carwin (and Brown), urging us to "hear such echoes without attempting to master and control them, without subject-ing them to an absolute historical or theoretical closure."[84] Of course it has been one of the main arguments of this chapter that Brown's national literary aesthetic almost never sought historical or theoretical closure because he was acutely aware of contingency—the unfinished business (with all of its uncertainties, conflicts, and debates) of his contemporary moment. I have also argued that Brown through his first-person narra-tors *performs* his thematics in his writings, and that the best way to get at his complex and sometimes contradictory politics is to approach these discursive performances as Brown's possibly ironic (and always self-consciously artful) creations, and not as transparent "evidence" of his own views. A brief look at "Memoirs" in the context of the post–Louisiana Purchase moment is in order.

In all probability, Brown drafted "Memoirs of Carwin" in 1798 and thought about completing and publishing it then.[85] If so, a reading of "Memoirs" in relation to governmental policy of the early 1800s doesn't really work. And yet Brown may well have revised and expanded the sketch during 1803–5; he may also have chosen to publish it when he did because he thought it was relevant to that particular historical moment. "Memoirs" is thus fair game for a post-Purchase reading that takes ac-count of debates on Native Americans. That said, it is important to note that "Memoirs" has only the one reference to the Mohowks, which comes when the fourteen-year-old Pennsylvanian Carwin, who had just failed to exhibit the competence of his older brother by letting cows escape from the pasture, enters "gloomy hollows," feels terror for all sorts of reasons (the likelihood of punishment from his father, the very gloom of the recess itself), and attempts to stoke up his confidence. His description of his recourse to Indian-ness is worth quoting in full: "These terrors are always lessened by calling the attention away to some indifferent object. I now made use of this expedient, and began to amuse myself by hallowing as loud as organs of unusual compass and vigour would enable me. I uttered the words which chanced to occur to me, and repeated in the shrill tones of a Mohowk savage . . . 'Cow! cow! come home! home!' . . . These notes were of course reverberated from the rocks which on either side towered aloft, but the echo was confused and indistinct" (the ellipses are Brown's). Within an hour, Carwin learns how to make the echo more distinct, and he returns one more time to the cliffs to explore "new tones and new positions."[86] This scene is described in the first of the ten install-ments of "Memoirs," and there is no further mention of an Indian (or reference to this scene). If Brown is trying to say something about the Indians in "Memoirs," the point would have been long lost by the time a reader had taken in all ten installments.

But let us assume that Brown had intended to publish "Memoirs" as a whole sometime around 1803 to 1805. Even if that were the case, there are several aspects of the text that would work against an interpretation of this scene as evidence of unambiguous, unexamined, closed-off support for white settler colonialism. Like Edgar Huntly, the second-son Carwin greatly resents those who have money (his father and the older brother who stands to inherit the family's wealth). It is significant in this respect that his imitation of the voice of a Mohowk should occur at the precise moment when he expects to be punished by his father, and that the recourse to the voice provides him with "pleasures" that "were an ample compensation for the ill treatment which I expected on my return." True, playing Indian is a fantasy of colonizers (and boys), but here, as in Edgar Huntly, we have an impoverished character who has linked his own re-bellious energies to the rebellious energies of those who are in the process of being displaced by settlers on the frontier. As we read on, Carwin eventually figures out how to ventriloquize various voices and to put those voices to the service of his own rebellious ambitions, such as by making a dog appear to speak when there is the possibility that such trickery could help him become an heir of his wealthy aunt. It should be underscored that in this case his inspiration for becoming a ventriloquist comes not from the Indians but from his reading of Milton's Comus, which prompts him to experiment with the "idea of a distant voice."[87]

Carwin soon takes up with the apparently Irish Ludloe, travels with him to Dublin, journeys to Spain, and does not return to the United States (until his arrival at the beginning of *Wieland*, that is). Ludloe has a mysterious plan to establish an "empire of reason" in "some unvisited region," but that region is not anywhere in or near the United States. As "Memoirs" moves to its climactic nonending (it just stops in the midst of things), the question at the forefront of the narrative is whether Carwin will be forced to reveal to Ludloe his "secret" powers of ventriloquism— powers that Ludloe clearly knows about already.[88] In these final installments, there is nothing about U.S. empire, nothing about the Indians.

That said, with its emphasis on Ludloe's colonizing plans, "Memoirs" could be read in relation to the new realities of American expansionism that came with the Louisiana Purchase. Hsuan L. Hsu, for instance, argues that "Memoirs" "reframes the domestic crisis of Brown's earlier novel [*Wieland*] within the international context of American expansionism."[89] And yet, Brown makes clear that Ludloe is not an American and that his project does not involve the Americas. Moreover, as we have seen in Brown's journalistic writings of the period, Brown in the early 1800s may have wanted the United States to have full access to the Mississippi, but he also resisted aspects of U.S. expansionism, particularly the exporting of slavery into the territories, which he feared would only intensify sectional strife. He was also concerned that unfettered territorial growth would make it impossible to develop the attachments among different sections and regions that, in a geographically compact republic, would help to sustain national union. Writing just a few years after the publication of the final installment of "Memoirs," Brown in *The British Treaty* thus mocked what he described as Jefferson's half-crazed, Ludloe-esque vision of endless empire, accusing him, with respect to the Louisiana Purchase, of "stretching the boundary north and west, so as to reach the polar circle and the Pacific Ocean," even though "centuries . . . must roll away before we can populate our old domain."[90] A similarly critical (Mohawk-like) voice of resistance informs "Memoirs" as well.

In "Memoirs," Brown moves his sights well beyond the Americas and offers no clear vision of any sort of political program involving the rise of a continental empire. Much of what happens in the fragment seems accidental and mysterious, and the fact that Carwin to the very end remains resentful toward both his family and the appalling, empire-building Ludloe helps to link him, as Edgar and Edny were linked, to the very Indians that he initially sought to imitate. We never learn if he is forced to reveal his "secret" to Ludloe; generically consistent with the unbounded nature of a fragment, Carwin's final words confess to his unresolved confusion: "I vainly endeavored to conjecture."[91] Multiple plots could develop from these conjectures, but Brown supplies not a one, keeping personal and political outcomes in a state of perpetual suspense.

In other of his post-1803 writings, Brown focuses more intensively on continental borders and territories, mostly as an unambiguous critic of Jefferson's "empire of liberty." While Jefferson believed that continued U.S. expansion would promote industry and virtue, and perhaps even contribute to what he termed the "diffusion" of slavery (even as he continued to hold onto his approximately 200 slaves and defend the South's right to enslave blacks), Brown remained concerned about what he referred to in his Louisiana pamphlet as the "bane in our vitals"—the presence of black slaves in the United States nursing desires for revenge against the whites who enslaved them.[92] Sharply departing from Jefferson by promoting a politics of antislavery in his magazine writings of the early 1800s, Brown sympathized with the efforts of black revolutionaries and suggested that he was of a shared mind with the northern Federalists who were prepared to recognize the independent nation of Haiti. His opposition to Jefferson's embargo, which he regarded as a southern-based attack on northern merchants, may also have been motivated by his disgust that Jefferson had worked into it a declaration of nonintercourse with Haiti in order to appease the French.[93]

Brown regularly positioned himself against what he regarded as the South's (and Jefferson's and Madison's) politics of section. His fictional French consul of *Address*, after all, advises Napoleon to exploit southerners' fears of a slave conspiracy and (drawing from France's experience in Saint Domingue) identifies the existence of slavery itself as the nation's main point of vulnerability. In the preface to his 1804 translation of Volney's *A View of the Soil*, Brown talks of "the weakness of the *south*, from the prevalence of slavery"; and a year later, in an essay in the *Literary Magazine* titled "How Far Do Slaves Influence Political Representation in America," he portrays southern slave interests as continuing to pose a grave threat to the future of the nation. Focusing on the constitutional compromise that gave the southern states three-fifths of a person representation for each of their slaves, he offers a statistical analysis of how that policy has been affecting the political life of the nation, and he grimly predicts that American freedom may become a relic of the past: "The day is not far, when the southern and western states will have more representatives in congress and electors of presidents for slaves only, than the northern will have for all its free people."[94]

Brown and other northerners feared that the sectional conflict over slavery could eventually lead to a break between North and South, and they blamed the South for putting the Union in such jeopardy. In an 1803 issue of the *Port Folio*, known for its Federalist politics, an anonymous writer expressed concerns similar to Brown's in declaring that the Louisiana Purchase may help to give rise to a southern confederacy that would undermine the new nation, or at least the nation as defined by the Northeast: "Louisiana is too distant to be of any use to the Atlantic States. . . . The riches, and youth, and virtue of the old states, will go yearly to settle, and improve a country too distant for them to govern; and, before one tenth part of the money it cost will be reimbursed, it will not only be independent itself, but it will draw the western country after it."[95] While this anonymous writer is concerned about the possibilities of disunion, Jefferson in early 1804 could blithely write Joseph Priestly: "Whether we remain in one confederacy, or form into Atlantic and Mississippi confederacies, I believe not very important to the happiness of either part." From Jefferson's point of view, such a split in the Union would come about only if the Atlantic states chose to pursue it, and if they did, as he remarked in a letter of 1803 to a southern friend, the choice was clear: "[W]hy should we take side with our Atlantic rather than our Mississippi descendants?"[96]

Later in the decade, Jefferson was less blithe, and Brown surprisingly more, when there did appear to be a threat to the Union, the moment in 1806–7 when Aaron Burr moved down the Mississippi with the apparent intention of taking Spanish Mexico and perhaps New Orleans and making the acquired territory a center for breakaway western territories. The axis here was more East-West than North-South, but Jefferson nonetheless regarded Burr as "a sort of honorary Federalist,"[97] while Brown pretty much dismissed him as little more than an interesting character. Writing in his 1808 *American Register, or General Repository of History, Politics, and Science*, Brown presents Burr as something like Ludloe and Carwin, "an outcast from ordinary society" for whom secrecy, concealment, and plotting are his modus operandi. Precisely because Burr's possible plot could only be revealed by gaining access to "many secret communications," Brown initially holds off on judging the "outcast." But ultimately he concludes that Burr, with his ragtag operation of around 100 "young and raw adventurers," posed no threat at all, remarking that even the government's prosecutors had come to the conclusion that the Republicans in power had overstated the crisis. As a result, Brown writes, "apprehension gave place to shame, terror to ridicule, and credulity to wonder at the circumstances by which it was misled."[98] For Brown, the principal threat to the Republic would come not from subversives like Burr but from what he increasingly came to regard as sectionalists like Jefferson and Madison, particularly as such policies as the embargo seemed to him a plot against the nation's economic well-being.

In the debate over which sectional side best represented the nation, Brown remained firmly with the Northeast, which he regarded as exemplifying the principles of free trade and free labor. He had earlier elaborated his position on sectional matters in a review of William Robertson's *The History of America*, printed in the May 1799 issue of *Monthly Magazine and American Review*, where he differentiates North from South through an allegorical contrast of New England and Virginia. "The founders of Virginia were," he says, "for the most part, the refuse of their country, banished by their vices, or allured by their avarice," while "New-England forms a considerable contrast to Virginia," informed as it was by "the fruits of the national and commercial spirit of the English," though on "an higher principle."[99] The idea that New England to some extent embodied the highest principles of the nation became central to New England thought around the time of the embargo and contributed to the dissent of New England Federalists during the War of 1812 and eventually to the Hartford Convention of 1814, where some Federalists debated the possibility of disunion.[100] Sectional tensions would flare once again during the 1819–21 period, a time of renewed (literary) nationalism. The literary consequences of those tensions will be taken up in the next chapter.

Brown in the final years of his relatively short life came to put his faith in the "higher principles" of commerce as a way of developing a united and moral empire, and in that regard he shared the perspective of the former Federalist Joel Barlow, whose 1807 *Columbiad*, a revision of his 1782 *Vision of Columbus*, contemplates the prospects of the United States in the wake of the Louisiana Purchase. (In a footnote to the poem, Barlow states that he began the revision at the time of the Purchase.) Like Brown in his magazine articles of the early 1800s, Barlow presents a damning image of the French enslavers who sought to bring "the shades of vassalage and sloth" to "Louisiana's lovely clime." Presenting slavery as the evil "spot in that bright sun" of the new republic, he warns of the possibilities of vengeance coming from the slaves, implicitly presenting the revolution in Saint Domingue as presaging the possibility of a similar event in the United States. As Atlas, the guardian of the enslaved blacks, declares:

Nor shall these pangs atone the nation's crime;
Far heavier vengeance, in the march of time,
Attends them still; if still they dare debase
And hold inthrall'd the millions of my race;
A vengeance that shall shake the world's deep frame,
That heaven abhors and hell might shrink to name.

Challenging the hardening racism of the time, Barlow suggests that racial differences are merely superficial, the result of environmental differences based in "climate, soil, and sky." Thus he proclaims: "Equality of Right is nature's plan; / And following nature is the march of man." By the end of the poem he presents a millennial vision of the nations themselves disappearing, blending together in global unity:

Each land shall imitate, each nation join
The well based brotherhood, the league divine,
Extend its empire with the circling sun,
And band the peopled globe within its federal zone.

In this new world order, there would be no distinctive races, just "the total race," one language, interlinked commercial empires ("commerce join'd"), and a world congress that includes all countries and peoples, including what he calls "impervious Afric."[101]

As we have seen, similar antislavery views can be found in Brown's magazines of the period. Similar views of commerce and empire can be found in his last published pamphlet, *An Address to the Congress of the United States, on the Utility and Justice of Restrictions upon Foreign Countries. With Reflections on Foreign Trade, in General, and the Future Prospects of America* (1809). Published a year before his death, the tract, which once again voices Brown's opposition to the embargo, lacks the vituperative energy of his other political writings of the 1800s, though one imagines that a festering anger at Jefferson lies beneath its surface. Instead, it is surprisingly reflective and prophetic on a host of matters related to what Brown terms "the Future Prospects of America." In the manner of Barlow (and in language that also bears an eerie resemblance to the utopian postnational language of Ludloe), Brown makes the case for a global commercial empire that will move U.S. citizens beyond domestic and foreign conflicts. He offers this millennial vision: "One of the consequences of extended empire is to pull down those barriers which separate mankind from each other; to enlarge that circle which each man calls his country; to take away the grounds of dissension and rivalship; to create one nation out of many; to blend into one system of friendly, and especially of commercial intercourse, tribes that formerly looked upon each other as natural and hereditary enemies."[102] This future-oriented millennial voice is a far cry from the bellicose voice of the countersubversive narrator of the Louisiana pamphlets, but in some ways it is of the same tenor, suggesting in its own imperial way the benefits of a U.S. expansionism that will one day help to bring the world together in a social and economic order that is somehow beyond nation, beyond borders, beyond class, and, as the odd reference to "tribes" works to suggest, beyond race and ethnicity. Most of Brown's writings of the period running from 1798 to 1809 resist emplotment into a grand national narrative and make an art of unknowingness. But for Brown in this final tract, the contingencies of empire are resolved, at least for the moment, with the help of an American dream.

2

Circulating the Nation

David Walker, the Missouri Compromise,
and the Appeals of Black Literary Nationalism

The debates on the Missouri Compromise, I will be arguing in this chapter, were crucial to the development of African American literary nationalism during the 1820s and 1830s, and they had a pronounced influence on the development of a more broadly conceived American literary nationalism as well. As was the case during the 1790s and early 1800s, U.S. nationalism remained highly conflicted and contingent, and it therefore would be mistaken to say that there emerged a clear and distinctive "national narrative," as Jonathan Arac terms it, informed by "an American ideology . . . that was played out . . . by the national expansion that brought the United States all the way to the Pacific coast and threatened to go further into Central America and the Caribbean."[1] The Missouri crisis made clear that there was no single "American ideology" at this time but instead fiercely contested notions of what such an ideology might be. There were expansionists and antiexpansionists, regionalists and sectionalists, unionists and nullifiers, and a host of other groups who laid claim to the mantle of nationalist. U.S. nationalism was still in formation and up for grabs, and one wonders, when reading literary manifestos by southerners such as William Gilmore Simms or by the African American contributors to *Freedom's Journal*, exactly who would have been regarded as the key architects of a national narrative, and how that national narrative would have developed and been interpreted, had history unfolded somewhat differently than it did.

Of course the period running from 1815 to the early 1830s has generally been regarded as a period of consensus, a literary era of good feelings, as it were, precisely because of the outcome of the War of 1812. As Spiller remarks, "The so-called War of 1812 may have been inconclusive on the sea and in the world of politics, but in the development of a national cultural consciousness it was a milestone." According to this standard account, which continues to hold considerable sway, the resurgent U.S. nationalism of the postwar moment helped to renew efforts to foster a distinctively American literature that was republican, progressive, and informed by the principles of the Declaration of Independence and the Constitution (however those principles might have been interpreted by different constituencies). The founding of the *North American Review* in 1815 has typically been seen as a seminal moment in the development of a national literary culture, despite the fact that its editors were New England Federalists, many of whom had opposed the war with England, for it was in the pages of the *North American Review* that the need for a renewed American literary nationalism was most urgently proclaimed. In "Essay on American Language and Literature," for example, which appeared in the journal's November 1815 issue, Walter Channing called on Americans to produce "a literature of our own," even as he worried over the difficulties of producing such a literature in relation to English literary traditions. As is well known, from the perspective of British literary nationalists, a separate and distinctive U.S. literature would be slow in coming, if not an impossibility, because of the self-evident greatness of British literary traditions. But the triumphalist American literary-nationalist response to Sydney Smith's mocking query of 1820—"In the four quarters of the globe, who reads an American book?"—was that a number of people were beginning to read American books, and that the international success of Irving's *Sketch-Book* (1819–20), William Cullen Bryant's *Poems* (1821), and James Fenimore Cooper's *The Spy* (1821) showed that American literature *had* begun to take its place among the literatures of more established nations (even if that literature seemed highly indebted to British literary traditions).[2]

I am not questioning the important role that responses to England played in the development of American literary nationalism. But such a story is partial and fails to attend to the very real rifts in the national culture that revealed themselves right around the time that Smith published his attack on U.S. literary culture in the *Edinburgh Review*—the rifts that have recently led historian Sean Wilentz to redub the 1820s and 1830s the "Era of Bad Feelings."[3] Moreover, it ignores what could be termed a hemispheric or diasporic perspective that looks beyond national borders to the southern Americas and Africa, even as borders and boundaries remained central to efforts to define and imagine the future of the U.S. nation.

Bad feelings about borders and boundaries surged in 1819, when Missouri applied for admission to the Union as a slave state, and national leaders were once again debating what to do with the lands obtained by the Louisiana Purchase. As Brockden Brown might have predicted, sectional conflict on Missouri quickly gave the lie to the supposed post-1815 national consensus, with northerners and southerners attempting to stake out their positions on whether the nation should be slave or free and how best to interpret the nation's founding documents. These pivotal debates had important consequences for U.S. literary nationalism. David Waldstreicher remarks that " 'the nation' is never just an idea or a thing; it is also a story, an encompassing narrative or set of competing narratives with the potential to crowd out other narratives that may have rather different political implications."[4] At the conclusion of the chapter, I will consider the construction and reconstruction of American literary nationalism with respect to efforts by northerners and southerners to represent themselves as the incarnation of the U.S. nation. Suffice it to say here that, following the debates on Missouri, such literary sectionalism gained a heightened urgency as each side attempted to "crowd out" the other.

Nationalist discourses were not limited to the sections; such discourses were also deployed by U.S. blacks and Native Americans. Donald E. Pease asserts that "socially disenfranchised figures" challenge "the national narrative" by way of what he terms "postnational narratives, [which] actively contested its social arrangements."[5] My reading of intranational conflict as crucial to the formation of ofttimes competing national narratives puts into question the very idea of a postnational narrative, however transnational or diasporic such narratives can appear to be. It may be more accurate to say that, as was true for the sectionalists, the producers of such discourses sought to define the national narrative on their own terms at a time when that narrative seemed particularly open to reinterpretation.

One of the specific challenges facing African American literary nationalists, however, was that their community (unlike, say, communities based on sectional, regional, or tribal allegiances) was itself hard to define, given its scattered and fragmented nature. All the more reason, then, that early national and antebellum black nationalists often appropriated discourses of U.S. nationalism. As Xiomara Santamarina explains, black leaders' "goal of uniting a 'scattered' community paralleled the task of U.S. nationalists who sought to consolidate a splintering polity into a coherent unity."[6] The question confronting African American leaders was how to define, shape, and disseminate their own nationalist vision in relation to a larger national narrative. By dislocating, relocating, and in many respects just plain ambiguating connections between race and nation, David Walker, in his *Appeal, in Four Articles; Together with a Preamble, to the Coloured Citizens of the World, but in Particular, and Very Expressly, to Those of the United States of America* (1829), creatively attempted to do just that.

Walker's *Appeal* is generally regarded as one of the most influential and explosive black-nationalist documents authored by an African American. Urging the slaves to "kill or be killed,"[7] Walker has gained a reputation for militancy, even though much of the *Appeal* is concerned with countering white racial prejudice and developing strategies for black empowerment in the United States. Whether viewed through the lens of militancy or uplift, it is fair to say that Walker has emerged, in Sterling Stuckey's words, as the "father of black nationalist theory."[8] But in light of what I am suggesting about the contending nationalisms of early national culture, we might ask: what was that theory, and how did Walker present it? We can begin to answer these interrelated questions by considering a passage in Article I of the *Appeal* on Walker's reading. He remarks:

> I saw a paragraph, a few years since, in a South Carolina paper, which, speaking of the barbarity of the Turks, it said: "The Turks are the most barbarous people in the world—they treat the Greeks more like *brutes* than human beings." And in the same paper was an advertisement, which said: "Eight well built Virginia and Maryland *Negro fellows* and four *wenches* will positively be *sold* this day, *to the highest bidder!*" And what astonished me still more was, to see in this same *humane* paper! ! the cuts of three men, with clubs and budgets on their backs, and an advertisement offering a considerable sum of money for their apprehension and delivery. I declare, it is really so amusing to hear the Southerners and Westerners of this country talk about *barbarity*, that it is positively, enough to make a man *smile*.

More is going on in this passage than a sardonically gleeful attack on the hypocrisy and blindness of southern enslavers. By discussing his newspaper reading, Walker positions the *Appeal* in relation to what could be termed the newspaper print culture of the 1820s. It is worth noting that the newspaper Walker refers to is southern, a portion of which he in effect now circulates in the North and then recirculates nationally in this appropriated and ironically rearticulated form. Throughout the *Appeal* there are numerous references to northern and southern newspapers, all suggestive of Walker's aspirations to achieve an authority for his text rivaling that of the nation's increasingly influential newspapers. Moreover, with his references to North and South, East and West, Walker seeks to display his own newspaperlike ability to circulate throughout the nation in ways intended to be as threatening as possible to his imagined white readers. I will be discussing Walker's black literary nationalism in a number of contexts and from a number of different perspectives, focusing in particular on the tensions in his writing between a black nationalism conceived in relation to a conflicted U.S. nationalism and a black nationalism conceived diasporically. There is no easy way to "locate" Walker's black nationalism. Nevertheless, it can be said that whether considered nationally or transnationally, or as an interplay of the two, black nationalism for Walker was ultimately a matter of expanding his (and African Americans') circulatory orbit through the power of print.[9]

In his invaluable *To Awaken My Afflicted Brethren: David Walker and the Problem of Antebellum Slave Resistance*, Peter P. Hinks asserts that the "*Appeal* issued from a well-established tradition of black antislavery and religious oratory."[10] Although I would not want to deny the importance of those traditions to the *Appeal*, my emphasis will be on exploring the close relationship between the burgeoning print culture of the period and Walker's contributions to an emergent, and sometimes conflicted, black literary nationalism. Walker and other black activists regarded print, rather than oratory, as promising to link together the disparate and scattered African American communities of the early Republic. Significantly, beginning in 1827 Walker served as an authorized subscription agent for John Russwurm and Samuel Cornish's *Freedom's Journal*, the first African American newspaper, and he continued to demonstrate his commitment to the African American press by working as an agent for *The Rights of All*, a short-lived newspaper edited by Cornish between May and October 1829. Both newspapers underscored the crucial connections among black literary production, uplift, and community. Published in three editions between September 1829 and June 1830, the *Appeal* appeared right around the time of the demise of *Rights*, as if Walker were attempting to carry on the mission of that journal by circulating his own call for black uplift and community.

Appeals to circulation as a desideratum, material practice, and sign of national belonging were among the principal African American responses to the congressional debates of 1819–21 on Missouri. Those debates, as I will be elaborating in the first section of this chapter, intensified the conflict between proslavery and antislavery forces, raised new questions about the problematics of borders on both the state and national level, and engaged numerous Americans in the ideological challenge of rethinking the meaning of the American Revolution and Constitution—indeed, the meaning of the nation itself. The debates also generated a tremendous amount of print. As the press historian Carol Sue Humphrey observes, "Missouri's application for statehood in 1818 sparked a major debate over the status of slavery in the United States, and the press provided a major mechanism for communicating the various arguments." That process of communication contributed to two significant and interrelated developments: the founding of several hundred newspapers and the increasing sectionalization of those newspapers. Among the newly created newspapers were Philadelphia's antislavery *National Gazette and Literary Register* and Charleston's proslavery *Southern Patriot, and Commercial Advertiser*. Whereas earlier newspapers were closely tied to particular parties, which sometimes crossed sectional lines, newspapers around the time of the Missouri crisis came to reflect, as David Paul Nord notes, "the disaggregation and decentralization of the country."[11]

Lurking beneath the glories of Henry Clay's nationalistic "American System," then, were unresolved tensions concerning matters of territory, section, nation, race, and citizenship. These tensions were exacerbated not only by the initial debates on the Missouri Compromise of 1820 but also by the follow-up controversy that ensued when in late 1820 the Missouri state legislature submitted a proposed constitution to Congress with a provision barring free blacks and mulattoes from entering the state. The debate on that provision, which was widely reported in the newspapers of the time, brought into focus a number of crucial questions on the matter of blacks' citizenship and the implications of the Constitution's three-fifths clause. Were free blacks citizens of the United States? Did they have the right to travel from state to state? Did they have any rights at all? These are some of the large questions addressed in the post–Missouri Compromise writings of David Walker and other free blacks of the period, and the responses to these questions were varied, often pivoting on issues of location. Some African Americans called for a violent response to white enslavers and a reconception of the very idea of the nation in terms of a racialized (black) diaspora; others embraced the nonviolent possibilities of black emigration or colonization to Africa or Haiti; and still others, particularly northern free blacks, renewed calls for a commitment to a nationalist strategy of uplift in the United States. As was the case with U.S. nationalism, there was no single black nationalism at the time, and yet there was common ground among various African American activists on blacks' rights to the privileges of circulation.

This chapter is structured around David Walker as a key figure of black circulation and African American literary nationalism. Born in the late eighteenth century in Wilmington, North Carolina, Walker was a freeman who, sometime between 1815 and 1820, made his way to South Carolina. As a literate free black, he had ready access to transcripts and summaries of the congressional debates on Missouri as they circulated in the southern and national newspapers of the time, and his writings suggest the crucial importance of those debates for his thinking about black resistance. Walker was not the only African American in South Carolina who took note of the Missouri debates. Denmark Vesey and other free blacks of Charleston reportedly read the debates with keen interest. Inspired by the antislavery rhetoric espoused by some northern politicians, they may have conceived of a black conspiracy that would have burnt Charleston to the ground and eventually brought the conspirators to Haiti. (The recent historiographical debate on whether or not the Vesey conspiracy was "real" will be addressed below.) The evidence suggests that Walker was in Charleston during the time of the possible conspiracy, that he knew Vesey, and that if there had been a conspiracy, he may have been in on the plot. But even if Vesey's plot had been the fabrication of anxious white South Carolinians, as Michael P. Johnson has recently argued,[12] the published version of the trial transcript itself, ironically enough, provided Walker and other African Americans with a model of resistance in which black revolutionism and community were conceptualized both within and beyond the U.S. nation.

The chapter then follows Walker's own continued circulation as he moved from Charleston to Boston and there became involved with black-uplift organizations and the emergent black press. Walker's participation as an authorized sales agent for *Freedom's Journal* was crucial to his black literary nationalism, particularly as it took expression in his *Appeal*—a text, I argue, that engaged the interrelated issues of black citizenship and mobility central to the Missouri debates, Vesey's alleged conspiracy, and the rise of the black press. Though a diasporic consciousness has an important place in the *Appeal*, Walker never relinquished his hopes for a United States–based black nationalism, and at times, such as in his rhetorical performances of race, he conveyed his hopes for a nationalism that could move beyond race. But as the full title of the *Appeal* suggests, he also felt a connection to the "Colored Citizens of the World," and however suspicious he may have been of race as a scientific category, he recognized its political uses in the fight against racism and in the struggle to build black community, whether in the United States or elsewhere. The unresolved conflicts between nationalism and transnationalism, U.S. citizenry and colored "citizenry," that inform and ultimately energize the *Appeal*—the conflicts, in short, underlying Walker's efforts to (dis)locate race and nation—would remain at the center of African American culture long after Walker was found dead at his Boston home under suspicious circumstances in 1830.

Inoculating Missouri

Between 1819 and 1821, U.S. political leaders addressed questions of slavery, citizenship, and race in the halls of Congress during the debates on Missouri. The specific issues of black citizenship and circulation came to the fore during negotiations on the so-called second Missouri Compromise of 1821. But first a few words on the more famous Missouri Compromise of 1820, which, like the second compromise, captured the attention of Walker, Vesey, and other African Americans of the time.

When New York congressman James Tallmadge Jr. proposed amendments to the Missouri statehood bill of 1819 that would have banned the future introduction of slaves into Missouri and freed all children born as slaves in the new state by the age of twenty-five, a furor erupted in Congress. The subsequent debates of 1819–20, which historian Robert Pierce Forbes terms "probably the most candid discussion of slavery ever held in Congress," forced congressional leaders to address issues of territorial expansionism, sectional identity, federal versus state powers, and the very workings and ideological foundations of the nation itself. For many in the North, what was at stake in the Missouri controversy was sectional balance, a desire to maintain the North's preeminence as an economic center, as well as an increasing sense that slavery was inconsistent with the nation's founding ideals. Southerners also invoked the nation's founding ideals. Linking northerners' efforts to undermine the principle of states' rights to the Hamiltonian federalism that the 1799 Virginia and Kentucky Resolutions had contested two decades earlier, southern orators, along with the aged Thomas Jefferson, who famously termed the Missouri debates "a fire bell in the night," invoked the Declaration of Independence to assert their duty to oppose what they regarded as the authoritarianism of the national government. And they invoked the three-fifths clause of the Constitution to argue that northern restrictionists were undermining the Constitution itself. After much debate, in March 1820 a compromise was achieved with the help of Congressman Henry Clay of Kentucky and Senator Jesse B. Thomas of Illinois that allowed Maine to enter as a free state and Missouri as an unrestricted state, while banning slavery in the territory of the Louisiana Purchase north of 36°30'.[13]

But controversy flared again in December 1820 when Missouri's legislators submitted to Congress their proposed state constitution with a provision prohibiting free blacks and mulattoes from entering the state. In the tradition of Congress's 1790 and 1802 naturalization bills, which had limited citizenship to free white persons, Missouri's constitutional convention concluded that blacks never were and never could become citizens, and that the "free negro" therefore had no place in the new slave state because, by the very logic of the Constitution itself, the free black simply did not exist as a legal entity. Desirous of keeping their slaves untainted by what they regarded as the oxymoronic (and threatening) free black, the framers of the Missouri constitution required their new legislature, in the words of the proposed constitution, to "pass such laws as may be necessary . . . to prevent free negroes and mulattoes from coming to and settling in this State, under any pretext whatsoever."[14] The inclusion of this anti-immigration provision prompted a debate in Congress on the larger issue of black citizenship in the United States, with the discussion centering on whether the provision was in violation of Article IV, Section 2, of the U.S. Constitution: "The citizens of each State shall be entitled to all privileges and immunities of citizens in the several States."[15]

Though the time between Missouri's proposed constitution of December 1820 and the second Missouri Compromise of February 1821 was relatively short, the controversy on the issues raised by Missouri's constitution had far-reaching implications for considerations of race and citizenship in the United States, which were not to be "resolved" until the *Dred Scott* ruling of 1857. Again, it should be emphasized that a "national" position on the question of black citizenship simply did not exist. Not surprisingly, as one of the few occasions during the first three decades of the new nation in which Congress addressed the issue of black citizenship, the debates captured the attention of the free-black community. Historian Glover Moore notes that the "Negro population of Washington . . . flocked to hear the congressional debates."[16] The debates were also widely disseminated in the nation's proliferating newspapers and were read with great interest by literate blacks. We can recover a sense of what Vesey, Walker, and other free blacks would have encountered in the newspaper accounts of the period by considering the transcripts of the speeches printed in *Annals of Congress*, a number of which were subsequently reprinted in the *National Intelligencer*, *Niles' Register*, and a great many local newspapers.

For opponents of Missouri's constitutional provision barring free blacks and mulattoes from entering the state, the issues were relatively simple: the Missouri state constitution violated the U.S. Constitution by denying constitutionally affirmed privileges and immunities to U.S. citizens, specifically, the right of citizens to circulate from state to state. In articulating such an argument, therefore, those opposed to Missouri's ban on black immigration found themselves making claims in the halls of Congress that free blacks either were or had the potential to become citizens of the nation. To be sure, those northern congressmen who opposed Missouri's constitution were not calling for the repeal of the naturalization bills of 1790 and 1802. But they did make the case for common-law notions of ascriptive citizenship across the color line, arguing for the crucial importance of native birth in determining an individual's qualifications for citizenship. Moreover, these congressmen set forth arguments that African Americans had made in the past and would repeatedly make in the future (perhaps as inspired by these very debates): that blacks' contributions to the nation, whether as laborers or as soldiers in the Revolutionary War and War of 1812, had earned them the right to citizenship. Senator David L. Morril of New Hampshire, for example, proclaimed on 11 December 1820 that "this provision in the constitution of Missouri is in direct hostility to the Constitution of the United States," and that it would be particularly heinous to exclude "soldiers of color" from "their Constitutional 'privileges and immunities.'" He also voiced a concern shared by a number of northerners that southern efforts to limit the rights of free blacks were part of a larger challenge to northern whites themselves, and, by extension, to the futurity of the nation: "If you can prescribe one class of citizens, you may another. Color no more comes into consideration to decide who is a citizen than size or profession. . . . Where is your 'free ingress and regress from State to State?' Your national existence is lost; the Union is destroyed." Not quite as alarmist as Morril, Congressman William Eustis of Massachusetts similarly linked citizenship to patriotic service, noting that during the Revolutionary War the "freemen entered our ranks with the whites," and that it would therefore be immoral to tell them, "after having shed their blood, in common with the whites," that they "are not to participate in the rights secured by the struggle." In Massachusetts, Eustis proudly asserted, free blacks "are considered citizens equally as whites." And what was true for Massachusetts, Eustis proclaimed, should be true for the nation; after all, he reminded his auditors, the preamble to the Constitution does not begin, "We the *white* people."[17]

For the southerners (and some northerners) supporting Missouri's proposed ban on black immigration, there was no need for the Constitution to be explicit on the matter of race and citizenship, since they took as a given the white racial identity of the nation. Rejecting the notion that native birth confers citizenship, these congressmen and senators maintained that citizenship for blacks could come about only if the existing white citizenry chose to grant citizenship to a class of people who, as they said the 1790 Naturalization Law made clear, were not regarded as citizens at the time of the adoption of the Constitution.[18] Virginia senator William Smith remarked on 8 December 1820 that "the Constitution and laws of the United States . . . furnish a mass of evidence, which nobody could doubt but a sceptic, that free negroes and mulattoes have never been considered as a part of the body politic." Tellingly, he went on to argue that from what he had observed of the North, there was no significant difference of opinion among northerners and southerners on this matter, insofar as most northern blacks were denied the right to participate in state militias, local elections, and juries. Ridiculing the northern antislavery notion that the Constitution and Declaration were race blind by adducing the material facts of northern culture itself, Smith demanded of those northerners who sought to deny Missouri its alleged right to ban free blacks from the state: "If this was a declaration of independence for the blacks as well as the whites, why did you not all emancipate your slaves at once, and let them join you in the war? But we know this was not done." A similar argument about northern hypocrisy was elaborated in a speech of 9 December 1820 by Congressman Alexander Smyth of Virginia, who also spoke of how northern blacks were denied basic rights of citizenship. Because blacks in the North are "everywhere inferior to the white man," he triumphantly maintained, the northern argument that blacks' constitutional rights would be usurped by Missouri's constitution was fundamentally illogical, as such violations could only occur "to citizens who are, in their own States, entitled to all the privileges and immunities of citizens." Even Maine senator John Holmes, a supporter of Missouri's proposed state constitution, agreed with Smith's claims about blacks' essential lack of citizenship in the North, concluding that the very idea of a black citizen "is an absurdity too gross and palpable to be seriously entertained." As he rhetorically remarked on the intentions of the Founders: "That the framers of the Constitution intended that blacks and mulattoes might be members of Congress or Presidents, is a supposition too absurd to be for a moment maintained."[19]

If blacks historically lacked the status of citizens in the United States, southerners and some northerners maintained, then arguments that Missouri was violating the Constitution's privileges and immunities clause were nothing short of incoherent and hypocritical. Of course some northern legislators challenged these contentions, and the debate continued for another month or so until it came to a crashing halt when Congressman Charles Pinckney of South Carolina finally spoke out on the issue. Holding special pride of place in Congress for having participated in the 1787 Constitutional Convention, and thus for his putative ability to disclose the original intentions of the Founders, Pinckney proclaimed in a speech of 13 February 1821 that he himself had authored the privileges and immunities clause, and that he could therefore say with absolute certainty that it was absurd to think it had any application to blacks: "I perfectly knew that there did not then exist such a thing in the Union as a black or colored citizen, nor could I then have conceived it possible such a thing could ever have existed in it; nor, notwithstanding all that is said on the subject, do I now believe one does exist in it." For Pinckney, the debate on Missouri's proposed constitution revealed northerners' "total want of knowledge of the distinction which has, from time immemorial, existed in the civilized world, between the black and white race, and the strong and immoveable line which has separated, and will forever continue to separate, them in the Southern and Western States of the Union." The only way that the senior South Carolinian could explain such ignorance on the part of northerners, he glumly remarked, was that they must harbor a "wish to dissolve the Union."[20]

Pinckney's intervention made clear to most congressmen that a second Missouri Compromise was needed to bring the debate on Missouri's state constitution to a close. The March 1821 compromise forged by Clay and a joint committee of the Senate and House of Representatives made some concessions to both sides but essentially allowed the Pinckney view of citizenship to prevail. Asserting that Missouri's ban on the ingress of free blacks "shall never be construed to authorize the passage of any law . . . by which any citizens of either of the States of this Union shall be excluded from the enjoyment of any of the privileges and immunities to which such citizen is entitled under the Constitution of the United States," the joint committee's vaguely worded compromise bill ultimately permitted Missouri to do whatever it wished with respect to free blacks. As historian George Dangerfield wryly observes, "[I]t became a 'fundamental condition' of the admission of Missouri that her *unamended* Constitution should require the General Assembly to pass laws excluding free Negroes and mulattoes[,] ... but that no law, so passed, should ever be interpreted as meaning what it did mean."[21] The results of such an uneven compromise were predictable: Missouri was able to ban just about all free blacks from the state by demanding that they have on their person their respective state's naturalization papers (which the states tended not to produce), while the issue of black citizenship in the United States remained unresolved.

And yet, however much the second Missouri Compromise lent itself to the Missouri legislators' racist ends, its vagueness allowed for the possibility of opposed interpretations. Those conflicting interpretations, which ultimately focused on material issues of circulation and location with respect to race, remained alive in the congressional and newspaper transcripts available to readers across the nation. Antislavery northerners like New Hampshire congressman Josiah Butler linked the privileges of universal circulation to the very existence of the Republic, declaring that the "right, which every citizen of every State has of emigrating to and becoming a citizen of another State, is the bond of social intercourse and harmony among the several States. Without this privilege, each State would become a distinct nation of people, ... [and] the passions of the people of each state would soon be in martial array against one another." But a "right" that could be regarded by one section as essential to the futurity of the Union could be regarded by the other as a threat to that very futurity. Virginia congressman Alexander Smyth, who insisted that blacks were "aliens" beyond the pale of U.S. citizenship, addressed in calculatedly chilling terms the dangers that unlimited black circulation would pose to the nation:

I will ... put an extreme case. Suppose that leprosy—a disease certainly communicated by the touch—should appear in Philadelphia, and that 10,000 persons should be affected before proper means had been taken to stop its progress; would the corporation of Philadelphia, or the Legislature of Philadelphia, have a right to send those lepers into Delaware; and would they have a right of "settling" there, as one of the privileges of citizens of the United States, against the will of the government of Delaware? I think it will scarcely be contended that Delaware would not have a right to oppose an intrusion so fatal to her health; and, if she would have a right to oppose it, Missouri has an equal right to oppose the intrusion of free negroes dangerous to her peace.

Invoking the yellow fever epidemic of Philadelphia of 1793, which in the popular (white) imagination had been linked to the revolutionary "germs" spread by the contemporaneous black rebellion in Saint Domingue, and invoking as well Philadelphia physician Benjamin Rush's well-known notion that black skin was the result of leprosy, Smyth conceived of freely circulating black bodies as a type of virus against which the nation required various forms of inoculation (border patrols, legislation against ingress, and so on). Free blacks in particular, he declared, who were "everywhere inferior to the white man," needed to be contained and controlled, regarded as "denizens" but never as citizens, for they posed a threat to the "peace" of a slave state like Missouri by making the supposedly content slaves unhappy with their lot.[22] According to the trial transcript of Denmark Vesey's slave conspiracy of 1822, Vesey made just such an attempt to "infect" the free and enslaved blacks of Charleston by exposing them to nothing less than the debates on the Missouri Compromise.

Cunning Denmark Vesey

The Vesey conspiracy occurred approximately one year after the Missouri debates, and in certain ways it was inspired by those debates. But did such a conspiracy truly exist? Antebellum southerners seemed to think so, as did many African American leaders of the nineteenth century. In 1964, however, historian Richard C. Wade argued that the Vesey conspiracy was the concoction of fearful white South Carolinians who used the trial of Vesey and his putative accomplices as a way of executing some of Charleston's black leaders. That interpretation was roundly rejected by Sterling Stuckey and most other historians of black culture, who worked with letters and other archival materials to reassert the importance of Vesey to the history of black revolutionary nationalism in the United States.[23] But in 2001 Michael P. Johnson resurrected Wade's argument, proclaiming in no uncertain terms that there was no conspiracy, that Vesey was simply "a fall guy for both the court and the witnesses who repeatedly testified against him," that the black witnesses in particular were "eager for their own reasons to pay homage to the enduring power of white supremacy," and that all pre-2001 historians arguing for the existence of the conspiracy can be regarded as the "unwitting co-conspirators" of Charleston's murderous white-supremacist court.[24] As these dismissive remarks suggest, one of the more troubling aspects of Johnson's analysis is the way that he mocks historians for using the trial transcript as evidence of a conspiracy, while at the same time making claims (such as that black witnesses were eager to pay homage to white supremacy) without a shred of supporting evidence. Leaving aside the question of whether there was a "real" conspiracy (and conspiracies, by their very nature, are always difficult to detect), we can say that if, as Johnson alleges, white South Carolinian elites deliberately put Vesey and his supposed accomplices on trial in order to reinforce their power, this was an act of surpassing stupidity. For the result of their actions was to create in the widely circulated published version of the trial transcript the figure of a heroic black revolutionary whose "cunning," as described by one of the black witnesses, continued to inspire blacks long after the authorities put him to death.[25] In this respect, I would argue, contra Johnson, that those like myself who detect in the trial transcript the voices of a black revolutionary and his coconspirators are colluding not with the South Carolina authorities of the early 1820s but rather with the many African Americans, including David Walker, who were inspired by Vesey.

Walker almost certainly met Vesey, for he resided in Charleston during the late 1810s and early 1820s when Vesey emerged as a leader among the free and enslaved blacks of Charleston. As Hinks and Egerton point out, Walker's references in the *Appeal* to religious meetings in South Carolina suggest not only that he was in the area but also that he may have attended Vesey's Charleston's Cow Alley African Methodist Episcopal Church and (assuming there had been a conspiracy) known of his plot.[26] Even if Walker had left Charleston by 1822, the conspiracy was so widely reported in the newspapers of the time that it inevitably would have influenced his thinking about the importance of black communication networks and physical resistance. But if Vesey had inspired Walker, he would have troubled him as well, for there were limits to Walker's militance, and he was not eager to leave the United States. Nevertheless, the Vesey conspiracy, or reports thereof, would have provided Walker and other African American leaders with new ways of thinking "postnationally" or diasporically about a hemispheric black nationalism, and new ways of thinking about the power of print in constructing and publicizing that nationalism.

To briefly summarize the alleged conspiracy: Denmark Vesey, who in all likelihood was born in Africa during the 1760s, was purchased in Saint Thomas by Joseph Vesey in the early 1780s and brought to South Carolina shortly thereafter. In 1799 he won the East-Bay Lottery and subsequently bought his own freedom, which he could do because slaves in South Carolina at that time still had some rights to their own property. The evidence suggests that Vesey soon developed a revolutionary politics that was shaped by his African Methodist Episcopal affiliations, his links with the conjuror Gullah Jack and other "ethnic" blacks of Charleston who practiced East African religious rituals, his admiration for the rebels of Saint Domingue and the new nation of Haiti, and his marshalling of U.S. Revolutionary ideals. Working with a small number of leaders, Vesey allegedly (and probably in fact) formulated a plot for a black uprising in Charleston on 14 July 1822 (Bastille Day), in which his coconspirators planned to rise up against the masters at midnight, kill as many of the white inhabitants as possible, loot and set fire to commercial areas, and then set sail to Haiti with money and goods taken from the city. As suggested in the trial transcript, the overarching goal of the conspiracy was to initiate a mass slave uprising in the South and to create a diasporic black nationality in the southern Americas that eventually would become *the* defining nationality of the American hemisphere. The conspiracy failed, according to the transcript, when William Paul, one of Vesey's associates, revealed the plot to another slave, who then revealed it to his master. These betrayals led to the arrest of Vesey and most of his associates, and after a summary trial, thirty-five blacks were hanged and thirty-seven transported out of the state. As would be true for the Nat Turner rebellion of 1831, the civic authorities clamped down on the slaves and free blacks in the wake of the purported conspiracy, banning their churches and putting greater controls on their access to print. And as would also be true for the Turner conspiracy, white civic authorities, in their efforts to explain what they regarded as the unexplainable ("contented" slaves rebelling against "benevolent" masters), determined to place the principal blame for the conspiracy beyond the borders of the southern slave states.

Specifically, they blamed the alleged conspiracy on the antislavery opinions espoused by northern politicians during the debates on Missouri, and they were particularly concerned about the circulation of those views in the newspapers of the day. In a column on the Vesey conspiracy printed in the 31 August 1822 issue of the *National Intelligencer*, for instance, the writer suggested that discussion of "the hateful 'Missouri question'" should be "suffered to sleep," given the distinct possibility that the debates helped "in promoting the servile insurrection in South Carolina." A column printed one week later in the 7 September 1822 *South Carolina State Gazette* singled out for blame the antislavery New York congressman Rufus King, stating that King and others must have known that "extracts of speeches on the Missouri question" would have worked to "promote insurrection." As the columnist rather eloquently put it: "'The Devil can quote scripture'—and propositions about liberty and equality (particularly when made to bear upon a particular class) suited exactly the ends of those who grasped at the brightest names, and even tore the inspiration page, to sanction deeds of darkness."[27]

Southern opinion on the dire influence of the Missouri debates on the Vesey conspiracy was confirmed in the trial transcript itself. The short book that emerged from the trial, *An Official Report of the Trials of Sundry Negroes, Charged with an Attempt to Raise an Insurrection in the State of South Carolina* (Charleston, 1822), authored and edited by Lionel H. Kennedy and Thomas Parker, the presiding magistrates, made clear that northern whites would have to take primary responsibility for the conspiracy. In their prefatory overview, "A Narrative of the Conspiracy and Intended Insurrection, Amongst a Portion of the Negroes in the State of South Carolina, in the Year 1822," Kennedy and Parker have virtually nothing to say about the U.S. Revolutionary, transnational, ethnic, or racial dimensions of Vesey's plot. While they remark on Vesey's use of Scripture to inspire the free blacks and slaves, they primarily contend that Vesey was able to gain adherents by appropriating, circulating, and (in their view) "distorting certain parts" of the "speeches in Congress of those opposed to the admission of Missouri into their union," mainly by persuading enslaved blacks "that Congress had actually declared them free, and that they were held in bondage contrary to the laws of the land."[28]

Arguably, Kennedy and Parker focus on the Missouri debates because that context was central to their fictionalization of a conspiracy that, as Johnson asserts, never was. But for those inclined to think that the conspiracy was genuine (and recent studies by Egerton and Paquette suggest that it was), the trial transcript can be read as a hybridized text that, though shaped by white editors, also recorded blacks' voices, agency, and political perspectives. It is both a white-supremacist document that was intended to bring closure to what the magistrates regarded as an aberrant event in South Carolina slave culture *and* a black freedom document in which many of the black defendants attempted to speak beyond the confines of Charleston by grounding their black revolutionism in the antislavery sentiments espoused by some northern leaders during the debates on Missouri.[29] One anonymous black participant attested that at meetings led by Vesey and his associates, "it was said that *some white men said Congress had set us free,*" and that, because of southern intransigence, "a large army from Santo Domingo and Africa were coming to help us." According to another witness, Vesey drew on the Missouri debates to proclaim "that all men had equal rights, blacks as well as whites." The most telling witnesses pointed in very specific ways to the linked role of the Missouri debates and print culture in fomenting the insurrectionism of Vesey and his accomplices. The black William, who was eventually acquitted, told of how he went to the dwellings of Vesey's coconspirator Monday Gell "to hear what was going on in Congress, as we expected that Congress was going to set us free, and as what was going on was printed in all the papers, so that black as well as white might read it." Jacob Stagg, who was eventually convicted and executed for his alleged participation in the conspiracy, similarly affirmed to the court that Monday Gell recruited blacks with the help of newspaper accounts of antislavery speeches by northern congressmen: "THE PRISONER stated that Monday read daily the newspapers, and told him that Congress was going to set them free (alluding to the Missouri question); he said, to hear about that carried him to Monday's."[30]

In addition to presenting blacks' desires for freedom in relation to the egalitarian sentiments supposedly voiced by antislavery northern congressmen, the transcript suggests, as with the above-cited reference to "a large army from Santo Domingo and Africa," that Vesey had also conceived of his revolutionary conspiracy in transnational or diasporic terms as a black rebellion against a white slave power. In this respect, one of Vesey's great achievements as an organizer of black rebellion in the United States, at least as depicted in the transcript, was his ability to reconfigure black community away from the ethnic or national particularisms of Africa and the New World in order to champion the notion of a united black community that had the potential of achieving its own sense of nationhood in the Americas.[31] Vesey was particularly attracted to Haiti, and thus he shared a good deal with the New Englander Prince Saunders and other African Americans who, during the 1810s and 1820s, were advocating African American emigration to the independent republic of Haiti out of a conviction that African Americans and Haitians shared a common racial identity and destiny.[32] And yet even as Vesey directed his coconspirators' attention to the southern Americas, Kennedy and Parker's transcript emphasizes that what he found most inspiring were the arguments by antislavery northern politicians during the debates on Missouri in support of blacks' rights in the United States.

Though the magistrates' efforts to blame northern congressmen and a national print culture for the Vesey conspiracy was surely self-interested, a way of remaining blind to the evils of slavery and the possibilities of black agency, that does not mean they were necessarily wrong in their interpretation, especially if we take the black voices in the trial transcript seriously and not as part of a white fabrication. Those voices would suggest that the debates on Missouri, by exposing not only the antislavery beliefs of certain northerners but also the fractures in the supposedly unified nation, helped both to legitimate and precipitate the conspiracy—or, at the very least, helped to legitimate the black anger and desire for community that gave rise to the fear of that conspiracy. As Egerton remarks on Vesey's apparent interest in developing an "American" black nationality in Haiti: "Reading the [Missouri] debates in Charleston—and they were widely covered in both newspaper and pamphlet—Vesey came to understand that America was two countries, and that the North, if not hospitable to African Americans, might prove a bit tardy in riding to the defense of the Southern planter class."[33] We could also say that by reading the debates, Vesey came to understand how print could help him in his efforts to create a unified black community, both by circulating texts among literate blacks and by reciting those texts to the illiterate, as we see in the transcript's account of his efforts to use New York congressman Rufus King's widely reprinted antislavery speech for his own political ends.

Unsurprisingly, Kennedy and Parker accused Vesey of distorting the speeches of King and others, and in an effort to underscore that point, they included as a supplement to their edited trial transcript the confession of Jack Purcell, which was supposedly offered just before his execution. Because of the centrality of print to the (printed) confession, I offer an extended quotation from Purcell's confession as documented in *Official Report*:

If it had not been for the cunning of that old villain Vesey, I should not now be in my present situation. He employed every stratagem to induce me to join him. He was in the habit of reading to me all the passages in the newspapers that related to Santo Domingo, and apparently every pamphlet he could lay his hands on, that had any connection with slavery. He one day brought me a speech which he told me had been delivered in Congress by a Mr. King on the subject of slavery; he told me this Mr. King was the black man's friend, that Mr. King had declared he would continue to speak, write, and publish pamphlets against slavery as long as he lived, until the Southern States consented to emancipate their slaves, for that slavery was a disgrace to the country.[34]

Of course this reads like anything but the spontaneous remarks of a man on the verge of being hanged. Purcell may have said something to this effect during the trial, but the final "confession" appears to have been worked up to support the perspective of the magistrates that northerners were dangerously interfering with southern polity, to the point where "Santo Domingo" revolutionaries and northern politicians could be regarded as one and the same. And yet that doesn't necessarily mean that Purcell's remarks shouldn't be taken seriously as a record of blacks' perspectives on the Missouri debates. Egerton believes that Vesey made use of King's speech, while all along understanding "that Congress never actually debated emancipation where slavery already existed. . . . He realized, too, that selected passages from the debates might help him to recruit followers."[35] Whether or not he "distorted" the debates, the Vesey of the trial transcript attended to the radical implications of northerners' attacks on slave culture and sought to keep in circulation those portions of the debates that underscored the evils of slavery and the possibilities of its demise.

Because Rufus King had such an important place in the Vesey trial transcript, it would be useful to take a closer look at his speeches on Missouri as reprinted in the 4 December 1819 issue of *Niles' Register,* one of the crucial sources for subsequent newspaper reprintings in the North and South. To be sure, King cannily maintained in his prefatory remarks to the editors of *Niles'* that he simply wanted to establish Congress's legal right to prohibit slavery in the new territories, and that he would never have "assent[ed] to any measure that would affect the security of property in slaves, or tend to disturb the political adjustment which the

constitution has established respecting them." But in the speeches themselves, King outlined a broad critique of the institution of slavery, and
then insisted on the right of Congress to abolish it. He rejected the notion
that slaves should be thought of as "property," given that "the term property in its common and universal meaning does not include or describe
slaves"; he remarked about slavery itself that "Enlightened men . . . regret
its existence among us, and seek for the means of limiting and mitigating
it"; he anticipated the antislavery arguments of Frederick Douglass, William Wells Brown, Harriet Beecher Stowe, and many others by identifying
as one of the chief evils of slavery the "breaking up and separation of . . .
families"; and he concluded by identifying slavery as a key threat to the
nation because of the way it undercut the value of free labor, mocked "the
principles of freedom," and made the United States vulnerable to "foreign
assailants" by limiting the nation's ability to "raise soldiers, or to recruit seamen."[36]

If Vesey had distorted King's message when he allegedly read his
speeches to Charleston's illiterate blacks, that distortion was a matter
of degree and not of kind. By appropriating and recirculating King's
speeches, the Vesey of the trial transcript, somewhat in the manner of
Benjamin Banneker, Douglass, and Wells Brown, participated in a long
tradition of African Americans' appropriations of those discourses of U.S.
nationalism that best promised to improve blacks' situation within the
United States. At the same time, the compilers of the trial transcript
attempted to show that in his planning of the conspiracy, Vesey drew on
discourses of Haitian nationality in an effort to forge a hemispheric black
nationalism beyond the U.S. nation. Influenced by the debates on Missouri as reported in various newspapers and journals, and by the accounts of the Vesey conspiracy in the trial transcript and elsewhere, David
Walker and other African American literary nationalists of the 1820s and
1830s similarly worked with sometimes competing ideological notions of
race and nation, though most favored the forms of circulation, textual and
otherwise, that they believed had the potential of developing a black
nationalism within (or in relation to) the United States.

Circulating Agents and the Rise of the Black Press

Whatever the historical facts of David Walker's whereabouts at the
time of the alleged Vesey conspiracy, he clearly came to understand the
importance of print to the development of a black-nationalist conscious-

ness. That understanding may have been sparked by his reading of some or all of Kennedy and Parker's widely disseminated trial transcript, which emerged as a principal source for subsequent newspaper accounts and other renderings of the alleged Vesey conspiracy, such as James Hamilton's *An Account of the Late Intended Insurrection Among a Portion of the Blacks of this City* (1822). Walker arrived in Boston sometime between 1822 and 1825; Hamilton's account, a slightly reconceived and abridged version of Kennedy and Parker, was reprinted twice in Boston at around the same time.[37] The debate on black circulation had earlier made its way to Boston, for the issue was of national significance and not limited to Missouri. As historians James Oliver Horton and Lois E. Horton note, "Ohio, Indiana, Michigan, and Illinois either banned black immigration outright or imposed heavy bonds to ensure 'good conduct' from those blacks allowed to enter the state."[38] In Massachusetts, a legislative committee proposed in 1821 that blacks should be prohibited from entering the state on the grounds that they posed a danger to the social order and would drain money from the public charities. If the bill had come before the Massachusetts legislature in late 1822, it quite possibly would have been adopted.

Precisely because Massachusetts did not pass an anti-immigration law, Walker was able to move to Boston in the aftermath of the Vesey conspiracy. The exact date of his arrival remains unclear, but we do know that in 1826 he was initiated into the Boston order of the Prince Hall Free Masons. Walker also came to have a key role in the Massachusetts General Colored Association (MGCA). Both the Prince Hall Masons and the MGCA attempted to improve the situation of local and national free blacks through the promotion of temperance and literacy, placing a special emphasis on the importance of creating black literary societies, reading rooms, and publishing venues.[39]

Crucial to the evolving goals of the African American groups and organizations Walker joined in Boston was an effort to use print to counter the increasing prestige of the American Colonization Society (ACS), which sought to make the United States into an all-white nation by encouraging free blacks to emigrate to their supposedly "native" Africa. For leaders of the ACS such as Henry Clay, reports of the Vesey conspiracy only further strengthened their conviction that free blacks and whites could not coexist in the United States. In an effort to publicize their views, in 1825 the ACS founded a monthly journal, the *African Repository and*

Colonial Journal. Walker noted in his *Appeal* that he read the *African Repository and Colonial Journal* "from its commencement to the present day."[40] Though opposed to the *Repository's* politics, Walker and other free-black leaders were inspired by the journal's regular accounts of the historical greatness of Africa (which, unlike the colonizationists, they took to legitimate African Americans' place in the United States) and by the editors' efforts, as declared in the lead editorial of the August 1825 issue, to circulate their ideas to "both the Southern and Northern States."[41]

Similar desires for a national reach were among the primary goals of the first African American newspaper, *Freedom's Journal,* which began publishing in New York City in March 1827, the year New York State abolished slavery. Edited by the Jamaican-born John Russwurm, a graduate of Bowdoin College, and the New York Presbyterian minister Samuel Cornish, *Freedom's Journal* attempted to do for black nationalism what Benedict Anderson argues newspapers do for the nation: develop "a deep, horizontal comradeship."[42] In the inaugural issue, the editors underscored just how important it was for blacks to have a newspaper to plead their "own cause," particularly as such a newspaper would help to forge connections among its scattered readers: "It is our earnest wish to make our Journal a medium of intercourse between our brethren in the different states of this great confederacy." In the same issue the editors reported on "a respectable Meeting of the People of Colour of the City of Boston, held at the house of Mr. David Walker, on Monday evening 20th ult. for the purpose of taking into consideration the expediency of giving aid and support to the 'FREEDOM'S JOURNAL.'" At that meeting, the participants passed a resolution on the new newspaper pledging "to use our utmost exertion to increase its patronage."[43]

To some extent influenced by the *African Repository and Colonial Journal,* Russwurm and Cornish attempted to develop black pride by printing articles, similar to those in the *Repository,* that celebrated the African origins of Western culture.[44] In the manner of the much-publicized Denmark Vesey, the editors conceived of blacks not only "in the different states" but also around the world as a racially unified people, presenting Haiti in particular as a site of black-nationalist pride in the Americas. In a commencement address at Bowdoin College on 6 September 1826 titled "The Condition and Prospects of Haiti," Russwurm had predicted that Haiti would "exhibit a picture of rapid and unprecedented advance in population, wealth, and intelligence," and in the newspaper itself, he called for an end to white Americans' "unmanly attacks upon a brave and hospitable people," hailing the freedom fighters of the Haitian revolution as "our brethren of St. Domingo."[45]

Given the regular references to the blacks of Africa and Haiti, one might ask of *Freedom's Journal*'s masthead epigraph, "Righteousness Exalteth a Nation," what exactly was "the nation" in the eyes of the editors? This question of nation would remain an important one in the journal, and surprisingly Russwurm would eventually make the case that blacks should consider emigrating to Liberia under the auspices of the ACS. But at least at the outset of the journal's publication, its editors were mainly interested in challenging the *African Repository*'s colonizationist agenda by presenting strategies for black elevation in the United States.

Of central importance to their program of black uplift was a commitment to African American literary nationalism, for the editors believed that black literary achievement would counter whites' racist stereotypes of blacks as uneducated "savages" who should remain apart from the national community. Thus Russwurm and Cornish regularly ran essays in their journal on neglected black writers. In an article on Phillis Wheatley in their "Original Communications" column, for instance, the editors celebrated a poet "who by her writings has reflected honour upon our name and character, and demonstrated to an unbelieving world that genius dwells not alone in skins of whitish hue." Similarly, in "The Surprising Influence of Prejudice," an essay running on the opening pages of the issue of 18 May 1827, the anonymous author surveyed the accomplishments of the many black writers—Wheatley, Francis Williams, Quobna Ottobah Cugoano, Olaudah Equiano, Ignatius Sancho, and Benjamin Banneker, among others—who had been able to achieve literary prominence in spite of whites' antiblack prejudices. As reported in the 25 April 1828 issue of *Freedom's Journal*, Walker appealed to Boston's blacks to make similar efforts, focusing on "the disadvantages the people of Colour labor under, by the neglect of literature—and concluded by saying, that the very derision, violence, and oppression, with which we as a part of the community are treated by a benevolent and Christian people, ought to stimulate us to the greatest exertion for the acquirement both of literature and of property." Walker's commitment to African American literary nationalism as a form of "property" was evidenced most clearly in his efforts to help purchase the freedom of the enslaved North Carolina poet George Horton, a cause célèbre of the journal. The editors wrote in an issue of August 1828 that Horton, whose poems had begun to circulate in newspapers, "has astonished all who have witnessed his poetic talent." Two months later they noted: "We feel proud in announcing the name of *David C. Walker* of Boston, Mass. as a subscriber to the fund about to be raised for the purchase of George M. Horton, of North Carolina." Despite Walker's best efforts, Horton remained a slave for life.[46]

As the Horton case suggests, the editors regarded corporeal and textual circulation as crucial to black literary nationalism and their larger program of black elevation. *Freedom's Journal* itself was of course the editors' own contribution to African American literary nationalism, and in order for the journal to have any impact, it had to circulate outward from New York City. For good reason, then, the editors regularly highlighted the importance of circulatory freedom in their editorials, to the extent that it could be argued that black circulation became *the* crucial topic addressed in the newspaper, that the topic (or thematic) was inseparable from the paper's politics of black literary nationalism, and that it had its most compelling sources in continued concerns about black citizenship and circulation raised by the debates on Missouri and the figure of Vesey. In a column appearing in the 7 September 1827 issue of *Freedom's Journal*, the editors, in their own act of textual recirculation, reprinted an anti-Missouri speech from 1820, in which an anonymous northern politician chides the free states for capitulating to the desires of the slave power in "trampling on the natural rights of myriads of our fellow mortals, in defiance of the eternal principles of justice and equality."[47] Similar concerns informed a major essay serialized in *Freedom's Journal* from 22 February 1828 to 21 March 1828: James Forten's 1813 *A Series of Letters by a Man of Color.*

Termed by one historian "perhaps the most fully articulated attack on racial prejudice and slavery in the early republic," Forten's *Letters* in the context of its republication in *Freedom's Journal* can seem to be addressing the very issues that were central to the circulatory politics of the black press in the wake of the debates on Missouri.[48] In their prefatory note to the first installment of the republication, the editors themselves highlight the politics of circulation, instructing their readers that Forten's text was "originally published in the year 1813, in Philadelphia . . . when a proposition came before the Legislature of Pennsylvania, to register all free persons of Colour within the state, and also to prevent others from the different states settling within her borders." Because of the effectiveness of Forten's tract in helping to defeat that proposition, the editors remark, "we are anxious that [it] could circulate far and near, and be perused by friend and foe." The republication of Forten's 1813 *Letters* in 1828 also makes it appear to be a prescient "response" to Missouri, as Forten addresses many of the same issues that arose during the debates on Missouri's own anti-immigration provision. Invoking the Revolutionary War (which Forten depicts as a battle against a slave power) and the Constitution, Forten proclaims in 1813 and in effect reproclaims in 1828: "It cannot be that the authors of our Constitution intended to exclude us from its benefits, for just emerging from unjust and cruel emancipation, their souls were too much affected with their own deprivations to commence the reign of terrours over others." Convinced that constraints on mobility were in direct violation of the Constitution's aspiration to protect the "rights and privileges" of all Americans, Forten adopts a rhetoric of sentimentality in an effort to prompt white readers to sympathize with the plight of blacks who would be deprived of what he presents as the basic rights of citizenship: "[Y]e rulers of the black man's destiny, reflect upon this; our children must be registered, and bear about them a certificate, or be subject to imprisonment and fine. You, who are perusing this effusion of feeling, are you a parent? . . . [T]o you, we submit our case." But of course as reprinted in *Freedom's Journal*, the case is essentially being submitted to black readers and their white antislavery supporters, who would have been acutely concerned about even greater constraints on free blacks, including the possibility that, as a natural consequence of the Missouri Compromise, "we may expect shortly to find a law . . . authorizing the Constables to seize and confine everyone who dare walk the streets without a collar on his neck."[49]

Among those free blacks walking the streets "without a collar on his neck" were those entrusted by Cornish and Russwurm with the charge of circulating *Freedom's Journal* from town to town and state to state. After all, if the newspaper failed to get into the hands of subscribers, it simply would not exist in the way that the editors had imagined: as a material synecdoche for the black national body that they hoped to bring into a fuller and more vital existence. Throughout its two-year run, the editors thus ran regular columns on the crucial connections among circulation, financial survival, and the forging of black community, while providing updates in every issue on a principal figure of circulation, the "Authorized Agent," the very role that David Walker would take on in his efforts to promote and increase the circulation of the journal.

In the inaugural issue of *Freedom's Journal*, the same issue that published the account of the meeting at Walker's house in which Boston's blacks pledged themselves to increase the newspaper's circulation, Russwurm and Cornish printed on the last page a list of fourteen "Authorized Agents" charged with precisely that task.[50] Among those agents was David Walker. Implicit in the boxed listing of these agents, who were all based in northern states and the District of Columbia, was a suggestion of their representative relationship to the relatively small subscribing body. One of the dramatic developments charted by the paper through its succeeding issues was the steady increase of the list of authorized agents, with the small box at the bottom of the page eventually growing to one full column. As the editors made clear by regularly printing such lists, the agents, in the manner of skillful plotters, were gradually extending their reach into the southern states and beyond, thereby flouting the race-based anticirculatory politics of the second Missouri Compromise. The list of authorized agents in the issue of 23 March 1827 included a new agent in Haiti; twenty-two agents were listed in the issue of 3 August 1827, including an agent in Virginia. In the issue of 14 September 1827, Russwurm informed readers of the journal that Cornish was leaving his co-editorship position in order to devote himself to his ministry, but that he would continue to serve as "General Agent" overseeing the now twenty-three authorized agents.[51] Cornish's departure may have been motivated by his dissent from Russwurm's increasing attraction to Liberian coloniza-tionism, but he stayed on as general agent until the final issue. Perhaps as a result of his work, the list of agents continued to grow: the issue of 16 November 1827 noted the addition of two agents each in Virginia and Maryland, and the issue of 11 January 1828 noted the addition of three new agents in North Carolina and one in England.

For Russwurm, the work of the authorized agents was absolutely central to the financial survival of the paper. But equally important was the authorized agents' role in extending a sense of black community beyond the borders of the northern states. In this respect, there was a connection between Russwurm's promotion of the authorized agent, on the one hand, and his interest in Liberia, on the other, as Liberia became for him an attractive alternative to a nation that seemed intent on denying free blacks even the basic rights of mobility. As he remarked in an 1828 essay titled "Colonization": "If the free states have passed no laws as yet forbidding the emigration of free persons of colour into their limits; it is no reason that they will not, as soon as they find themselves a little more burdened." Increasingly interested in an unencumbered black nationality in Liberia, he attempted to extend the geographical range of his newspaper through his authorized agents. Over the next year or so, new agents continued to be added to the list, including one in Upper Canada and even one in New Orleans. By the time Russwurm decided to commit himself to "the expediency of emigration to Liberia," as he announced in his farewell editorial of 28 March 1829, he had a total of thirty-eight authorized agents from four countries, including a number from the southern states.[52] Although Walker rejected Russwurm's emigrationism, he remained committed to the mission of disseminating a blacknationalist newspaper. In addition to persisting with his work as an authorized agent, in late 1828 he began to advertise his clothing store in the paper, a sign of his commitment to economic programs of black uplift in the United States. That advertisement appeared in every issue of the six-month run of *The Rights of All*.

Cornish began publishing *Rights* approximately two months after the demise of *Freedom's Journal*. In an anticolonizationist editorial in the inaugural issue of 29 May 1829, similar to the editorials in the inaugural issue of *Freedom's Journal*, he emphasized the importance of advocating "the rights, & interests of the coloured population" in the United States. Again, literal circulation of the paper is crucial to this agenda, and he makes a special plea to potential black readers not to "withhold [their] patronage from this publication, it being devoted to all the interests of the coloured population." As with *Freedom's Journal*, Cornish places the burden of extending the paper's subscription base on the shoulders of the authorized agents: "The first number will mostly be sent to the care of the several agents, who will please to obtain the names and residences of the subscribers, and hand them their papers." On the final page of the first issue, Cornish lists thirty-two "Authorized agents," including David Walker. Among the thirty-one other agents are people based in Haiti, England, Canada, North Carolina, Virginia, Louisiana, the District of Columbia, and Maryland.[53]

Because of the precarious financial standing of Cornish's paper, over the next several months he paid particular attention to the role of the authorized agents in keeping the paper afloat, stating rather urgently in the issue of 12 June 1829: "The Agents throughout the country, are requested to extend the circulation of this paper." In his most sustained reflection on the connection between the authorized agents, the circulation of his paper, and his hopes for the development of black community in the United States, Cornish remarks in the issue of 18 September 1829: "[L]et the executive committees employ one general agent, whose duty it shall be to continue travelling from one extremity of our country to the other, forming associations, communicating with our people and the public generally, on all subjects of interest, collecting monies and delivering stated lectures on industry, frugality, enterprise &c., thereby linking together, by one solid chain, the whole free population, so as to make them think and feel, and act, as one solid body, devoted to education and improvement."[54] As was true for *Freedom's Journal*, that publicized, textualized, and disseminated voice is imagined as having the power to link (and create) "brethren."

A similar vision of black community linked (and created) by print informs Walker's one extant speech, "Address, Delivered before the General Colored Association of Boston," which appeared in the 19 December 1828 issue of *Freedom's Journal*. In this speech, delivered on the occasion of the "first-semi-annual meeting" of the MGCA, Walker laments the "yet unorganized condition" of blacks in the United States, and asserts that the primary goal of the MGCA should be "to unite the colored population, so far, through the United States of America, as may be practicable and expedient; forming societies, opening, expanding, and keeping up correspondences." Of note here is the emphasis on written communication, the belief that the circulation of "correspondences" would help to achieve black-nationalist goals in the United States. But, as expressed in this speech, Walker has larger aspirations as well of developing the sort of diasporic community emblematized by the authorized agents' extensions into Haiti, Canada, and England, with the hope of even further and wider extensions to come. Thus by the end of his speech he moves from what could be termed a U.S. black nationalism, a concern for what he terms the "[t]wo millions and a half of colored people in these United States," to a Denmark Vesey–like Pan-Africanism, as he salutes "our brethren, the Haytians" and enjoins "the dejected, degraded, and now enslaved children of Africa . . . to take their stand among the nations of the earth."[55] Approximately one year after delivering this speech, and right around the time of the demise of *The Rights of All*, Walker, with the help of his own authorized agents, would attempt to circulate his own "correspondence" to U.S. blacks and their "brethren" in his black literary-nationalist *Appeal*.

The Circulatory Routes of the Appeal

Border crossing, circulation, and black community are central to Walker's *Appeal*, which can be thought of as taking up the mission that Cornish's *The Rights of All* was forced to leave off. Like Cornish, Walker in the

Appeal attempts to "speak to our brethren at a distance." Such an effort to "speak" in print to blacks in various regions and sections, and in this way "[link] together, by one solid chain, the whole free population," emerges as one of the principal goals of the *Appeal* (as it was of African American literary nationalism). As suggested by the book's evocative full title, *David Walker's Appeal, in Four Articles; Together with a Preamble, to the Coloured Citizens of the World, but in Particular, and Very Expressly, to Those of the United States of America,* Walker seeks to legitimate blacks' claims to a U.S. national narrative that, like the sectionalists of the time (and Denmark Vesey), he attempts to shape on his own terms, while simultaneously making a transnational, community-creating appeal to blacks in the Americas and throughout the world. As I discuss below, crucial to the *Appeal* are strategies of rhetorical performance that work to trouble categories of race and enlarge the parameters of nation. And yet more often than not, as signaled by his opening reference to *"My dearly beloved Brethren and Fellow Citizens,"*[56] Walker's concerns are centered on African Americans in the United States and are conceived in relation to the issues of territory and citizenship brought to the fore by the Missouri controversy and its aftermath.

First published in September 1829, the *Appeal* is best known for its aggressive response to Jefferson's racism in *Notes on the State of Virginia* (1785), its effort to develop black pride by linking blacks to ancient Egyptians and contemporary Haitians, its hortatory calls for black uplift, and its militancy. My initial focus, however, will be on figures of circulation, which are integral to the book's provocative performance of race and nation. As with the emergent black press of the period, circulation in the *Appeal* is often literally about efforts to put bodies and texts in motion.

The preamble to the *Appeal* begins in this way: "Having travelled over a considerable portion of these United States, and having, in the course of my travels, taken the most accurate observations of things as they exist— the result of my observations has warranted the full and unshaken conviction, that we, (coloured people of these United States,) are the most degraded, wretched, and abject set of beings that ever lived since the world began" (1). In a gesture intended to show his disdain for current restrictions on black mobility, Walker, in the manner of Russwurm and Cornish's "authorized agents," presents his literal circulation throughout the nation as quest for knowledge, community, and authority. His travels thus pose a distinct challenge to white culture, as he explains in Article I, "OUR WRETCHEDNESS IN CONSEQUENCE OF SLAVERY" (7), because blacks in the United States, unlike the enslaved Israelites of ancient Egypt, are denied such basic privileges. As Walker points out, the Israelites to a certain extent were offered a place in Egypt, and could intermarry across "racial" boundaries and traverse "over all the land" (8) of what U.S. Christians would regard as the biblically archetypal evil slave nation. Thus in Article II, "OUR WRETCHEDNESS IN CONSEQUENCE OF IGNO-RANCE" (19), he presents blacks' lack of free mobility in the United States as one of the main signs of their degradation: "If any of you wish to know how FREE you are, let one of you start and go through the southern and western States of this country, and unless you travel as a slave to a white man . . . or have your free papers, (which if you are not careful they will get from you) if they do not take you up and put you in jail, and if you cannot give good evidence of your freedom, sell you into eternal slavery, I am not a living man" (28).

Noteworthy here is Walker's emphasis on "free papers," or print. In addition to making claims for the importance of geographical and social mobility, Walker insists on the need for blacks to develop the very skills that could be used to produce such "free papers" as *Freedom's Journal* and *The Rights of All*. Throughout the *Appeal*, literacy is presented as funda-mental to African Americans' ability to contest whites' efforts to limit their freedom. Responding in Article I to Jefferson's remarks on why (white) Roman slaves were able to become notable writers while Ameri-can (black) slaves have heretofore failed to distinguish themselves in the same way, Walker asserts, "Every body who has read history, knows, that as soon as a slave among the Romans obtained his freedom, he could rise to the greatest eminence in the State" (16). And he remarks that anyone who has read U.S. laws knows that blacks do not have similar oppor-tunities. The "heart-rending" (33) results of such racist exclusions were on display, Walker notes, when he recently "examined school-boys and young men of colour in different parts of the country, in the most simple parts of Murray's English Grammar, and not more than one in thirty was able to give a correct answer to my interrogations" (33). Angered by his observations of how whites "keep us ignorant" (33), even as he boastfully calls attention to his transgressive ability to circulate in "Boston, New-York, Philadelphia, or Baltimore [and] . . . further south or west" (33), Walker remarks on his vitriol: "No doubt some will say I write with a bad spirit" (20).

Walker's choice of the word "write" over "speak" in ironically referring to his "bad spirit" is appropriate, for throughout the *Appeal* he emphasizes the textuality of his analytical performance. Even the hyperbolic typeface —the repeated multiple exclamations, pointing fingers, and so on—is primarily intended for the reading eye. But there is an important oral dimension to the *Appeal* as well, and Hinks's argument that "Walker's *Appeal* has its roots in an oral, not a print, culture" is best supported by the relatively short Article III, "OUR WRETCHEDNESS IN CONSE-QUENCE OF THE PREACHERS OF THE RELIGION OF JESUS CHRIST" (35).[57] Attacking the hypocrisy of nominally Christian preachers, Walker himself assumes the persona of a preacher declaiming against what he terms the "mockery of religion . . . conducted by the Americans" (43), focusing in particular on the situation in South Carolina. In what may be a reference to South Carolina authorities' razing of Denmark Vesey's AME Church in 1822, he describes the *"patrols"* in South Carolina that would attack praying blacks and "beat them until they would scarcely leave life in them" for "the audacity to be found *making prayers and supplications to the God who made them! ! ! !"* (37). At the same time, he tells of how blacks were allowed to attend proslavery camp meetings. After describing a sermon by a South Carolina preacher who instructs the slaves on their biblical duty to obey their masters, Walker, in the manner of a Jeremiah, concludes his discussion of whites' manipulations of religion with an apocalyptic prediction of impending divine retribution: "I call God—I call angels—I call men, to witness, that your DESTRUCTION *is at hand,* and will be speedily consummated unless you REPENT" (43).[58]

There is something wonderfully audacious about Walker's willingness here to appropriate the preacherly role and stand in judgment of white religious and cultural authorities. Although the admonitions exist in print and have a compelling presence on the page, it is difficult not to "hear" Walker's prophetic words. Even so, Walker makes it clear that he is responding not just to a sermon that he claims to have heard at a camp meeting in South Carolina but also to his reading of southern newspapers, which, almost despite themselves, provide accounts of the horrors of slavery. For when he writes about southerners that they "have newspapers and monthly periodicals, . . . on the pages of which, you will scarcely ever find a paragraph respecting slavery" (39), Walker means to underscore the fact that slavery is so assumed as a positive good that southern journalists, even when reporting on runaway slaves, feel no need to comment on the institution from the critical perspective of the fugitive. The failure of the South and, more generally, the nation to discuss slavery in a print context replete with dissenting minority voices can therefore be taken as the main subject of the *Appeal*'s longest section, the concluding Article IV, "OUR WRETCHEDNESS IN CONSEQUENCE OF THE COLO-NIZING PLAN" (45). This section consists almost entirely of Walker's remarks on various newspaper articles, which he puts into conversation with one another and thus recontextualizes and recirculates in his *Appeal*. Anticipating the similarly ironic strategies of recontextualization in Brown's *Clotel* (1853), Walker attempts to reenvision and critique the nation from the vantage point of the marginalized and silenced, whom he reveals are not so marginal and silent after all.[59]

Article IV focuses on the national "conversation" among blacks and whites about the ACS's project of colonizing the free blacks to Africa. That project was announced at the founding of the ACS in December 1816 and reported in the Washington, D.C., newspaper the *National Intelligencer*, the preeminent newspaper of the time.[60] In his journalistic Article IV, Walker quotes several times from the 24 December 1816 account of the ACS in the *National Intelligencer*, asserting that Clay and others formulated "a plan to get those of the coloured people, who are said to be free, away from among those of our brethren whom they unjustly hold in bondage, so that they may be enabled to keep them the more secure in ignorance and wretchedness, to support them and their children, and consequently they would have the more obedient slaves" (47). As Walker develops his analysis of the newspaper account of the meeting, it becomes clear that the colonizationists' plan is of a piece with the proposals of the Missouri legislators: to limit interactions among the free and enslaved blacks and thus to thwart the growth of African American community. As in earlier sections of the *Appeal*, Walker in effect converses with the dominant white culture through a politics of textual (re)circulation, regularly underscoring the printed or textualized dimension of his response to the ACS: "I shall now pass in review the speech of Mr. Elias B. Caldwell, Esq. of the District of Columbia, extracted from the same page on which Mr. Clay's will be found" (51). Like Clay, Caldwell talks of the importance of denying blacks knowledge so as to keep the overall black populace in "the condition of brutes" (52), and Walker goes on to describe the *National Intelligencer*'s report of John Randolph's similar plea to separate the educated free blacks from the uneducated slaves.[61] He then prints a letter by Philadelphia's Richard Allen, the noted founder of the African Methodist Episcopal Church, which excoriates the racist work of the ACS in denying blacks' claims to U.S. citizenship. Significantly, Walker cites as his source for Bishop Allen's letter the 2 November 1827 issue of *Freedom's*

Journal (56); and after reprinting selections from the letter, he once again reminds his readers of its source: "I have given you, my brethren, an extract verbatim, from the letter of that godly man, as you may find it on the aforementioned page of Freedom's Journal" (58).

To some extent, the battle of words between Allen and the ACS is presented as a newspaper war, or public debate, which now comes to life as publicized by Walker in the *Appeal's* Article IV. In his placement of the *Freedom's Journal* letter immediately after the excerpts from the *National Intelligencer*, Walker makes it appear that Allen is responding directly to those articles, which, in effect, *is* the case in the textual context of the *Appeal*. Allen exposes the hidden aim of the supposedly reformist ACS, which is to improve the lot of the slave masters: "Is it not for the interest of the slave-holders to select the free people of colour out of the different states, and send them to Liberia? Will it not make their slaves uneasy to see free men of colour enjoying liberty?" (57). Having attacked the politics of the ACS, Allen asserts African Americans' rights to U.S. citizenship in no uncertain terms: "This land which we have watered with our *tears* and *our blood*, is now our *mother country*, and we are well satisfied to stay where wisdom abounds and the gospel is free" (58). Walker echoes Allen's criticisms, presenting blacks as even more legitimately of the land than whites: "America is more our country, than it is the whites—we have enriched it with our *blood and tears*" (65). And then Walker turns to another newspaper article from the black press, adducing "the language of the Rev. Mr. S. E. Cornish, of New York, editor of the Rights of All," in asserting that any black who (like Russwurm) supports the agenda of the ACS " 'should be considered as a traitor to his brethren, and discarded by every respectable man of colour' " (67). At the same time, Walker offers his resounding support for *Rights*, and without acknowledging the recent failure of that newspaper, he makes an "appeal" for its "circulation": "Let me make an appeal brethren, to your hearts, for your cordial co-operation in the circulation of 'The Rights of All,' among us. The utility of such a vehicle conducted, cannot be estimated. I hope that the well informed among us, may see the absolute necessity of their co-operation in its universal spread among us" (67). The circulation of the paper would serve the national ends of the thrice-stated "among us" of this proclamation, thereby countering both the removal politics of the ACS and the anticirculatory politics of the second Missouri Compromise.

Walker of course is doing his own work of circulating key articles from the black press in the *Appeal*. He makes one final reference to a black newspaper near the end of his book when he urges his readers to "See my Address, delivered before the General Coloured Association of Massachusetts, which may be found in Freedom's Journal, for Dec. 20, 1828" (71). The very idea of "seeing" a speech once again points to the crucial place of print in an age of oratory, for without print that speech would not have circulated beyond the confines of the MGCA. The reference to what for many would have been a rather obscure speech also points to the role of black newspapers (and Walker's book) in publicizing black perspectives and making those perspectives integral to national debate.

The role of publicity in the formation of national communities is central to Jürgen Habermas's influential notion of the public sphere. In *The Structural Transformation of the Public Sphere*, Habermas idealizes a moment in eighteenth-century British culture when (he claims) various public institutions—coffee houses, literary societies, novels, and newspapers—contributed to the emergence of a rational, participatory public culture. In Habermas's formulation, newspapers were of particular importance in helping to develop this culture, for "the press institutionalized regular contacts and regular communication." A number of critics have challenged Habermas for what they regard as his elitist or hegemonic conception of the public sphere. Houston A. Baker Jr. contends, for example, that Habermas's notion of a participatory public sphere is inapplicable to African Americans, most of whom were either socially disenfranchised or regarded as property: "Insofar as the emergence and energy of Habermas's public sphere were generated by property ownership and literacy, how can black Americans, who like many others have traditionally been excluded from these domains of modernity, endorse Habermas's beautiful idea?" And yet what Walker proposes, I want to suggest, is that his readers regard the black public, particularly as developed and publicized by its newspapers, as a constitutive part of a public sphere that is anything but monolithic. In the *Appeal*, Walker underscores the crucial importance to democratic culture of what Nancy Fraser terms "*subaltern counterpublics*," placing a special emphasis on the public-ness of that counterpublic. Within Walker's dialogical model, black newspapers and the *Appeal* itself must be viewed as essential participants in an ever-widening national conversation on slavery, race, and citizenship.[62]

Walker signals his own efforts at widening the arena of participatory democracy in the United States when he turns his attention from his African American readers, whom he has been addressing directly through-out the text, to his white readers, whom he has been addressing both as "Fellow Citizens" and oppressors. Circulation is once again key to Walker's rhetorical and political aims, for Walker can only address whites if he has confidence that his book *will* be widely circulated in the culture. In some respects, what Walker has to say to the whites who happen to be reading the book is relatively reassuring. Ostensibly refuting Jefferson's famous prophesy in *Notes* that a racial war of extermination would be the inevitable result of emancipation, Walker remarks in Article IV that blacks ask whites "for nothing but the rights of man, viz. for them to set us free, and treat us like men, and there will be no danger, for we will love and respect them, and protect our country" (66). With the reference to "our country," Walker once again asserts African Americans' rights to citizen-ship in a nation that they helped to create, and he goes on to offer a series of bright idealizations of the possibilities of blacks and whites coexisting in the United States. "What a happy country this will be, if the whites will listen" (70), he declares, and at a time of apparent conflict, he waxes utopian in imagining such harmonious possibilities: "Treat us then like men, and we will be your friends. And there is not a doubt in my mind, but that the whole of the past will be sunk into oblivion, and we yet, under God, will become a united and happy people" (70).

Here is the Walker who has been celebrated by Hinks and others for his racial egalitarianism, humanism, pacifism, integrationism, and U.S. nationalism. According to Hinks, Walker "was certain that the best hope blacks had for their healthy and happy participation in an interracial, republican America lay in peace and conciliatory gestures toward whites, not in aggressive denunciation and warfare."[63] And yet if that is so, why does Walker repeatedly offer such denunciations? Perhaps he does so because he cannot put his faith in such interracial bromides, at least not in 1829 and 1830, and at this key moment of the *Appeal* he is asserting precisely the opposite of what Hinks contends: that the best hope *whites* have for their healthy and happy participation in an interracial, republi-can America lies in peace and conciliatory gestures toward blacks, not in aggressive denunciations and warfare. While Walker may convey a hopefulness about the harmonious possibilities that would ensue should whites treat blacks like human beings, he has considerable doubts about whites' capabilities of acting in such a way at this particular historical moment, with or without the help of God. For the fact is that, despite his efforts to develop a black counterpublic through his circulatory strategies, there is virtually nothing in the *Appeal* suggestive of U.S. whites' willingness or ability to conceive of blacks as human beings, to listen to what they have to say, or to consider them as possible friends or fellow citizens.

VIEWED IN THIS LIGHT, Walker's avowed hopes for a development that he must know will not occur in the immediate future can be interpreted as a moment of counterfactual narration, an attempt to imagine or create a different history from what he suspects will be the social reality at the time of the *Appeal*'s publication—a narrative moment of "undoing" that seeks to encourage change by insisting on the possibility that blacks and whites over time can, through conscious deliberation, alter the social landscape. Theorist Jeremy Waldron has linked the trope of undoing to debates on reparations, arguing that reparations to historically victimized groups can be taken as attempts to reshape the future through acts that symbolically undo the past.[64] It is significant that Walker's counterfactual imagining of a reformed social order brought about by white civility and interracial harmony has at its center a call that even he must have regarded as quixotic and untenable at the present moment: a demand that whites issue a national apology for their crimes against black people and offer something like what we might call affirmative action and reparations. Admitting that he is setting forth what will be regarded as "unexpected, strange, and wild . . . propositions," he nonetheless asserts: "The Americans may say or do as they please, but they have to raise us from the condition of brutes to that of respectable men, and to make a national acknowledgment to us for the wrongs they have inflicted on us" (70). Immediately after making these demands, Walker conveys his awareness of the unlikeliness of such demands being met in the foreseeable future by defining himself in relation to Africa: "If they are anxious to know who I am, know the world, that I am one of the oppressed, degraded and wretched sons of Africa, rendered so by the avaricious and unmerciful, among the whites" (71). Moving from hopeful affirmations of interracial brotherhood to aggressive assertions of whites' wrongdoings against blacks, from a U.S. nationalistic engagement with the public culture of print to bold proclamations of his Africanness, Walker as a sort of synecdochic textual embodiment of a contending black counterpublic can seem well nigh discombobulating (or dislocating) in his shifting affirmations and commitments.

These rhetorical moves at the end of the text are distinctively *literary* moments, displaying Walker's skillful deployment of voice, persona, and conjectural narrative, along with his sense of the limits of circulation as a political strategy at a time of hardening racism in U.S. culture. Concerned that blacks will have to do battle against a white-supremacist national culture for some time to come, Walker, in addition to offering a glimpse of an alternative history of undoing, seeks to undermine the very stability of the linkage of (white) race and U.S. nation that informs white-supremacist culture, and the two Missouri Compromises, through a complex *performance* of race and nation. We should therefore resist critical efforts to stabilize the text, whether as an unambiguously clear assertion of black-nationalist separatism, on the one hand, or as a more integration-ist program of black uplift, on the other.[65] The *Appeal* is relatively indeterminate or, perhaps more accurately, protean with respect to race and nation, in part because Walker wants his text to ramify in different ways among different readers as it circulates in various social, cultural, geographical, and even historical contexts, and in part because he wants to escape the trap of reproducing the essentialist racial thinking of his culture.[66] In this sense, circulation for Walker is less about privilege than disruption.

Throughout the *Appeal*, Walker appeals to his blackness, stating near the end of the book, in one of his angriest performative moments, "My colour will yet, root some of you out of the very face of the earth! ! ! ! ! !" (72). But is color the same as race in Walker's text? For the most part, Walker presents race as a concept that is imposed on peoples of color by the whites in power. It has no stable or essential meaning and thus can be held up for mockery and irony. When Walker states in the preamble of the *Appeal*, for instance, that his text is directed toward those "who can dispense with prejudice long enough to admit that we are *men*, notwithstanding our *improminent noses* and *woolly heads*" (4), he ironically invokes the "scientific" empiricism deployed by Jefferson in *Notes*, using the italics to underscore the absurdity of viewing such alleged physical differences as proof of the existence of separate species or races. Likewise, he mocks Jefferson in Article I when he notes that the ancient Egyptians, unlike Jefferson and his followers, never sought to distinguish themselves from the Israelites "by telling them that they were not of the *human family*" (10). In his efforts to display "race" as a category that comes into being through the efforts of one group to marginalize or dominate another, Walker shows how he can perform just such an act of racialization by troping on Jefferson's famous disquisition on black racial inferiority in *Notes*. Walker elaborates a long history of white imperialism, domination, and involvement with the slave trade and then concludes in the manner of Jefferson (echoing his words in *Notes*): "I therefore, in the name and fear of the Lord God of Heaven and of earth, divested of prejudice either on the side of my colour or that of the whites, advance my suspicion of them [whites], whether they are *as good by nature* as we are or not" (17). While clearly using irony to forge a sense of black community, the equally important suggestion here is that such "racing," whether done by Jefferson or Walker, depends upon the existence of a receptive interpretive community.[67]

In fascinating ways, then, the *Appeal* seeks to develop black racial pride in the late 1820s and beyond by challenging the very concept of race itself. In the *Appeal*, Walker's references to color are often more metaphorical than essentialist, references to concepts of morality and spirit rather than to biology. For instance, when Walker proclaims that "[t]he world will have an opportunity to see whether it is unfortunate for us, that our Creator *has made us* darker than the *whites*" (12), he invokes racial difference while at the same time undermining that concept by metaphorically linking the notion of darkness to whites. Blacks, he archly suggests, are darker by color; whites, who, by the very comparison, are also dark, are darker by deed.

And yet, as the Missouri debates made clear, there is nothing metaphorical about oppression, and color does define race in the antebellum United States as a marker of inferiority or superiority, marginality or citizenship. Defined by whites as a separate race, blacks perforce are required by the racist culture to live in a subordinate or enslaved relation to whites. Within the racialized black group, Walker develops a "racial" pride even as he would seem to remain skeptical about the concept of race as propounded by the dominant culture. He emphasizes the importance of such pride as a response to whites' racism: "They think because they hold us in their infernal chains of slavery, that we wish to be white, or of their color—but they are dreadfully deceived—we wish to be just as it pleased our creator to have made us" (12). On the one hand, then, Walker denounces and ironically undercuts racial thinking; on the other, he strategically embraces race both as a marker of the shared experience of oppression and as a pragmatic tool for creating a community united in its struggle against such oppression.

Walker's depiction of nation in the *Appeal* is just as indeterminate and protean, just as performative and strategic, as his depiction of race. Throughout the book he appeals multiply not simply to a fixed and absolute category of nationhood but to a U.S. nationalism, an African American nationalism, and a diasporan post- or transnationalism. Of course in his discussion of colonization, Walker insists on African Americans' rights to citizenship in the U.S. nation. Although the claiming of those rights is one of the fundamental arguments of his book, there is nothing stable about nation in the *Appeal*. In the manner of the heroic figure of Denmark Vesey, Walker presents a diasporic vision of the linkages among oppressed "coloured people," arguing that it is "an unshaken and for ever immovable *fact*, that your full glory and happiness, as well as all other coloured people under Heaven, shall never be fully consummated, but with the *entire emancipation of your enslaved brethren all over the world*" (29). More specifically, he discusses African Americans' close ties to "our brethren" (56) in Haiti, proclaiming that the relatively new nation is "the glory of the blacks and terror of tyrants" (21). Careful about overly celebrating African Americans' links to Africa, lest he appear to be supporting the arguments of the colonizationists, he nonetheless echoes the sentiments expressed in the *African Repository and Colonial Journal* that blacks should take pride in their connection to "the sons of Africa" (19), referring to the African continent as "our mother country" (57) and "native land" (56), thereby begging the question of blacks' connections to the United States. As was true for the Vesey of the trial transcript, there is something revolutionary about such a rhetorical move to configure blackness and nation in opposition to what Walker clearly regarded as a white-supremacist U.S. nation. But whatever the claims that Walker wishes to make on Africa and / or black diaspora, there is a clear suggestion that the United States has equal if not greater claims on his imagination.

It is worth emphasizing, then, that perhaps even despite itself, the *Appeal* is also inspired by the liberatory potential of Jefferson's Revolutionary nationalism. In one final act of textual recirculation, Walker invokes a particular aspect of that potential in the closing pages of the *Appeal*, as he reprints the portion of the Declaration of Independence that calls for a revolutionary emancipation when a "long train of abuses and usurpation" (75) is imposed upon "one people" (74). In the manner of the Vesey of the trial transcript, Walker turns to a key text of U.S. nationalism, a text that had its initial incarnation in newspapers, and a text that Jefferson surely never intended as a call for black revolutionism, as a way of inspiring and legitimating the development of a militant black (African American) nationalism.[68] Aggressively positioning black community against white community, he demands of white Americans: "Do you understand your own language? . . . Compare your own language above, extracted from your Declaration of Independence, with your cruelties and murders inflicted by your cruel and unmerciful fathers and yourselves on our fathers and on us." And more: "Hear your language further! ☞ 'But when a long train of abuses and usurpation, pursuing invariably the same object, evinces a design to reduce them under absolute despotism, it is their *right*, it is their *duty*, to throw off such government, and to provide new guards for their future security'" (75). Warning in jeremiadic fashion of the imminence of a black revolutionism in which God would take His vengeance against a sinful nation, Walker concludes his text as it begins, with an image of himself as a traveling observer whose circulation throughout the country has provided him with firsthand evidence for his scathing critiques and judgments. Referring to the efforts of southern clergy and masters to preach submission, Walker exclaims: "If any man wishes to hear this doctrine openly preached to us by the American preachers, let him go into the Southern and Western section of this country—I do not speak from hear say—what I have written, is what I have seen and heard myself. No man may think that my book is made up of conjecture—I have travelled and observed nearly the whole of those things myself." Walker's ability to travel, observe, report, and circulate the facts of blacks' situation in the United States stands as his large transgressive challenge to racist whites of all regions. "Americans," Walker writes, "may be as vigilant as they please, but they cannot be vigilant enough for the Lord, neither can they hide themselves, where he will not find and bring them out" (76). The lowercase "he," perhaps a slip, allows for a conflation of Walker and God as all-seeing witnesses and avengers.

Although the *Appeal* concludes with a call for black vengeance against white sinners, it does so within the ideological frame of the nation's Declaration of Independence. Walker's decision to conclude his text by quoting from Jefferson's originary Declaration brings us back to the question of the relationship between Walker's politics of print and his politics of black nationalism. Anticipating Benedict Anderson's notion of the connection of newspapers to the formation of the nation, Walker's nationalism champions the circulation of black texts and bodies and views that circulation as central to linked efforts to develop black citizenship and community. An inevitable result of what Stuckey terms "Walker's disregard for geographical barriers,"[69] however, is that such circulation can be viewed as both an expression of "American" mobility and a challenge to the U.S. nation, particularly at those moments when the *Appeal* suggests Walker's larger hemispheric concerns about the "coloured persons" (63) of the West Indies and South America. With his final remarks on the failure of the United States to live up to its founding ideals, Walker brings the focus back to the situation of African Americans. Nevertheless, there remains an animating tension in Walker's rhetorically canny *Appeal*, and his equally canny efforts at circulating it, between nationalistic notions of "our country" (65) and transnational or diasporic notions of "[our] *enslaved brethren all over the world*." This tension would continue to inform the complex rhetorical and cultural work integral to the creatively resilient black (literary) nationalism of the nineteenth century.

ON THE ONE HAND, then, the *Appeal* can be read in relation to the Denmark Vesey conspiracy, whether actual or invented, as a Pan-African text of black separatism and revolutionism; on the other, it can be read in relation to the rise of the black press as an antiracist text of black uplift aspiring to make African Americans part of the national community through the work of circulation and publicity. Or, as I am suggesting, it can be read in relation to both as a highly performative response to the key debates on race, nation, and citizenship of the 1820s. With his appropriations and recontextualizations of numerous newspaper articles in particular, Walker seeks to place African American perspectives at the center of U.S. public culture, even as he exposes the contradictions and mendacity at the heart of that culture. Central to the circulatory power of the *Appeal* is precisely the way that it conveys, from the title page on, multiple commitments that some might find contradictory and others mutually reinforcing.

As is well known, circulation and publicity were not only textual thematics of the *Appeal*, but also material strategies of an author intent on getting his text into the hands of as many readers as possible. Published in Boston in September 1829, the *Appeal* quickly made its way to Savannah, Georgia; Wilmington, North Carolina; Charleston, South Carolina; and even New Orleans. In his efforts to disseminate his book, Walker was clearly inspired by the concept of the "authorized agent" that was so central to the distribution of *Freedom's Journal* and *The Rights of All*; and it is noteworthy that the *Appeal* was discovered in many of the same cities listed by Cornish and Russwurm in their ever-expanding lists of authorized agents. As W. Jeffrey Bolster and others have documented, Walker adopted a number of tactics for circulating the text outside of Massachusetts. One of his most effective was to deploy free black seamen as his authorized agents in the South. In the wake of the alleged Vesey conspiracy, some southern states began to incarcerate black sailors during their visits, though many of these sailors continued to have exchanges with the free and enslaved blacks of port cities and were able to get the *Appeal* into the hands of southern blacks. By the time of the June 1830 publication of the third edition of the *Appeal*, southern efforts to ban Walker's tract had intensified. Appearing as it did during the debates on the tariff and nullification, the book, as Hinks notes, "seemed only to evince further the existence of a distant enemy menacing the South." In North Carolina, authorities were particularly cognizant of circulation as a form of subversive infiltration. In attempting to halt the text's distribution by approving an "Act to prevent the circulation of seditious publications," North Carolina officials imposed regulations reminiscent of the Missouri state constitution. As part of its revised "Free Negro Code," the North Carolina legislature voted to quarantine black sailors, to forbid the entrance of other free blacks into the state, and to make it illegal for North Carolina's free blacks to return to the state should they choose even temporarily to cross its borders.[70]

The material dimension of the *Appeal's* politics of circulation is addressed directly in the third edition, for by the time of this republication, Walker, in the manner of a newspaper reporter, was able to report on the reception of the *Appeal* in southern culture. In a prefatory note to this edition, Walker presents the dissemination of his text as an imperative for blacks throughout the world: "It is expected that all coloured men, women and children, of every nation, language and tongue under heaven, will try to procure a copy of this Appeal and read it, or get some one to read it to them, for it is designed more particularly for them" (n.p.). An extensive footnote in Article IV, added to the June 1830 edition, elaborates on what Walker had already commented on in the first and second editions, that if whites "find us with a book of any description in our hand, they will beat us nearly to death—they are so afraid we will learn to read, and enlighten our dark and benighted minds" (65). In the new footnote, Walker once again displays his own powers of infiltration by commenting, almost as if he were there, on police efforts to stop the spread of the *Appeal* in the South. He rhetorically queries: "Why do they search vessels, &c. when entering the harbours of tyrannical States, to see if any of my Books can be found, for fear that my brethren will get them to read. Why, I thought the Americans proclaimed to the world that they are a happy, enlightened, humane, and Christian people" (72). And he supplies his own answer: "But perhaps the Americans do their very best to keep my Brethren from receiving and reading my 'Appeal' for fear that they will find in it an extract which I made from their Declaration of Independence, which says, 'we hold these truths to be self-evident, that all men are created equal,' &c. &c. &c" (72).

Concerns among southern whites about a revolutionary rearticulation of the Declaration as a black freedom document speak to lingering fears raised by the debates on Missouri (and the subsequent alleged Vesey conspiracy), in which northern congressmen, as Glover Moore observes, "invoked the concept of natural law and the most famous American document which expounded it—the Declaration of Independence—to sustain their ... positions."[71] Precisely such invocations of the Declaration during and immediately following the debates on Missouri led Thomas Jefferson, who himself had publicized the Declaration in colonial newspapers, to link the Declaration to a philosophy of states' rights. Walker's debate with Jefferson in *Appeal* can thus be read as yet another aspect of that text's waging of a newspaper war in the wake of the Missouri controversy. Perhaps more importantly, however, Walker's appropriation of the key founding text that remained pivotal to the development of U.S. nationalism reminds us once again that there were no self-evident truths about the meaning of that nationalism.

Walker Sleeps, Yet He Lives

I have been using the debates on Missouri to help us rethink the African American literary nationalism of the *Appeal*, but we might now use those debates, and the *Appeal* itself, to reconsider U.S. literary nationalism during this period more generally.

According to the influential nineteenth-century literary historian Moses Coit Tyler and the numerous critics who have followed his lead, the 1820s and 1830s saw the emergence of a distinctively "American" U.S. literature in the writing of New Englanders, which culminated in such literary-nationalist texts as Emerson's "The American Scholar" (1837) and "The Poet" (1844). It is worth noting, however, that when Emerson delivered his "The American Scholar" address in the late summer of 1837, he was speaking at a time of intense partisan conflict over such issues as the gag rule on the presentation of antislavery petitions in Congress. Lee Rust Brown argues that "Emerson's ambition to found an originally American literature within the scope of his own writing project was no less responsive to . . . American urgency than the political efforts of Daniel Webster . . . to cement a whole national identity in the face of divisive interests and ruinous passions." Arguably, when Emerson in "The American Scholar" imagines a unified "nation of men . . . inspired by the Divine Soul which also inspires all men," he is subsuming conflict to a "transcendental" vision that Christopher Newfield maintains helped to advance the "corporate individualism" of northern market culture. Emerson no doubt had larger aims as well, but when he remarks in "The Poet" that the true American poem would bring together "the northern trade, [and] the southern planting," one suspects that he was not imagining the northern economy in subordinate or even equal relation to southern slavery.[72]

Whether Emerson's vision of unity is ultimately what one critic terms "a powerful sectional nationalism" is beyond the purview of this chapter.[73] But, returning now to the 1820s and early 1830s, what we can say is truly "national" about the literature of New England is the desire, similar to Walker's and other African American literary nationalists, to lay claim to "America." Such texts as Daniel Webster's "First Settlement of New England" (1820), Catharine Maria Sedgwick's A New-England Tale (1822), Edward Everett's, "First Settlement of New England" (1824), Sarah Hale's Northwood; A Tale of New England (1827), Rufus Choate's "The Importance of Illustrating New-England History by a Series of Romances like the Waverley Novels" (1834), and Sedgwick's The Linwoods (1835) can be seen as engaged in a not-so-innocent project of presenting U.S. nationalism as synonymous with New England values and perspectives. Daniel Webster influentially proclaimed in "First Settlement of New England," for example, that New England did more than any other "portion of the country . . . to bring the Revolutionary struggle to a successful issue," hailing New England as the incarnation of national liberty for continuing to fight against the authoritarianism and evils of the southern slave "traffic." Sedgwick's The Linwoods similarly advances a vision of the importance of New England character to the liberty of the nation. Set during the Revolutionary period, the novel focuses in large part on the progress of the New Yorker Isabella Linwood in overcoming her anti–New England prejudices. As she writes in a letter to a friend: "I have an antipathy to the New-Englanders—a disloyal race, and conceited, fancying themselves more knowing in all matters, high and low, especially government and religion, than the rest of the world." Eventually, however, she falls in love with Eliot Lee of Massachusetts, described by the narrator as the "lineal descendant from one of the renowned pilgrim fathers." The concluding marriage of a woman who is "fit to grace a peerage" to a man who is "the portionless son of a New-England farmer" allows Sedgwick to instruct her readers on the virtues of New England "industry and frugality." Among the industrious and frugal are the black "servants" Jupiter and Rose, who remain faithful to their masters/employers throughout the novel. Such loyalty is among the benefits accruing to liberty-loving, nationalistic New Englanders "in a country," Sedgwick remarks, "that is sure to smile upon these qualities."[74]

But of course the South did not smile upon such qualities in New Englanders. Any consideration of a U.S. national narrative at this time must take account of the fact that, as William Gilmore Simms argues in "Americanism in Literature" (1844), southern literary nationalists viewed their own project as fully "American." That is precisely the perspective that informs the writings of Nathaniel Beverley Tucker, one of the most significant "southern" writers to emerge in the aftermath of the Missouri controversy.[75] Born in Virginia, Tucker settled in the Missouri Territory in 1816, where he was appointed judge of the Northern Circuit, and in letters and newspaper articles written during the debates on Missouri, he championed Missouri's right to enter the Union on its own terms as a slave state. Responding to the tariff debates, Nat Turner's rebellion, and the nullification crisis of the early 1830s—all of which he regarded as the inevitable consequences of the Missouri Compromise—he came to conceive of secession as a properly "American" and liberty-loving option for resisting the federal government's attempts to abridge states' rights. In 1836, three years after returning to Virginia, Tucker, now a professor of law at the College of William and Mary, published his first historical novel, George Balcombe, set in Virginia and Missouri, which advanced his states' rights doctrines. Despite the novel's "sectional" agenda, Edgar Allan Poe, in a review in the Southern Literary Messenger, declared George Balcombe "the best American novel."[76] The fate of "America" itself is at stake in Tucker's better known The Partisan Leader: A Tale of the Future, which was also published in 1836.

Written in an effort to derail Martin Van Buren's presidential campaign, the melodramatic and highly engaging The Partisan Leader depicts a dystopic future United States in which Van Buren, now running for his fourth term, reigns as a kind of monarch in "his palace," representing a "sectional faction" of Northeast merchants and power brokers "who served the crown." Outraged by such sectional domination, the Deep South states have seceded, with the drama focusing on what the leaders of the border state Virginia will decide to do. Tucker's principal political argument is clear: the southern confederacy represents the best hope for preserving the American nation as conceived by its founders, for as the novel's hero Bernard Trevor remarks on the Van Buren administration, *"the acts of the Government were violations of the constitution."* The novel thus distinguishes between the nation (embodied by the confederate states) and the state (embodied by Van Buren's federal government), celebrating the former while damning the latter. In depicting the progress of Bernard Trevor's nephew Douglas Trevor in eventually choosing his uncle's states' rights constitutionalism over his father's federal Unionism, which "deride[s] the idea of State sovereignty," Tucker presents southern secession as in the tradition of the American Revolution. As in Sedgwick, the black servants / slaves are presented as supportive of the vision of the white leaders. The "Yorkers" remain yoked to Van Buren, who eventually attempts a military occupation of Virginia. To oppose Van Buren is thus to stand up for "the great principles of the American Union, which had been trampled on by the Federal Government."[77] It is not surprising, then, that the novel should have been republished in Virginia in 1862 in an effort to bolster southern nationalism. But one section's nationalism could be another's sectionalism; the novel was also republished in New York in 1861 in order to demonstrate to northern readers that the South all along had been plotting to destroy the Union.[78]

Published approximately five years before *The Linwoods* and *The Partisan Leader*, Walker's *Appeal* asserted its own forms of literary nationalism and, to invoke Toni Morrison's famous formulation, may have been a shaping presence behind the white sectional nationalisms of the 1830s and 1840s, whether in the South or New England.[79] It is significant in this regard that both Sedgwick and Tucker presented loyal black "servants" in their fictions, almost as if they were haunted by Walker, Vesey, Nat Turner, and the general specter of black revolutionism.

Walker was of course a more obvious shaping influence on subsequent African American writing. Within African American literary-nationalist traditions, the death of Walker in 1830 shortly after the publication of the third and final edition of *Appeal* made him into a mythic figure, as rumors abounded that he had been killed by whites who sought to silence him. The most prominent African American interpreter of Walker in the immediate wake of his death was Maria W. Stewart, who in her 1831 "Religion and the Pure Principles of Morality" invokes "the most noble, fearless, and undaunted David Walker" as a presiding deity over her own black-nationalist work. "Though David Walker sleeps," she remarks in her sermonic essay, "yet he lives, and his name shall be in everlasting remembrance." Marilyn Richardson observes that Stewart "drew from Walker's impassioned manifesto an ethic of resistance to physical and political oppression," but that she also "moved beyond Walker's influence . . . in insisting upon the right of women to take their place in the front ranks of black moral and political leadership." Indeed, in the *Appeal*, Walker appears to envision education and leadership as the province of men, and at one point even conveys his apparent anger at slave women for somehow being more complicitous with slave culture than slave men. Reprinting an anecdote from "the Columbian Centinel of this city, for September 9, 1829" (23), Walker tells of how a black woman helped a slave driver survive an attack by resistant slaves. Walker lambastes "the *ignorant* and *deceitful actions* of this coloured woman" (24), while saying barely a word about the slave driver, who happens to be a black man. In her most famous speech, "An Address, Delivered at the African Masonic Hall, Boston, Feb. 27, 1833," Stewart turns the tables on Walker's indictment of black women, castigating black men for seemingly acquiescing to white-supremacist culture, while again depicting Walker as a lone beacon of resistance: "But where is the man that has distinguished himself in these modern days by acting wholly in the defense of African rights and liberty? There was one, although he sleeps, his memory lives."[80]

Among the ideas bequeathed to Stewart by Walker is the tension between a U.S. nationalism and a diasporic concept of what Stewart refers to as the "sons and daughters of Africa" who had "sprung from [the] learned and enlightened nation" of Ethiopia. But the overall emphasis of her lectures and essays of the period is on pursuing full rights of citizenship for blacks in the United States. Thus, like Walker, she links her black-nationalist project to the egalitarian ideals that she asserts were articulated in the nation's founding documents. She remarks in her 1831 "Religion and the Pure Principles of Morality" that "according to the Constitution of these United States, he [God] hath made all men free and equal," and she sums up her political goals in her 1833 address to Boston's black Masons: "Let every man of color throughout the United States, who possesses the spirit and principles of a man, sign a petition to Congress, to abolish slavery in the District of Columbia, and grant you the rights and privileges of common free citizens."[81] With the *Appeal*'s emphasis on literacy, Stewart and other black leaders could regard Walker's text in the context of the uplift strategies of African American literary nationalism.

Not surprisingly, at the first national negro convention, which convened the year Walker died, and at subsequent conventions, one of the main concerns addressed by participants was the need to establish a national black newspaper or journal that would link together the scattered black communities of the U.S. nation.

Not all African American leaders were convinced of the wisdom of persisting in their efforts to improve blacks' prospects in the United States. The New York minister Nathaniel Paul, regularly listed as an "Authorised Agent" in *Freedom's Journal*, moved to Canada in 1830 to experiment with the newly formed black community at Wilberforce, and he then moved back and forth between Wilberforce and England before returning to the United States only two years before his death in 1837. Hosea Easton, who, as reported in the 25 April 1828 *Freedom's Journal*, chaired the meeting in which Walker called on blacks to develop their literary capabilities, remained uncertain about whether African Americans had much of a chance in a nation in which antiblack racism was endemic to the culture. A close friend of Walker's, Easton in 1837 published his major work, *A Treatise on the Intellectual Character, and Civil and Political Condition of the Colored People of the U. States; and the Prejudice Exercised towards Them: With a Sermon on the Duty of the Church to Them*. In the manner of Walker, Easton presents a history of white crimes against peoples of color and speculates on the possibility that whites may be inherently depraved: "Their whole career presents a motley mixture of barbarism and civilization, of fraud and philanthropy, and patriotism and avarice, of religion and bloodshed." Anyone looking for "true greatness," Easton states, "must decide in favor of the descendants of Ham." Though his Afrocentric pride led him toward diasporic imaginings, Easton, like Stewart, ultimately hoped for the development of a black nationalism, and black citizenship, in the United States. As he remarked in the *Treatise*'s concluding chapter, "On the Claims of the Colored People to all the Civil, Religious, and Social Privileges of this Country": "The claims set up are founded on the fact that they are Americans by birth and blood. Complexion has never been made the legal test of citizenship in any age of the world."[82] Walker had made a similar point in his discussion of Roman slavery in Article I of the *Appeal*.

Whether explicitly affirmed (as with Stewart) or implicitly noted (as with Easton), Walker remained a persistent influence on subsequent African American writing. That influence was remarked upon by Frederick Douglass in 1893, near the end of his own career, when he proclaimed at the 1893 World's Columbian Exposition in Chicago: "Speaking for the Negro, I can say, we owe much to Walker for his appeal." As Douglass had elaborated ten years earlier in "Our Destiny Is Largely in Our Own Hands," a lecture delivered to a predominately black audience, one of Walker's great contributions was the role he played in establishing the importance of black perspectives in the battle against slavery: "Walker, a colored man, whose appeal against slavery startled the land like a trump of coming judgement, was before either Mr. Garrison or Mr. Lundy."[83] During the 1857–93 period in particular, as I will be discussing in chapter 4, the U.S. nationalist and putatively color-blind cosmopolitan Frederick Douglass was now and again attracted to the notion of a diasporic black nationalism bearing some resemblance to that of his sometimes adversary Martin Delany. Walker can be taken as one of the major influences on this neglected aspect of Douglass's career.

Douglass did not comment extensively on Walker until 1883. However, he did print an essay on Walker in the 14 July 1848 issue of the *North Star* titled "A Brief Sketch of the Life and Character of David Walker." That essay was by Henry Highland Garnet, and it initially appeared in *Walker's Appeal, with a Brief Sketch of His Life. By Henry Highland Garnet. And also Garnet's Address to the Slaves of the United States of America*, which was published earlier in 1848 by Garnet with the help of the radical abolitionist John Brown. In his preface to the book, Garnet makes large claims for the influence of Walker on African American politics and writings of the 1830s and 1840s: "When the history of the emancipation of the bondmen of America shall be written, whatever name shall be placed first on the list of heroes, that of the author of the Appeal will not be second." In the "Brief Sketch" itself, he presents Walker as a freedom fighter "ardently attached to the cause of liberty" whose ever-circulating text came to pose *the* major threat to the southern slave power.[84]

In reprinting the *Appeal* in 1848, along with his own militant text of 1843, Garnet was clearly attempting to harness Walker to the service of recirculating his own "An Address to the Slaves of the United States of America." The "Address" famously calls on the slaves to use violence against the slaveholders, but in certain respects it seems lacking in the racial solidarity that informs the *Appeal*. "Slavery has fixed a deep gulf between you and us," Garnet remarks on the distance between free black and slave, and from his more comfortable position of relative freedom he can seem rather preachy when proclaiming to the slaves: "You had far better all die—*die immediately*, than live slaves, and entail your wretchedness upon your posterity." Though Garnet appears not to have fully learned the community-building lessons of Walker, he nonetheless celebrates Denmark Vesey as "a martyr to freedom," sympathetically describes the enormous difficulties facing the enslaved blacks in contesting slavery on their own, and perceptively views slavery in relation to new developments in national expansionism, which he presents as working against the interests of all U.S. blacks: "You cannot remove en masse, to the dominions of the British Queen—nor can you pass through Florida, and overrun Texas, and at last find peace in Mexico. The propagators of American slavery are spending their blood and treasure, that they may plant the black flag in the heart of Mexico, and riot in the halls of the Montezumas."[85]

If Walker and Garnet sought to harness the circulatory power of their texts to create black community, the ongoing expansionism that came to be understood as Manifest Destiny seemed intent on keeping that community divided, scattered, and ineffectual, and thus on establishing firm hierarchies of white over black and other peoples of color. That expansionism went hand in hand with a renewed American literary nationalism, based in New York City, which attempted to bring the sections together by insisting on precisely what Walker, Stewart, Garnet, and many other African Americans sought to use their circulatory strategies to sunder: the manifest connections between race (whiteness) and the U.S. nation. The troubling of those connections by African American writers also emerged as one of the more surprising projects of the writer who for a while was celebrated by the Young America literary nationalists as the preeminent "American" author of the time: the Jacksonian Democrat Nathaniel Hawthorne.

3

Genealogical Fictions

Melville and Hannah Crafts in Hawthorne's House

The July 1844 issue of the *United States Magazine and Democratic Review* (generally known as the *Democratic Review*) featured a sketch by Nathaniel Hawthorne titled "A Select Party." In it, a "Man of Fancy" imagines a festive get-together in "one of his castles in the air," a castle, the narrator declares, that is "more real than the earth." Numerous guests show up for the party, including the "Oldest Inhabitant," a man-about-town gossip, a meteorologist, and that most improbable of figures, a "Scholar without pedantry." All is going well, until an "uninvited" guest causes the Man of Fancy to experience "dire terror." As the narrator describes the scene:

> He was particularly startled by the vision of a deformed old black woman, whom he imagined as lurking in the garret of his native home, and who, when he was an infant, had once come to his bedside and grinned at him, in the crisis of a scarlet fever. This same black shadow, with others almost as hideous, now glided among the pillars of the magnificent saloon, grinning recognition, until the man shuddered at the forgotten terrors of his childhood. It amused him, however, to observe the black woman, with the mischievous caprice peculiar to such beings, steal up to the chair of the Oldest Inhabitant, and peep into his half-dreamy mind.
>
> "Never within my memory," muttered the venerable personage, aghast, "did I see such a face!"[1]

Central to this passage is the suggestion of the Man of Fancy's and Oldest Inhabitant's shared efforts to deny the historical presence of the old black woman and "others almost as hideous" within their "native home." The face that is never seen is the face that is always there, the "black shadow" that has the force of the uncanny. In calling attention to this "hideous" old black woman and her compatriots, Hawthorne may well be sharing his own anxieties about the blackness at the heart of Salem, Massachusetts, or the nation itself. And yet, in presenting her in such an actively impish role, Hawthorne seems more in allegiance with the grinning black woman than with the whites who shudder at her presence.

But the sketch does not stop with the "aghast" Oldest Inhabitant. Almost immediately after the description of the old black woman comes a description of whiteness, as the Man of Fancy takes note of a personage whom no one else notices: "a stranger" who has "a high, white forehead." Ironically, the narrator reports that this white-browed man is "the Master Genius, for whom our country is looking anxiously into the mist of time, as destined to fulfil the great mission of creating an American literature. . . . From him, whether moulded in the form of an epic poem, or assuming a guise altogether new, as the spirit itself may determine, we are to receive our first great original work, which shall do all that remains to be achieved for our glory among the nations."[2] The search for a writer who would incarnate the genius of the nation had of course long been central to American literary nationalism and had been given a renewed emphasis in Emerson's "The Poet," published the same year as "A Select Party." In "The Poet," Emerson affirms the nation's need for a writer of genius, but he concludes: "I look in vain for the poet whom I describe." Hawthorne's suggestion in "A Select Party" that such a Master Genius is present but unseen had an impact on Herman Melville, who, in his celebration of Hawthorne's "blackness" in his 1850 "Hawthorne and His Mosses," identified "Young Goodman Brown" and "A Select Party" as the two Hawthorne stories that best display an American genius comparable to anything that can be found in Shakespeare or Spenser. Melville generously asserts in "Mosses" that the Man of Genius is Hawthorne, though one imagines that he saw himself as that neglected Master Genius, feeling a dismay similar to the narrator's that "none pay reverence to the worker of immortality."[3]

By bringing together in "A Select Party" both the specter of blackness and "the great mission of creating an American literature," Hawthorne addressed (however obliquely and ironically) the large concerns of the very journal that published his sketch, the *Democratic Review*, which itself yoked the cause of American literary nationalism to the project of developing a white U.S. nationalism. The same issue of the *Democratic Review* with "A Select Party," for example, had an anonymous essay titled "The Re-Annexation of Texas: In Its Influence on the Duration of Slavery," whose author asserted that the incorporation of Texas into the Union would help the nation both to expand its borders and rid itself of blacks. Such would be the high population density of Texas, the writer predicts, that "slavery shall cease to exist," and blacks in search of "a land of political freedom and social dignity under a genial sky" will make their way to their "more appropriate home in Mexico."[4] Around that same time, however, a number of contributors to the *Democratic Review* began to argue that the United States should take some or all of Mexico, thus keeping under debate in the journal the question of just where blacks' proper "home" should be. But in "A Select Party," Hawthorne makes clear that African Americans have always been at home in the United States. In the context of the July 1844 issue of the *Democratic Review*, the sketch thus raises questions about the nationalists' denial of the blackness within their own homes and, with its noting of the old black woman's familiarity with the bedroom, teasingly raises questions about the racial purity of the white fathers and (especially) the children of the white fathers, the kinds of questions that would be addressed more explicitly in William Wells Brown's *Clotel* (1853).

Clotel is one of a number of compelling genealogical fictions of the 1850s, works that, like Harriet Beecher Stowe's *Dred* (1856) and Frank J. Webb's *The Garies and Their Friends* (1857), highlight the social and cultural consequences of a history of racial entanglement in America. Lee Quinby writes that genealogical fictions "[break] the hold of official truth and the metaphysics of memory, putting in their place the truth of countermemory."[5] There is no more haunting "countermemory" in all of Hawthorne's fiction than the grinning old black woman of "A Select Party." Similar such emphases on countermemories and the possibilities of mixed bloodlines are absolutely central to the genealogical fictions of the 1850s that I will be examining in this chapter—Hawthorne's *The House of the Seven Gables* (1851), Melville's *Pierre* (1852), and Hannah Crafts's *The Bondwoman's Narrative* (ca. 1855)—all of which can be read as responses to the cultural nationalism of the 1840s and 1850s and its attendant racist and expansionist ideologies. These novels expose the pure white bloodlines touted by white nationalists as little more than fictions, thereby encouraging readers, as Brown does in *Clotel*, to develop a skeptical relationship to mythified stories of foundings and transmissions, especially as those stories are put to the service of making contemporary hierarchies (racial, economic, and national) seem logical, just, and *destined*. To be sure, works such as *The House of the Seven Gables* and *Pierre*, which focus so intensively on white characters, are not immediately thought of in relation to debates on slavery and race. But as Teresa

Goddu has shown, questions of race have always been at the center of what she describes as the gothic tradition of American romance, a tradition that appropriated a central trope of the Continental version of the gothic—the twisted genealogical lines materialized in the twisting passages of the castle—as a way of exploring how "the ghosts of America's racial history" continue to haunt the present. That haunting extends to questions of racial identity. Haunted by the past, Hawthorne explores in *House* the futility of Colonel Pyncheon's project of planting a family that had "his race and future generations fixed on a stable basis," and, two years before *Clotel*, he addresses themes that one wouldn't expect of a staunch Democrat, such as the immorality of master-slave relationships and, in the figures of Judge Pyncheon and Chanticleer, the absurdity of making pretensions to racial superiority and purity. Goddu argues that when African American writers worked with gothic modes during the 1850s, they took a very different perspective from Hawthorne and other "haunted" white genealogical romancers, for they could choose to "haunt back."[6] But I will be suggesting that there is no reason to believe that African American writers couldn't be haunted by race as well, and that white romancers couldn't haunt back, too.

More than most white writers of the period, Hawthorne haunted back, and in *The House of the Seven Gables* he turned against the Anglo-Saxonist exceptionalism that was at the heart of the cultural nationalism associated with the *Democratic Review* (and thus, by association, with himself as a star contributor to the journal). Celebrated by John O'Sullivan and others as the literary nationalist par excellence, Hawthorne has greater differences from the various racist nationalists who were advancing his career than most critics have been willing to allow. In his 1849 sketch "Main-street," after all, Hawthorne depicts what he terms "the Anglo-Saxon energy" as frighteningly destructive, commenting on "how the aforesaid Anglo-Saxon energy is now trampling along the street, and raising a positive cloud of dust beneath its sturdy footsteps."[7] Despite the fact that Hawthorne's historical tales and sketches of the 1830s and 1840s are rife with ironies about U.S. millennial destiny and—in tales such as "The Birthmark," "Rappaccini's Daughter," and "A Select Party"—equally rife with ironies about racial identity, there has emerged "a critical consensus," as Arthur Riss puts it, "concerning Hawthorne's notorious insensitivity to the historical problem of U.S. slavery." Recent critics have been especially condemnatory, presenting Hawthorne as "a voice of America's repressive culture" whose "studied ambiguity" ultimately conveyed a "desire for a monocultural utopia" and an unambiguous commitment to an "American exceptionalism that could ignore contradictions like slavery and Indian removal."[8] Hawthorne no doubt had a stake in the Democrats' nationalist vision and was willing to profit from his friendships with party leaders. Like most northern whites, including those known for their progressive politics, he kept his distance from blacks, occasionally voiced racist sentiments, and took some comfort in racial hierarchies. Even so, he remained suspicious of many of the orthodoxies of his day, regarding slavery in particular as one of the world's "evils."[9] His suspicions inform even his seemingly most upbeat and socially conciliatory fiction. In a capacious discussion of Hawthorne as a cultural critic, Joel Pfister remarks that "Hawthorne was capable of being sexist, anti-Semitic, racist, and insufferably middle class—a purveyor of customs. Most important, he had an admirable self-critical inclination to explore beyond his own ostensible ideological preferences."[10] Hawthorne's efforts to explore concepts of race and nation beyond the frame of what can sometimes seem to be his complacent Democratic politics will be one of the main subjects of this chapter.

I begin with a consideration of the literary nationalism of Young America. Hawthorne, as the ironic imaginings of "A Select Party" help to suggest, was not so easily appropriated by John O'Sullivan and the other Young Americans of the *Democratic Review*, and in *House*, I argue, he poses a surprising challenge to the Anglo-Saxonist and exceptionalist assumptions of mid-nineteenth-century U.S. (literary) nationalism. Gretchen Murphy maintains that Hawthorne's *House* "produced a hegemonic way of locating the nation in the 1850s," and that "over the next century that exceptionalist fantasy . . . secured *House's* place in the canon, where it could more powerfully reinforce interpretations of political history and literary tradition." For Murphy, in other words, Hawthorne's *House* in effect helped to secure the neighborhood (the United States' hegemonic position in the hemisphere) by "conceal[ing] the troubling implications of U.S. empire [and] composing an imaginary return to insularity and purity."[11] In an effort to reimagine the political and literary trajectories supposedly initiated or revitalized by *House*, I will be offering an alternative literary genealogy, one that focuses on how the novel's demystifying narrative, ironic scopic strategies, and insistence on the difficulties of tracing bloodlines subversively dislocates race and nation in the American 1850s by pointing to the fictiveness of insularity and purity.

The chapter then turns to two novels specifically inspired by *House*,

Melville's *Pierre* and Crafts's *The Bondwoman's Narrative*, exploring in particular how these genealogical fictions take up and extend the work of racial and national questioning that Hawthorne models in *House*. Melville and Crafts, I show, are to a certain extent *in* Hawthorne's *House* as they write their own novels, admirers who choose to open some doors of the "fine old chamber" (Melville's playful term for *House*) that Hawthorne prefers to keep closed.[12] In crucial respects, as will become apparent, my readings of *Pierre* and *The Bondwoman's Narrative* are in large part readings of Melville's and Craft's readings of *House*. As a study of an episode in American literary nationalism, then, this chapter will be making less a counterfactual than a counterintuitive claim that Hawthorne deserves consideration along with, say, William Wells Brown as an author who wrote a genealogical fiction that aggressively and, in terms of literary history, influentially sought to counter the assumptions about whiteness that were at the heart of the expansionist ideology of the 1840s and 1850s, inspiring at least two other powerful genealogical fictions of the period that in their own ways also sought to expose the contradictions and incoherence of the all-too-representative literary nationalism of O'Sullivan and Young America.

The Democratic Creed

In the first two chapters of this book, I have attempted to rethink familiar accounts of nineteenth-century U.S. literary nationalism by focusing on conflicts within U.S. nationalism. But as conflicted as that nationalism may have been, one might nonetheless ask how such conflicts would have been apprehended by those who absorbed the brunt of the nation's emergent power. For instance, at the moment in 1847 when the U.S. Army occupied Mexico City, were the Mexican people able to see any rifts in what would have appeared as monolithic power? Obviously, the Mexican people would have had difficulties discerning such conflict, in part because conflict is usually not on display in invading armies, and in part because conflict *was* more muted during the 1830s and 1840s. Though debates on race and nation remained central to U.S. culture, these debates, for a while at least, were subsumed to an exuberant Jacksonian nationalism that championed the United States as a white republic destined to spread its regenerative, progressive reach across the continent and beyond.[13]

No one better expressed the optative nationalism of the time than John

O'Sullivan, who founded the *Democratic Review* in 1837 and edited it through most of 1846. As exemplified in the inaugural issue's introductory essay, "The Democratic Principle—The Importance of Its Assertion and Application to Our Political System and Literature," O'Sullivan self-consciously and insistently linked politics and art. Warning Americans against the corrupt, putatively antidemocratic values of England, O'Sullivan sought to develop a canon of U.S. writers—Hawthorne, William Gilmore Simms, George Bancroft, and others—whose works would foster a nation-defining *"democratic republicanism."* His literary nationalistic efforts contributed to the emergence by the mid-1840s of the New York–based literary-nationalist "Young Americans," who, in their zeal for democratic progress at a time when democratic movements throughout Europe were being thwarted, modeled themselves on such European revolutionary groups as Young Italy and Young Hungary.[14] O'Sullivan and his fellow Young American literary nationalists possessed what historian Anders Stephanson has called "a strongly destinarian conception of the United States"; and it was precisely this ebullient, millennial conception of U.S. continental destiny that led O'Sullivan to imagine the possibility of the United States making a "natural" expansion into the Southwest that would not necessarily require a war with Mexico.[15] O'Sullivan's highly influential brand of nationalist exceptionalism can best be illuminated through a brief examination of his journal.

In the tradition of his 1837 inaugural essay, O'Sullivan regularly printed literary manifestos in the *Democratic Review* on the centrality of democratic and "home" principles to American literature. In the anonymous 1842 "Democracy and Literature," the writer (perhaps O'Sullivan's fellow Young American, the editor and critic Evert Duyckinck) celebrated not the cosmopolitan man of letters but the "Patriot," declaring that U.S. authors must write for U.S. readers: "National honor, national admiration, is more eagerly coveted by him than a wide and undistinguishing regard." Asserting that the "spirit of Literature and the spirit of Democracy are one," the critic urges his readers to break their thrall to English writers and to embrace "our writers of the first class, Bancroft, Channing, Hawthorne, &c.," for these three authors in particular "have not only spoken out freely their belief in the stability and integrity of the Republic, but have also expressed themselves plainly in the terms of the democratic creed." That "creed" went hand in hand with what O'Sullivan and his cohort regarded as the (white) writer's "natural sympathy with his race."[16]

A linking of writing, democratic politics, race, and nation would become central to the *Democratic Review*'s eventual support of the war against Mexico, which took as its racial warrant the work of Samuel Morton and others identified with the American school of ethnology. As a group, these ethnologists gained international stature for writings that purported to offer scientific proof of what historian Reginald Horsman terms "the innate superiority of the American Anglo-Saxon branch of the Caucasian race."[17] Central to the arguments of many of these ethnologists was the theory of polygenesis—a belief that blacks and whites and other racial groups had separate moments of creation that help to explain the differences among the races. The scientific racialists supported their theories through close study of the physical, social, and mental characteristics of peoples of differing racial types. For instance, the Philadelphia physician and researcher Samuel Morton, president of the Academy of Natural Sciences, published a series of comparative analyses of skull size and shape that attempted to demonstrate the physical basis for what he argued was the superior intelligence of whites, and thus why throughout "all recorded history, races were frozen in place, with whites at the top and blacks at the bottom." His influential *Crania Americana* (1839) and *Crania Ægyptiaca* (1844) inspired the research and writings of the Swiss evolutionary theorist Louis Agassiz, a professor of zoology and geology at Harvard whom Hawthorne and other Massachusetts intellectuals admired. Though neither Morton nor Agassiz took proslavery positions, their insistence, in the words of Agassiz, that it is "mock-philanthropy and mock-philosophy to assume that all races . . . are entitled to the same position in human society," added further "scientific" support to those who advocated a politics of white supremacism, whether in terms of slavery or expansionism, or a combination of the two.[18]

A vision of "whites at the top and blacks at the bottom" informed the many essays in the *Democratic Review* championing a national program of continental expansion. In 1845 O'Sullivan famously declared that it was the United States' "manifest destiny to overspread the continent allotted by Providence for the free development of our yearly multiplying millions." In this same 1845 essay, he referred to the people of Mexico as "imbecile and distracted," and he grouped all peoples of color under the rubric of "negro" while scoffing at the notion that "the negro race" possessed "equal attributes and capacities with our own." Hailing "the advance guard of the irresistible army of Anglo-Saxon emigration," O'Sullivan conceived of U.S. nationalism in relation to an untroubled conception of whites spreading to the southern and western reaches of the continent and assuming a "national" domination. Caleb Cushing stated the proposition of Anglo-Saxon superiority most baldly in an essay on Mexico in the June 1846 issue of the *Democratic Review*: "*Race* is the key to much that seems obscure in the history of nations. Throughout the world, the spectacle is everywhere the same, of the whiter race ruling the less white, through all gradations of color."[19]

The very concept of "gradations of color," however, points to whites' anxieties, expressed in the *Democratic Review* and elsewhere, that the United States could become a nation of mixed-race peoples precisely because of the success of its expansionistic policies. In an anonymous article titled "Do the Various Races of Man Constitute a Single Species?," appearing in the 1842 *Democratic Review*, the author initially asserts a confident ability to discern differences between the races: "What a striking contrast does the coarse skin and greasy blackness of the African, present to the delicate cuticle and the exquisite rose and lily that beautify the face of the Georgian!" But almost immediately thereafter the writer concedes that such contrasts are rare, and that it is "often impracticable to determine, independent of the individual's locality, to what of the human race he belong." Numerous other essays published in the *Democratic Review* conveyed similar concerns about racial mixing and the stability of the races themselves. Thus some contributors argued that the United States should only temporarily occupy Mexico in order to ensure that the purity of the white Anglo-Saxon conquerors would not be tainted by their (sexual) interactions with "5,000,000 ignorant and indolent half-civilized Indians, [and] with 1,500,000 free negroes and mulattoes."[20]

But how pure was the nation in the light of its connections to a long history of colonialism and slavery in the Americas? According to the black abolitionist Henry Highland Garnet, the ongoing United States–Mexican War made clear that there was only one way of understanding Manifest Destiny at the present moment: as an onward march to the ultimate dilution, even abolition, of whiteness. As he proclaimed in a lecture of February 1848, which he published later that year as *The Past and Present Condition, and the Destiny, of the Colored Race*: "*This western world is destined to be filled with a mixed race.*" Composing his lecture at a time when a U.S. military victory over Mexico seemed imminent, Garnet concluded that, precisely because of that probable victory, the prospect of a white Anglo-Saxon U.S. nation had never looked more hollow. For by taking some or all of Mexico, Garnet archly remarks, troping on the concerns of the nationalists of the *Democratic Review* and elsewhere, the

United States would only be adding to its total population of the "Colored race." With a nod to David Walker, Garnet asserts that because whites have always been a violent and dominating race, the addition of the "dark-browed and liberty-loving" Mexicans to the population of the United States promises to bring about "the triumph of freedom in the hemisphere," especially when what he describes as an already "mixed" white race sexually intermingles with the Mexicans. Turning Manifest Destiny on its head, Garnet concludes his talk by confidently proclaiming that "this republic, and this continent, are to be the theatre in which the grand drama of our triumphant Destiny is to be enacted": the coming into majority rule of the peace-loving and truly republican "Colored race."[21]

As I will discuss in the next chapter, Frederick Douglass in the early 1870s would advance similar ideas as part of the hemispheric nationalism undergirding his support for U.S. annexation of Santo Domingo. Suffice it to say here that Garnet's 1848 lecture had little impact on whites' thinking of the time, and that even with the circulation of similar such writings by Martin R. Delany and other black abolitionists, an overall confidence remained among most white Americans that the national domain could be extended southward and westward as part of whites' providentially sanctioned national destiny to populate the continent. As historian Thomas Hietala puts it: "[T]he expansionists looked forward to the time when blacks, Indians, and Mexicans would completely disappear from the continent and whites would take sole possession of it."[22] Most contributors to the *Democratic Review* shared such confidence about the national destiny, though O'Sullivan had qualms about moving too quickly. Convinced that U.S. expansion should occur "naturally" over a longer period of time, and without the race mixing that he feared would inevitably accompany intrusions into Mexico, O'Sullivan never did endorse the war. In part because of his hesitations, he was ousted as editor of the *New York Morning News*; shortly thereafter, in late 1846, he surrendered the editorship of the *Democratic Review*.

Following O'Sullivan's departure, the *Democratic Review* became even more aggressive in its conjoining of expansionism, Anglo-Saxonism, and U.S. literary nationalism. In a February 1847 essay titled "The War," for instance, the anonymous writer celebrated the "virtues of the Anglo-Saxon race," insisting that it is the "inevitable destiny" that the "Mexican race" will suffer "the fate of the aborigines of the north"—a fate presented as decreed by Providence. One month later, Duyckinck published the first installment of his series "Nationality in Literature," which called for the "literary growth" of a native literature, or what he called an "empire of thought," that would develop apart from English literature and express "the spirit of the country" through "home themes." Although he does not explicitly address questions of race, the emphasis on "home" invokes the fairly traditional linkage of the genealogical house, the nation, and the body that would come to inform Hawthorne's *House*.[23] In the essay, which celebrates not Hawthorne but Cornelius Mathews as the exemplary American writer, Duyckinck shares his progressive vision of "this greater country that is to be; this nation of churches and school-houses, as well as canals and railroads," proclaiming that the continental growth of the nation and "the literary growth of this country" will go hand in hand.[24]

As is well known, Nathaniel Hawthorne embraced Jacksonian democracy while a student at Bowdoin College during the early 1820s, became friends with a number of the men who would emerge as the leading Democrats of their time, found employment with the help of Democrats, and eventually wrote the campaign biography of his friend Franklin Pierce, which led to a plum political appointment as U.S. consul to Liverpool in 1853. Much to the detriment of his critical reputation, Hawthorne's 1852 campaign biography, *The Life of Franklin Pierce*, and his earlier association with the jingoistic and racist writers of the *Democratic Review* have worked to suggest an untroubled commitment to the compromising Unionism of the proslavery majority wing of the Democratic Party. While I readily concede that anyone reading through all of Hawthorne's journals and letters (or, for that matter, the journals and letters of Emerson, Margaret Fuller, and many other leading white cultural figures in the Northeast) would be hard-pressed not to find unattractive statements about race, I want to raise questions about the ahistorical flattening of Hawthorne's views on slavery by complicating our sense of his Democratic politics.[25]

It is conventionally argued that the Democrats supported the slavery system, but there was actually much dissent among Democrats about slavery, and that dissent was consistent with the radical energies that contributed to the founding of the Democratic Party. Influential Democratic writers of the 1820s and 1830s, such as William Leggett, George Henry Evans, and Thomas Morris, attacked monopolies and other forms of concentrated power and saw connections between the "monstrous" First Bank of America and the slave power. In a recent revisionary study, historian Jonathan Earle provides substantial evidence that Free-Soil politics, and not the expansionism of the *Democratic Review*, should be taken as the culmination of the Jacksonian principles that Hawthorne and many others had initially found so inspiring during the late 1820s. David Wilmot, the Pennsylvania congressman whose proviso came close to banning slavery from the territories taken from Mexico, was a Democrat. The Wilmot Proviso passed the House on a vote of 77 to 58, and there was significant support for the proviso in the Senate as well. Though the proviso was eventually defeated, the closeness of the congressional vote suggests that the expansion of slavery was not a given at the time, and that it would be a mistake to put all Democrats into the proslavery or compromise-with-slavery folds. Numerous Democrats who had fought the First Bank and other monopolies found themselves moving toward the emerging Free-Soil Party, and these Free-Soilers, Earle writes, "opposed the perpetuation of slavery wherever it existed, rejected racist arguments justifying bondage, and insisted on the basic humanity of African Americans."[26]

Such beliefs were central to Horatio Bridge's *Journal of an African Cruiser*, which was serialized in the *Democratic Review* in 1845 and published later that year as part of the Wiley and Putnam "Library of Choice Reading" series edited by Duyckinck. The book is strongly antislavery, as is consistent with Bridge's naval assignment to enforce the Ashburton Treaty's ban on the slave trade in Africa, and there is considerable evidence that Hawthorne wrote substantial portions of the book for his friend. In a letter of 2 March 1845 to Duyckinck, Hawthorne states that he has a "pretty large license" to work with Bridge's journals, and he remarks about his editing: "I have re-modelled the style, where it seemed necessary, and have developed his ideas, where he failed to do it himself, and have put on occasional patches of sentimental embroidery." Some of that "embroidery" may have concerned matters of race. In this respect, one of the more interesting aspects of the book is its "sentimental" depiction of equality across the color line. Bridge writes of his interactions with the black people of Liberia: "One thing is certain. People of color have here their fair position in the comparative scale of mankind. The white man, who visits Liberia, be he of what rank he may, and however imbued with the prejudice of hue, associates with the colonists on terms of equality. This would be impossible (speaking not of individuals, but of the general intercourse between the two races) in the United States." Bridge then meditates on the implications of his vision of human equality in a passage that may have been authored or "embroidered" by Hawthorne: "I have dined at tables of many colored men in Liberia, have entertained them on shipboard, worshipped with them at church; walked, rode, and associated with them, as equal with equal, if not as friend with friend. Were I to meet those men in my own town, and among my own relatives, I would treat them kindly and hospitably, as they have treated me." Bridge concludes that the lack of social equality in the United States "is sad; but it shows forcibly what the colored race have to struggle against in America, and how vast an advantage is gained by removing them to another soil."[27] Although Bridge uses this and other examples to make a case for Liberian colonization of African Americans, that argument is made in relation to his concerns not about black but about white inferiority—specifically, the inability of whites to follow the biblical golden rule because of their "prejudice of hue."

Of course Bridge (and Hawthorne) no doubt avoided dining with black people in the northern United States, or, given the stark reality of the color line in the North, simply never had the social opportunity. Still, given that there is virtually nothing in the *Democratic Review* attacking whites' "prejudice of hue," *African Cruiser* would have posed a significant challenge to the Anglo-Saxonist nationalism of O'Sullivan's journal. In this respect, the antislavery and antiracist sentiments expressed in Bridge's book, if they are indeed the work of Hawthorne, help to explain Hawthorne's decision to stray from the Democrats in the late 1840s and early 1850s on precisely the issue of slavery. While Hawthorne remained true to his close friend Franklin Pierce, there is evidence that he was increasingly sympathetic to the Free-Soil position, to the point that he would eventually sign a document offering his support following the passage of the Fugitive Slave Law. Hawthorne counted Free-Soiler Charles Sumner among his friends, and in January 1849 he arranged for Sumner to give a lecture titled "The Law of Human Progress" at the Salem Lyceum. Sumner had delivered the same lecture in July 1848 before the Phi Beta Kappa Society of Union College in Schenectady, New York, one month after he had delivered a blistering attack on the slave power, condemning "that combination of persons, or, perhaps, of politicians, whose animating principle is the perpetuation and extention of Slavery, with the advancement of Slaveholders." Hawthorne, in his capacity as the corresponding secretary for the Salem Lyceum, may have invited Sumner out of a commitment to free speech, but there are marked similarities in their vision of gradual reform that suggest a surprising congruence in their politics. In

"The Law of Human Progress," Sumner, known for his radicalism, urges a patient course in the manner that Hawthorne had advocated in his reformist tales of the 1840s: "Nothing is accomplished except by time and exertion. Nature abhors violence and suddenness." Sounding very much like Hawthorne on social reform, he asserts as the great theme of his speech: "Gradual change is a necessary condition of the Law of Progress." Sumner has little to say about slavery in this particular speech, but he does address the question of race, conceding a bit to the racial scientists while holding onto the notion of human unity: "It is true, doubtless, that there are various races of men; but there is but one great Human Family, in which Caucasian, Ethiopian, Chinese, and Indian are all brothers, children of *one* Father, and heirs to *one* happiness."[28]

There is no record of Hawthorne's response to this lecture, but the fact is that he maintained his admiration for Sumner into the 1850s. Writing Longfellow on 8 May 1851, Hawthorne confides that he is dismayed by the Fugitive Slave Law, which Pierce had supported, and that even though he is suspicious of political abolitionism, he is heartened by Sumner's successful campaign for the Senate: "How glad I am that Sumner is at last elected!" Two months later, in one of the letters that is regularly cited as evidence for his racism, Hawthorne elaborates to his friend Zachariah Burchmore on the politics of slavery, race, and free soil: "I have not, as you suggest, the slightest sympathy for the slaves; or, at least, not half so much as for the laboring whites, who, I believe, as a general thing, are ten times worse off than the Southern negros. Still, whenever I am absolutely cornered, I shall go for New England rather than the South;—and this Fugitive Law cornered me. Of course, I knew what I was doing when I signed that Free-Soil document, and bade farewell to all ideas of foreign consulships, or other official stations."[29] Despite his avowed lack of sympathy for the slaves, this is a contradictory letter that reveals a more progressive Hawthorne than we usually imagine. His remark on the slaves is qualified with respect to the white working class (with the suggestion that that his lack of sympathy is relative and not absolute), and then is further qualified by a statement of his opposition to the Fugitive Slave Law (which suggests some commitment to antislavery), and then is qualified even further by the surprising revelation that he has signed a Free-Soil document that threatens to keep him permanently unemployed. Significantly, he signed that document shortly after he published *The House of the Seven Gables*.

Hawthorne's *House* has traditionally been regarded as his most upbeat celebration of the nation's middle-class values, a wholesome book that, unlike *The Scarlet Letter*, would not give his wife, Sophia, or anyone else a headache.[30] But as a genealogical fiction, it deserves to be better understood as a novel that poses considerable challenges to the racial-nationalist orthodoxies of the day. Begun right around the time the Fugitive Slave Law was adopted as the law of the land, and completed shortly before Hawthorne expressed a surprising solidarity with the Free-Soilers, *House* can be read, in part, as a questioning of the blood-based Anglo-Saxonist nationalism of the O'Sullivan Young American crowd and of the many others, Democrat or otherwise, who shared their views. Read against the grain of our fixed "knowledge" that Hawthorne was an inveterate racist and Democratic flunky, *House* emerges as a novel that, like *Clotel*, offers surprisingly fresh possibilities for rethinking the nation's mixed-race past, present, and future. My reading of the novel, a prologue to my *House*-inflected readings of *Pierre* and *The Bondwoman's Narrative*, will focus on Hawthorne's complex narrative and epistemological strategies for troubling genealogical histories, and the way those strategies, rather than firming up the white nation, point to the limits and even absurdities of such blood thinking. At the very least, the novel suggests that if "[h]uman blood . . . should run in hidden streams,"[31] some digging beneath the surface is in order. Melville and Crafts may dig deeper than Hawthorne, but, in the literary history that I am (re)constructing in this chapter, Hawthorne leads the way.

The Work of Blood

So let me begin my discussion of *The House of the Seven Gables* by making some broad claims about the novel. Hawthorne's *House* does not demonstrate the superiority of one race over another and, in particular, it does not demonstrate the superiority of Anglo-Saxon "blood" over other blood. Despite its use of the rhetoric of race, the novel remains highly unclear, even suspicious, about whether race even exists as a meaningful category of human identity and difference. And despite its related use of the racialized rhetoric of evolutionary biology, which is often deployed ironically anyway, the novel expresses remarkable skepticism about conceptions of historical progress that imagine a coherent and unbroken movement toward a racially inscribed *telos*. With its undermining of the very notions of race and progress that undergird the concept of Manifest Destiny, the novel thus positions itself at a skeptical distance from the expansionism and literary nationalism of the 1840s and 1850s. In this and other respects, the novel is unrelentingly *political* in its vision of race and nation, pointing to the self-serving expediency of an exceptionalism based on concepts of Anglo-Saxon superiority and providential design. Moreover, the novel's narrative strategies encourage resistant readings of the "accepted" social truths of racial and class hierarchies and thus can be tied to a democratic reading practice that we tend to undervalue in Hawthorne but that has its sources in the radical antiaristocratic Jacksonianism of the 1820s and 1830s that attracted him to the party in the first place.

Central to Hawthorne's method in *House,* as he announces in the preface, is his perspective as a gothic romancer, which allows him to "enrich the shadows of the picture" (those hidden aspects that are sometimes overlooked or taken for granted) so that he might "connect a bygone time with the very Present that is flitting away from us."[32] But those connections are often contingent and fanciful, he insists at the outset, dependent upon what he terms the "artistic arrangement" (5) of incidents or episodes. Rejecting the sort of narrative that would depict "a chain of events" (5) in which one event leads irrevocably to the next, Hawthorne forcefully declares that "it is not our purpose to trace down the history of the Pyncheon family, in its unbroken connection with the House of the Seven Gables" (20). From beginning to end, especially through the key trope of sudden death, Hawthorne presents ruptures and breaks in his narrative of the family history, even as he teasingly suggests continuities through his use of paintings and daguerreotypes that seem to offer visual proof of "unbroken connection" between, say, Colonel Pyncheon of the early 1690s and Judge Pyncheon of the present moment. But as I will discuss below, Hawthorne just as forcefully suggests that pictures are only pictures until a perhaps overzealous interpreter makes them into vehicles that may or may not reveal genealogical truths about heritability. ·

The idea of traits being passed from one generation to another invokes notions of biological succession central to Anglo-Saxonist destinarianism. And yet it is worth underscoring that Hawthorne's biblically based theme that "the wrong-doing of one generation lives into the successive ones" (2) implies a historical vision, and politics, altogether different from the determinism of the evolutionary biologist. Again and again the narrator suggests that moral wrongs do harm in their own time and beyond, and that one can begin to address such wrongs not by surrendering to their historical or biological inevitability but instead by interrogating the narratives that work to conceal them. In this respect, one of the large goals of the romance, at least as Hawthorne sets it up at the very start, is to make crimes visible in relation to the human motivations and contingencies that helped produce them. From what I would term Hawthorne's radical Jacksonian perspective, such scrutiny in the here and now allows for the possibility of change. In order to encourage such change, the genealogical fiction writer working in the Jacksonian mode must develop strategies for unfixing that which is "massive, stable, and almost irresistibly imposing," that which is regarded as part of the "natural" social order—the very narratives generated and sustained by those of "established rank and great possession" (25).

The narrator in his opening stroll down Pyncheon Street attempts to do just that, as he pauses before Pyncheon House and Pyncheon Elm to meditate on "the circumstances amid which the foundation of the house was laid" (6). But how explore those circumstances if, as the narrator claims, there is "[n]o written record" (7) beyond the fact that Colonel Pyncheon obtained a government grant to take the land that was once Maule's Lane? The answer is to tell a story that is "derived chiefly from tradition" (7) and "rumors" (16). Like some of the pictures of the novel, oral traditions take on a life and existence apart from the official narratives developed by those in power, emerging as a democratic form of what Peter Bellis terms "subversive counter-memory."[33] Drawing on such counter-memory, the narrator tells a democratic story of "the work of blood" (8), describing how Colonel Pyncheon took advantage of his elite-class status to expropriate the plebeian Maule's land by having him executed during the Salem witch crisis of 1692. Maule's curse on Colonel Pyncheon, that "God will give him blood to drink!" (8), does its own democratic work of blood, for the Colonel dies of apoplexy (or Maule's blood) on the day that he plans to celebrate the opening of his house with the town's elites.

Still, there is a sense that the Colonel, through the very founding and building of the house, has achieved his broad aims. As the Reverend Mr. Higginson's funeral oration makes clear, Pyncheon sought to perpetuate his blood in the manner of those blood thinkers who link conceptions of pure white "common antecedents" and "common descendants" to what Etienne Balibar has termed the "nationalization of the family."[34] Higginson speaks to such protonationalistic desires for genealogical stability when he declares that the surviving house of the dead Pyncheon helps to ensure that his "race and future generations [are] fixed on a stable basis . . . for centuries to come" (17). However, in his democratic opening, the narrator alternatively suggests that a belief in the power to extend one's family into the future in such unbroken fashion depends upon the same sort of greed (and conviction of blood superiority) that motivated the Pyncheons to take Maule's property; and given that the Colonel's descendants' desire to extend their domain is linked to their desperate efforts to locate an Indian deed that supposedly would provide additional lands for those of "Pyncheon blood" (18), Hawthorne would seem to be commenting not only on the greed and blood pride of seventeenth-century white colonialism but also on the greed and blood pride of mid-nineteenth-century white expansionism.

Blood and greed remain central to the Pyncheon family history. Approximately thirty years before the present of the novel, a Pyncheon bachelor determined to make amends to the Maules is apparently murdered, and one of the Pyncheon bachelor's nephews, Clifford, has been sent to prison for the seeming crime, while the other, Judge Jaffrey Pyncheon, eventually emerges as "an honor to his race" (24). Significantly, though the Pyncheons' "race" has remained highly visible in the culture, they hardly embody the pure genealogical succession that the Colonel had imagined when he attempted to fix the "race and future generations . . . on a stable basis . . . for centuries to come." It is crucial to note, for instance, that unlike the inbreeding Ushers of Poe's "The Fall of the House of Usher" (1839), the Pyncheons over the decades have married well outside of their family, and the Pyncheons central to the present of the action—Hepzibah, Clifford, Jaffrey, and Phoebe—are not in the direct line of Colonel Pyncheon (which has long come to an end); instead, they are various "little offshoot[s] of the Pyncheon race" (69). Their blood already has been dispersed, mixed, dissipated. As for the Maules, this family or "race" would seem to have disappeared from the American scene. That said, in language that Melville would draw on for *Pierre*, the narrator comments on how difficult it is to trace a family over time, comparing the "original" Maule's bloodlines to the ebbing flow of a river: "His blood might possibly exist elsewhere; here, where its lowly current could be traced so far back, it had ceased to keep an onward course" (26).

As presented by the narrator, then, with the help of popular legend, there are two genealogically figured "racial" families in the novel, the Pyncheons and the Maules, and one of these families, or races, would seem to have triumphed over the other. But how biologically distinct or distinctive are these racially described families? And to what extent is Hawthorne invested in a blood-based or racial politics of heredity?

In influential early analyses of this topic, Roy Male claimed that Hawthorne "assumed that hereditary factors are somehow transmitted 'in the blood,'" and Frank Kermode similarly asserted that Hawthorne believed in different and separate racial "types."[35] And yet if *House* emphasizes anything, it is just how difficult it is to trace the flow of blood in order to make such "scientific" differentiations. Heredity may provide one possible way of understanding Judge Jaffrey Pyncheon's similarities to Colonel Pyncheon, but the narrator more importantly emphasizes that the key connection between the Judge and the Colonel is their similar imbrication in their respective cultures' institutions of power, as manifested by the apoplexy that now and then plagues some figures in the genealogical house of Pyncheon (but not the marginalized Hepzibah, Clifford, or Phoebe). The narrator does call attention to blood and heredity with respect to the Maules, asserting that the Maule "race" was marked by "an hereditary character of reserve" (26). But as the history of the Pyncheons' dispossession of the Maules reveals, that "reserve" has much to do with the Maules' realization that the adoption of a canny offstage presence best enables them to plot their revenge.

Given that the novel's democratic narrator and purveyors of "gossip" disdain the Pyncheon elites—who, after all, are the blood thinkers of the novel—the Pyncheons' "eugenicism" and expansionism must be taken as one of the novel's *subjects*, not its *donnée*. Rather than advocating blood thinking in the manner of the Pyncheons, Hawthorne takes pains throughout *House* to raise questions about the very notion of blood purity and superiority that the Pyncheons deploy to legitimate their power over others. A key figure of their prideful ambition is the portrait of Colonel Pyncheon that remains hanging in the House of the Seven Gables. As will be the case in *The Bondwoman's Narrative*, a novel that also raises searching questions about the privileging of whiteness in contemporary national formations, the patriarch's portrait evinces an ambition to naturalize connections between blood (the genealogical house) and rank (the house itself and the additional money and property vouchsafed by such connections between blood and rank). Seeking to enforce that ambition upon subsequent generations, the Colonel writes into his will that his portrait must remain "affixed to the wall of the room in which he died" (21) for as long as the house, genealogical and otherwise, survives. Accordingly, the portrait stands as the dead Colonel Pyncheon's iconographic assertion that there will always be a Colonel Pyncheon, which is to say that there will always be a white patriarch reigning over the house.

The question is whether there will always be a Colonel Pyncheon because of the genealogical transmission of blood.

To be sure, the portrait initially appears to announce that the resemblances between Judge Jaffrey Pyncheon, the current principal representative of the Pyncheon line, and Colonel Pyncheon are all about genealogical transmission; for when Hepzibah, from within the House of the Seven Gables, turns from her sighting of the flesh and blood Judge Pyncheon to the portrait of Colonel Pyncheon hanging on the wall, the narrator remarks: "While gazing at the portrait, Hepzibah trembled under its eye. Her hereditary reverence made her afraid to judge the character of the original so harshly, as a perception of the truth compelled her to do. But still she gazed, because the face of the picture enabled her—at least, she fancied so—to read more accurately, and to a greater depth, the face which she had just seen in the street" (59). Hepzibah sees the Judge as the incarnation of the Colonel, and thus as "the very man to build up a new house! Perhaps, too, to draw down a new curse!" (59). But even as she discerns a blood connection between these two Pyncheons, the narrator, through the parenthetical "at least, she fancied so," disrupts overconfident notions that blood determines character. After all, if her theory of transmission made sense, it would have equal implications for Hepzibah and Clifford, who are just as much in the genealogical line of Colonel Pyncheon as Judge Jaffrey Pyncheon. With the mention of Hepzibah's "hereditary reverence," Hawthorne signals that her thinking has more to do with the Judge's accrued cultural power than with insights into blood; and the fact that her meditation is stimulated by a picture suggests that she is operating less in the mode of the evolutionary biologist (or geneticist) than of the romancer (or reader of romance). As Christopher Castiglia points out, that initial portrait of the founding Pyncheon, which here and elsewhere appears to be presented as a seemingly accurate image imported from the past, is "itself an interpretation shaped by historically changeable aesthetic conventions." In gazing at the ancient portrait and thinking about its connections to Jaffrey, Hepzibah, as will be the case with Phoebe later in the novel, is ultimately comparing Jaffrey not to the original Pyncheon but to a picture that is a "a counterfeit of its necessarily absent original."[36] Such an interpretive connection may have a certain psychological or moral accuracy, but it is hardly the sort of "science" that would win plaudits from the likes of Samuel Morton and his fellow craniologists.

And yet Hawthorne did turn to contemporaneous scientific thinking

on heritability, popularized by the French naturalist Jean Baptiste Lamarck, for two main figures of inheritance and transmission in the novel:
the garden (with its imagery of planting and seeds) and the animals within
the garden (Chanticleer and the family of fowl). Even here, though,
Hawthorne seeks to show that genetics complicates rather than clarifies
questions of bloodlines. For instance, mixture and uncertainty are absolutely central to the imagery of the garden. Aspiring to plant a family
whose pure bloodlines would be sustained over the centuries, the Pyncheons also plant a garden. The overlapping imagery of family planting
and garden planting is introduced at the outset of the novel with the
narrator's observation "that the act of the passing generation is the germ
which may and must produce good or evil fruit, in a far distant time" (6).
Here, deeds are kinds of seeds, and transmission can be understood as
the consequences of actions. In the several extended passages on the Pyncheons' garden, there are indications that Hawthorne is interested in
understanding transmission genealogically as well, though the recurrent
imagery of "entanglement and confusion" (73) underscores just how
difficult such a project would be. In an earlier tale, "Rappaccini's Daughter" (1844), Hawthorne had described the entanglement among Rappaccini's plant species as a "lurid intermixture," and in doing so, Anna Brickhouse suggests, he conveys his anxieties about "genealogical uncertainty"
by suggesting an "equation of racial mixture with poisonousness."[37] But
with its critique of Giovanni's unwillingness to commit himself to the
woman he loves, the tale also adumbrates the dangers of succumbing to
such paranoiac beliefs, given the inescapable reality of the "entanglement
and confusion" of racial intermixture. In House, Hawthorne certainly
works with allegorical notions that particular plants, such as Alice's poesies, are connected to particular people and thus can be understood to
represent the Pyncheon "race" in the way that Maule's Well represents the
Maule "race." But the various descriptions of the garden's confusion, and a
submerged confusion at that, emphasize that the seeds and roots of some
flowers mix with the seeds and roots of others, and that the waters of
Maule's Well likewise take on other waters. In this light, the merging of
Alice's poesies with Maule's Well, viewed by some readers as Hawthorne's
forecasting of a purifying (or eugenicist) happy ending of the novel, might
more accurately be taken as a figuring of a mysteriously lurid intermixture
of that which is already intermixed.

Where purity does seem to be preserved is in the novel's most insistently eugenicist figure: that of the Pyncheons' Chanticleer and his fellow

fowl, who are presented as a familial "race" bred in the way that Colonel Pyncheon hoped to breed the Pyncheons: through a form of inbreeding that would perpetuate the aristocratic blood purity that he regarded as legitimating the Pyncheons' claims on Maule's and the Indians' lands.[38] Hawthorne underscores the parallels between the Pyncheons as "the better specimens of the breed" (19) and their "self-important" (152) fowl by comically exaggerating Chanticleer's Pyncheon-like qualities. In this way, as Shawn Michelle Smith notes, Hawthorne casts the Pyncheons' "obsession with blood purity and ancestral inheritance as the cornerstone of aristocratic malady."[39] Both the fowl and the Pyncheons are presented as degenerating, but the Pyncheons' degeneration has nothing to do with inbreeding; it is linked instead to their conception of themselves as aristocrats who shouldn't have to exert themselves because of their claims on the extensive lands supposedly deeded them by Indians. True, Hawthorne does preserve a notion of genealogical transmission in his presentation of the tendency of some Pyncheons toward apoplexy, even as he connects apoplexy to a nonheritable greed. But throughout the novel he underscores the fact that the breeding of the fowls is controlled by their owners, while the Pyncheons have long strayed from the founding patriarchal line. Concepts of genetic purity may be vaguely workable within a controlled population of birds, but the emphasis in *House* is on how bloodlines in human populations become too mixed-up, too hidden, to account in clear ways for the behavior that supposedly is passed along through a house or "race."

Racial imagery is everywhere in *The House of the Seven Gables*, and Hawthorne's use of that imagery, I am arguing, generally destabilizes racial categories and the narratives based on such categories, whether he is addressing matters of family (the respective "races" of the Pyncheons and the Maules) or, by implication, the binary of whiteness and non-whiteness underpinning the literary nationalism of Young America. Like the image of the "hidden streams" that Hawthorne associates with racial genealogies, race as conceived by Hawthorne in the imaginative interstices of his novel is almost entirely fluid and even a matter of conjecture. Not for nothing does he state in the preface that the "personages of the Tale . . . are really of the Author's own making, or, at all events, of his own mixing" (3). Whereas Colonel Pyncheon aspires to fix "his race and future generations" (17) on the stable basis of "the Pyncheon blood" (18), Hawthorne indicates just how unstable, mixed, or even "black" that blood might be. In the preface, Hawthorne asserts that the House over time "grew black" (6), and that imagery of blackness extends to the family: Jaffrey, we are told, inherited from the "dark, high-featured countenance" (43) of the Colonel, indeed, from the "black and heavy-browed" (81) House of the Seven Gables, a "black stain of blood" (23). Thus while Jaffrey regularly displays "a white neckcloth of the utmost snowy purity" (116), it is the darkness or blackness that prevails. Like the house itself, Jaffrey is "dark-browed," and like the founding patriarch, he has a "dark, full-fed physiognomy" (118).

One way of reading Jaffrey's "blackness" would be through allegory, the historically conventional connection of blackness and evil. As critics such as Walter Benn Michaels, Gillian Brown, David Anthony, and Paul Gilmore have argued, it is also possible to read that "blackness" in relation to marketplace capitalism, on the grounds that the market, by reducing individuals to creatures of mere economic desire, makes them over into metaphorical slaves of appetite who, by virtue of being figured as types of slaves, have lost their "whiteness." Gilmore has made this argument most compellingly, arguing that Hawthorne in *House* "projects the threat of an unrestrained, market-driven manhood onto racial blackness." In this read-ing, even Hepzibah to some extent becomes "black" once she opens her shop and begins selling Jim Crow gingerbread men, which themselves become markers of her implication in an "enslaving" market economy. But blackest of all, in this analysis, is Judge Jaffrey Pyncheon, whose "economic and political grasping," Gilmore argues, is imaged "in terms of racial blackness."[40] After all, there would seem to be little difference between his grasping and the grasping of the Italian organ grinder's monkey, which has a "man-like expression" as it extends its "small black palm" (164) for money.

But here it must be asked: if the characters tied to the market are "black," where are the "whites" of the novel? After all, the novel makes clear from the very start, with Hepzibah's opening of her shop, that there is no escaping the market. Without completely rejecting Gilmore's argu-ment, I would underscore that what Hawthorne is doing in his genealogi-cal fiction is excoriating Jaffrey's economic and political grasping, which, in terms of his family's history, has its foundation in a conception of his white Anglo-Saxon superiority, by undercutting the purity of that white-ness. Rather than using racial imagery to locate what Gilmore calls "in-nate racial character,"[41] Hawthorne for the most part uses that imagery to unfix notions of innate racial character and thus to unsettle those houses (or nations) founded in racial certainties and absolutes. The fixing of race, as I will be elaborating in the final section of this chapter, would seem to be *our* project and not Hawthorne's.

Consider, for example, just how fluid race is at one of the cruxes of the novel: Holgrave's (Maule's) story of Alice Pyncheon as told to Phoebe Pyncheon. There are obvious and much-discussed parallels between Holgrave's mesmerical telling of his story to Phoebe and the story's account of Matthew Maule's mesmerical "enslavement" of Alice. In both cases, we have characters who are using their "Black Art" (84) against paragons of white femininity. In the story itself, Maule's "strange power of getting into people's dreams" (189) and the "witchcraft of [his] eye" (189) are connected to the oppositional, antiaristocratic, democratic energies of the novel consistent with Hawthorne's own Jacksonian disdain for the aristocrat, as well as to the oppositional energies that could be connected to the power of vodoun and black rebellion.[42] It is significant in this regard that Matthew Maule is linked to black Scipio and in certain respects is presented as "blacker" than Scipio. As Anthony notes, Scipio is depicted for the most part in terms of the "basic tropes of minstrelsy and racial performance."[43] But it is precisely the sense that race is performed, or mediated by mass-circulated images, that makes race such a provisional and hard-to-define category in the story (and overall novel). As Holgrave recounts, Scipio, when unnerved by Maule's effrontery at using the front entrance, adopts the class superiority of his master, demanding of Maule: "[W]hat for do you look so black at me?" Maule's response only further undercuts fixed notions of race: "Do you think nobody is to look black but yourself?" (188). If anyone can look or even be "black," then what exactly does the term mean? And if the Maules are presented as one "race" and the Pyncheons as another, then what is the difference between the two when Gervayse Pyncheon, a slaveholder himself, is willing to "sell" his daughter to Maule with the hope of recovering the lost Indian deed, while Maule, angered by what he incorrectly takes as Alice's class superiority, is willing to use his mesmerical skills to make her into what Holgrave calls "Maule's slave" (208). The two "races" seem at one here; they are both drinking each other's blood. In a Hegelian mode, Hawthorne, in what can be taken as a powerful antislavery allegory, reveals the enslaving dimensions of mastery itself.[44]

In his account of the violation of Alice by "black" Maule (with the help of Alice's "black" father), Holgrave further complicates questions of bloodlines both within and beyond the frame of the story. Telling of how Gervayse married a "lady of fortune" (190) in England, he chooses not to convey details of the new Mrs. Pyncheon's genealogical history. It remains unclear whether she is even English, for she and Gervayse educate their "exotic" (191) daughter in Italy.[45] Given that their daughter dies, that would seem to be the end of the supposedly direct flow of the Pyncheon bloodlines, for Gervayse is the grandson of Colonel Pyncheon, the boy who discovered the dead Colonel under his portrait. So the question given new impetus by this story is where did the other Pyncheons of the novel come from? What exactly is their connection to the founding line, and how "pure" was that founding line anyway?

The death of Judge Jaffrey Pyncheon shortly after the telling of the story brings these questions sharply into focus but, as anticipated in the tangled imagery of the Pyncheon garden, with no clear answers in sight. Presented as the very embodiment of what his allegedly murdered uncle had regarded as the "black stain of blood" in the Pyncheon family tree, Judge Pyncheon would appear to be in the genealogical line of the Colonel, given the nature of his actions and the "blackness" that matches the "dark countenance" (36) of the Colonel's portrait. Like the Colonel, the Judge himself dies of apoplexy while in the throes of greed, and thus Hawthorne holds onto notions of biological determinism or heritability as a possible way of thinking about Pyncheon genealogies, while at the same time signaling that greed can do great damage to the body. The one thing that Hawthorne clearly is *not* suggesting in the racial imagery of the overall novel is that Anglo-Saxon whiteness transmits itself across the centuries in a "pure" form that makes one family, nation, or "race" better than or essentially different from another. Sitting beneath the dark portrait of Colonel Pyncheon, the dead Judge initially exhibits what the narrator terms a "singularly white" countenance. But that countenance soon changes from white to a "swarthy whiteness" (276) and a "swarthily white visage" (295). Anthony provocatively posits that the narrator's mocking descriptions of the dead judge's transformation puts on display "a failed last moment in the maintenance of upper-class whiteness."[46] From beginning to end, I would add, the novel places a special emphasis on demonstrating precisely the difficulty, indeed the impossibility, of maintaining such a genealogical fiction given the unknowability of bloodlines and the inevitability of blood intermixture.

But if Hawthorne uses his descriptions of the Judge's blackening white face to undercut fictions of whiteness, what are we to make of the novel's ending, which, in its happy and escapist marriage of Holgrave/Maule and Phoebe, has been regarded by many readers as Hawthorne's own escape from the darker and more challenging implications of his novel? Gretchen Murphy laments Hawthorne's seeming return to what she calls "an exceptionalist national identity," and Shawn Michelle Smith, who admires the novel's critique of the aristocratic obsession with blood purity, nonetheless claims that the novel's concluding "celebration of 'healthy' marriages" implicates Hawthorne in the white Anglo-Saxonist supremacism of expansionist and proslavery writers—and much more. Punningly stating that Hawthorne through his ending "plants the seed of a theory of biological inheritance newly articulated by biological racialists in the first half of the nineteenth century," Smith links him not only to Colonel and Judge Pyncheon, but also, through the image of the seed, to what she describes as the "eugenicists' romance of Anglo-Saxon superiority at the turn of the century."[47] A novel that attempts to trouble notions of untroubled genealogies, and that unambiguously lampoons the prideful blood thinking of the Pyncheons, is here unproblematically linked, via what Hawthorne in the preface mockingly terms "a chain of events," to the eugenicism and imperialism of the culture approximately fifty years later. And yet if we resist linking *House* to particular cultural narratives that may have sprouted from the seeds of mid-nineteenth-century Anglo-Saxonism and instead, as I have been urging, read the novel at its moment of production as a critical engagement with the fictions of a "pure" and "better" Anglo-Saxonism, the ending is not as conventional as it seems. Arguably, it enacts the characters' own forms of counter-expropriation even as it continues to trouble "manifest" notions of national and racial destiny.

To be sure, *House*, in the way of Shakespearean romance, concludes on a hopeful note, as the "wild reformer" (313) Holgrave, perhaps the one surviving Maule, announces his more "conservative" (315) perspective on social change shortly after proposing to Phoebe Pyncheon. Even so, again in the way of Shakespearean romance, the conflicts at the heart of the novel maintain their hold on the imagination. Moreover, the ending itself is not as straightforwardly "purifying" or future oriented as may initially appear. Oddly and even incongruously, Hawthorne, in celebrating the apparent end to a long cycle of violence and retribution, provides the seemingly marginal elderly townsperson Uncle Venner with a central place in the novel's happy (re)construction of family. Why is it that Hawthorne leaves us not with two characters—a loving couple—choosing to live together happily ever after, but with five characters, three of whom are elderly, two of whom are brother and sister, and one simply the friendly town vagrant? Hawthorne's disposition of Uncle Venner in particular raises questions about what sort of "family" has emerged in this supposedly conventional resolution and suggests the close connection of *House* to other popular domestic/sentimental novels of the period. As Cindy Weinstein observes, in such works as Susan Warner's *The Wide, Wide World* (1850) and Maria Cummins's *The Lamplighter* (1854), the "generic goal is the substitution of freely given love, rather than blood, as the invincible tie that binds together individuals in a family."[48]

And there are further questions: Why, in the prophetic pictures ending the novel, is there no mention of the children to come from Holgrave/ Maule and Phoebe or of a desire to "plant" a family? And what are we to make of the impending marriage between Holgrave and Phoebe anyway? Given that they are initially presented in the novel as exemplars of two different "races," it is difficult not to see some hinting at cross-racial mixing in the final coming together of the lovers, especially when we recall Holgrave/Maule's connections to traditions of voudon. Significantly, the only progeny mentioned at the novel's end are those that will be produced by the Pyncheon fowls at the Judge's country seat, which implies that Holgrave and Phoebe represent the possibility of something much different from the fowl, especially given the fowl's metaphorical connections to the pure Pyncheon line as imagined by Colonel Pyncheon. The break from that Pyncheon is signaled most decisively in the novel's final image of the Colonel's portrait. Sprung open by Holgrave to reveal the recess with the missing deed, "the portrait, frame and all, tumbled suddenly from its position, and lay face downward on the floor" (316). He who had meant to shape (or frame) the racial/familial genealogical line of the Pyncheons well into the future, he who had hoped to plant the seed for the prideful breeding embodied by Chanticleer and his hens, he who had hoped to use his sense of blood superiority as a pretext for taking hold of thousands of acres of Indian lands finds his final fate with his face smashed to the ground.[49] In all sorts of ways, then, it seems fair to say that, though there is a certain forced happiness to the conclusion, the group going off to the Judge's country seat will operate very differently from the Colonel, the Judge, and others in the grasping Pyncheon line in ways that are consistent with the novel's overarching suggestion that real estate does not "naturally" belong to those who lay claim to it on paper.[50]

Jaffrey Pyncheon, of course, used his country seat as an outpost from which he could plan additional expropriations of land and capital as legitimated by his conception of class and blood privilege. Those ambitions are mocked at the close in a variety of ways, and not simply through the death of the Judge and the revelation of the worthless Indian deed, but also through the bizarre (and wildly exhilarating) scene near the end of the novel when Clifford and Hepzibah take flight on a railway car. For as Clifford breaks away from the House of the Seven Gables, he emerges as the expansionist par excellence, the person committed to "moving at whirlwind speed" (256) in the manner of those crossing the continent. "More! More! More!," John O'Sullivan had proclaimed in a well-known editorial. "Yes, more, more, more will be the unresting cry, till our national destiny is fulfilled and the whole boundless continent is ours."[51] When first introduced into the novel, Clifford, under the intoxicating influence of his first good cup of coffee in thirty years, similarly cries: "More, more!" (107). Taking flight on the train weeks later, he celebrates two of the dizzying technological changes of the time—the train and the telegraph—and, in the manner of O'Sullivan and Young America, sees no bounds to the possible growth and interconnectedness of the nation. As he remarks on the wonders of the telegraph: "Lovers, day by day—hour by hour, if so often moved to do it—might send their heart-throbs from Maine to Florida" (264). Hietala notes that "the conquest of distance was as important to the Democrats as the conquest of Indians and Mexicans"; and indeed, O'Sullivan himself wrote in 1845 that the very technological changes that Hawthorne has Clifford celebrating six years later were central to Anglo-Saxon continental expansionism, declaring that a "vast skeleton framework of railroads, and an infinitely ramified nervous system of magnetic telegraphs," is precisely what was needed to link together the developing white communities of the ever-expanding United States.[52] But when the enthusiastic Clifford is reminded by the gimlet-eyed interlocutor that trains and telegraphs serve very particular interests, less of "lovers" than of "speculators in cotton" (264), he abruptly recoils from the romantic energies that he had been celebrating, an exhausted and confused old man.

Clifford's ultimate vision, then, which he proclaims on the train and which is underscored throughout the novel, is that "real estate . . . is the broad foundation on which nearly all the guilt of this world rests" (263). In that light, no one linked to prevailing structures of power can ever really be free of guilt, and for Hepzibah, Clifford, Uncle Venner, Holgrave, and Phoebe to reside at Judge Pyncheon's country seat is only as "criminal" as residing on any plot of ground. And yet there are clear indications that these characters are moving in a different direction from the Judge. The five characters who will be residing for an undisclosed length of time at the Judge's former house do not engage in blood talk; they have no immediate aspirations to do anything other than begin to make sense of their rapidly transformed situations. Their relocation suggests a larger dislocation indicative of an unclear but more hopeful future. Family, community, and national histories remain to be written; new seeds may be in the process of being planted, but no one at the end of the novel can declare with any sort of confidence what those seeds are, how they are to be nourished, or what will eventually sprout from them. Entanglement and confusion remain the order of the day, and there's nothing necessarily poisonous about that.

Blackened Hands

Or would Melville beg to differ on precisely this point, given that his novel of genealogical entanglement and confusion ends with poison? Published less than a year after *The House of the Seven Gables*, Melville's *Pierre*, in part because of that ending, has generally been taken as a novel that "responds" to *House* by pointing to its limitations. Brenda Wineapple speaks for many when she writes that "*The House of the Seven Gables* finds its inversion in *Pierre*."[53] The idea that Melville to some extent parodies *House* through a series of strategic inversions could be supported, for example, by noting that Hawthorne's announced generational theme of *House* is revoiced in *Pierre* by the morally shallow and hypocritical Reverend Falsgrave: " 'The sins of the father shall be visited upon the children to the third generation.' "[54] But that revoicing could also be taken as Melville's wink to Hawthorne on what he and Hawthorne both knew were the sorts of moral bromides that Hawthorne felt he had to offer his readers in a preface. Rather than seeing Melville as trying to subvert or "invert" Hawthorne, I will be arguing that *Pierre*, in sometimes outrageous fashion, follows up on *House*'s challenge to a blood-based exceptionalism by boldly exposing the nation's hidden history of racial entanglement. *Pierre* extends *House* rather than gutting and remodeling it.

Although Hawthorne and Melville are often presented in the critical literature as diametrical opposites on the political spectrum (Hawthorne as "conservative" Democrat; Melville as "radical" cosmopolitan), there are notable convergences in their lives, careers, and politics during the late 1840s and 1850s that would help to explain the ease with which these supposedly very different types were able to assume a friendship in the summer of 1850. Melville had close ties with a number of the literary-nationalist Democrats, and as radical as he might have been in his fiction, he was relatively unengaged with the day-to-day workings of his political world. There is no known equivalent in Melville's life, for instance, to Hawthorne's signing of a Free-Soil petition, and the letters Melville wrote friends and family during the 1840s and 1850s are for the most part without political content. But a letter that Melville wrote his brother Gansevoort shortly after President James K. Polk declared war on Mexico (and nearly three weeks after Gansevoort, unbeknownst to Melville, had died in England after arranging the British publication of *Typee* [1846]) provides a significant exception. Gansevoort was a Democratic politician who passionately supported U.S. expansionism, but in the letter to his brother, Melville poked fun of the military pomp and self-righteousness attending the "state of delirium about the Mexican War," reminding Gansevoort of war's ultimate reality: "Nothing is talked of but the 'Halls of the Montezumas.' And to hear folks prate about those purely figurative apartments one would suppose that they were another Versailles where our democratic rabble is meant to 'make a night of it' ere long. . . . But seriously something great is impending. . . . Lord, the day is at hand, when we will be able to talk of our killed & wounded like some old Eastern conquerors reckoning them up by thousands." In his sketches and fiction of the late 1840s, Melville similarly raised questions about U.S. imperial ambitions, satirizing Mexican War hero General Zachary Taylor in "Authentic Anecdotes of 'Old Zack'" (1847), for instance, by focusing less on Taylor's military exploits than on "his present bulk" (figured as a kind of corporeal expansionism). In a particularly acute moment of cultural critique in *Mardi* (1849), Melville conveys his doubts about Manifest Destiny through a jeremiadic warning that his questing characters find inscribed in an "anonymous scroll": "And be not too grasping, nearer home. It is not freedom to filch. Expand not your area too widely, now. Seek you proselytes? Neighboring nations may be free, without coming under your banner." The novel comments as well on the evils of slavery in Dominoro (the South), a critique that would be developed the following year in the antiflogging passages of *White-Jacket* (1850). Thus when Melville declares in that novel in a millennialist mode, "[W]e Americans are the peculiar, chosen people—the Israel of our time; we bear the ark of the liberties of the world," it is difficult not to hear more than a touch of irony.[55]

And yet even as Melville mocked U.S. notions of a divinely sanctioned Manifest Destiny and developed an antislavery perspective in his early writings, he, like Hawthorne, had close ties to the Democrats associated with the Young America circles of the *Democratic Review* and the *Literary World*. Melville's association with key figures in the Young America movement clearly did not indicate an uncritical acceptance of their Anglo-Saxonist expansionism. Still, because of his friendship with some of the leading figures of the movement, it would have been difficult for him to dissociate himself from the sometimes shrill nationalism that these cultural figures espoused; and the fact is that he, like Hawthorne, had an important place in their American literary-nationalist program. Melville's first novel, *Typee*, was published by Duyckinck in Wiley and Putnam's "Library of American Books" series; it was Duyckinck and his Young America friends who arranged for Melville to meet Hawthorne at a Stock-bridge picnic on 5 August 1850; and it was Duyckinck who arranged later that month for the publication in the *Literary World* of "Hawthorne and His Mosses," Melville's American literary-nationalist paean to Hawthorne. Posing as a Virginian enamored of the "mystical blackness" of the great New England writer, Melville offers a cross-sectional appreciation of a writer whom he presents, like the stranger in "A Select Party," as having vindicated the promise of the nation's genius. For all of the suspicions of U.S. exceptionalism that Melville voices in his letter to Gansevoort, his "Old Zack" essays, and his early fiction, he speaks in this essay as a Young America literary nationalist, proclaiming that "no American writer should write like an Englishman" and linking the promises of American literature to a larger vision of U.S. empire: "While we are rapidly preparing for that political supremacy among the nations, which prophetically awaits us at the close of the present century; in a literary point of view, we are deplorably unprepared for it; and we seem studious to remain so." By adopting the voice of a Virginian, Melville to some extent distances himself from these views, which perhaps he is satirizing; though if that were the case, there is no evidence that anyone at the time discerned the satire.[56] Instead, there was excitement among Hawthorne's friends, family, and admirers about the advocacy of Hawthorne as the incarnation of American genius and wonder about who that advocate might be.

A relatively short and intense friendship ensued between Hawthorne and Melville from late 1850 through 1852. Melville shared with Hawthorne his struggles to complete *Moby-Dick*, which he dedicated to Hawthorne, and Hawthorne, like Melville, was chagrined by Duyckinck's unappreciative review of *Moby-Dick* in the *Literary World*.[57] If Melville had second thoughts about the literary program of Young America, that review certainly prompted him to make his break, and he would satirize Duyckinck's tame version of American literary nationalism in *Pierre*. Meanwhile, Hawthorne shared *The House of the Seven Gables* with Melville, and though we do not have Hawthorne's side of the correspondence, we have Melville's letter to Hawthorne on his initial reading of *House*. For those who see *House* as a genteel performance, it can seem that Melville had been reading some other novel, or else (as I prefer to think) reading it more deeply than most. In his letter on *House*, Melville declares in the spirit of "Hawthorne and His Mosses": "There is the grand truth about Nathaniel Hawthorne. He says NO! in thunder; but the Devil himself cannot make him say *yes*." Melville's most specific comment on the novel comes in the letter's P.S.: "The marriage of Phoebe with the daguerreotypist is a fine stroke, because of his turning out to be a *Maule*. If you pass Hepzibah's cent-shop, buy me a Jim Crow (fresh) and send it *to* me by Ned Higgins." It is striking that Melville finds Hawthorne's much-criticized ending a "fine stroke." And it is striking as well that he invokes Jim Crow without referring to issues of slavery and race, though he enigmatically remarks elsewhere in the letter that while musing on the novel, "I have landed in Africa."[58] That said, Melville's conjoining of the marriage and Jim Crow suggests that he was interested in the conjunction of genealogical history and race, issues that, as he well understood, were central to Hawthorne's *House*. Melville would pursue these concerns on his own terms in *Pierre*, the novel he began shortly after reading *House* and that in certain respects did land him in Africa.[59]

There are numerous parallels between *House* and *Pierre* as genealogical fictions, such as the use of portraiture to illuminate (and call into doubt) family history and the use of rumor in unfixing that history. Both novels frame questions of blood in relation to what Hawthorne presents as aspirations to "plant" a family through a kind of eugenicist breeding. Given the importance of motifs of breeding to both novels, I would suggest that the "seed" of *Pierre* may well have been the description in *House* of Chanticleer's "two wives" and their one chicken, which "looked small enough to be still in the egg, and, at the same time, sufficiently old, withered, wizened, and experienced, to have been the founder of the antiquated race." That bred chicken can be taken as a prefiguration of Pierre. Hawthorne describes the mother chicken's relationship to the new exemplar/progenitor of the "race" in this way:

Its mother evidently regarded it as the one chicken of the world, and as necessary, in fact, to the world's continuance, or, at any rate to the equilibrium of the present system of affairs, whether in church or state. No lesser sense of the infant fowl's importance could have justified, even in a mother's eyes, the perseverance with which she watched over its safety, ruffling her small person to twice its proper size, and flying in everybody's face that so much looked toward her hopeful progeny. No lower estimate could have vindicated the inde-fatigable zeal with which she scratched, and her unscrupulousness in digging up the choicest flower or vegetable, for the sake of the fat earth-worm at its root. . . . By degrees, the observer came to feel nearly as much interest in this chicken of illustrious race, as the mother-hen did.[60]

Invested in her chicken as both the exemplar and possibly last of the "illustrious race," and obsessively wanting to protect it from harm, the mother hen of course speaks to the Pyncheons' pride in their "race" but also anticipates Melville's Mary Glendinning, whose obsession with her son operates in precisely these terms. Like the mother hen, she regards her only child Pierre as the incarnation and last best hope of her "race" (the Glendinnings), is reluctant to let him out of her sight, and attempts to help him prosper in relation to "church or state" by arranging his marriage to the docile and seemingly "angelical" (25) and "white" (183) Lucy. From the opening of the novel to her despairing renunciation of her son, Mary "glorifie[s] the rare and absolute merits of Pierre" (15), seeing him as "the choicest guild of his race" (16) and therefore in need of constant guidance so that he remains true to what she would like to believe is a genealogy "wherein is no *flaw*" (11). But let us not forget about Chanticleer's second "wife"!

The possibility that Pierre's heretofore highly revered father may him-self have had a second "wife," or mistress, haunts both Mary Glendinning and her son, and I want now to jump into the midst of things by looking at a key scene at the midpoint of *Pierre* that to some extent parallels the dislocating moment late in *House* in which the dead Judge Pyncheon is transformed from white to "swarthy" beneath the ambiguous portrait of the Colonel. Nowhere are Pierre's concerns about the racial identify of his father (and himself) more acutely on display.

Preparing to journey to New York City with the black-haired, "olive"-complected (46) Isabel Banford and the disgraced pregnant servant

Delly Ulver, after having just broken off his engagement with Lucy Tartan of the "white cottage" (186), Pierre, at the suggestively named Black Swan Inn, contemplates a chair portrait of his father from his happier bachelor days. Convinced by the circumstantial evidence of Isabel's story that his father had had a premarital affair and fathered Isabel, Pierre suddenly comes to see all that his prideful mother has been celebrating—the glorious Glendinning family genealogy, and indeed his own identity as exemplar of the race—as little more than a fraud. As in *House*, portraits speak to the family history, but they can only speak so much. Studying the portrait, Pierre feels mocked by his father's "ambiguous, unchanging smile," and he is particularly disturbed by a "certain lurking lineament in the portrait . . . [that] was visible in the countenance of Isabel" (196). Enraged by what he thinks he has learned about his father, Pierre drops the canvas into a flaming hearth, taking satisfaction in "the first crispings and blackenings of the painted scroll." But when his father's blackened face on the canvas seems to look at him "in beseeching horror," Pierre makes a last-minute unsuccessful effort to save the portrait, which leaves one of his hands "burnt and blackened" (198). He later notices that Isabel's hand also has somehow blackened. At the Black Swan Inn, Pierre discovers (or so he thinks he discovers, for the novel remains forever ambiguous on the matter) that what links him to Isabel is not just that they have a common father (if in fact they do) but, as suggested by their mutually blackened hands, a common "race" (if in fact one can ever know one's racial identity).[61] Melville's subtle troubling of the connections between whiteness and familial identity in early national and antebellum culture, his exploration of the (dis)connections among genealogical history, racial identity, and ultimately national identity, particularly in the first half of the novel, emerge in significant ways from his imaginative response to Hawthorne's *House*.

Both *Pierre* and *House* begin with detailed genealogical histories, and Melville's use of such history anticipates the novel's depictions of Pierre's and Isabel's blackened hands. Initially speaking in the jingoistic voice of the American literary nationalist, Melville in the opening book patriotically mocks the English "Peerage Book" (9), comically undercutting the very notion of pure, heroic, and known English genealogies of royalty and aristocracy by reminding his readers of the branches extending from Charles II and his mistress Nell Gwynne and then back to "the thief knights of the Norman" (10). And yet the first American genealogies that the narrator discusses after his comical remarks on the miscegenated character of the English Peerage Book reveal a confluence of sources that raise questions about national purity. The narrator refers to "the old and oriental-like English planter families of Virginia and the South; the Randolphs for example, one of whose ancestors, in King James' time, married Pocahontas the Indian Princess, and in whose blood therefore an underived aboriginal royalty was flowing over two hundred years ago" (10). As with the river imagery Hawthorne deploys with respect to the Maules, the emphasis here is on the ebb and flow and mixing of blood, with the ironically developed notion that the Randolph blood is simultaneously miscegenated and pure. In the context of such paralleling accounts of English and American mixing of blood, the narrator then turns to the house of Glendinning, declaring, as Hawthorne states about the Pyncheons, that the family aims to "perpetuate itself," despite the difficulties of transmitting traits and property from generation to generation in a country lacking a "chartered aristocracy, and . . . law of entail" (8). Appearances proclaim that they have succeeded in their quest, for their "special family distinction" (12) has become both the joy and onus of Pierre's strong-willed mother, who remains committed to the "fair succession of an honorable race!" (194). But in the crucial subsequent account of Pierre's paternal grandfather, a slave master, which looks forward to the accounts of the "blackenings" of his son's portrait and his grandson's hand, Melville suggests that the Glendinning "race" may not be so fair and honorable after all.

In *House*, there is an emphasis on the Pyncheons' legal deeds with Indians; in *Pierre*, the emphasis is initially on the Glendinnings' deeds against Indians, specifically the violent actions along "the historic line of Glendinning" (5) that, to Pierre's young mind, helped to establish the greatness of "his race" (6). Telling a story that has become central to Pierre's own sense of family and self, the narrator comments on how Pierre's paternal great-grandfather had fought Indians for possession of the land, and how his paternal grandfather, General Glendinning, "had annihilated two Indian savages by making reciprocal bludgeons of their heads" (29–30).[62] In addition to establishing a violent racial authority over the Indians, the General was also successful in establishing authority over his black slaves.

But in the evocative discussion of the Glendinning estate around the time of the American Revolution, the narrator ironically romanticizes the violence of slave ownership as a love altogether similar to the love that the General has for his horses.[63] Slaves and horses are closely linked on the

General's estate, and there are half-joking suggestions from the outset of the novel that slaves, horses, and even Glendinnings share parallel (and perhaps intersecting) genealogies. The narrator asserts that "on the lands of Saddle Meadows, man and horse are both hereditary"; and in the initial description of Pierre taking a ride with his beloved Lucy Tartan, the narrator remarks that Pierre is "seated where his own ancestor had sat, and reining steeds whose great-great-great-grandfathers grand old Pierre had reined before" (32). Reminiscent of Hawthorne's linking of the Pyncheons to Chanticleer, the rhythms of this description work to connect the genealogy (and breeding) of the horses with the genealogy (and breeding) of the Glendinnings. In this regard it is significant that Pierre himself is introduced in Book I as a kind of horse: "Pierre neighed out lyrical thoughts, as at the trumpet-blast, a war-horse paws himself into a lyric of foam" (14). He is also presented as having a "complexion inclined to brown" (17). The novel subsequently provides a secret history of sorts that helps to make sense of the associative grouping of horses, slaves, and Glendinnings.

"Now, this grand old Pierre Glendinning," the narrator proclaims, "was a great lover of horses." Year after year on Christmas day he expressed his love by making special visits to the stables to spend what are implicitly presented as sexualized encounters with the animals under his command. For during these holiday visits, "no one grained his steeds, but himself. . . . He said that no man loved his horses, unless his own hands grained them" (30). The horses, according to the narrator's account, love his visits, as do the slaves, who occasionally are given responsibility for the grooming but more often than not do their best to make sure the horses are prepared for the General. They act out of love and fear: "Woe to Cranz, Kit, Douw, or any other of his stable slaves, if grand old Pierre found one horse unblanketed. . . . Not that he ever had Cranz, Kit, Douw, or any of them flogged . . . but he would refuse to say his wonted pleasant word to them; and that was very bitter to them, for Cranz, Kit, Douw, and all of them, loved grand old Pierre" (30). As the account makes clear, the slaves' "love" of the General has much to do with his patriarchal dominance.[64] But what exactly does the master do to the horses/slaves with "his own hands"? Or, to put the question differently: how does a patriarchal master express his "love"?

Melville hints at answers to these questions in his description of the General later in life after he has decided to forgo morning rides of his beloved "saddle beast" because of the changes age have wrought on his body: "But time glides on, and grand old Pierre grows old: his life's glorious grape now swells with fatness; he has not the conscience to saddle his majestic beast with such a mighty load of manliness" (31). The suggestion of the phallic imagery here is that, not unlike the southern slave master, the General when in vital health, during the time in his younger days when his "glorious grape" swelled with something more potent than mere "fatness," saddled his "beast" with his "mighty load of manliness"; and the implication of the sexual imagery, given the General's representative status as a Glendinning patriarch and the blending of slaves and horses as interchangeable property, is that Pierre and other Glendinnings and the horses/slaves themselves may all be thought of as "one branch" or "family cousins" (21). Maurice S. Lee notes that the "antebellum era linked horses and slaves as branded, bred, and brutish chattel—a fact decried on the masthead of the *Liberator*, which conflated slave and horse auctions."[65] That conflation, which informs Melville's sly presentation of the General's seemingly sexual history with the horses, points to the General's possibly sexual history with his slaves. As with the English Peerage Book, Melville cunningly implies, when one looks closely at the twistings and turnings of the genealogical histories of the masters and the slaves, one discerns mixture and shared origins among high and low (specifically, among Pierre and the colts/slaves). But that sexual and racial history can only be hinted at, for as the historian Joel Williamson writes, "The great difference between miscegenation by white men and that by white women was, of course, that maternity could not be hidden with the same ease as paternity."[66] Hidden paternity, one of the central tropes of antislavery discourse, and of course the donnée of William Wells Brown's presentation of Thomas Jefferson in *Clotel*, is central to the unfolding of *Pierre's* plot as well. Through the tantalizingly enigmatic genealogical history in the opening books of the novel, Melville suggests that Pierre's vision of his blackened hand (and father) should perhaps be regarded as having the force of revelation.

And yet, in the manner of Hawthorne's emphasis on the hidden streams of the Pyncheons' and Maules' bloodlines, Melville ultimately only teasingly raises the possibilities of miscegenated (and unknown) genealogies rather than offering some specific "proof" of Pierre's "black" blood.[67] Like Hawthorne, Melville is ultimately concerned less with establishing firm genealogical lines through an uncovering of secret deeds than in exploring, indeed emphasizing, what Joan Dayan has termed "the mottled discourse of racial identity."[68] There is no character in the novel whose identity is more "mottled" than Isabel's, and no character who incarnates more resonantly what Pierre refers to as that "darker, though truer aspect of things" (69).

As in *House*, "dark things" (76) are suggested through pictures, even as pictures are presented as ambiguous and highly mediated markers of histories that cannot be completely recovered or known. In a series of narrative set pieces that provide an ambiguous history of the origin of Isabel's blackened hand, Pierre is described at age twelve overhearing his father on his deathbed asking after a daughter, and then is described several years later contemplating the two surviving portraits of his father: a large formal portrait made when the father was married, and a pre-marriage, smaller, informal chair portrait surreptitiously sketched by a cousin. It is the smaller one, much beloved by Pierre's Aunt Dorothea and loathed by Mary Glendinning, that, until he chooses to burn it, fascinates Pierre, who regularly gazes at it in an attempt to discern the father's "secret published in a portrait" (79). There are hints of that secret, for Dorothea tells Pierre that the portrait was sketched at a time when Pierre's father was involved with a young French woman who had fled her "native land, because of the cruel, blood-shedding times there" (75). Pierre's aunt offers no specific information about the young lady, who eventually disappears from sight (with the suggestion that she may have become pregnant with Pierre's father's daughter), and no specific information about the revolution from which she fled, which could just as easily have been the revolution in Saint Domingue as Paris. The chair portrait thus possibly attests to an interracial love far more provocative than the cross-"racial" love between a Pyncheon and a Maule.

The story that Isabel subsequently tells Pierre over the course of two visits only further heightens a sense of her "blackness." Like a slave who has been sired by the plantation master, the "Franco-Africanist figure of Isabel," as Brickhouse terms her, has no sense of her identity in relation to her father, though she's eventually taken to a farmhouse where she is visited by a man who secretly whispers to her the word "Father" (124).[69] Significantly, the secret space of the Ulver farmhouse, both the site of the father's supposed visit and the site where Isabel now tells her story to Pierre, has a homologous relation to the General's stables, from which outsiders similarly are banned. In the manner of the ex-slave of numerous slave narratives, Isabel tells Pierre how she taught herself to read and write, and how she used this knowledge to read "Isabel" on a guitar from the house of the Glendinnings and thus to discern possible connections between herself and the family of the big house. Although Isabel voices her concern that her "soul hath cast on thee the same black shadow that my hair now flings on thee" (190), Pierre chooses to embrace his "black shadow." Pierre's instantaneous love for the dark Isabel, even as he is aware of its possibly incestuous nature, in effect ratifies his "blackness," for like the typical biracial brother of antislavery fiction, he chooses to align himself with his apparent half-sister and in this way redeem the violated mother. Melville's remarks later in the novel on the defiant Enceladus, the son of a series of incestuous and mixed "marriages" and a figure whom Pierre regards as a version of himself, suggest that Melville views his "mulatto" hero, as Nancy Bentley argues a number of antislavery writers regarded similar such mulatto figures, "as the heroic oedipal son of a white father."[70] (It is worth underscoring, however, that the whiteness of the "white" father, as in *Clotel* and other antislavery texts, remains deliberately ambiguous.) In this respect, Pierre's love for Isabel can be taken as an expression of his rebelliousness, and not just against his "blackened" white father and prideful white mother. After he "imprint[s] repeated burning kisses upon her," he and Isabel remain "coiled together, and entangledly stood mute" (192). Like the mutes of "Benito Cereno," they stage their own mutiny against the tyranny of the "white-browed and white-handed" (99), choosing to leave the hypocritical country world of Mary Glendinning and the Reverend Falsgrave for the tumult of Young America's New York City.[71]

IN HER FINE ANALYSIS OF INTERSECTING domestic motifs and themes in *Pierre* and *House*, Wyn Kelley takes Pierre's and Isabel's rebellious departure for New York City as that point in the novel when "Melville leaves Hawthorne and the world of middle-class house and home far behind."[72] As my close attention to *Pierre's* first half suggests, I am in general agreement with Kelley's assessment. And yet if we read "house and home" in relation to the Young America literary nationalism that I am maintaining both Hawthorne and Melville respond to in their genealogical fictions, Melville does not leave that world as far behind as it might seem.[73] It is telling, for example, that Pierre's first great success in New York City as a Young American author comes about through the publication of what the narrator terms his "delightful love-sonnet, entitled 'The Tropical Summer'" (245). Here the literary work clearly invokes U.S. expansionist aspirations of the period, not only for parts of Mexico but also for an "American" Caribbean, a point underscored by the fact that

Pierre uses the profits from his sonnets to purchase cigars "perfumed with the sweet leaf of Havanna" (262).[74] Of course Pierre quickly turns against his facile success as a genteel author, lighting his cigars "by the sale of his sonnets, and . . . by the printed sonnets themselves" (263). But Melville's amusing parody of Young America gentility and "Perfect Taste" (245) should not obscure that he is also raising larger questions about the nation's imperialistic program of hemispheric expansionism, linking it to the amoral "virtuous expediency" (214) described in "Chronometricals & Horologicals," wherein the possible author Plotinus Plinlimmon assails those "professed Christian nations" which greedily extend their rule and "glory in the owning" (207).

The *House*-inspired blood themes and motifs of *Pierre*'s domestic first half also remain of importance to the novel's urban chapters, particularly with respect to questions of Pierre's identity. In a letter of 1849 to Duyckinck, Melville commented on the intimate connection between identity and genealogy: "The truth is that we are all sons, grandsons, or nephews or great-nephews of those who go before us. No one is his own sire."[75] Following Isabel's vague account of her life history and Pierre's resolution to journey to New York City and masquerade as her husband, *Pierre*'s narrator, working with and against Emersonian notions of self-reliance, comments similarly on the limits of individual identity: "[S]urely no mere mortal who has at all gone down into himself will ever pretend that his slightest thought or act solely originates in his own defined identity" (176). And yet while in the city, Pierre attempts to refute or rebel against such a notion, for it is increasingly clear that he wants somehow to liberate himself from his family's genealogy, however muddled that genealogy may be, through heroic acts of self-making.

In describing Pierre's efforts at disentanglement, Melville, as critics have observed, presents Pierre as a kind of American Hamlet. But he also presents him as an American Othello. After all, in a retrospective account of the earlier times when the younger Pierre sensed that his beloved cousin Glendinning Stanly's affections were beginning to be directed toward others, the narrator remarks: "Jealousies are felt. The sight of another lad too much consorting with the boy's beloved object, shall fill him with emotions akin to those of Othello's; a fancied slight, or lessening of the every-day inclinations of warm feelings, shall prompt him to bitter upbraidings and reproaches; or shall plunge him into evil moods" (217). Pierre's later rage at "Cousin Glen" in the city is presented in almost stereotypical terms as the putatively unmanageable rage of what Shakespeare's Emilia, following Othello's murder of Desdemona, calls "the blacker devil."[76] Thus when Pierre is stopped at the entrance to Glen's house by Glen's deferential black servant, the juxtaposition of "blackened" Pierre and black servant, in a scene that directly parallels Holgrave's account of Matthew Maule's confrontation with black Scipio, works to underscore Pierre's Othello-like anger. Moved by a "savage impulse in him" (239), Pierre attacks Glen in the manner of a rebellious slave, "leaping toward him like Spartacus" (239). He wants to stab Glen so that he can "let out all thy Glendinning blood" (239); and in this context it should be noted that Pierre's early love letters to Glen were written "throughout with red ink upon black; . . . [because] one pen and one pigment were insufficient" (219). Images of red and black, along with the telling reference to "pigment," evoke both blood and skin. Such imagery, coupled with the Othello analogue and the allusion to Holgrave's story of Alice Pyncheon in *House*, further suggest the possible mixtures in Pierre's own bloodlines.

Following the news of his mother's death and her decision to disinherit him, Pierre feels "the very blood in his body had in vain rebelled against his Titanic soul" (341). He cannot stand alone as an autonomous Titan precisely because of what Melville punningly refers to as the "vain" (vein) that unfixes his genealogical identity. Isabel continues to insist upon the "blackness" of that vein. Concerned about Lucy's possible arrival, she orders her "brother" Pierre to examine her cheek, which she describes as "all dark, dark, dark" (314). The narrator then refers to Isabel's "ebon tresses" and "ebon eyes" (314) and, following Lucy's arrival, directs attention, by way of contrast, to Lucy's "two thin white hands" (325) and "marble-white" (329) complexion. Pierre's unorthodox and perhaps incestuous union with the dark Isabel and the light Lucy then motivates "this American Enceladus" (346) to meditate on ur-acts of incest and miscegenation, as he contemplates the unions between Coelus and Terra (heaven and earth) and Old Titan and Terra (his mother), which produced Enceladus, "both the son and grandson of an incest" (347).[77] Thoughts of mixture put Pierre into a "mixed . . . mood" (347), an appropriate psychological frame for a final (re)consideration of his own racial or genealogical identity.

Melville, in the manner of *House*, once again works with portraits to explore and unsettle racial identity. Out for a walk, Pierre and Isabel come to a gallery where they become obsessed with two paintings: a copy of Guido's *Cenci* and an unknown painter's rendition of *The Stranger*, which hang "from the opposite walls, [and] exactly faced each other" (351).

Melville, Crafts, and Hawthorne's House {159}

Isabel and Pierre are initially drawn less to Beatrice Cenci, whose portrait silently speaks to horrific acts of incest and parricide, than to the image of the Stranger, fascinated as they are by his racialized identity: " 'The Stranger' was a dark, comely, youthful man's head. . . . [T]he dark head, with its crisp, curly, jetty hair, seemed just disentangling itself from out of curtains and clouds" (351). In the ambiguously dark face of the Stranger, Isabel detects "certain shadowy traces of her own unmistakable likeness; while to Pierre, this face was in part as the resurrection of the one he had burst at the Inn" (351). Gazing at the dark stranger, who "gazes" at the conventionally light Beatrice Cenci of "blue eyes and fair complexion" (351), they believe they are viewing a symbolic reenactment of the father's sexual act that gave rise to their own incestuous predicament. Moreover, the emphasis on Cenci's lightness and the Stranger's darkness makes clear that what we're also witnessing in the cross-alignment of the portraits is a figuration of a racial crossing that, as long as the portraits remain positioned face to face, perpetually implies not only Pierre's and Isabel's miscegenated identities but also the miscegenated identities of unknown men and women of preceding, current, and subsequent generations.

Not surprisingly, then, given the "resurrection" of the "dark" father, a genealogical imagery of blood is central to the bloody denouement of the novel. Earlier, as part of this recurring imagery, Pierre had concluded that Lucy was "without shadow of flaw or vein" (317), with the implication that a "flaw" could be detected only at the site of a hidden vein. Imagery of veins comes to the fore in the novel's final chapters. With the ironic suggestion that there is a "shadow of flaw" in Pierre's veins, the narrator refers to Pierre's "rebellious blood" (341) when he resolves to kill Glen and Lucy's brother Fred shortly after viewing *The Stranger*. Charlie Millthorpe, Pierre's country friend and now fellow (Young America) apostle, watches the American Othello pass by in a rage and remarks: "There was ever a black vein in this Glendinning; and now that vein is swelled. . . . Shall I go to his rooms and ask what black thing this is that hath befallen him?" (358). Referring to Pierre by the name of his genealogical house, Millthorpe encourages a reading of the subsequent murder of Glen, the last of the Glendinnings, as a kind of racial civil war within a house divided (Hawthorne of course presents his own house divided in *House*). Pierre's rebellious anger at Glen, particularly as depicted in relation to his "black vein," has significant parallels with the anger of the rebellious slave at his "white" brother(s) as depicted in antislavery fiction of the period. Also reminiscent of that fiction are the suicides described in the novel's final pages, for as Werner Sollors observes, "[T]he mulatto suicide is the cultural given in American settings."[78] In this respect it is important to note that Melville blackens Pierre's and Isabel's suicides. Contemplating Pierre's dead body, Millthorpe states: "The dark vein's burst, and here's the deluge-wreck." Our final image of Pierre is of a young man shrouded in blackness, for Isabel's "long hair ran over him, and arbored him in ebon vines" (362).

When Isabel offers Pierre poison, she takes it from "the secret vial nesting" at her bosom (360). To some extent that "vial" serves as a metonym of her secret vein. But by referring to Isabel's hidden "nest" of poison, Melville also links her to Shakespeare's Cleopatra, who suicidally placed a poisonous asp at her breast. Pierre too is linked to an Egyptian forbear, as he had given the name "Memnon Stone" to the stone he fancifully enjoyed imagining as a sort of tombstone, thereby honoring Memnon, "that dewey, royal boy, son of Aurora, and born King of Egypt, who, with enthusiastic rashness flinging himself on another's account into a rightful quarrel, fought hand to hand with his overmatch, and met his boyish and most dolorous death beneath the walls of Troy" (135). For those who conceive of Pierre as an American Hamlet, Melville encourages a more historically complex reading: Hamlet as an Anglicized Memnon, a genealogical analogue that further underscores Pierre's connection to Egypt. Shakespeare's *Hamlet*, the narrator notes, can itself be thought of as coming out of Africa, for "the English tragedy is but Egyptian Memnon, Montaignized and modernized" (135).

By associating his blackened heroes with Egypt, Melville participates in a larger antebellum cultural conversation on race. Insistent on establishing absolute racial differences between blacks and whites, racial ethnologists of the American school regularly argued, in the words of Samuel Morton, that Egypt "was originally peopled by a branch of the Caucasian race" and that "the complexion of the Egyptians did not differ from that of the other Caucasian races." In a compelling response, Frederick Douglass, in "The Claims of the Negro Ethnologically Considered" (1854), attacked Morton and his followers while asserting "a near relationship between the present enslaved and degraded negroes, and the ancient highly civilized and wonderfully endowed Egyptians." (As discussed in chapter 4 below, during the 1880s Douglass continued to seek out ways of refuting Morton.) Like Douglass, Melville in the closing chapters of *Pierre* underscores the "miscegenated" origins not only of the United States but of Western culture, thereby suggesting the representativeness of Pierre's "blackness." It is in this broader conception of Western culture that Melville extends the racial thematics of *House*. Significantly, in *The Marble Faun* (1860), which, with its use of the Cenci legend, can be taken as a "response" to *Pierre*, Hawthorne extends his own racial thematics, suggesting an alliance with Melville on the question of Egypt when his narrator praises Kenyon for the realism of his sculpture of Cleopatra: "The face was a miraculous success. The sculptor had not shunned to give the full Nubian lips, and other characteristics of the Egyptian physiognomy."[79]

"Out of some past Egypt," Melville writes in *Pierre*, "we have come to this new Canaan" (33). In the image of the blackened hands and darkened "veins" of a particularly heroic American family, a family of Revolutionary descent, Melville poses a Hawthorne-inspired challenge to the genealogies that mean to establish the exceptionalist nature of the "new" republic by separating it from longer racial histories. Etienne Balibar writes that the "symbolic kernel of the idea of race (and of its demographic and cultural equivalents) is the schema of genealogy, that is, quite simply the idea that the filiation of individuals transmits from generation to generation a substance both biological and spiritual and thereby inscribes them in a temporal community known as 'kinship.' "[80] That privileged substance, with respect to Young America's expansionistic United States, was a supposedly divinely favored whiteness, which Melville much more vigorously and explicitly than Hawthorne exposes in his domestic potboiler as having highly precarious historical, cultural, religious, psychological, and biological foundations. By exploring racial matters in domestic fictions, the most popular novelistic mode of the period, Melville and Hawthorne together illuminate the ways in which domesticity was deployed to define and regulate the national "family," distinguishing between the whiteness inside and the "blackness" without. But in their complementary genealogical fictions of the early 1850s, both writers depict racial and, by extension, national identity as incoherent and tottering on the point of collapse, for the blackness "outside" appears to be lodged uneasily inside the homes of the post-Revolutionary generation.

Trappe(d)

Representations of the tangled interracial histories of various genealogical houses, including those of a Revolutionary hero like Thomas Jefferson, were of course also central to the more explicitly antislavery writings of the period. In *Clotel*, for example, published one year after

Pierre, William Wells Brown provides a comic anecdote about Daniel Webster's difficulty in obtaining accommodations because his "dark features" led a landlord "to suppose him a *coloured man*." In the context of the miscegenated histories depicted in *Clotel*, the landlord's misidentification of Webster's "race" may not have been a misidentification after all. It is all the more ironic, Brown suggests, that it should have been a dark-complected person like Webster who had championed the Fugitive Slave Law of 1850, a law that, given Webster's darkness, was potentially just as threatening to him as to fugitive slaves. Similarly, Brown points out in his account of the white slave Salome that in the wake of the Fugitive Slave Law any "white" woman with a tinge of color could also be remanded into slavery. As Brown boldly (and threateningly) titles one of his chapters: "TO-DAY A MISTRESS, TO-MORROW A SLAVE."[81]

The specter of such a dramatic shift in racial identification and social status is at the heart of *The Bondwoman's Narrative*, a novel or narrative written sometime after *The House of the Seven Gables* and *Pierre*, but almost certainly before the Civil War, by a person who signed "herself" Hannah Crafts, who was perhaps a free northern white woman (a "mistress") but more likely a former slave, and who, by the novel's end, presents herself, or her fictional persona, as a kind of mistress. Published for the first time in 2002 in an edition edited by Henry Louis Gates Jr., *The Bondwoman's Narrative* shares many of the gothic tropes and dislocating strategies of *House* and *Pierre* and also the genealogical/racial/ gothic tropes and motifs one finds in much antislavery writing of the period and in at least one British genealogical fiction, Dickens's *Bleak House* (1852–53). Scholars have demonstrated the importance of Dickens to Crafts's literary imagination;[82] I will be arguing that, as with Melville, Crafts's creative reading of Hawthorne had a significant impact on her representation of genealogical houses and bloodlines. As in my discussion of *Pierre*, I will address not only parallels between *Bondwoman's* and *House*, but also Crafts's efforts to extend *House*'s implicating racial thematics. In particular, I focus on her efforts to expose the "hidden streams" and passageways of southern slave culture through the genealogically obsessed Mr. Trappe. For her characterization of the wealthy lawyer Trappe, Crafts drew on the characterization of the predatory Tulkinghorn in Dickens's *Bleak House*. But with his black suit, cane, scholarly proclivities, and sadistic penchant for watching over others, Trappe is perhaps even more compellingly an amalgam of Chillingworth and Judge Jaffrey Pyncheon.

Before considering Trappe, however, an additional remark on *Bond-woman's* Hawthorne connection is in order, for this connection points to the narrative's participation in the debates of the time on expansionism and slavery. Though critics remain uncertain about whether the text should be read as a novel or semifictionalized slave narrative,[83] there is general agreement that one of *Bondwoman's* characters, the North Carolina slave master and aspiring politician Mr. Wheeler, was modeled on the historical John Hill Wheeler, a Democrat from North Carolina who had close ties to Hawthorne's friend Franklin Pierce. In 1853 President Pierce appointed Wheeler secretary to sign land warrants and later that year named him American Minister to Nicaragua. Early in 1854, Wheeler traveled to Nicaragua with his wife and sons, where he became a supporter of the filibusterer William Walker's efforts to seize control of that country. Like the literary nationalist John O'Sullivan, Wheeler admired Walker because he was convinced that adding Nicaragua to the United States was consistent with adding Texas and other territories to the expanding southern slave empire. But because filibustering remained a controversial policy, Wheeler was recalled to Washington, D.C., in 1855. Shortly after his return, three of his slaves escaped with the help of abolitionists. (Gates suspects that one of those slaves, Jane Johnson, may have been "Hannah Crafts"; others disagree.)[84] In a high-profile case, Wheeler won a ruling in a federal court that upheld his property rights to the slaves, but they remained in hiding and he was never able to reclaim them.[85]

In *Bondwoman's*, the character Wheeler is presented not as an office-holder but as an office seeker, and a failed one at that. One reason that he fails is that he is believed to be "black." Enraged by her husband's inability to obtain a patronage position, Mrs. Wheeler lashes out at the office seekers of the time: "They want a secretaryship, they want a clerkship, they want to be foreign ministers, they want to be consuls, they want to be Governors of Territories, they want a Custom House appointment [!] and if nothing better offer they will gladly accept even a commission to keep Lights, or attend the mail."[86] Enlarging her criticism, she then mocks the expansionist ambitions of the nation's leaders: "They would build new ships and hire new steamers, they would go to war and make peace[,] they would take Cuba, or Canada, or Dominica, they would have a rail-road to the Pacific, and ship Canal across the Isthmus, they would quell the Indians and oust the Mormon" (197). The main requirement, or legitimation, for all this empire building, as becomes clear when Wheeler's "blackness" does him in, is whiteness—whiteness secures all. In this larger context of U.S. empire, let us turn to Crafts's and Trappe's respective (and very Hawthornean) plumbing of bloodlines.

Trappe is introduced at a crucial genealogical moment early in the novel, when the current master of the Lindendale plantation in Virginia, where the first-person narrator Hannah is a house slave, brings his new bride home. (Neither the master nor mistress are ever given names; and because the character Hannah is only called Hannah, I will use "Hannah" when I am emphasizing the role of the character and "Crafts" when I am emphasizing the role of the writer who created "Hannah.") Like Pierre with respect to Isabel, Hannah is intrigued by the mistress's "mystery," the sense that there is "something indefinable about her" (29). But she is equally intrigued by Trappe, an old man dressed in black who remains perpetually by the mistress's side. Like Chillingworth, Trappe is an elderly scholar who is most at home among "books and papers" (35), who has been spurned by a younger woman (the lady herself, who refused to marry him), and who seems driven by a sadistic desire for revenge. Hawthorne describes Chillingworth as "delving among [Dimmesdale's] principles, prying into his recollections, and probing every thing with a cautious touch, like a treasure-seeker in a dark cavern."[87] Crafts similarly describes Trappe as having "spent his life in hunting, delving, and digging into family secrets, and when he has found them out he becomes ravenous for gold" (45).

The family secret that Trappe has apparently discerned is that the mistress is "black," which would mean that should she successfully pass as white and produce an heir, the house of Lindendale would by the culture's definition of such matters be blackened. The mistress herself reveals to the sympathetic Hannah that the "shadow darkening her life" (34) is precisely that of race. According to the mistress, at the time of her birth there were parallel female births at the plantation, and when the white infant died, the black nurse took the newly born "black" baby girl—the present white mistress—and put her "by her lady's side, when that Lady was to[o] weak and sick and delirious to notice that the dead was exchanged for the living" (44). (The cradle-switching motif of Crafts's unpublished novel presciently anticipates similar motifs in Lydia Maria Child's *A Romance of the Republic* [1867] and Mark Twain's *The Tragedy of Pudd'nhead Wilson* [1894].) Such was the entanglement of white and black families on the plantation that both babies appeared white to the eye, and thus, according to her story, no one noticed the switch, not even the father. Somehow, though, Trappe discovered the switch by studying family papers at the time of the father's death.

But has Trappe really discerned the truth in the shadows? Hannah pursues this question by skeptically asking the mistress: "Can you be certain that his information is correct . . . and that he does not merely seek to torment and trouble you?" (44). The mistress concedes that there is only one thing "wanting to complete the chain of evidence, and that is the testimony of an old woman, who it seems was my mother's nurse, and who placed me in her lady's bed" (44). This is a rather significant missing piece of testimonial evidence, and the ambiguities raised by the lack of evidence are worthy of *Pierre* (and "A Select Party"). Nonetheless, as the mistress tells Hannah, Trappe "confirmed" the fact of the mistress's blackness when, several years earlier, he showed her a portrait of a slave named Susan, whom the mistress views as an image of herself, even "though I have never sate [sat] for my likeness to be taken" (47). Just as Phoebe and Hepzibah see in the portrait of Colonel Pyncheon the congruent identities of the founder of the Pyncheon house and his distant descendant Judge Jaffrey Pyncheon, the mistress sees in the portrait of Susan her own congruent identity with a predecessor and concludes that she is under Trappe's control. Refusing to be humbled, "exposed," and enslaved, the mistress eventually makes her escape from Trappe in the same way that Dimmesdale escapes from Chillingworth, through a dramatically willed death that is portrayed as a form of victory: "A gleam of satisfaction shone over her face. There was a gasp, a struggle, a slight shiver of the limbs and she was free" (100).

In the haunting Trappe, then, there is a disturbing mix of sadistic will to power, knowledge, and greed. As a "black" man in white culture, he himself seems haunted, and there are indications in the repeated mentions of his "keen black eyes" (63) and black clothes that his knowledge of racial entanglement is a form of self-knowledge, that he knows whereof he speaks. Crafts ultimately presents the knowledgeable Trappe as a figure of terror—he who (in the manner of the genealogical fictionalist) exposes the instability, fluidity, and uncertainty of a culture that bases itself on rigid racial dichotomies and binaries; and he who threatens to reveal to white culture that which it already knows about itself and strives to suppress: "Many and many are the family secrets" that the genealogical seeker can "unravel" (98). Nowhere is the tension between knowledge and suppression more apparent than in the novel's opening chapters describing the founding of the house of Lindendale—the very house whose "purity" Trappe would seem to have preserved in all its whiteness through his exposure of the mistress. And it is here that we can see the decisive influence of Hawthorne's *House* on Crafts's own novel of divided houses.

Prior to the actual arrival of Trappe and the bridal party at the house of Lindendale, Crafts, through Hannah, provides a lengthy description of the founding of both the physical and genealogical house. As in Hawthorne's *House*, the two foundings go hand in hand. Like Colonel Pyncheon, the Hawthornean-sounding Sir Clifford De Vincent, the founding patriarch of Lindendale, establishes a house with a mission similar to Colonel Pyncheon's (and the house of Glendinning): to perpetuate what he believes are his family's "better" white bloodlines. As in *House*, portraits are crucial to the genealogical imperatives of the founder. When he first formally occupies the house, Sir Clifford hangs his and his wife's portraits in the mansion's main drawing room, and, like Colonel Pyncheon, he pronounces "a severe malediction against the person who should ever presume to remove them, and against any possessor of the mansion who being of his name and blood should neglect to follow his example" (15). Insisting upon the conjunction of name and blood, Clifford wants the iconic display of husbands and wives to attest to the untroubled transmission of the founder's putatively pure white blood through successive generations. His wishes would seem to have been fulfilled, for "each inheritor had contributed to the adornments of the drawing-room a faithful transcript of his person and lineaments, side by side with that of his Lady" (16). Hannah's description of the painting of a representative mother/bride shows how the gallery appears to be serving its purpose: "Over the pale pure features of a bride descends a halo of glory; the long shining locks of a young mother waver and float over the child she holds; and the frozen cheek of an ancient dame seems beguiled into smiles and dimples" (16).

But perhaps these smiles denote something other than happiness, something other than transmission of purity. For as Hannah describes the portrait gallery's visual proclamation of "pale pure" whiteness, she notes in the gallery's portraits, in the manner of Pierre gazing at the chair portrait of his father, a "shadow flitting past through the gloom" (15). Describing herself as "standing face to face with their pictured resemblances and looking into the stony eyes motionless and void of expression as those of an exhumed corpse" (16), she is interrupted by the white housekeeper, who brusquely asks what she is doing in the gallery. "Looking at the pictures" (17), Hannah declares, to which the housekeeper replies: "[A]s if such an ignorant thing as you are would know any thing about them" (17).

But she *does* know something more about them, which helps to explain her visual interrogation; specifically, she knows that behind the portraits lurks a crime that the official portraits cannot completely conceal as long as rumor—which also helps to disclose unofficial histories in *House*—holds sway.[88] As Hannah reveals, the portrait gallery of Lindendale is not the only site at or near the house that marks family genealogy. The family tree, the linden planted by Sir Clifford when he, like Colonel Pyncheon, "planted" his genealogical house, also evokes that history, but from the very different perspective of the slaves. That history, similar to what is hinted at in the account of Pierre's paternal grandfather, is the history of the violent entanglement of master and slave, a violence that speaks not only to the physical cruelty of the master but also to the tenuous basis of the master's white house.

As in *House* (and *Pierre*), there are two genealogical lines, in this case the white masters and the black slaves, which have become entangled because of the "sins of the fathers." The story seems relatively simple: at around the time that Sir Clifford established his portrait gallery, he tied the elderly slave Rose and her beloved dog to the linden tree because Rose had refused to drown her dog. The language that he uses to order this punishment parallels Colonel Pyncheon's demonizing of Matthew Maule: "Now take this old witch, and her whelp and gibbet them alive on the Linden" (22). After six days of suffering, both Rose and her dog die. The story of Sir Clifford's torture-murder of Rose is as much a primal first "portrait" of the genealogical house/tree as the idealized portraits in the mansion's gallery. Significantly, Hannah asserts that though the portrait gallery tells the family history to the public, it is the linden that tells the family history to the slaves: "The servants all knew the history of that tree" (20). And the story is not so simple after all.

In an account that may have sources in Frederick Douglass's description in *Narrative* (1845) of the beating of his Aunt Hester and/or Stowe's description in *Uncle Tom's Cabin* (1852) of Cassy's tangled sexual history, Crafts portrays the close connection between the master's physical and sexual violence against slave women, a violence that casts its shadow over the family tree (represented by both the linden and the portrait gallery). According to the narrator, the linden, literally the family tree, "had its roots . . . manured with human blood. Slaves had been tied to its trunk" (20). The suggestive talk of black blood mixing into the family tree points to the sexually violative nature of the entanglement between Clifford and Rose. Rose had been the nurse of Clifford's son, hinting at her possible maternal relation, and she herself had had a daughter, hinting at Clifford's possible paternal relation. When the daughter becomes older, she is sold into slavery in Alabama, and the aggrieved Rose attaches herself to the dog that had been her daughter's pet, with the dog becoming "to her what a grandchild is to many aged females" (22). Given this history, we can read Clifford's order that she drown her "grandchild" as suggesting the possibility that Sir Clifford had raped not only Rose but also her daughter, thereby producing a granddaughter that Clifford or his wife would have wanted killed at birth in order to preserve the purity of the house (and also to protect the family from the threat of light-complected baby swapping that may have occurred with the new mistress). Whatever the facts of this occluded history of entanglement, Rose refuses the master's orders and is bound to the tree, along with the dog. In Hawthorne's *House*, Matthew Maule, just before his execution, proclaims about Colonel Pyncheon (and by implication the house of Pyncheon): "God will give him blood to drink!"[89] Just before her death, Rose makes a similar curse on Clifford's genealogical house: "I will hang here till I die as a curse to this house, and I will come here after I am dead to prove its bane" (25). Blood is important to this curse as well, for Rose in crucial respects "appears" as the blood that remains veiled by the portraits, the blood that Trappe discerns coming from outside the house of Lindendale in the form of the new mistress, the blood that, appropriately enough (given *Bondwoman's* important source in *House*), streams from the master's self-inflicted "ghastly wound in his throat" (74) when he learns that his wife is "black," and the blood that will be revealed as permeating the "roots" and "branches" of Lindendale in the later story of the Cosgroves.

Before turning to the Cosgroves, however, we should consider the intervening account of the Wheelers in Washington, D.C., which, precisely because of its setting in the federal city, presents a more fully national vision of racial haunting and instability than we get in *House*. It is significant that Hannah observes Trappe in Washington watching over the nation's capital in his "coat of seedy black" (158) and that their encounter should occur shortly after she purchases a fashionable whitening powder for her new mistress, Mrs. Wheeler (as if Trappe, in watching over the scene, somehow knows better about "whiteness"). That powder, which promises to remove all facial markings that even hint at blackness, provides one of the fine comic moments in the novel. Like the white women on display in the Lindendale portrait gallery, the white women of the District aspire to present themselves (to invoke *Pierre*) as "without blemish, unclouded, snow-white, and serene."[90] Described as having "tangled" (149) curly hair (in the novel a marker of blackness),[91] Mrs. Wheeler applies the "very fine, soft, and white" (165) powder to her face before journeying across town to appeal to a government administrator for a civil-service position for her husband. Failing in her quest, she returns a transformed woman. Hannah remarks: "[T]he servant admitted a lady, who came directly to Mrs. Wheeler's apartment. I was greatly surprised; for though the vail, the bonnet, and the dress were those of that lady, or exactly similar, the face was black" (165). Or as Mr. Wheeler more directly puts it to his wife: "Your face is black as Tophet" (166).

The transformation of Mrs. Wheeler from white to black has parallels in Hawthorne's description of the swarthy Judge Pyncheon and in Melville's descriptions of various Glendinning blackenings. It is also strikingly similar to the scene in Frank J. Webb's *The Garies and Their Friends* when the white supremacist George Stevens is subjected to racist ridicule after he is tarred by street toughs.[92] The reader wants Stevens to learn from his sufferings about the contingencies of race and the hardships facing the free blacks of Philadelphia, but instead he removes the tar, reasserts his whiteness, and renews his efforts to foment a murderous riot in black neighborhoods. Similarly, the reader wants the racist Mrs. Wheeler to gain some sympathetic wisdom from what Crafts punningly terms "A Turn of the Wheel" (157). Instead, she lashes out at her slave Hannah for failing to warn her that a vengeful chemist had put into circulation a powder that would "blacken the whitest skin" (167). Furious at her husband's attempts to defend Hannah, Mrs. Wheeler states: "Slaves generally are far preferable to wives in husbands' eyes" (167). If that is the case, as suggested by the novel's hidden history of Lindendale, then over time "white" and "black" would lose their distinctive biological meanings, and the ideological defense of slavery and the ideological concept of the United States as a white nation simply would not make any sense. That is also the implication of the story of the Cosgroves that the Lindendale's house slave Lizzy subsequently tells Hannah when she meets her in Washington, D.C.

According to Lizzy, Cosgrove, the new master of Lindendale, is "haunted" (171) because he feels responsible for having killed his wife. But the person in Lizzie's story who is most haunted is Cosgrove's English aristocratic wife, proud of what she would like to believe is the pure white "English and aristocratic blood in her veins" (175). Like the English aristocratic wife of Holgrave's story of Alice Pyncheon, Mrs. Cosgrove lives in a house of blackness. And as in *House*, the passages of her house are analogized to what Hawthorne terms "passages of family history." In search of Clifford and clues as to what has been transpiring at the House of the Seven Gables, Hepzibah "trode along the foot-worn passages and opened one crazy door after another,"[93] only to find nothing and learn nothing. Crafts's Mrs. Cosgrove, by contrast, discovers something crucial about family passages when she opens closed doors in the house's "remotest corners" (179). Wandering through "long galleries and winding passages" (178), she eventually comes to a "door that seemed to be fastened within" (179). Pushing it open, she discovers the family secrets that arguably have a history going back to Sir Clifford's founding of Lindendale: white-to-the-eye "black" children, specifically "two boys, with round fat cheeks, great blue eyes, and plump little hands, quite as beautiful and fresh and healthy as if the most favored lady in the land had been their mother" (182)—the sons of her husband and a light-complected slave woman.

There are other "white" children—passages and doors without end—and all are the issue of Cosgrove's violative unions with his female slaves. Attempting to rid her house of blackness by expelling the slave woman and her two boys, Mrs. Cosgrove has a violent encounter with her husband that leaves her seriously injured. Shortly thereafter, in an oddly sentimental turn, she discovers religion and forgives her husband before succumbing to her injuries. But the reconciliation cannot hide the truth that this genealogical house has failed to achieve the vision of its founder. Exposed by the slaves, Sir Clifford is now exposed by his heirs. Accordingly, in a scene that draws on *House*, the linden is cut down and the portraits tumble from the walls within, finding a fate similar to Colonel Pyncheon's.

The fall of the house of Lindendale raises large questions, similar to those that drove the probing Mrs. Cosgrove mad, about whether there are any "whites" to be found in the South. That is precisely the white racial nightmare informing the account of Trappe's death near the end of the novel. Ironically, the fugitive slave Hannah overhears the story of Trappe's "assassination" (232) as recounted by slave traders who are delighting in his death. They regard Trappe, and not themselves, as having "no principle" (232), for as one of the traders remarks: "[H]e would not have hesitated a moment to sell his own mother into slavery could the case have been made clear that she had African blood in her veins. No blood-hound was ever keener in scenting out the African taint than that old man" (232). The image of the genealogical investigator as "blood-hound" is telling here, given that the novel also portrays actual blood-hounds in pursuit of fugitive slaves. As a Chillingworth-like bloodhound, Trappe pursues fugitives not through swamps, rivers, and forests, but through paper trails of blood. Crucially, those he pursues are always the culture's "whites." The implied concern of the slave traders is that someone as skilled in genealogical history as Trappe may well have the ability to discover the papers that would raise questions about *any* mother's racial identity. In the world of Trappe (as in the world of the genealogical fictionalist), no "white" is safe. Thus the traders are pleased that the sons and brothers of formerly "white" women have taken revenge on the man who consigned their relatives to slavery, shooting Trappe in the brain. No longer need southerners fear that Trappe will visit their houses! And well they should have been fearful, for *Bondwoman's* has failed to depict one convincing instance of a racially unmixed family. The destabilizing work of Crafts and Trappe would seem to go hand in hand.[94]

In this respect, it is ironic that while Hannah presents various women with whom she experiences a sense of solidarity, the character she most resembles in the novel is Trappe. Like Trappe, she has "a silent unobtru-sive way of observing things and events, and wishing to understand them better than I could" (5); like Trappe, she watches over characters as she attempts to discern their (racial) identities, and she experiences a certain gratification in her powers of surveillance. Hannah presents herself as someone who needs to use the tools of a Trappe to resist his traps. But even apart from Trappe, she reveals herself, on the order of Hawthorne's Holgrave, as someone who takes great pleasure in uncovering the secrets of others. For example, during the short period of her enslavement at the Henry plantation, she becomes obsessed with watching the behavior of the newly betrothed slaves Charlotte and William, convinced that William, who lives on another plantation, has been visiting the house at night. She wants to know more: "I determined at once to fathom the mystery." She secretly follows Charlotte, admitting to her readers that she never asked herself "by what right I presumed to interfere with the secrets of a house where I was myself admitted only by tolerance" (134), even as she feels unease at "the use, or necessity, or even the expediency of my instituting an espionage on the actions of one every way my equal, per-haps my superior." When she finds that Charlotte is harboring the escaped William, she reveals the information to Mrs. Henry, despite her "conscience of cruelty and wrong" (136) in betraying these slaves. It is the antislavery slave owner Mrs. Henry who decides not to meddle; and it is Hannah who seems cruel when she rejects Charlotte and William's appeal to join them in their escape.

Attempting to present herself as anything but cruel, Hannah regularly announces the importance of religion to her character, and her ability to experience, as she puts it, "a manner of sympathy and consideration for every one" (11). But the power of sympathy, even at its most benevolent, is also somewhat Trappe-like, based as it is on the sympathizer's assumption that by virtue of a superior kind of imagination he or she can know the other.[95] Moreover, as we have seen in the case of Charlotte and William, there are limits to Hannah's sympathy.

Hannah's most disturbing failure of sympathy comes near the end of the novel, when the Wheelers return to their North Carolina plantation and Hannah confronts head-on the putatively large gap between house and field slaves. The field slaves, she says, "toil beneath the burning sun, scarcely conscious that any link exists between themselves and other portions of the human race," and thus possess a "mental condition" that can be "briefly summed up in the phrase that they know nothing" (200). She asserts that the house slaves, by contrast, are "of a higher and nobler order than those belonging to the fields" (202). Like Frederick Douglass and many other antislavery writers, Crafts allows that "[d]egradation, neglect, and ill treatment had wrought on them [the field slaves] its legitimate effects" (200); but her insistence on such absolute differences between the two groups of slaves is surprisingly extreme. It is at its most extreme when Mrs. Wheeler vindictively expels her from the plantation house and attempts to force her to become the wife of the field slave Bill. Hannah describes herself as experiencing "horror unspeakable" at the thought of being "doomed to association with the vile, foul, filthy inhabitants of the huts, and condemned to receive one of them for my husband" (205).

Hannah's revulsion at the field slaves will no doubt become one of the critical cruxes of *Bondwoman's*. As Gates remarks somewhat defensively in his introduction to the novel, the revulsion makes good sense in terms of class and gender issues. Hannah expresses her outrage at the prospect of "marriage" to Bill, asserting that marriage should be "voluntarily assumed" (205). An involuntary marriage prescribed by a slave owner, Gates rightly notes, would constitute a form of rape, and he remarks on this scene: "Rarely, if ever, in the literature created by ex-slaves has the prospect of rape, and the gap in living conditions between house and field, been put more explicitly and squarely."[96] But I wonder if that gap hasn't also been put melodramatically to the service of Crafts's own racial anxieties. Given that the novel has heretofore focused on a history of white masters raping their slaves, why hadn't Hannah expressed revulsion or fear at the prospect of one of her white owners sexually violating her? Does she regard a black rapist as worse than a white rapist? Or perhaps that is not really the main issue here. For having made her point about the forcible nature of the marriage, Crafts nonetheless has Hannah describe the situation at Bill's cabin in language that deflects attention onto other matters as well. The paragraph is worth quoting in full:

> Bill's cabin was in the midst of the range of huts, tenanted by the workers in the fields. In front was a large pool of black mud and corrupt water, around which myriads of flies and insects were whirling and buzzing. I went in, but such sights and smells as met me I cannot describe them. It was reeking with filth and impurity of every kind, and already occupied by near a dozen women and children, who were sitting on the ground, or coiled on piles of rags and straw in the corner. They regarded me curiously as I entered, grinned with malicious satisfaction that I had been brought down to their level, and made some remarks at my expense; while the children kicked, and yelled, and clawed at each other, scratching each other's faces, and pulling each other's hair I stumbled to a bench I supposed designed for a seat, when one of the woman [sic] arose, seized me by the hair, and without ceremony dragged me to the ground, gave me a furious kick and made use of highly improper and indecent language. Bill, who had retired to the outside of the hut, hearing the noise of the fray came hastily in. It was his turn then. He commenced beating her with a hearty good-will, and she scratched and bit him, furiously. In the rough and tumble they knocked over two or three of the children, besides treading on the toes of some of the women, who irritated by the pain started up and joined the contest which soon became general. (208–9)

However much Crafts might wish to attribute the "reeking" filth to the degradation forced upon enslaved blacks by whites, she seems to discern in the cabin something essentially repulsive about the character of the cabin's inhabitants. But what is especially noteworthy here is that Hannah's revulsion seems focused less on Bill than on the dozen or so black women who immediately want to pummel her. She fears that she will become like these women, and those fears are precisely what Mrs. Wheeler had played upon when she banished Hannah to the fields in the first place: "With all your pretty airs and your white face, you are nothing but a slave after all, no better than the blackest wench" (205).

That white can be revealed as black is, I have been arguing, central to the trope of haunting that informs *Bondwoman's* and many other genealogical fictions of the 1850s, and that is what makes Trappe—the man who traffics in such revelations—such a central and frightening figure. The possibility of white being revealed as black is also one of *Bondwoman's* informing anxieties, and I want to suggest the possibility that Crafts may be tapping into these anxieties not only to undermine the ideological premises of white supremacy but also because these are fears that she herself possesses. I am aware that this is a potentially troubling claim that cannot be easily supported, given that we can be certain about very little (actually, nothing) about the "black" Crafts. But the disgust at blackness near the end of the book, when compared to Hannah's seeming obliviousness to the threat posed to her body by her white masters, seems out of proportion, as if she has discovered the nightmare of slavery in the slaves themselves and thus wants to resist the obvious fact that, as underscored by Mrs. Wheeler's taunting, she is one of them.

To be sure, when Hannah undertakes her eventual escape from slavery (and the field slaves) by masquerading as a white man, she does offer sympathy and assistance along the way to two blacks, Jacob and his sister, who are attempting to escape from a South Carolina slave plantation. But before her relationship to these fugitive slaves is put to much of a test, the sister dies and Jacob is shot while trying to steal a boat. At which point Hannah's former religious mentor, the white Aunt Hetty, takes her in and eventually sends her off to find refuge in a black community in New Jersey. In the happy final chapter, Hannah talks of how the "hand of providence" (237) also guided to the same community her mother and the former slaves she had once betrayed, Charlotte and William. Hannah has married an ordained Methodist preacher and has fulfilled her dreams in every way: "I found a life of freedom all my fancy had pictured it to be. I found the friends of the slave in the free state just as good as kind and hospitable as I had always heard they were. I dwell now in a neat little Cottage, and keep a school for colored children" (237).[97]

A happy ending, yes, but a disconcerting ending, too, completely inconsistent with the more troubled and ambivalent accounts we have of "freedom" at the end of Douglass's *Narrative*, Harriet Jacobs's *Incidents*, Harriet Wilson's *Our Nig*, and perhaps most pertinently, Webb's *The Garies and Their Friends*. *Garies* concludes with a happy marriage and group gathering of free blacks and their white abolitionist friends, though with the disturbing suggestion of black vulnerability in racist Philadelphia, as the half-crazed Mr. Ellis, the victim of white vigilantes, remains on the lookout for "another mob."[98] In *Bondwoman's*, the short interlude with Jacob and his sister and the closing chapter in New Jersey seem intended to counterbalance the fear and loathing of blackness expressed by Hannah (and Crafts) in Bill's cabin. But the concluding chapter's untroubled celebration of black uplift, "goodness," "undeviating happiness" (239), religious regeneration, and interracial harmony reads more like a white abolitionist fantasy than an affirmation of black community. Or perhaps we should simply read the ending as a final bow to Hawthorne, whose *House* also ends on a disconcertingly upbeat note. In that spirit, we can note that the final sentence of *Bondwoman's* invokes the collaborative nature of romance in a Hawthornean mode: "I will let the reader picture it all to his imagination and say farewell" (239).

WHATEVER ONE MAKES OF HANNAH'S ANXIETIES about being linked with the black field slaves, the ending of *The Bondwoman's Narrative* does emphasize a politics of black community. Such a politics also informs the story of the bloody linden tree central to the novel's representation of genealogical haunting, the story passed on by the slaves at Lindendale (and sympathetically passed on by Hannah). And yet because we do not know the "real" Hannah Crafts, it is ultimately impossible to make categorical claims about her own racial politics, affiliations, and anxieties, and because the novel was not published until 2002, we cannot make claims about reception and influence that would help to support particular cultural and literary readings. What are the differences, then, between reading *Bondwoman's* as the first novel written by a formerly enslaved African American woman and reading it as a novel by, say, a white abolitionist woman (or man) with extensive knowledge of the life histories of formerly enslaved African American women (and of Hawthorne)? The differences would seem to be profound. But are they? For one of the oddly disconcerting aspects of *Bondwoman's*—disconcerting insofar as Crafts seems to have anticipated the dilemmas of racial-identity politics with such prescience—is the way that it can trap its bookish, Trappe-like readers who insist on working with fixed racial categories in order to establish "authentic" identities. *Bondwoman's* suggests the intellectual limits of reading and conceiving of identity in this way, making it difficult to see the great difference between the scholar combing the archives in an effort to establish Crafts's "blackness" and a genealogical archivist like Trappe intent on disclosing whites' "blackness," even with the obvious differences in historical circumstances and motives. To put this differently, for I do not want to underestimate the value of attempting to learn more about the historical Crafts: the novel works to suggest that locating Crafts's race, as it were, ought not to make such a difference, particularly in the way that the figure of Trappe suggests the invidious implications of identifying race so categorically. In the novel, race itself becomes a trap, and thus one of the great values of having a newly discovered antebellum work that is to some extent "un-raced" is that it frees us from some of the traps, or Trappes, of our own contemporary moment.[99]

By focusing this chapter on Hawthorne's influence as a genealogical fictionalist, I have been attempting to challenge some of the analogous traps of the increasingly pervasive criticism in which Hawthorne has come to serve in almost allegorical fashion as the representative literary white racist of the antebellum period. Such an approach locks Hawthorne into predictable narratives of racism, Manifest Destiny, and imperialism and consequently robs his texts of a sociocritical dimension that, ironically enough, could be directed against Hawthorne himself (there is perhaps no sharper criticism of Hawthorne the racist than Hawthorne's own genealogical fictions). Hawthorne's Democratic politics are far more complicated than his Franklin Pierce campaign biography would suggest, and it is worth noting that in his own time he was admired by such feminist-abolitionists as Jane Grey Swisshelm, Amelia Bloomer, Grace Greenwood, and Charlotte Forten.[100] Though it is undeniably true that he, like a number of progressive thinkers of the period, was skeptical of political abolitionism, Hawthorne did some hard thinking on race and nation, and that thinking had an impact on Melville, Crafts, and perhaps other writers of the 1850s who themselves engaged the challenge of (dis)locating race and nation. Melville's and Crafts's respective occupations of Hawthorne's *House* help us to recover the Hawthorne who troubled many of the "certainties" trumpeted by his culture, including the idea that the U.S. nation should be understood, legitimated, and celebrated for its "pure" and superior whiteness. That may be the willed and expedient vision of Colonel and Judge Pyncheon and some of Hawthorne's Young America contemporaries, but it is not the vision that prevails in Hawthorne's most searching genealogical fictions.

Whiteness theorists such as Alexander Saxton, David Roediger, and Michael Ignatiev have presented the 1840s and 1850s as a time when whites were convinced of the superior value of whiteness and its essential difference from blackness. As Shelly Streeby has recently summed up the conclusions of these theorists: "[W]hiteness took hold as a unifying national and transcontinental structure of feeling."[101] But how unifying and transcontinental was such a notion? Were Hawthorne, Melville, and the possibly white Crafts among the lone dissenters, seeing whiteness as a troubled fiction that ultimately failed to unify across sectional, class, and gender lines, or were they tapping into a generally unacknowledged recognition (a political unconscious) of the limits of whiteness as a unifying or legitimating constituent of the nation? I would suggest that the latter may well be the case, and that from this perspective Hawthorne, Melville, Crafts, and other genealogical fictionalists of the 1850s could be regarded as surprisingly representative chroniclers of the pervasive cultural doubts about the meaningfulness of race as a defining mark of the nation's past, present, and future.

At the very least, genealogical fictionalists addressed broad concerns about a "structure of feeling" that may well have been more a structure of anxiety about how adding to the nation's total population of peoples of color through the expansion of slavery and the taking of considerable parts of Mexico made U.S. whites increasingly "perplexed," as Henry Highland Garnet remarked in his 1848 lecture *The Past and Present Condition, and the Destiny, of the Colored Race*, "in deciding where to draw the line between the Negro and the Anglo-Saxon." Because of the interracial sexuality that inevitably accompanied colonialism and expansionism, Garnet, as noted earlier in the chapter, thought the signs were right for the emergence of a "blacker" America. Thus at the very moment that he was despairing about the inevitability of Mexico becoming "annexed to this union," he was also able to imagine U.S. expansionism as bringing about the eventual end of white supremacy and "the triumph of freedom in the hemisphere."[102] Approaching matters from a very different political perspective, Frederick Douglass during the early 1870s similarly came to regard U.S. expansionism into the southern Americas as an opportunity to move beyond "race" and to bring about greater freedom in the hemisphere. But this was just one of several episodes in Douglass's hemispheric literary nationalism.

4

Frederick Douglass's
Hemispheric Nationalism, 1857–1893

This chapter takes as its starting point a little-known column, "The Colored People and Hayti," that Frederick Douglass printed in the January 1861 issue of his *Douglass' Monthly*. Announcing that the Haitian government had recently appointed James Redpath as its general emigration agent, Douglass provides the address of the office, 221 Washington Street in Boston, for those African Americans who wish to gain "necessary information" about the possibilities of emigrating to Haiti. During 1853–54, when Martin Delany and his supporters were advocating black emigration to the southern Americas, Douglass would occasionally print pro-emigration columns in his newspaper only to rebut them. Much had changed by 1861. As Douglass notes in the same piece, he had published a number of essays, official documents, and letters on Haitian emigration over the past several months, and "we notice that nearly all of our exchanges are favoring the movement." Consistent with this trend, Douglass subsequently inserts into his column an article from the *Worcester Spy* in which the writer contemplates the persistence of slavery in the United States, decries the "inhuman legislation" that "trample[s] out all of the few rights the free colored population have hitherto enjoyed," and then turns his eyes to the southern Americas and offers a prophecy on race and empire:

We believe the inevitable logic of events points plainly to the ultimate growth in the equatorial regions of the American continent, of an empire controlled by the mixed races of African blood. The islands of the American Archipelago are to-day virtually in possession of that mixed race. In all of the British West Indies the white population are vanishing—so with the other islands. Cuba, though now in the possession of slavery, is fast becoming Africanized, and must ultimately pass into the hands of a free colored race. St. Domingo, or Hayti, as it is more properly called, is governed by the colored race. The eastern or Spanish part is under the government of the Dominican Republic, and the western under that of the Haytian, administered by its present enlightened head, President Fabre Geffrard. These republics have maintained their independence for nearly seventy years, and have secured a recognition of their nationality from all the principal governments of the civilized world, with the solitary exception of this Union.[1]

Rather than undermine this prophecy, Douglass prints in the same issue a "Call for Emigration" released by F. E. Dubois, a black Philadelphian who recently had become Haiti's secretary of the interior, along with a column entirely authored by himself, "Emigration to Hayti," in which he admiringly describes Redpath at his Boston emigration office. Remarking that there are many good reasons for African Americans to consider emigrating to Haiti, Douglass offers a surprisingly upbeat assessment and even endorsement of the movement: "Let every emigrant go to Hayti with the purpose to give the country his best energies, and we will be bound that the country will take care of him and fulfill his highest expectations."[2]

Arguably, Douglass's apparent support of selective African American emigration to the black republic of Haiti has much to do with his long-standing concerns about U.S. whites' efforts to expand slavery into the Southern Hemisphere. In one of his initial columns in the *North Star*, he had attacked the "horrid conflict" with Mexico as a brazen effort to enlarge the domain of U.S. slavery, and he regularly warned in the *North Star* and *Frederick Douglass' Paper* that the United States, under pressure from southern slave owners, was "whetting his talons for the capture of Cuba." Following South Carolina congressman Preston Brooks's vicious caning of Massachusetts senator Charles Sumner in the chambers of Congress in May 1856, Douglass declared that the South's overarching goal was "to make Slavery national, so that the rule of the South shall become the rule of the North," and then he voiced an even greater apprehension about southerners' imperial ambitions: "They purpose to plant Slavery in South America, to overthrow the Black government of Hayti; and possess themselves of the West Indian islands, and to reduce this whole continent to the rule of slavery."[3] In the context of this specter of a white southern slave empire in the Americas, Douglass's reprinting in the January 1861 *Douglass' Monthly* of a writer envisioning an "African" empire in the southern Americas could be taken as a form of desire, conveying his hope that the slaveocracy would be met with spirited and united black resistance.

Or perhaps his interest in Haitian emigration suggests an aspect of Douglass's thinking that has heretofore been overlooked by Douglass's biographers: the importance of the Southern Hemisphere to his conception of an "American" nationality. In the same 1861 essay in which he offers his support to those African Americans contemplating emigration to Haiti, Douglass writes about black nationalism in a way that seems out of keeping with our traditional manner of thinking about Douglass as a U.S. nationalist. Sounding more like his sometimes rival Martin Delany in the aggressive black nationalist mode of "Political Destiny of the Colored Race on the American Continent" (1854), Douglass states:

> [L]et us go to Hayti, where our oppressors do not want us to go, and where our influence and example can still be of service to those whose tears will find their way to us by the waters of the Gulf washing all our shores. Let us be there to help beat back the filibustering invaders from the cotton States, who only await an opportunity to extinguish the island asylum of the deeply-wronged colored race. . . . As the poor slaves march towards the Gulf States in chains, it may be well for the free people identified with them to float towards the same point by sea, carrying with them the settled purpose, a purpose to be taught to their children and their children's children, to play a part in the liberation and elevation of their race.[4]

A Douglass who imagines a unified black nationality in the American hemisphere challenges the conventional view of Douglass as an African American nationalist who regularly sought to link that nationalism with his U.S. nationalism. It also challenges (or supplements) Waldo E. Martin Jr.'s influential account of Douglass as a cosmopolitan whose "ideal nation-state, society, and culture would have been raceless," and Paul Giles's recent account of Douglass as a transatlantic thinker whose British encounters helped him to develop "a transnational, comparative consciousness." Ifeoma Nwankwo is one of the few critics who has studied Douglass in relation to the southern Americas, attending to the ways in which his "relationship to the Black world beyond the U.S. shapes and is shaped by his relationship with Americanness, and his drive for full citizenship for African Americans." Ultimately, though, she sees that relationship as based on Douglass's unyielding commitment to the U.S. nation and thus on his "presumption that the battle for rights or citizenship in the particular national context is incommensurate with the articulation of a transnational notion of community."[5] I will be arguing for an even more capacious, unbounded, and experimental Douglass whose hemispheric imaginings and affiliations, or what I am terming his "hemispheric nationalism," modified, challenged, and at key moments dislocated his U.S. nationalism and pushed him to think more diasporically about race and nation.

There is a hint of this "hemispheric" Douglass in his 1853 novella "The Heroic Slave," which focuses on the actual 1841 slave revolt on the *Creole* led by Madison Washington. Prior to the publication of this work, Douglass had written very little on the southern Americas. He had discussed Mexico in relation to the Mexican War; he had published in the *North Star* several columns on Haiti by a corresponding editor and had himself lambasted "slaveholders and slave traders" for their efforts "to make Haiti appear before the world as feeble, indolent and falling to decay"; and he had offered occasional thoughts on Cuba with the emphasis (as with his writings on Mexico) on the threat posed to that nation by proslavery expansionists. During his 1845–47 tour of Great Britain, he had given several speeches on Madison Washington, celebrating his heroism and bravery in leading the 1841 revolt, but those speeches mostly honored the goodness of the British in offering sanctuary to the rebels in British-controlled Nassau. Douglass's emphasis is rather different in the ending of "The Heroic Slave." According to the white storyteller Tom Grant, when Madison Washington and his coconspirators arrive in Nassau, they are met by "a company of *black soldiers*," who declared that "they did not recognize *persons* as property." Joining with these soldiers, Madison and the former slaves "deliberately gathered up their baggage . . . poured through the gangway,—formed themselves into a procession on the wharf,—bid farewell to all on board, and, uttering the wildest shouts of exultation, they marched, amidst the deafening cheers of a multitude of sympathizing spectators, under the triumphant leadership of their heroic chief and deliverer, MADISON WASHINGTON." As Ivy G. Wilson remarks, the novella thus ends "with a displaced cadre of transnational blacks whose affiliations and affinities are determined less by their reference to the United States than by their relationship to other blacks in the diaspora."[6] Such connections became increasingly important to Douglass during the 1857–93 period.

This chapter looks at three episodes in Douglass's later career: his interest in Haitian emigration circa 1857–61; his support for Santo Domingo annexation circa 1871; and his conjoined interest in Rome and Haiti circa 1886–93. The latter decades of Douglass's career have long been neglected by critics, in large part because the works by Douglass that have achieved canonical status—the *Narrative* (1845), "What to the Slave Is the Fourth of July?" (1852), "The Heroic Slave" (1853), and *My Bondage and My Freedom* (1855)—were all published prior to those years. Though there are some admirers of *Life and Times of Frederick Douglass* (1881; rev. ed. 1892) and many admirers of Douglass's antilynching speech "The Lessons of the Hour" (1894), for most literary scholars Douglass's career in effect ended in 1855. There is also the problem that Douglass's politics after the Civil War, in which he often appears to be functioning as a Republican loyalist, can seem less dramatic and appealing than his earlier work as an abolitionist. The chapter attempts to recover some of the complexities of Douglass's political thinking during the post–Civil War years, including offering a new reading of his advocacy in the early 1870s of Santo Domingo annexation. As I will be arguing, however imperialistic Douglass may appear in pursuing that project, it was tied to his antiracism, inflected by his hemispheric nationalism, and intimately related to his long career as an African American literary nationalist.

In the tradition of Samuel Cornish, John Russwurm, David Walker, and other African Americans interested in the black press, Douglass's own African American literary nationalism was for many years expressed through his editing and circulating of black newspapers. In a column by "Dion" in the 23 September 1853 *Frederick Douglass' Paper*, the contributor laments "that while American literature is rapidly growing into universal appreciation, the name of no colored American has as yet been blazoned upon its rolls of heraldry" and goes on to remark that the best hope for the emergence of such figures is through the nurturing of various literary associations and enterprises "among our people," including newspapers. Douglass shared that view, and in the inaugural 3 December 1847 issue of the *North Star* he spoke of the crucial contributions that black authors, editors, and orators could make to the cause of black elevation: "In the grand struggle for liberty and equality now waging, it is meet, right and essential that there should arise in our ranks authors and editors, as well as orators, for it is in these capacities that the most permanent good can be rendered to our cause."[7] Much of the focus of this chapter on Douglass as a literary nationalist will be on his role as a newspaper editor, though in the final section attention will shift to the role of his autobiographies and speeches in expressing that nationalism. For it is in the revised 1892 *Life and Times of Frederick Douglass* and his late speeches on Haiti that his hemispheric nationalism is most clearly on display.

Writing in a counterfactual mode, Niall Ferguson comments on how (auto)biographers, historians, and critics tend to make sense of the chaos of history by imposing a narrative that achieves coherence by working backwards from an endpoint, as if that end were predetermined. Knowing what is going to happen in the future (of the past) allows for the construction of narratives that move from a particular past moment to a known future outcome in ways that can obscure the possibilities of alternative histories and narratives. But as Ferguson underscores: "The past—like real-life chess, or indeed any other game—is different; it does not have a predetermined end." Nevertheless, he says, the "professional writer writes with an ending in mind," and that "predetermined end" helps to shape the story and give meaning to what was actually much more inchoate and open-ended than such a teleological-driven narrative generally conveys.[8] Ferguson's comments are highly relevant to Douglass, who, like most autobiographers, shaped all three of his autobiographies to give meaning to his life through a sense of their endings. The meanings conveyed in those narratives, determined in large part by endings that underscore Douglass's emergence as an African American leader, have helped to shape subsequent Douglass biographies and have contributed to the neglect of aspects of Douglass's life that fail to fit the framework established by Douglass himself in his autobiographies. As will become apparent, I am particularly suspicious of the biographical value of sections of the 1881 *Life and Times of Frederick Douglass*, given that one of Douglass's goals in that autobiography was to enshrine himself as an African American leader who faithfully worked with the Republican Party. That narrative obscures and elides much of interest in his career running from the late 1850s through the late 1870s. The more revealing final section of the 1892 expansion of *Life and Times* ends with Douglass poised between the United States and Haiti. I move the story forward one more year in order to see what that does to our understanding of Douglass's hemispheric nationalism from 1857 to 1893. The chapter ends with Haiti and it begins with Haiti, which Douglass came to regard with renewed interest in the years immediately following the *Dred Scott* decision of 1857.[9]

In January 1859, Douglass, who had been struggling to meet the demands of his weekly *Frederick Douglass' Paper*, announced a new name for his journal, along with a more leisurely publication schedule. But as elaborated in his editorial comment in the inaugural issue of *Douglass' Monthly*, he continued to regard journalism as the prime sphere for advancing an African American literary nationalism and for challenging whites' persistent notion "that negroes have no patriotism, and no love of letters." Douglass addressed the importance of African American letters in the subsequent issue as well, calling attention to the founding in New York City of the *Anglo-African Magazine*, which he celebrates as the first journal by and for African Americans on literature, science, and statistics. Despite the fact that the New York monthly could be seen as posing a direct challenge to the preeminence of his own monthly, he wishes the editor, Thomas Hamilton, "every success in this praiseworthy effort to promote literature and learning among our people." Both the announcement of the change to *Douglass' Monthly* and his hailing of the advent of the *Anglo-African Magazine* suggest Douglass's ongoing work as an African American literary nationalist, particularly in the way he links "patriotism" to "love of letters." His patriotism would soon be expressed through an embrace of the Civil War as a war against slavery, and by late 1861 the war itself would become the fundamental concern of his monthly. Even during the Civil War years, however, Douglass would continue to call his readers' attention to African American writing, reserving his highest praise for William Wells Brown's *The Black Man, His Antecedents, His Genius, and His Achievements* (1863), which he extolls for making "a valuable contribution to the colored literature of the country," a literature that Douglass says is "destined to grow and increase to far greater strength and volume than any enemy has ever feared, or any friend has ever hoped of the colored man."[10]

Douglass's support for the Union war effort and his continued championing of African American literary nationalism have contributed to the picture that we have, reinforced by his later writings, of Douglass as an unwavering U.S. nationalist who regarded his black literary-nationalist work as a newspaper editor as integral to his work for black uplift in the United States. And yet despite Douglass's retrospective insistence on his steadfast allegiance to the U.S. nation, there is considerable evidence that beginning around 1857 he began to move in the direction of a David Walker or Martin Delany in thinking about race and nation more diasporically. During the 1840s and early 1850s, Douglass had vociferously opposed all colonizationist and emigrationist schemes while fighting for blacks' rights to citizenship in the United States. But with the 1854 Kansas-Nebraska Act's repeal of the provisions of the Missouri Compromise, the upsurge of violence in the Kansas and Nebraska Territories, the hardening in the South of the proslavery position, the increasing sway of white-supremacist racial "science," and the Supreme Court's *Dred Scott* ruling of 1857, Douglass had good reason to wonder about African Americans' future in the United States. David Blight suggests that, even with all of the discouraging developments of the mid- to late 1850s, Douglass sought to repress his doubts and work to improve blacks' situation in the United States because of his "psychological attachment to American nationalism."[11] As my analysis of Douglass circa 1857–61 will suggest, Douglass was not quite as attached to the United States as Blight and others would have it, and during the period 1859–61 in particular he used his monthly to explore the possibility of Haitian emigration.

Biographers' accounts of Douglass's ongoing commitment to an African American nationalism wedded to a U.S. nationalism, despite the pressing problems of the late 1850s, draw on Douglass's own testimony. But it has to be emphasized that Douglass most compellingly testified to his late 1850s and early 1860s faith in the U.S. nation after the fact, in his 1881 *Life and Times of Frederick Douglass*, which has virtually nothing to say about his editorial work for *Douglass' Monthly*. As a Republican appointee who had come under considerable criticism for his supposed mishandling of the Freedman's Savings and Trust Company, Douglass in the 1881 *Life and Times* wanted to present himself as an African American who continued to place his faith in the nation, despite the evident failure of Reconstruction. Thus, given that one of his goals in the autobiography was to depict white racists as disloyal national subjects, he suppressed some key details that could have been construed as evidence of his own seeming disloyalty, such as his pre–Civil War flirtation with Haitian emigration. Douglass's major biographers have generally followed Douglass's lead and said nothing about his interest in Haiti during this period. Blight is an important exception in acknowledging the interest, but he refuses to take it seriously, describing it as a short-term moment in which Douglass "caved in to emigrationism"—as if departing from U.S. nationalism was a weakness.[12] I maintain that an alternative way of regarding Douglass's interest in Haiti is to see it as helping him to enlarge and complicate his perspectives on race, nation, revolution, and the Americas, and as inaugurating a more contestatory, capacious, and complex relation to the American Revolutionary and American nationalist traditions that would continue to inform and complicate the thinking of the "patriotic" Republican Douglass of the post–Civil War years.

In *Life and Times*, Douglass certainly presents himself as dismayed by the sectional conflict on slavery, remarking that "[f]rom 1856 to 1860 the whole land rocked with this great controversy." Because his admiration for John Brown was already well known, he speaks with relative candor about this association, declaring that he knew the man, had talked to him about his various plans for black insurrection, and continues to regard him as one of the "greatest heroes known to American fame." But Douglass also insists in 1881, as he insisted in 1859, that he did not support the assault on Harpers Ferry, not only because it was impractical but also because he could not support a military "attack upon the federal government." It is precisely his continuing commitment to the federal government, or what we might call the nation-state, that he emphasizes in his 1881 recounting of this volatile cultural moment. Consistent with Douglass's desire to present himself as a U.S. nationalist, he portrays himself as having made an instant and unwavering commitment to the presidency of Abraham Lincoln. Thus, despite the fact that he published numerous essays in *Douglass' Monthly* castigating Lincoln for his seeming racism, his willingness to capitulate to the South, and his contemplation of a plan to colonize blacks to the southern Americas, Douglass in the 1881 *Life and Times* depicts the new president as a heroic liberator, celebrating him as a leader who, from the moment he was elected, sought "to exclude slavery from the territories of the United States, . . . with a view to its ultimate extinction."[13]

And yet right around the time of Lincoln's election, Douglass was developing plans to travel to Haiti, and he may well have been contemplating an actual move, whether short- or long-term. Douglass says nothing about this Haitian interest in *Life and Times*. But in an evocative sentence in the 1881 autobiography, he captures quite powerfully the sense of dislocation and despair that he and many other African Americans experienced in the wake of the *Dred Scott* ruling of 1857: "Standing outside the pale of American humanity, denied citizenship, unable to call the land of my birth my country, and adjudged by the Supreme Court of the United States to have no rights which white men were bound to respect, and longing for the end of the bondage of my people, I was ready for any political upheaval which should bring about a change in the existing condition of things."[14] Douglass's allusion to the *Dred Scott* ruling is of particular significance, for it was that ruling, more than anything else, that brought a heightened new concern to African Americans about their future in the United States, concerns that led many African American leaders, including Douglass, to explore the possibility of moving beyond the U.S. nation.

To briefly review the facts of this well-known case: Dred Scott, the slave of army surgeon John Emerson, first sued for his freedom in a St. Louis court in 1846, three years after the death of Emerson, for he remained the property of Emerson's wife. With the help of the sons of Peter Blow, his former owner, Scott argued that because he had lived for two years north of Missouri, in the free state of Illinois, he was entitled to his freedom in terms of the common-law precedent of the 1772 British *Somerset* case and a provision of the Missouri Compromise, both of which suggested that slaves became free by virtue of having lived in a free territory. He and his legal advisors argued for the freedom of his wife on the same grounds, and for his two daughters on the basis of their matrilineal descent from a free person. A St. Louis court declared Scott a free man in 1850, but the decision was appealed, and in 1852 the Missouri Supreme Court overturned the decision, ruling that each state had the authority to determine whether blacks are free or slaves, and that in Missouri they are slaves. Scott appealed the decision, which was upheld in 1854 by a U.S. circuit court, whereupon he appealed to the Supreme Court in the case that became known as *Dred Scott v. Sandford* (Sanford was the brother of Mrs. Emerson; the "d" in the Supreme Court case title was an error). In a 7–2 decision issued shortly after Democrat James Buchanan won the presidential election of 1856, the Court offered a broad ruling that spoke to Chief Justice Roger Taney's desire to adjudicate the issue of slavery in the United States once and for all. Taney and the majority decreed not only that individual states had the right to determine the status of blacks within their borders, but also elaborated the following three large propositions: (1) that Congress had no legal authority to regulate slavery, and that the Missouri Compromise was therefore unconstitutional; (2) that blacks had no constitutional claims to national citizenship, even if they were citizens of individual states (Taney declared that blacks "are not included . . . under the word 'citizens' in the Constitution, and can therefore claim none of the rights and privileges which that instrument provides for and secures to citizens of the United States"); and (3) that blacks, in Taney's notorious and oft-quoted words, were "so far inferior, that they had no rights which the white man was bound to respect."[15]

The Compromise of 1850 had raised a host of concerns among black abolitionists about the nationalizing of slavery, but most free blacks continued to assert that they had reasonably good prospects of one day becoming national citizens. But the *Dred Scott* decision in effect lifted the veil or mask, revealing to the free blacks their utter disfranchisement both in the present and foreseeable future.[16] In African American newspapers, conventions, speeches, and writings of the 1857 to 1863 period in particular, there is marked tonal shift, a despair that had not been expressed nearly as powerfully before about the relation of African Americans to the U.S. nation, a dislodging of the United States from the center of a (black) nationalistic consciousness, a renewal of emigrationist thinking (with specific interests in African and Haitian emigration), and an overall greater willingness, often an *exhilarating* willingness, to challenge the current national formation. Black abolitionist Robert Purvis, who had generally been optimistic about blacks' prospects, militantly declared in a *Dred Scott* speech of May 1857 that "the Government of the United States, in its formation and essential structure as well as in its practice, is one of the basest, most atrocious despotisms that ever saw the face of the sun"; and a year later the generally moderate Charles L. Remond remarked that the *Dred Scott* decision revealed the imperative of dissolving the Union. Around the same time that Still and Purvis were attacking the U.S. government, Martin Delany was developing a plan for African American emigration to the Niger region of Africa, and William Wells Brown and other blacks were looking toward Haiti as a site for a regenerative black nationalism in the Americas. In his 1863 history, *The Black Man*, praised by Douglass in his monthly, Brown celebrates black revolutionary freedom fighters—Dessalines, Denmark Vesey, the Cuban revolutionary poet Placido, Joseph Cinque—who conceived of themselves apart from U.S. national ideologies, and in the most powerful chapter of the book, "A Man Without a Name," presents himself in the wake of *Dred Scott* as a man without national identity, status, or name in the land of his birth. "What country, sir, have I?" he asks. "The Supreme Court of the United States, and the laws of the south, doom me to be a slave of another. There is not a foot of soil over which the *stars and stripes* wave, where I can stand and be protected by law."[17]

Douglass initially appears to be an exception to the despair with U.S. nationalism and the shift to a more violent, revolutionary, and even trans- or postnational discourse that emerged in African American writing and politics during the dislocating post–*Dred Scott* moment. After all, in a speech of May 1857 on the *Dred Scott* decision, he declares that "nothing in the present aspect of the anti-slavery question . . . should drive us into the extravagance and nonsense of advocating a dissolution of the American Union"; and he states as well that "thanks to the slaveholding wing of the Supreme Court, my hopes were never brighter than now." Central to the optimism of that address was his belief, despite the *Dred Scott* ruling, that the Constitution was a fundamentally antislavery document. That belief had helped to generate his break from William Lloyd Garrison in 1851; and in a May 1857 debate with the black Garrisonian Remond, Douglass seemingly willed a blindness to current legal developments in order to sustain his conviction that the Constitution was informed by a "higher law" commitment to the principles of equality as enunciated in the Declaration. In response to Remond's charge that "the Constitution of the United States . . . guarded the hellish institution of Slavery with a watchfulness and zeal greater than was ever done for any other institution in the world," Douglass responded that "the Supreme Court has again and again determined that where the rights of human beings are in issue the rights must be presumed as established until the contrary is distinctly proved." In a *Dred Scott* speech of the same month, Douglass elaborates his views of the Constitution more fully, stating that the authors of the Constitution deliberately created a freedom document by not making explicit references to slavery, and that the egalitarian spirit of the Constitution is best discerned in the preamble's commitment to "liberty and justice." In a nationalistic conclusion to a speech that presents Taney as essentially un-American, he calls on "the American people" to "live up to the Constitution, adopt its principles, imbibe its spirit and enforce its provisions."[18] This is the Douglass who, as described by Gregg D. Crane, "powerfully recasts the national narrative as a continuing confrontation of the challenge to read justice in terms of the national charter despite our history of injustice."[19]

But there is a more radical and revolutionary Douglass that we need to attend to as well, a Douglass who, as in "The Heroic Slave," is capable of thinking about race and nation beyond the parameters of the U.S. nation and who, when he turned his eyes southward, embraced the larger diasporic promise of an "American" black revolutionism. In "The Significance of Emancipation in the West Indies," his great August First speech delivered later in 1857 to over 1,000 African Americans in upstate New York, Douglass called for black freedom and black self-determination beyond the borders of the United States, beyond the U.S. national imaginary. This West Indies emancipation speech is rarely discussed or reprinted, and Douglass himself does not mention it in *Life and Times*.[20] Instead, critics interested in Douglass's oratory and thinking about revolution tend to focus on the Fifth of July speech of 1852, "What to the Slave Is the Fourth of July?," which invokes the ideals of the Declaration of Independence and thereby comfortably fits into the paradigm of Douglass as a reform-minded U.S. nationalist. A different sort of Douglass is on display in "The Significance of Emancipation in the West Indies," different even from the Douglass who had given numerous West Indies emancipation speeches before the *Dred Scott* ruling. As he regularly did in such August First speeches, Douglass in his 1857 address pays tribute to the British for their August First 1834 West Indies emancipation, stating, for example, that England should be honored for "bowing down, confessing and forsaking her sins." But whereas in his earlier August First addresses he had kept the focus on white British reformers, in the 1857 address he places additional emphasis on the role of the black revolutionaries of the West Indies in "fight[ing] for their freedom." It wasn't simply the British who liberated the slaves, he tells his African American auditors, but the slaves themselves who helped to bring about their own liberation. As he puts it: "This, then, is the truth concerning the inauguration of freedom in the British West Indies. Abolition was the act of the British Government. . . . Nevertheless a share of the credit of the result falls justly to the slaves themselves. . . . What Wilberforce was endeavoring to win from the British Senate by his magic eloquence, the Slaves themselves were endeavoring to gain by outbreaks and violence." In an August First speech of 1848, Douglass had celebrated the "peaceful emancipation," which he says was "marked by no deeds of violence." Rejecting the moral suasionism of the Garrisonian phase of his career, or the notion that "insurrectionary movements of the slaves [are] . . . prejudicial to their cause," Douglass in this 1857 address to New York African Americans extols the value of black revolutionary violence as modeled in the southern Americas, asserting that "abolition followed close on the heels of insurrection in the west Indies." In the transnational or black-nationalist manner characteristic more of Delany or Brown, Douglass celebrates black revolutionary leaders such as Nat Turner, Joseph Cinque, and Madison Washington, whom he says are "more worthy to be remembered than the colored man who shot Pitcaren at Bunker Hill."[21]

Given this 1857 celebration of the black freedom fighters of the Americas, it is not surprising that, in the wake of *Dred Scott*, Douglass would become increasingly interested in the southern Americas, particularly Haiti, as a site of black nationality and resistance. Both Delany in his 1854 "Political Destiny of the Colored Race on the American Continent" and William Wells Brown in his 1859–62 writings on Haiti argued that the presence of a black republic in the Southern Hemisphere would serve key ideological and strategic benefits, dramatically putting on display blacks' abilities to achieve republican freedom while remaining close enough to the United States to make the slaveholders uneasy about pan-African revolutionism. There is tantalizing evidence that, by the late 1850s, Douglass was beginning to share such views. Although he had previously objected to all black emigration and colonization projects, in an 1858 editorial in *Frederick Douglass' Paper* he offered his support for blacks who sought to leave the United States, as long as they made their decisions without being coerced by white colonizationists: "Let colored men go to Africa, and to St. Domingo, to Jamaica, Mexico, or elsewhere, just as they list, but let them be self-moved in the matter." But even as he allowed for the possibility of multiple sites of emigration, he increasingly focused on Haiti as his favored choice, especially compared to Africa, which he regarded with suspicion for a number of reasons, ranging from his rejection of essentialist claims of blacks' links to Africa as the "homeland" (the claims central to the American Colonization Society's project of shipping free blacks to Liberia) to his civilizationist view of Africa as an intellectual and cultural backwater. Considering Haiti in relation to Africa, he rhetorically queried: "How long shall we be called upon to establish a '*nation in Africa*,' as a condition to respectability? We have an African nation on our borders. A million of sable people have been governing themselves, in freedom and independence, more than half a century, right under our *national* nose; but America has never acknowledged her independence, and Colonizationists seldom point to Hayti as an example of what the black race are capable of."[22]

Douglass's evolving interest in Haiti, which goes unmentioned in *Life and Times* and the major Douglass biographies that follow Douglass's own U.S. nationalist script, can be traced in *Douglass Monthly*, where we find him coming close to suggesting that blacks' best hopes for achieving what he terms "all the rights claimed by the whitest man on the earth" lies in Haiti. There may well have been a rhetorical dimension to his promotion of Haiti, a wish to demonstrate some flexibility on the emigration issue in the light of the period's increasingly dire developments for African Americans. Or he may have been genuinely interested, though cautious about moving too quickly. Whatever Douglass's thoughts on the matter may have been, the fact is that in the wake of *Dred Scott*, Haitian emigration was becoming an increasingly tempting option for free blacks of the Northeast and was promoted by such charismatic leaders as James Holly, William Wells Brown, and John Brown's friend and associate James Redpath. Redpath's promotional work especially influenced Douglass, for during his late 1850s association with John Brown, Douglass had developed close ties with Redpath, who would become Haiti's main recruitment agent in the United States. Redpath, a white Scotsman, was an unlikely choice for such a position, and black nationalists like Delany were not hesitant about expressing their unhappiness that a white man had gained such a leadership role. A key figure in the radical abolitionist politics of the late 1850s, Redpath became increasingly convinced that Haitian emigration would help to undermine the slave power by developing an oppositional black nationalism across the Americas. Following two visits to Haiti in 1859, Redpath began working closely with Wells Brown through the Haitian Emigration Bureau in Boston, which Holly, with the help of the financial support of the new Haitian president Fabre Geffrard, established in 1860. Around that time, Redpath initiated his efforts to convert Douglass to the Haitian emigration cause.[23]

But even before Redpath attempted to lay claim to the celebrity African American abolitionist leader, Douglass had already evinced an interest in Haiti. Beginning in the spring of 1859, several months after he transformed *Frederick Douglass' Paper* to *Douglass' Monthly*, he devoted considerable space in his literary-nationalist monthly to the Haitian emigrationist movement, printing such essays as "All Going to Hayti" and "Haytian Emigration Again." These essays, and others that appeared in issues of 1859, displayed Douglass's conflicted views on Haiti (and the United States). Though he saw much to like about Geffrard's invitation to African Americans to emigrate to Haiti, particularly given that the Haitian government was offering financial support to the emigrants, he remained concerned that organized emigration movements would hurt the cause of African Americans who wished to remain in the United States. Thus in the May 1859 issue of *Douglass' Monthly* he could write in one article that circumstances "in Hayti certainly do look at the present moment rather inviting to a certain class of our colored friends," while writing in another that "we should sooner believe that the white and colored people of America can live in the peaceable enjoyment of equal rights, than that the black and mulatto races can go live in Hayti."[24]

In late 1859, following John Brown's attack on Harpers Ferry, Douglass was forced to flee the country, traveling to Canada and then England to escape the arrest warrant that could have brought him to the gallows as one of Brown's coconspirators. In various letters and essays written in the United States, Canada, and England, Douglass vociferously declared his innocence. But the larger political point that he insisted on in his writings of the time was the impossibility of a black being a traitor to the United States, given that, as he writes in his November 1859 "To My American Readers and Friends," the "American government refuses to shelter the negro under its protecting wing, and makes him an outlaw."[25]

Angered by New York State's failure to adopt an equal suffrage bill, while remaining skeptical about the Republican Party's commitment to African Americans and the antislavery cause, Douglass grew more interested in Haiti over the next year or so. He printed James Redpath's promotional brochure "Hayti and Colored Emigration" in the November 1860 issue of *Douglass' Monthly*; and (as discussed in the opening of the chapter) he printed three additional Haitian-related documents in the January 1861 issue: "The Colored People and Hayti," "Call for Emigration," and Douglass's own "Emigration to Hayti," in which he praised Redpath as "a man of ability." But Douglass's focus in "Emigration to Hayti" is on his changed emigrationist thinking in light of the fact that "the United States is in great trouble," and that a "glorious era has evidently dawned upon Hayti." Explaining that he had previously believed that "the place for the free colored people is the land where their brothers and sisters are held in slavery," he announces that he has come to modify his views and now sees the value of selective emigration at a time when "never, we think, has the feeling in favor of emigration been so strong as now." The time may be right for emigrationism, he says, not only because of the current situation in the United States, but also because "Hayti, under the Presidency of a wise and patriotic statesman, is entering upon a new career of improvement and prosperity. She is at peace at home, and within a year or two past, has rapidly risen to respect in the world." Though Douglass says that he is not yet ready to concede that "we are a doomed race" in the United States, he nonetheless concludes: "[W]e can raise no objection to the present movement towards Hayti. . . . If we go any where, let us go to Hayti." Like Wells Brown, he saw Haiti (as opposed to Africa) as especially appealing because of its geographical proximity to the United States. By emigrating to Haiti, Douglass remarks, African Americans would remain "within hearing distance of the wails of our brothers and sisters in bonds."[26]

In subsequent issues of his monthly, Douglass continued his promotion of Haiti, printing in the March 1861 issue such essays as "Cotton and Hayti," "Notes on Hayti," and "Haytian Emigration," with "Haytian Emigration" in particular presenting Haiti as a logical and appealing option for those currently deprived of their rights in the United States: "To you who have no foothold *here*," he states to his readers, "we should say, go *there*." Unwilling to emigrate himself at that time, he nonetheless suggests in "The New President" that political affairs in the United States have reached a point at which Lincoln must take on the slave power "or consent to be the despised representative of a defied and humbled government." In the subsequent April 1861 issue, Douglass in "The Inaugural Address" takes some solace in the fact that Lincoln, by offering tentative support for personal-liberty laws, has departed from "the gulf of infamy into which the *Dred Scott* decision sunk the Supreme Court of the United States," though even in this relatively conciliatory essay, Douglass remains concerned about Lincoln's unwillingness to fight for the emancipation of the slaves.[27]

The May 1861 issue of *Douglass' Monthly* presents the most intriguing interlinking of Haiti, *Dred Scott*, Lincoln, and the Civil War. The issue concludes with a short section titled "Emigration to Hayti," which prints three Haitian emigration circulars from James Redpath. But the issue's most fascinating essay is its lead article, Douglass's "A Trip to Hayti," in which he announces his plans to travel to Haiti with his daughter, asserting that developments in the United States following the *Dred Scott* decision have made it clear "to the minds of the free colored people in all the States . . . that the portents of the moral sky were all against us," only to conclude the essay with an abrupt shift to an embrace of the Civil War as a war of emancipation that makes such a trip, and possible emigration to Haiti, completely unnecessary.[28] The shifting nature of the essay is consistent with the conflicted politics of an issue that both urges its readers to support the Civil War as a war against slavery and continues to publicize Haitian emigration as an attractive option for free blacks. "A Trip to Hayti" also has a kind of hoax-like or fictional quality in the way Douglass begins by making one sort of claim and concludes by making a very different one, without bothering to rewrite and reconceive the over-all essay. Before taking a closer look at "A Trip to Hayti," however, it would be useful to discuss an aspect of Douglass's travel plans that he does not discuss in the essay: his former concerns and revived hopes about race and the Haitian nation.

Douglass apparently planned to travel to Haiti not only with his daughter Rosetta but also with Ottilie Assing, the white German intellectual who had translated *My Bondage and My Freedom* into German and who had become his almost constant companion, and perhaps lover, since 1857. In a magazine article for the *Morgenblatt*, published in April 1861, Assing informed her readers that she would be making "an excursion to Haiti, in order to learn by direct encounter about the conditions in this Negro republic." In her excellent biography of Assing, Maria Diedrich speculates that Douglass and Assing, in planning to travel to Haiti, may have hoped "for a radical new beginning for both of them together."[29] One of the reasons that Haiti would have held a special appeal for Douglass and Assing in 1861 is that its relatively new leader, General Geffrard, estab-lished his power by reaching out to mulattoes in ways that the previous leader, Faustin Soulouque, had not. Soulouque had turned against the mulatto population when he declared himself emperor in 1849, and it is for that reason that Douglass previously had found it difficult to imagine blacks and mulattoes living in harmonious relation in Haiti. Soulouque was deposed early in 1859, and it is worth noting that shortly before Douglass understood the full ramifications of the change of power, he expressed his concerns in his monthly that mulattoes like himself would face the risk in Haiti of confronting racists who thought he was not black enough. As he explains in "All Going to Hayti": "It would be a sad thing to some of us, who have been hated and persecuted the first half of our lives for being too black, to go there and be hated and persecuted during the last half of life for being *too white*."[30]

The fear of encountering such "anti-white" prejudice from Haiti's blacks would have been much less of a concern for Douglass, and for Douglass and Assing, under Geffrard. In the post-Soulouque moment, we may speculate, what Douglass most admired about Haiti was that it embodied both the potential of a black nationality in the Americas that challenged the white-supremacist culture of the United States, and, per-haps just as important, the potential of a composite or multiracial na-tionality that held out the hope for moving beyond race as an essential category of nationality. If that is indeed what appealed to Douglass, then we may take his pre–Civil War admiration of Haiti as a crucial source for his post–Civil War advocacy of what he termed "Our Composite Nationality," which I will discuss in greater detail below in relation to his 1871 support for Santo Domingo annexation.

In the light of Douglass's hopes and aspirations for what can perhaps be regarded as an oxymoronic "composite" black-nationalist Haiti under the leadership of Geffrard, let us return to Douglass's essay in the May 1861 *Douglass' Monthly* on his impending visit, which had been arranged and fully funded by Haitian authorities with the help of Redpath. "A Trip to Hayti" begins like this: "A dream, fondly indulged, long meditated, and now quite likely to be realized. At this writing, we are on the eve of starting for a visit of a few weeks to Hayti." Significantly, despite his admiration for what he regarded as Geffrard's multiracial vision, after declaring his intention to visit Haiti, he links himself as a black man to the late eighteenth-century revolutionaries of Saint Domingue, stating in the diasporic fashion of his 1857 lecture on West Indies emancipation that he is "much elated by the prospect of standing once upon the soil of San Domingo, the theatre of many stirring events and heroic achievements, the work of a people, bone of our bone, and flesh of our flesh." Like other Haitian emigrationist leaders of the time, such as Holly and Brown, Douglass makes a black-nationalist appeal to the merits of "the free, orderly and Independent Republic of Hayti," which emerged from its great revolution as a nation that "has been administered by a race denounced as mentally and morally incapable of self government." His mission, as he elaborates it, is not only to take a pleasant cruise and have a pleasant stay, but also to link himself to a black nation in the American hemisphere at a time of crisis. For in the wake of *Dred Scott*, he says, the "free blacks, are now, as never before, looking out into the world for a place of retreat, an asylum from the apprehended storm."[31]

But just as it seems that Douglass is on the brink of voyaging from the United States, he inserts a blank space in the middle of the essay and completely reverses ground. "[T]his is no time for us to leave the country," he proclaims, following the resumption of the essay, for the news of the current moment, that is to say the news of the outbreak of the Civil War (which he suggests he has just heard as he writes and typesets the essay), has, he now asserts, using a different sort of revolutionary discourse, "made a tremendous revolution in all things pertaining to the possible future of the colored people of the United States." Everything has changed! He would have completely rewritten this lead editorial, he states, except that the opening section had already been "put in type."[32] One wonders why, if he were able to create the blank space at the essay's transition and rework the conclusion, he could not have also cut or rewritten the opening; and in all probability the answer is that he must have deliberately chosen to retain that opening and to insert the blank space in order to preserve the conflicted quality of the essay. Presenting the essay in this striking visual format, Douglass conveys his own conflicts between the U.S. revolutionary nationalism that he had invoked so often in his career and the revolutionary black nationalism of the southern Americas that had recently come to inspire him.

In the context of the outbreak of the Civil War, the conflicted or bivocal nature of "A Trip to Hayti" would have suggested right from the start that African American fealty to the Union was not necessarily a given, that it would require that the war be conceived of as a war against slavery. In "Nemesis," a short essay in the same issue as "A Trip to Hayti," Douglass emphatically makes just that point, asserting that the Civil War is the result of "Our National Sin" of slavery, and that a war effort failing to address the fact that the free blacks had been "scourged . . . out of the temple of justice by the Dred Scott decision," and failing to put an end to "the deadly virus of slavery," is a war effort that can only be regarded as "labor lost." In "How to End the War," a short essay immediately following "Nemesis," Douglass sets forth his terms for waging the Civil War, terms that over the next several years he would actively seek to make Lincoln's terms (as they clearly were not at the outset): "*The simple way, then, to put an end to the savage and desolating war now waged by the slaveowners, is to strike down slavery itself*, the primal cause of that war." And yet he concludes this particular issue by printing three circulars by Redpath on "Emigration to Hayti."[33]

Douglass would continue to publish Redpath in subsequent issues. Despite his commitment to the Union and what he hoped would be a full-scale war against slavery, Douglass did not lose sight of Haiti. Thus I would emphasize that Douglass's advocacy of the Civil War in terms of an antislavery and redemptive nationalism was not simply a "return" to a tried-and-true U.S. nationalism but was rather of a piece with his more expansive hemispheric politics in the wake of *Dred Scott*. Entertaining the possibility of a black nationality in Haiti at a moment when, as he remarks in *Life and Times*, he was "adjudged by the Supreme Court of the United States to have no rights which white men were bound to respect,"[34] Douglass for a short period of time was imaginatively both within and beyond the nation, and thus was willing, however temporarily, provision-ally, and uncharacteristically, to relinquish his hold on settled notions of the U.S. nation. Having located himself in such a liminal space, he sub-jected the nation to a critique that to a certain extent developed from the perspective of Haiti.

In this regard, one might think of Douglass's "reconstruction" efforts as commencing not with the end but rather with the beginning of the Civil War, as he sought to use his monthly to make Lincoln and the North conceive of the Civil War as a war against slavery and the racist national-ism sanctioned by the *Dred Scott* decision. As opposed to Douglass's claims in *Life and Times* that he supported Lincoln from the very start, the evidence of the many anti-Lincoln essays that he published in his monthly suggests that Douglass remained divided about Lincoln, the war, and the nation, though intent on making Lincoln (and the North) live up to the liberatory promise of the war. Writing in the September 1861 issue, for example, he declared in "The Progress of the War" that "unless a new turn is given to the conflict, and that without delay, we might as well remove Mr. LINCOLN out of the President's chair, and respectfully invite JEFFERSON DAVIS or some other slaveholding rebel to take his place." There is every indication that by the summer of 1862 Lincoln was listen-ing to Douglass and other African American activists, for not too long after Douglass delivered one of his most blistering attacks, calling Lincoln and his advisors "weak, paltering and incompetent rulers" for failing to see that the only way to respond to what he terms "a slaveholding re-bellion" is to offer "a proclamation of Emancipation," Lincoln initiated work on the Emancipation Proclamation (and also established diplo-matic relations with Haiti). In an address on the Emancipation Proclama-tion published in the January 1863 issue of *Douglass' Monthly*, Douglass celebrated "the glorious morning of liberty about to dawn upon us," while at the same time anticipating the challenges that he would be facing over the next several decades: "Law and sword can and will, in the end abolish slavery. But law and sword cannot abolish the malignant slaveholding sentiment which has kept the slave system alive in this country during two centuries. Pride of race, prejudice against color, will raise their hateful clamor for oppression of the negro as heretofore."[35]

In the aftermath of the Emancipation Proclamation, Douglass sought to convince Lincoln, with whom he met during the summer of 1863, to make black troops part of the Union army. Lincoln himself came to conceive of the free blacks as having the potential to become an army of liberators, capable of marshaling the destructive force of the 4 million southern slaves. Throwing himself into the recruitment and war effort, Douglass permanently closed down his journal in June 1863, and in that final issue he voiced his ideals for a multiracial society in ways that once again directly responded to the *Dred Scott* ruling of 1857: "I shall advocate for the negro, his most full and complete adoption into the great national family of America. I shall demand for him the most perfect civil and political equality, and that he shall enjoy all the rights, privileges and immunities enjoyed by any other members of the body politic." This is Douglass in his recognizable role as a strategic U.S. nationalist. But revolutionary Haiti remained important to his thinking as well. In his 1863 broadside "Men of Color, To Arms!," which he used to recruit blacks into the Union army, he called on blacks to take advantage of "our golden opportunity" to use violence to overthrow slavery, appealing to blacks to fight in the Civil War in the name of the man whose goals were to raze Charleston, South Carolina, and lead his cohorts to Haiti. "Remember Denmark Vesey," Douglass enjoined.[36] Douglass himself would not forget Haiti, but when he reconsidered the United States in a hemispheric context in the years following the Civil War, Haiti was, for a while at least, pushed into the margins, more of a threat than a promise.

The State of Santo Domingo

In 1861 Douglass viewed Haiti as a possible site for the development of a black nationality in the Americas. In 1871, as editor and publisher of the *New National Era*, he conveyed an altogether different sense of Haiti, presenting the country as a possible site for the development of U.S. empire in the Americas. An enthusiastic supporter of President Ulysses S. Grant's efforts to annex Santo Domingo to the United States, Douglass, in a series of essays in his newspaper, extolled the benefits of U.S. expansionism and, in response to those who were concerned about Haitian sovereignty, posed a series of rhetorical questions: "But, it is asked, would annexation stop with Santo Domingo? Is not this but the entering-wedge to the extension of our authority over Hayti as well? . . . But what if such a result should follow? I can conceive of a fate far worse for Hayti than would be her annexation to the United States." Formerly regarded by Douglass as an inspirational black republic, the very model of black revolutionism and independence, Haiti is depicted here as a possible "State in this American Union"—an American Union that, should President

Grant's long-term annexationist project prove to be successful, would incorporate not only Santo Domingo but eventually Cuba as "part of the Great Republic of the Western World."[37] What happened to bring about such a change in Douglass's hemispheric vision? What sort of nation, or "American Union," or "Great Republic," is he imagining circa 1871, and what would be the racial dynamics of such a nation, union, or republic? These are the questions begged by Douglass's advocacy of Santo Domingo annexation, which became intimately linked with his short-lived editing and publishing of the African American newspaper *New National Era* and thus with his American and African American literary nationalism of the early 1870s.

As is well known, following the Civil War, Douglass placed his faith in the Republican Party as *the* party of the nation, the party that Douglass believed would ensure that the privileges of citizenship would be made available to all African Americans. Again and again, as in a speech of October 1870, he affirmed his enthusiastic support: "Gentleman, I am a republican, a radical Republican, a Black Republican, a Republican dyed in the wool, and for one I want the Republican party to live as long as I do."[38] But in committing himself so single-mindedly to the Republican Party, Douglass, so the argument goes, lost touch with working-class blacks and gave himself over to those who exploited his fame and influence to advance agendas that ultimately had little to do with his hopes for black uplift and a multiracial United States. This would appear to be especially true for his support of the Republican President Grant's advocacy of Santo Domingo annexation during the early 1870s. Waldo E. Martin Jr. asserts that Douglass's annexationism betrayed his implication in the ideology of Manifest Destiny and "offered the paradoxical spectacle of Douglass favoring the extinguishment of a black republic." Merline Pitre similarly sees Douglass as favoring "an American expansionist policy in language as strong as . . . that of ardent imperialists," concluding that in the "Santo Domingo episode Douglass got a short-range objective (ascendancy of the Republican Party) confused with one of his long-range goals—elevation and liberation of the black race." Douglass's most recent biographer, William S. McFeely, goes so far as to suggest that Douglass promoted Grant's annexation plan because "the attraction of a presidential appointment . . . was so alluring."[39] Given the general consensus on Douglass's implication in what seems to many the worst sort of racist imperialism, it is not surprising that Douglass's writings on Santo Domingo and his concomitant editing of the *New National Era* have been mostly ignored in Douglass scholarship. We clearly prefer the younger, seemingly subversive writer of "What to the Slave Is the Fourth of July?" (1852) to the older, seemingly co-opted Republican author of "Annexation of San Domingo" (1871).

The Douglass of the early 1870s *is* somewhat different from the Douglass of the early 1850s; but of course one of the arguments that I am making in *Dislocating Race and Nation* is that we need to attend to the multiple perspectives and contingencies, the messiness and confusion, that invariably constitute, complicate, and unsettle writers' careers. And we need to be wary of the limits of reading particular works in the context of the historical developments that we "know" will emerge from particular historical moments. Although Douglass came to support Santo Domingo annexation, even at the expense of Haitian sovereignty, the fact is that by the late 1880s, as in the late 1850s and early 1860s, he once again strongly supported Haiti as an independent black republic in the Americas. Is there a coherent narrative about Douglass's hemispheric nationalism that can be told from the early 1870s to the late 1880s? Perhaps not. Had events turned out differently in 1871, had Grant actually succeeded in annexing Santo Domingo, a different history of U.S. relations with the southern Americas would have emerged, and Douglass's writings on the subject would have taken on different meanings. But when Douglass wrote in support of Grant's annexation plan in 1871, he did not know that the plan would fail, he could not have predicted with absolute certainty the end of Reconstruction in 1877, and he would not have been able to reflect critically on his support for annexationism in the context of the forms of U.S. imperialism that would emerge by century's end.

In his 1881 *Life and Times*, Douglass presents his political and writing self in the early 1870s as part of a relatively coherent narrative of his life as an African American leader, depicting his editing of the *New National Era* and support for Grant's imperial venture in particular as mutually beneficial work in the service of black uplift. As he explains in *Life and Times*, he had hoped that his editing of the *New National Era* would contribute to African Americans' "improvement and elevation," and he maintains that precisely because of his work on the newspaper, "the colored people are indebted for some of the best things ever uttered in behalf of their cause." Douglass would no doubt count among those "best things" his numerous columns supporting Grant's efforts to annex Santo Domingo, which similarly argued that adding Santo Domingo to the United States would contribute to what he termed the "cause of the colored race." The question that remains unanswered, or avoided, in *Life and Times* is how the annexation of Santo Domingo would have accomplished such a goal, especially given that Douglass, even in his 1881 autobiographical recounting, sounds very much like the prototypical U.S. imperialist and nationalist who believes that the United States should "extend its dominion whenever and wherever such extension can peaceably and honorably . . . be accomplished." Wouldn't such expansionism ultimately threaten the "cause of the colored race"? That was precisely the contention of Douglass's friend Charles Sumner, the formidable antislavery senator from Massachusetts, who argued that Grant's quest to annex Santo Domingo "was a measure to extinguish a colored nation, and to do so by dishonorable means and for selfish motives."[40] Given Sumner's eloquent opposition, which Douglass presents fully and fairly in *Life and Times*, Douglass's support for Grant's project remains rather puzzling—or not puzzling at all if one regards Douglass during the early 1870s as merely a Republican hack.

Although Douglass in the section on Santo Domingo in his 1881 autobiography chooses not to address the question of race except in response to Sumner's opposition, he does assert that he had come to believe in 1871 that "there was no more dishonor to Santo Domingo in making her a State of the American Union, than in making Kansas, Nebraska, or any other territory such a state."[41] I would suggest that it is precisely Douglass's conception of Santo Domingo as an eventual state of the Union, with voting rights for citizens and full representation in Congress, that points to the radical implications of his annexationism, which followed in certain key respects from Grant's own radical thinking. In all probability, the two men never actually shared their views on the subject, but both regarded Santo Domingo annexation in relation to their large and somewhat inchoate goals of black elevation not only in the United States but in the greater American hemisphere. In order to recover Grant's and Douglass's hemispheric vision, which was also central to Douglass's (literary) nationalism of the period, we need to turn from the 1881 autobiography to consider the debate on Santo Domingo annexation as it was conceived and articulated (and sometimes not articulated) circa 1869–71, the same years that Douglass was championing an African American literary nationalism in the *New National Era*.

The project of developing a multiracial United States with equal rights for all—the project, that is to say, that seemed to be embodied in the key post–Civil War constitutional amendments—was absolutely central to the black newspaper the *New Era* (the initial incarnation of the *New National Era*), which would become Douglass's main forum for expressing his views on Santo Domingo. Established in 1869 by the Washington, D.C., pastor and black abolitionist J. Sella Martin, the paper's first issue appeared on 13 January 1870, right around the time of the adoption of the Fifteenth Amendment, with Douglass listed on the masthead as corresponding editor. As announced in the "Prospectus of the New Era," the newspaper was "devoted especially to the promotion of the Political, Educational, Industrial, and Economical interests of the Colored People of the United States, and to their Moral and Religious Improvement." Although the prospectus stated that the paper's columns would be open to all who wished to discuss "questions of vital importance," it also made clear that the editors of the *New Era* were "colored men, and the contributors will be mainly colored."[42] Thus, as had been the case with numerous African American newspapers of the antebellum period, the multiracial project would be advanced from the perspective of African Americans who would take it upon themselves both to address strategies of black uplift and to continue to make the case for blacks' rights to all of the privileges associated with national citizenship.

Douglass's initial writings in the newspaper display his commitment to a politics of demonstration. In his first piece for the *New Era*, "Salutatory of the Corresponding Editor," which appeared in the issue of 27 January 1870, Douglass proclaims that in the post–Civil War era "the entire capability of our race to win the confidence, respect, and friendship of all patriotic men will be demonstrated." Over the first four months of the newspaper, literature had a central place in the editors' efforts to showcase blacks' capabilities. The editors serialized two novellas by Frank J. Webb, "Two Wolves and a Lamb" and "Marvin Hayle," and printed several essays on black writing. In a forceful piece titled "The Negro and American Literature," published in the 3 March 1870 *New Era*, the black critic George Rice insisted on the crucial interconnections between American literature and African American literature. Sounding very much like the American literary nationalists of the 1790s and 1840s, Rice laments that "[w]e have as yet to create a literature purely American," and then he adds from his perspective as an African American literary nationalist that it is crucial for black writers to consider their own writing in relation to the nation's still "unfinished" task of creating a distinctively "American" literature. The essay is thus fairly traditional in the way that it links writing and nation, and, viewed in relation to antebellum African American literary nationalism, it is traditional as well in arguing that blacks must display their "genius and talent" in order to confute whites' racist preconceptions.[43]

Concerned that the *New Era* was failing to gain the attention of whites and blacks alike, Martin and his editorial associates talked Douglass into assuming the editing and publishing responsibilities in late 1870, with the hope that his prestige would help to bring in additional cash contributions and subscribers. In many respects Douglass continued to emphasize a politics of demonstration, arguing, for instance, that the role of "Colored Newspapers" is to prove "to the world that colored men are capable of something more than a mere physical existence, . . . thought as well as action." But he also attempted to present an even more capacious and interracial vision of the national. In the same issue of 8 September 1870 in which Douglass introduces himself as the new editor of the paper, he foregrounds his concern about the "national" by renaming the newspaper the *New National Era* and stating that it now aspires to be "a national journal in its truest and broadest sense." The broader reach of the newspaper was reflected in the authors Douglass chose to print when he assumed control of the paper: African American writers, but also a greater range of white, canonical figures such as William Cullen Bryant, John Greenleaf Whittier, Charles Dickens, Alice Cary, and T. S. Arthur. He even reprinted a celebratory piece on Nathaniel Hawthorne from the *Atlantic*.[44]

But after Douglass formally announced in the issue of 15 December 1870 that he had officially assumed the role of both publisher and editor of the *New National Era*, literature would not have quite the prominence in the newspaper that it once had. During 1871 Douglass printed articles on Frances Harper, William Wells Brown, and Benjamin Banneker, and he continued his practice of reprinting the poems and writings of well-known white writers. But he channeled much of his editorial energy toward supporting President Grant's efforts to annex Santo Domingo, and the question of Santo Domingo quickly became *the* central concern of the newspaper during the first year or so of Douglass's stewardship as editor and publisher. In some respects this is not very surprising, for Douglass had offered active support for a number of Grant's initiatives prior to taking editorial control of the paper. What is surprising is the extent to which Douglass threw himself into the political fray. Douglass clearly saw important connections between Santo Domingo annexation and the black-uplift and African American literary-nationalist mission of his newspaper. Moreover, there were overlaps in his and Grant's thinking about race and the American hemisphere that help to explain Douglass's support for what some of his friends and political associates saw as abhorrent foreign policy.

President Grant initially proposed annexing Santo Domingo, or what is now generally called the Dominican Republic, to the United States in 1869. At that time, Santo Domingo occupied around two-thirds of the island of Hispaniola, with Haiti occupying the other third. The U.S. businessmen William Cazneau and Joseph Fabens, who had significant economic interests in Santo Domingo, used their influence to convince Grant to send one of his top aides, General Orville Babcock, to Santo Domingo in July 1869 to negotiate with the corrupt Dominican president Buenaventura Báez. As a result of those negotiations and the follow-up negotiations between Báez and Secretary of State Hamilton Fish, an initial annexation pact was informally agreed upon in early 1870. But on 15 March 1870, the Senate Foreign Relations Committee rejected the pact, and it was subsequently rejected by the full Senate in June 1870.[45]

That defeat led Grant to redouble his efforts. Though the Senate remained opposed to annexation, Grant gained Senate approval in December 1870 to send a commission of inquiry to Santo Domingo; and in mid-January 1871, several months after he became editor and publisher of the *New National Era*, Douglass accepted the position of assistant secretary to the commission. Following a nearly two-month visit from late January to late March 1871, the commission filed a report offering its enthusiastic support for all aspects of Grant's annexation plan, insisting that the San Domingans were equally enthusiastic about "becoming part of the people of the United States." Grant submitted the *Report of the Commission of Inquiry to Santo Domingo* to Congress in spring 1871, confident that it "more than sustains all that I have heretofore said in regard to the productiveness and healthfulness of the republic of San Domingo, of the unanimity of the people for annexation to the United States, and of their peaceable character." Despite having relatively subordinate roles, Douglass and Secretary A. A. Burton signed a testimonial in the *Report* affirming "that in all they have seen and heard they have met with nothing inconsistent with the foregoing report as signed by Commissioners Benjamin F. Wade, Andrew D. White, and Samuel G. Howe"; and Douglass himself contributed a short section entitled "Summary of testimony taken by F. Douglass among American colonists at Samana," which affirmed that there was unanimity among these colonists in favor of annexation.[46] Despite the endorsement of the commission, the Senate defeated an annexation proposal on June 1871. Though it took Grant some time to take the full measure of this second major legislative defeat, that vote essentially ended the possibility of Santo Domingo annexation during his presidency.

The principal opponents of Grant's proposal were the Republican senators Charles Sumner and Carl Schurz. Sumner couched his opposition almost entirely in terms of what he reported to William Lloyd Garrison was the measure's "heartless indifference to the colored race." Several weeks before the commission traveled to Hispaniola, Sumner voiced his objections in a four-hour speech in the Senate that some, including Douglass, regarded as calumnious. Comparing Grant to the proslavery Democrats Franklin Pierce and James Buchanan, Sumner expressed particular concern about the threat Santo Domingo annexation posed to Haiti, which he called "the only colored government now existing in the world, a republic seeking to follow our great example." At the center of his speech was an anti-imperialistic insistence that Santo Domingo was for the San Domingans. As he proclaimed: "Already by a higher statute is that island set apart to the colored race. It is theirs by right of possession; by their sweat and blood mingling with the soil; by tropical position; by its burning sun, and by unalterable laws of climate. Such is the ordinance of nature, which I am not the first to recognize."[47]

But what exactly did Sumner mean when he invoked that "higher statute" or "ordinance of nature" that supposedly delegated the tropical island to the "colored race," and to whom was he referring as the "first" to recognize such things? In an important revisionary study of the 1870–71 debates on Santo Domingo, historian Eric T. L. Love has argued that among the first and certainly most influential of the evolutionary biologists to make such claims was Louis Agassiz, who emigrated to the United States from Switzerland during the 1840s and assumed an influential position at Harvard later in the decade. Love contends that, however wrongheaded Grant's annexation plan may have been, it was motivated in part by an antiracist idealism and was opposed by anti-imperialist racists who were concerned about a plan that would add "tropical" blacks to the U.S. nation. Such concerns had their sources in Agassiz's and others' notions of polygeny, the theory that peoples of different races had different moments of creation at different places in the world and thus "naturally" belonged in those different places. Agassiz elaborated his views on the subject in "The Diversity of the Origin of the Human Races" (1850), an essay that, as noted in chapter 3, Hawthorne may have read and had his own doubts about. In the essay, Agassiz makes the case for racial differences and hierarchies, arguing for white racial superiority and for the importance of fulfilling the mandates of nature by keeping whites apart from blacks. As Stephen Jay Gould has shown in his analysis of Agassiz's personal letters of the Civil War period, Agassiz, who was opposed to slavery, was repulsed by black people and convinced of the need to continue practices of racial segregation in the wake of emancipation. In a series of letters to the Boston reformer Samuel Gridley Howe, Agassiz warned of the dangers that blacks and various mixed races posed to the nation and shared his hopes that blacks would "gradually die out in the North." Howe, as mentioned, was one of the three commissioners appointed by Grant to report on Santo Domingo, and it is to Howe's credit that Agassiz's letters would seem to have had little impact on his thinking about Santo Domingo or his willingness to work with Douglass. Agassiz also regularly corresponded with Charles Sumner, and though it is clear that Sumner was motivated by more than simply racialist environmentalism in his opposition to annexation, his conception of an "ordinance of nature" that made the tropics by "a higher statute" the province of blacks is of a piece with Agassiz's thinking. As Love points out, Agassiz already had had an impact on Sumner when in 1867 he helped to convince him to support the Alaskan purchase on the grounds that, as Agassiz asserted in a letter to Sumner, the cool climate of Alaska would be conducive to the "settlement of our race."[48]

Similar though more vitriolically stated concerns about the dangers posed by "tropical" peoples to "our race" were central to Missouri senator Carl Schurz's opposition to Santo Domingan annexation. In a speech delivered in the Senate on 11 January 1871, Schurz addressed what he called the "grave question" of annexation: "[I]s the incorporation of that part of the globe and the people inhabiting it quite compatible with the integrity, safety, perpetuity, and progressive development of our institutions, which we value so highly?" His answer was a resounding no, with the overarching suggestion that the nation would be better off with no blacks at all. Given that, as he remarks on the prospect of geographical annexation, morality would stand in the way of any plan to "exterminate" the San Domingans themselves, the U.S. nation, in Schurz's view, would face the distinct challenge of attempting to "incorporate them with our political system," should Grant's plan be approved. But it is precisely the problem of incorporating people "who have nothing in common with us" that is the true horror for Schurz, for, in the manner of the *Democratic*

Review writers unnerved by the prospect of adding "Mexican" or "Indian" races to the "white" United States, he imagines that "in the course of time and by the process of assimilation the Anglo-Saxon will lose more than the Africo-Indo-Latin mixture will gain." Warning that San Domingans will blacken the nation in all sorts of ways, Schurz offers a nightmare scenario of what would follow from Grant's annexation, or incorporation, of Santo Domingo as part of the United States: "[F]ancy the Senators and Representatives of ten or twelve millions of tropical people, people of the Latin race mixed with Indian and African blood; people who . . . have neither language, nor traditions, nor habits, nor political institutions, nor morals in common with us; fancy them sitting in the Halls of Congress, throwing the weight of their intelligence, their morality, their political notions and habits, their prejudices and passions, into the scale of the destinies of this Republic."[49] Although Sumner was far more willing to convey his respect for peoples of color, he reportedly expressed similar concerns about race and the tropics during a secret senatorial meeting of March 1871, stating that "[t]o the African belongs the equatorial belt," and that the people of Santo Domingo "were a turbulent, treacherous race, indolent and not disposed to make themselves useful to their country or to the world at large."[50]

Viewed in relation to Schurz's racist anti-imperialism in particular, Grant's desire to annex and eventually make a state of Santo Domingo can seem oddly progressive, which is not to excuse the self-righteous paternalism, nationalist exceptionalism, or economic shadiness that also lay behind his annexationism. But antiracism was among the principal goals of his initiative. Grant privately articulated such goals in a "Memorandum" of 1869 or 1870 that he wrote for his own contemplation and saved in his personal files, wherein, in the manner of a Ben Franklin exercise, he listed "Reasons why San Domingo should be annexed to the United States." As might be expected, he identified economic advantages as one of his "Reasons why." But we see a more surprising Grant when he comes to considerations of slavery and race. He notes in his list that annexation would help to end slavery in the southern Americas by making the United States less dependent on goods from Cuba and Brazil; and he gives as another of his reasons for supporting Santo Domingo annexation a desire to address the problem of racism in the United States: "The present difficulty, in bringing all parts of the United States to a happy unity and love of country grows out of the prejudice to color. The prejudice is a senseless one, but it exists. The colored man cannot be spared until his place is supplied, but with a refuge like San Domingo his worth here would soon be discovered, and he would soon receive such recognition to induce him to stay; or if Providence designed that the two races should not live to-gether he would find a home in the Antilles."[51] Practical politician that he was, Grant did not at any time during his public advocacy of annexation proclaim that he sought to contest whites' "senseless" prejudice against color, or to instruct whites on how crucial blacks were to the economic health of the United States. But these goals were clearly central to his vision of the eventual statehood, as opposed to perpetual U.S. colonial domination, of Santo Domingo. To be sure, Grant's grudging concessions that Providence *may* have designated blacks for the tropics and that Santo Domingo may end up as a site for black emigration reveal that he, too, was influenced by the environmentalism of the polygenesis-inspired anti-imperialists. In that respect, his hope that whites might one day overcome their irrational antiblack prejudices so that the United States could prosper as a multiracial nation is all the more impressive.

Grant offered this hope at a time when white southerners were welcoming the upsurge of the Ku Klux Klan's violence against blacks, and when white northerners, eager for reconciliation with the South, seemed increasingly indifferent to the struggles of African Americans.[52] Douglass had argued that the large goal of the Civil War should be "National regeneration," but in the late 1860s and early 1870s there appeared to be a return in the dominant culture to a prewar insistence on connections between whiteness and the nation. As was the case in such antebellum journals as the *Democratic Review*, postwar mainstream journals in the North continued to underscore the centrality of Anglo-Saxonism to the American character. Even the *Atlantic Monthly*, which was edited by a number of former abolitionists, linked Anglo-Saxonism to its renewed calls for an American literary nationalism. In 1870, the year that Grant probably wrote his private memorandum on Santo Domingo, the *Atlantic's* literary editor Thomas Wentworth Higginson, who had commanded a black regiment during the Civil War, wrote that he wanted an American literature "pervaded with Americanism," by which he meant democratic principles, a faith in "national self-government," and a recognition that a "broad Anglo-Saxon manhood . . . is the basis of our national life."[53]

J. Sella Martin's and Douglass's brand of American and African American literary nationalism in the *New Era* and the *New National Era* sought to counter this upsurge of political and literary Anglo-Saxonism in both its political and literary guises, and in this context Douglass's commitment to Santo Domingo annexation can be seen as inextricably linked to an aggressively resistant African American (literary) nationalism that bore some similarities to David Walker's. At a time when U.S. whites were attempting to insulate themselves from blacks, Douglass, as with his interest in Haiti in the late 1850s and early 1860s, was thinking diasporically, imagining connections between African Americans and blacks of the southern Americas that would revitalize and strengthen both communities. A crucial difference between these two historical moments is that, with Haiti, Douglass imagined a flow of desire that extended from north (the United States) to south (Haiti), whereas with Santo Domingo, he imagined a circuit of desire moving back and forth between north (United States) and south (Santo Domingo). The regenerative possibilities of such two-way flows became the main focus of his writings on Santo Domingo annexation in the *New National Era*.

Two weeks after announcing that he had become the new publisher of the *New National Era*, Douglass printed "The San Domingo Flurry," which offered enthusiastic support for Grant's plan to send a commission of inquiry to Santo Domingo. Two weeks after that, Douglass printed one of his most fascinating essays on the controversy, "Annexation of San Domingo." Published in the 12 January 1871 issue of the *New National Era*, and not reprinted since, the essay appeared shortly before Douglass was appointed to the commission, and thus at a time when he felt free to speak his mind as an individual with no official connection to the government. More than any other piece that Douglass would write on Santo Domingo, the essay conveys his conception of annexation as a profoundly antiracist venture, one that would counter whites' renewed Anglo-Saxonist nationalism by adding a fully enfranchised black state to the American Union. The Douglass of this essay thus shares much with the Grant of the private memorandum, voicing precisely the sorts of arguments and sentiments on race and nation that Grant felt he had to keep to himself in order to advance his own antiracist agenda.

At the core of "Annexation of San Domingo" is the argument that annexation would be beneficial for African Americans and San Domingans alike, and that it should not be pursued unless it comes "without dishonor, rapine, and bloodshed." Annexation, Douglass contends, would help to bring about the end of racial conflict and racial imbalance in the United States by adding a new state, a "black sister of Massachusetts," and annexation would help San Domingans, whom he believes want annexation, by allowing the United States to "transplant" to Santo Domingo "the glorious institutions which have lifted the grand Old Commonwealth to her commanding elevation."[54] There is of course much that is controversial and, from our current perspective, troubling about Douglass's insistence on the value of making Santo Domingo into a "black sister of Massachusetts." But it is in his talk of a black Massachusetts where we can discern his efforts to challenge the environmental racism of Schurz and his like-minded colleagues by, in effect, dislocating race from geography. As Douglass understood, there was much at stake in refuting the notion that blacks best thrived in tropical climates, for such a belief ultimately served the interests of racists who believed that blacks could never economically compete in places like Massachusetts, New York, and Pennsylvania and thus should continue the manual agricultural labors in the South that they had been forced to perform as slaves. By contesting such environmentalism through his support for Santo Domingo annexation, Douglass implies that blacks and whites are equally capable of prospering in any part of the globe, and in this way he seeks to dissolve the lines between north and south, the United States and the tropics.

Douglass cannily develops his arguments by initially working with the terms of the environmentalists only to subvert those terms through a liberalist appeal to the power of human reason. Thus, like Grant, he claims that Santo Domingo annexation would encourage some blacks to move to the southern Americas, with the result being that "the tropics will gain rather than lose a part of its appropriate population." But it is precisely through his ironic invocation of the word "appropriate" that Douglass means to dismantle the polygenesist environmentalism central to the racialist, or racist, geographical determinists. To that end, he again deploys the word in relation to the notion that whites do not belong in the tropics, or that whites would become lazy and depraved in the tropics, playfully calling on whites to meet the challenges of the tropics in the way that blacks have met the challenges of North America: "If it is objected that white men will go there, we say the more the better. If the negro can stand the white man upon the white man's own appropriate belt of the earth, where climate and other conditions are against the negro, the latter can certainly stand him, when enjoying all the advantages of a sunny climate suited to a dark man." Here is racial tolerance pushed to comical extremes, with blacks given the opportunity to be as forbearing to whites as Douglass wished whites would be to blacks. But then he turns against the environmentalism implied by the use of the word "appropriate" by adducing a basic biological fact: "The temperature of a healthy man's blood is about the same whether we find him within twenty-nine degrees of the north pole or under the equator." Not only do men of various races possess the same body temperature in the same places, but they also have equal capacities for rational thought and practical action that allow them to overcome supposedly "inappropriate" environments. As he explains: "Man alone, of all the animal world, can brave all climates, latitudes, longitudes, and altitudes. . . . He has reason, and can by its aid make it warm where it is cold; calm where there is wind; dry where it is damp; cool where it is warm, and in every way adjust himself to his circumstances. This is true of men, black as well as white." Given this important truth, Douglass concludes that environmental determinism must be regarded as a pseudoscience that limits racial mobility and cross-racial interactions and thus artificially produces the very inequalities that it claims exist naturally in nature: "But we are opposed to this parcelling out the earth to different varieties of men—locating one here and another there, and deeming this one and that out of its place, here or there." Rather than arguing for separate nations or separate racial identities, Douglass thus extols what he terms the "blessing" of "the *composite character* of the nation."[55]

In his well-known speech of 1869, "Our Composite Nationality," Douglass underscored the value of blending blacks, whites, Asians, and Native Americans and other racial and ethnic peoples as part of an effort to make the United States "the perfect national illustration of the unity and dignity of the human family that the world has ever seen." In 1871 Douglass continued to believe that the ideals of such a racially and ethnically mixed nation could best be achieved by the United States, though not necessarily within its then-constituted states and national borders. Though Douglass in his 1869 speech and 1871 promotion of Santo Domingo annexation can seem imperialistic in his celebration of the "outspread wings of the American eagle," he nonetheless insists on challenging those beliefs in white Anglo-Saxonist superiority that U.S. leaders had typically invoked to motivate and legitimate the nation's southern expansionism. In "Our Composite Nationality," he rejects such genealogical fictions, basing America's "right" to extend its dominion on a transnational humanism that knows no borders, abjures the use of force, and ultimately involves a dialectic of migration and incorporation: "The great right of migration and great wisdom of incorporating foreign elements into our body politic, are founded not upon any genealogical or ethnological theory, however learned, but upon the broad fact of a common nature."[56] As the tension between "migrating" and "incorporating" might suggest, Douglass clings to an idealistic notion of U.S. expansionism that is less about conquest than cross-influence and cross-desire. Such a dialectical notion of hemispheric influence would become increasingly important to the essays on Santo Domingo that he published in the *New National Era.* After all, the image of Santo Domingo as a black sister of Massachusetts forcefully conveys the idea that San Domingans would constitute part of the United States, would influence policy, and would further add to the nation's composite character. The gendering of San Domingo as female also points rather suggestively to the positive benefits of miscegenation, which Douglass would take up as one of his great antiracist themes around the time of his marriage to the white Helen Pitts in 1884.

Douglass's hopeful (and arguably naive) vision of a hemispherically expansive and "composite" United States became a central topic of his newspaper upon his return from Santo Domingo in late March 1871. In the first piece that he printed after his return, "The San Domingan Commission" (30 March 1871), he asserts that Sumner made a grave error in opposing Santo Domingo annexation *before* the U.S. Commission of Inquiry presented its report. Two issues later, Douglass filled the entirety of the newspaper's front page with excerpts from the *Report.* But his main effort to promote annexation in the larger context of a "composite nationality" came in a series of eight letters on Santo Domingo running in the *New National Era* from 13 April 1871 to 15 June 1871. The first letter was untitled, the second was titled "Letter on Santo Domingo.—No. 2," and the third and subsequent letters were titled "Santo Domingo," with the sequential number (No. 3, etc.) following the title. These letters, which have been neglected in Douglass scholarship, are complex meditations on questions of race and nation in the postemancipation moment and can be regarded as key contributions to the black-nationalist and black-uplift agenda of Douglass's *New National Era.* As a surprisingly compelling (if ultimately doomed) effort to imagine the development of a composite (trans)nationality in the Americas, the letters themselves can be taken as an important contribution to the African American literary nationalism of the post–Civil War period.

In some respects the letters have the "official" feel of the *Report* itself, for Douglass at times sounds as if he were still speaking as a representative of the commission. In the rhetorical mode of an editor who is aware that he is writing to black and white readers alike, he eventually does address race, but not before moving in the formulaic way of the *Report* through the various advantages of Santo Domingo annexation for the U.S. nation. And so in "Letter on Santo Domingo.—No. 2" he talks of the "marvelous fertility" of the island, emphasizing the resources that would come to the nation through annexation. "Santo Domingo—No. 3," which focuses on the "industry, enterprise, and progress in Santo Domingo," seems similarly intended for skeptical white readers, or readers who would have shared Schurz's views on the putative laziness of tropical blacks.[57] It is not until "Santo Domingo—No. 4" that Douglass addresses issues of race and nation directly, presenting annexation, as Grant did in his private memorandum, as serving antiracist and antislavery ends.

Writing in "No. 4" from what he now terms "a colored man's point of view," Douglass here chooses to respond to the contention of Sumner and his supporters that "humiliation" and sadness would result from "the extinction of a colored nationality" in Santo Domingo. Douglass makes clear that in the context of his advocacy of "large and composite nationalities," the great promise of Santo Domingo annexation lies precisely in the willingness of the United States to regard black islanders as both semi-independent, in the manner of a state, and as part of an expanding hemispheric nationality that knows no borders and is improved by the addition of yet another composite part. In this regard, the "extinction" of nations (other than the United States) could be viewed as a positive good; and given his insistence on San Domingans' rights to determine their own fate, his even larger argument is that a shared participation in a composite American nationality, and not extinction, is what annexation is all about. As he rhetorically remarks: "Talk of humiliation, talk of extinction and degradation! It is groundless and preposterous! What State in the world would be degraded by being made the equal of Massachusetts and New York? What people need be ashamed of American citizenship?" Or, to put this another way, which black islander would feel degraded being made into the political equal of Charles Sumner or Carl Schurz? As for those whites who would be appalled by a black Massachusetts, or a black New York, becoming part of a "large and composite nationality"— which is to say, becoming something like the phantasmagoric nation of Schurz's nightmares—Douglass states that "the vast and overwhelming opposition to the measure comes not from friends of human equality, but from its bitterest enemies," who are filled "with so much horror" at the prospect of adding to the nation's population of peoples of color that they want to insulate the United States from the larger hemisphere. It is this racist fear of the blacks of the Americas as the "touch contagion," Douglass asserts, that ultimately is "at the bottom of this pretended respect for the rights of nations."[58]

In subsequent letters, Douglass attacks Schurz's racist environmentalism, which he sees as providing the ideological rationale for the resistance to Douglass's (and Grant's) vision of a composite U.S. nationality. He also addresses substantive moral concerns, making clear that his support of Santo Domingo annexation is predicated on a belief (which history probably would have shown was mistaken) that annexation would help to bring about the end of slavery and racism in the Americas. As he maintains in "Santo Domingo—No. 7," annexation would "enable us the better to discourage slavery and promote the freedom of mankind." From Douglass's perspective, annexation would also help to begin to put the relationship between the people of the United States and the tropics on a more equitable and moral footing. It is precisely Schurz's unwillingness to confront the United States' continued implication in the slave system that raises Douglass's ire, for he sees in the senator's words and deeds a willed blindness to his complicity in the exploitation of blacks in the American hemisphere. As he sarcastically notes: "Senator SCHURZ, the most brilliant of all the Senatorial assailants of Santo Domingo, denounces the tropics with lips warm, and person fragrant, with his Havana cigar," and Schurz enjoys his cigars and coffee without ever "stopping to inquire where these things come from, or by what process they are produced." As Douglass goes on to explain, the idea that "free labor cannot succeed in a tropical climate," the idea that slavery is needed to produce the very products that Schurz enjoys on a day-to-day basis, "was the apology for slavery while slavery lasted." For Douglass, annexation "will speedily demonstrate the possibility of freedom and industry in that island," and as is consistent with his sense of black nationalism as a politics of demonstration, he maintains that annexation would help to refute the beliefs that contribute to the persistence of antiblack racism in the United States.[59] As Douglass sees it, blacks of the southern Americas and African Americans would all profit from an arrangement that would link them together as part of a multiracial and transnational U.S. nationality in the Americas. Such was Douglass's hemispheric nationalism in 1871.

But where would such a nationality leave Haiti or the San Domingans? Given Sumner's resistance to Grant's annexation plan on the grounds that it posed a threat to Haitian nationality, we need to consider Douglass's thoughts on the subject in his fifth and sixth letters on Santo Domingo. As we have seen, in the wake of the *Dred Scott* decision, Douglass clearly was inspired by the revolutionary black republic of Haiti. Here was a black nationality in the Americas, Douglass argued in the late 1850s and early 1860s, that African Americans could take pride in and perhaps even consider as an alternative to U.S. nationality. But in 1871 Douglass views Haiti quite differently. Though he remarks that "the colored people of the world over are indebted to Hayti more than to any other country for the little respect meted out by the nations of the Caucasian race towards those of African descent," he ultimately regards Haiti as having "failed to keep pace with the civilization of the age." Much of his commentary on Haiti in the Santo Domingo letters therefore focuses on what he calls the black republic's "superstition," the way that, as he puts it, "Catholicism and Voodoism and Fetichism flourish within her borders."[60] Douglass would be writing altogether differently about Haiti in the late 1880s and early 1890s, but during the early 1870s he made the pragmatic decision, buoyed by his confidence in the progressive potential of the post–Civil War moment, to distance himself from Haiti in the Santo Domingo letters, perhaps because he regarded the black republic as reinforcing the views of white racists about the detrimental, antiprogressive affects of the tropics. Moreover, Douglass at this time may well have concluded that black Haiti was not composite enough.[61]

Although Santo Domingo annexation was basically killed in Congress in June 1871, Douglass and Grant clung to the possibilities of annexation. Douglass developed a stump speech, "Santo Domingo," which he first delivered in 1871 and presented through 1873, the year that he surrendered the publishing and editing responsibilities of the *New National Era* to his son Lewis H. Douglass and the original founding editor, J. Sella Martin. In a version of the talk presented in St. Louis in January 1873 and re-printed in the 23 January 1873 issue of the *New National Era*, Douglass once again described the annexation plan as something different from Manifest Destiny or brute U.S. imperialism. For Douglass, Santo Domingo annexation was about a hemispheric nationalism in which various peoples of the Americas recognize their common aspirations and shared humanity. In continuing to call for Santo Domingo annexation, Douglass thus invokes the cosmopolitanism that throughout his career would have such a pronounced impact on his views of race and nation, appealing to "that side which allies man to the Infinite, which in some sense leads him to view the broad world as his country and all mankind as his country-men." In such a world, race is no longer the defining term of nation, and nations (or at least all those other than the United States) lose their primacy: "Greatness does not ask the nation or race of the human race—it kindles the enthusiasm of all."[62]

But even as he offers this visionary hope for a global human oneness that has as its starting point the forging of a oneness in the American hemisphere, Douglass, who regularly acknowledged the fact of his white paternity, refused to set aside the terms central to U.S. nationalism as understood by white nationalists and literary nationalists of the time. Thus, in the manner of Higginson in the *Atlantic*, he remarks in the same 1873 speech on the progressive worth of the "Saxon and Protestant civilization" that, as he presents it, has helped to raise the United States beyond the "ignorance, weakness, and barbarism" supposedly characterizing some black nations of the southern Americas (such as Haiti); and he scoffs once again at Sumner's concerns about "wiping out a colored nationality," asserting that the benevolent aim of U.S. policy is to lift the San Domingans, among others, "to our high standard of nationality."[63] At the endpoint of his campaign for Santo Domingo annexation, Douglass reveals himself as committed to the paradoxes of a postnational U.S. nationality and a raceless composite nationality driven progressively forward by the forces of Anglo-Saxonism. There are all sorts of good pragmatic reasons behind Douglass's somewhat bizarre thinking at this time, which led him to diminish black Haiti in the name of a "composite nationality" that he hoped would counter the white supremacism asserting itself with a vengeance as he was championing Santo Domingo annexation and an African American literary nationalism in the *New National Era*. There would be a return to Haiti in the years following the 1877 compromises and betrayals that led to the end of Reconstruction—a return marked by a striking reappraisal of the independent black republic. But first there would be Rome.

Saint Peter's Black Toe

Douglass visited Rome in 1887 and described his sojourn in the concluding section of the 1892 *Life and Times of Frederick Douglass*, an expanded version of his 1881 autobiography of the same name. Typically, nineteenth-century American travelers to Rome were drawn to the art and history of the city, and even to aspects of Roman Catholicism, while at the same time recoiling from what they portrayed as the decadence and duplicity of Protestant culture's traditionally seductive antirepublican enemy. Accounts of such conflicted responses to Old World culture and art had long been central to American literary nationalism, and much of what Douglass has to say about Rome in the 1892 edition of *Life and Times* suggests a desire to present himself as the archetypal U.S. traveler in the mode of such nationalists.[64] Although he suffers an initial disappointment when arriving in newer areas of Rome, which remind him of "Paris, London, or New York," Rome very quickly becomes "Rome": "[T]he Eternal City, seated on its throne of seven hills, fully gave us all it had promised, banished every disappointment, and filled our minds with ever-increasing wonder and amazement." But even as he confesses his attraction to the city's spiritual grandeur, he voices skepticism and concern about the possibly mendacious, despotic, and aristocratic character of the Roman Catholic Church. He wryly notes that "[r]eligion seems to be in Rome the chief business by which men live," and he condemns the "fanaticism . . . encouraged by a church so worldly-wise as that of Rome." The doubleness of his response, both critique and attraction, is nicely captured in his remarks on St. Peter's. Commenting on "the wealth and grandeur within," Douglass points out that "the Church of Rome today receives gifts from all the Christian world, our own republican country included." Yet despite his portrayal of the church as a money power, he finds himself succumbing to the atmosphere of "ethereal glory" at St. Peter's, and he concludes his remarks on a note of admiration: "St. Peter's, by its vastness, wealth, splendor, and architectural perfections, acts upon us like some great and overpowering natural wonder. It awes us into silent, speechless admiration."[65] Decadent and yet mesmerizingly beautiful, the simultaneously worldly and timeless St. Peter's offers a solace, Douglass suggests, currently unavailable in Protestant-republican America.

In 1887, Douglass needed solace. With the end of Reconstruction and the subsequent rise of Jim Crow laws, antimiscegenation statutes, and public lynchings of African Americans, Douglass, as in the years immediately following the *Dred Scott* decision, once again had grave doubts about the future of blacks in the United States. He also had vocational concerns, for with the election to the presidency of the Democrat Grover Cleveland in 1886, he was forced to resign his position as recorder of deeds for the District of Columbia. And there were personal concerns as well: a continuing public controversy about his marriage to a white woman, Helen Pitts, whom he had married in 1884 at the age of sixty-six, less than two years after the death of his first wife, Anna. A graduate of Mount Holyoke College, Pitts worked as Douglass's secretary when he was recorder of deeds in the early 1880s, and their marriage was greeted with considerable outrage: Douglass was reviled by blacks and whites (including Pitts's family) for marrying someone outside of his "race." In response to his critics, Douglass, as he had on many other occasions, aggressively challenged binaristic notions of racial difference, asserting, for example, in an interview printed in the 26 January 1884 issue of the *Washington Post*: "I am not an African, as may be seen from my features and hair, and it is equally easy to discern that I am not a Caucasian." Consistent with his statements on the matter since the 1840s, he argued for the importance of transcending race, declaring in the same interview: "You may say that Frederick Douglass considers himself a member of the one race which exists."[66] Writing about his marriage in 1892, just a few years before the Supreme Court's *Plessy v. Ferguson* decision would once again enshrine whiteness as the crucial identifying mark for the privileges of national citizenship, he cagily begins the new section added to the 1881 *Life and Times* by listing the various questions he is repeatedly asked about his racial status and marriage: "In what proportion does the blood of the various races mingle in my veins, especially how much white blood and how much black blood entered in my composition? . . . Whether I considered myself more African than Caucasian, or the reverse? Whether I derived my intelligence from my father, or from my mother, from my white, or from my black blood?"[67] The implication of this rhetorical opening is that Americans will be on the path to addressing their race problem only after they come to realize the intellectual and moral bankruptcy of such questions.

When Douglass departed for Europe with Helen in late 1886, then, he may have simply been seeking a short-term escape from troubles on the home front. Additional purposes for the tour became clearer to Douglass soon after he arrived in England, for it was at that time that he decided to add Rome and Egypt to his itinerary.[68] The evidence suggests that Douglass initially intended to use his visit to Egypt as a kind of fact-finding expedition that would help him to argue, in the manner of Martin Delany and many other nineteenth-century black leaders, that Western civilization had key sources in Africa and thus that those of African descent had legitimate claims to what Douglass in a letter to his son Lewis Douglass referred to as "the moral support of Ancient Greatness."[69] As he writes in the 1892 *Life and Times*, "I had . . . an ethnological purpose in the pursuit of which I hope[d] to turn my visit to some account in combating American prejudice against the darker colored races of mankind, and at the same time to raise colored people somewhat in their own estimation and thus stimulate them to higher endeavors."[70] It is ultimately in Rome, not Africa, that Douglass finds what he most values and believes will be of the greatest use in making his antiracist arguments in the United States: a conjunction of mixed-blood peoples (the Romans) along with the rise of Western civilization. And yet in the 1892 *Life and Times*, Douglass's presentation of the importance of blackness to Western civilization relates less to a reinvigorated celebration of a composite U.S. nationality than to a surprising re-embrace of a hemispheric nationalism that has Haiti at its center.

But let us keep the initial focus on Douglass's travels of 1886–87. Douglass and his wife began their tour in England in late September of 1886, stopping first at Liverpool and then making their way to London, where they met Anna and Ellen Richardson, the British sisters who had helped to purchase Douglass from slavery in 1846 for $711, and Julia Griffiths Crofts, the now-widowed white woman who had been Douglass's editor (and alleged paramour) during the early 1850s.[71] In October the Douglasses traveled to Paris, where they remained for eleven weeks, touring the city with, among others, Theodore Stanton, the son of Elizabeth Cady Stanton, and Theodore Tilton, who had left the United States in 1883 after his scandalous lawsuit failed to establish that Henry Ward Beecher had had an adulterous affair with his wife. During their stay, Douglass and his wife visited a number of people and landmarks that spoke to Douglass's interest in slavery and race: Haitian students from the French colonies whose intelligence and sophistication, Douglass wrote to a friend, testified to "the possibilities of the colored race"; a statue honoring Alphonse Marie Louis de Lamartine; and Gustave Doré's statue of the mixed-race writer Alexandre Dumas. According to Stanton, who published an account of his Parisian tours with the Douglasses in the journal *Open Court*, when Douglass viewed the statue of Lamartine, he dwelt "on the fact that the poet-President signed in 1848 the decrees that freed all the slaves of the French colonies, and his eyes were attracted by the resemblance of Lamartine's face to that of Lincoln"; and when he viewed the statue of Dumas he was unmoved, for he "remembered how this son of a negress had never spoken a word or written a line in defense of his mother's race."[72]

Although Paris clearly stimulated Douglass's thinking on racial matters, he devotes relatively little attention to describing the city, focusing instead on Rome and Egypt. In the 1892 *Life and Times*, he sets up the significance of his journey from Paris to Rome in terms of issues of race and civilization, referring to "the country lying between Paris and Rome" as "the cradle in which the civilization of Western Europe and our own country was rocked and developed," and describing the necessity of traveling even farther east to study its birth. In making this journey, he states, the traveler moves on a continuum from nations exhibiting relative whiteness to nations exhibiting relative blackness, with the implication being that there is no essential purity of races. In a passage crucial to Douglass's conception of the role of black people in Western history, he writes about the journey from Paris to Rome as a journey toward "blackness": "As the traveler moves eastward and southward between these two great cities, he will observe an increase of black hair, black eyes, full lips, and dark complexions. He will observe a southern and eastern style of dress, gay colors, startling jewelry, and an outdoor free-and-easy movement of the people." He presents these physical characteristics and signs of racial gradation as consistent with his "ethnological" project of using his eastward journey to develop arguments about the indebtedness of relatively white Western Europe to relatively black Northern Africa. For example, he notes that, like blacks in Egypt (and the American South), workers in France and Italy congregate together at night and carry their supplies on their heads. This provides evidence, he says, that refutes notions of "inferiority peculiar to the Negro," showing that "[e]ven if originated by the Negro," various cultural practices have "been well copied by some of the best types of the Caucasian. In any case, it may be welcomed as a proof of a common brotherhood."[73]

Douglass of course had long been thinking about race and cultural origins. As mentioned in chapter 3, in one of his best-known antebellum lectures, "The Claims of the Negro Ethnologically Considered" (1854), he had sought to counter the racist, polygenist arguments of the leading exponents of the so-called American School of ethnology—Josiah Nott, Samuel Morton, George Gliddon, and others—who had made avowedly scientific claims about the racial and cultural inferiority, separate creations, and absolute difference of blacks in relation to whites. Intent on demonstrating that Egypt's contributions to Western civilization had everything to do with the white blood of its inhabitants, Samuel Morton, for example, in his influential *Crania Ægyptiaca* (1844), asserted that the "Valley of the Nile, both in Egypt and Nubia, was originally peopled by a branch of the Caucasian race." In "Claims," Douglass ridiculed Morton for trying "to prove that the ancient Egyptians were totally distinct from the negroes, and to deny all relationship between," and he argued instead for "a near relationship between the present enslaved and degraded negroes, and the ancient highly civilized and wonderfully endowed Egyptians." Convinced that the scientific racism of the American School's ethnologists was being put to the service of legitimating racial hierarchies in the United States, Douglass proclaimed that "the whole argument in defence of slavery, becomes utterly worthless the moment the African is proved to be equally a man with the Anglo-Saxon."[74]

During the 1880s and early 1890s, Douglass was still fighting the battle against scientific racism, for the good reason that such thinking continued to hold considerable sway in U.S. culture, serving as crucial underpinnings to what he described as "the steady march of the slave power toward national supremacy since the agonies of the war."[75] In his 1892 account of his 1886–87 travels to Europe and Africa, Douglass celebrates both the black sources of Western civilization and the multiracial origins and development of the West. Given the symbolic place of his marriage in this social and political program, it is not surprising that he should seek to underscore the mixed-raced identities of Europeans and Africans (and, by extension, Americans), presenting mixture rather than purity as crucial determinants of civilization and progress.

In this regard, it is significant that when Douglass sailed to Europe in 1886 on the aptly named *City of Rome*, he should have spent a full day reading Ralph Waldo Emerson's *English Traits* (1856). (According to his "Diary, 1886–1894," Douglass was able to devote himself to Emerson on 20 September 1886 because his wife was confined to their cabin with seasickness.)[76] In the chapter in *English Traits* titled "Race," Emerson challenged the central tenets of the Scottish physician Robert Knox's 1850 book *The Races of Man: A Fragment*, which tried to prove, in Emerson's words, "that races are imperishable." Refuting Knox, Emerson maintains that the idea of a pure or unchanging race is a fiction, for the progress of Western civilization, he declares, "eats away the old [racial] traits." Especially gratifying to Douglass would have been Emerson's remarks on racial gradation and mixture. Emerson writes: "[T]hough we flatter the self-love of men and nations by the legend of pure races, all our experience is of the gradation and resolution of races, and strange resemblances meet us everywhere." Even the English, he says, have a "composite character [that] betrays a mixed origin." In contemplating English racial types, Emerson notes that "the Roman has implanted his dark complexion." It is precisely such intermixture, such "composite character," Emerson concludes, that contributed to England's emergence as one of the world's great civilizations and powers.[77] In his diary entry on Emerson, Douglass remarks, "I . . . have been glad to find my own views of the civilization of England supported by one so thoughtful and able as the Sage of Concord" (20 September 1886).

Emerson's discussion of the darkness of the Romans, and the overall mixed racial character of Europe, no doubt helped to corroborate Douglass's own account, approximately forty years later, of Rome's racial dynamics. For it is in Europe's Rome, as much as in Africa's Egypt, that Douglass takes note of racial mixture and blackness. Douglass made an initial two-week visit to Rome, arriving on 19 January 1887 and soon meeting up with the small black expatriate community that found Rome a congenial political and aesthetic refuge from a racist United States. This group included the sculptor Edmonia Lewis, who had been living in Rome since the late 1860s, and Sarah Remond, an abolitionist who was the sister of Douglass's close friend Charles Remond, the abolitionist lecturer.[78] In the enthusiastic spirit of these Rome-enamored expatriates, Douglass in *Life and Times* focuses much of his attention on describing his fascination with the relics of ancient Rome and the practices of the contemporary Roman Catholic Church. But he also talks about racial and cultural difference. Contemplating the Arch of Titus, he laments the fate of the Jews in losing their "beloved Jerusalem," and he suggests that his ability to sympathize with the Jews has much to do with the fact that as an African American he has suffered similar indignities based on racial prejudice: "[N]one who have never suffered a like scorn can adequately feel for their humiliation." He then moves from a lament for the Jews' sufferings to a discussion of the holiness and bravery of Saint Paul and Saint Peter, and this discussion culminates in a playfully arch image of worshippers paying their respects to the "black" statue of Saint Peter at St. Peter's: "I had some curiosity in seeing devout people going up to the black statue of St. Peter—I was glad to find him black, I have no prejudice against his color—and kissing the old fellow's big toe, one side of which has been nearly worn away by these devout and tender salutes of which it has been the cold subject."[79]

The joke here of course is that the bronze of the statue has blackened to such an extent that Douglass can present a picture of Saint Peter and his worshippers that inverts conventional images of white supremacy. Given the rise of public lynchings of blacks during the 1880s, there may even be a phallic visual pun in the image of whites kissing the saint's extended black toe. But more is going on in the passage than just a comic (and bawdy) racial inversion. Consistent with his conception of the Continent as becoming blacker as the traveler moves east, the image of a black Saint Peter that Douglass presents in *Life and Times* speaks to his own efforts to "blacken" traditional accounts of European and Christian history by questioning assumptions of whiteness. Along these lines, it is important to note that Douglass's description of the statue of Saint Peter in his 1892 autobiography departs considerably from his 1887 diary entry on the statue. When he wrote up the account in the early 1890s for the revised *Life and Times*, Douglass made a conscious decision to "blacken" Saint Peter, for his initial 1887 diary entry on the statue makes no mention of Saint Peter's "blackness." Instead, he matter-of-factly describes the "men and women . . . crossing themselves, and some kissing the toe of St. Peter, which toe has already been nearly kissed away" (24 June 1887). Whereas Douglass in 1886–87 seems approving of Emerson's notion in *English Traits* of the perishability of the races, there is much in the revised 1892 autobiography that underscores the persistence of blackness.

Douglass concludes his account of the Roman Catholic worshippers of the "black" Saint Peter by remarking, "It is doubtless a great comfort to these people, after all, to have kissed the great toe of the black image of the Apostle Peter." Having reinforced his imaging of a black Saint Peter, he then underscores, in an anticipation of the pragmatic, ethnographic mode of William James's *Varieties of Religious Experience* (1902), the psychological and spiritual similarities between whites' religious practices in Rome and blacks' religious practices in the United States: "I felt, in looking upon these religious shows in Rome, as the late Benjamin Wade said he felt at a Negro camp meeting, where there was much howling, shouting, jumping: 'This is nothing to me, but it surely must be something to them.'"[80] In his subsequent discussion of his travels to Egypt, Douglass takes a similar cultural relativistic approach, linking that which has traditionally been viewed as "white" with that which has traditionally been viewed as "black."

In *Life and Times* Douglass remarks that what he hoped to gain by journeying from Rome to Egypt in February 1887 was evidence in support of his "ethnological" vision: "I had a theory for which I wanted the support of facts in the range of my own knowledge. But more of this in another place." Douglass never did write up a major statement on ethnology in some other place, but we can speculate that he planned to revisit the main arguments of his 1854 "The Claims of the Negro Ethnologically

Considered" by collecting the empirical information that would support his thesis, as elaborated in "Claims," that "Greece and Rome—and through them Europe and America—have received their civilization from the ancient Egyptians," and that the Egyptians "were, undoubtedly, just about as dark in complexion as many in this country who are considered genuine negroes."[81] And yet, consistent with his notion of racial continuum and gradation, by the time he makes his way to Egypt, he believes that he has entered a realm of greater but not "pure" blackness. Shortly after arriving in Cairo, he writes in a diary entry of 18 February 1887: "I do not know of what color and features the ancient Egyptians were, but the great mass of the people I have yet seen would in America be classed with Negroes. This would not be a scientific description but an American description." In a letter of 20 February 1887 to his son Lewis, Douglass makes a similarly jaundiced point about the unscientific, culturally inflected nature of racial categories in the United States, observing that the Egyptians "are very much like the mulatto, and would be taken for such in the United States." Douglass's thinking on Egypt and race may well have been influenced by David Walker, who in his 1829 *Appeal* proclaimed that "the Egyptians, were Africans or coloured people, such as we are—some of them yellow and others dark—a mixture of Ethiopians and the natives of Egypt—about the same as you see the coloured people of the present day."[82] In this regard it should be recalled that as a mulatto Douglass earlier in his career had personally linked himself to Egypt, noting in the third chapter of his 1855 *My Bondage and My Freedom* that his mother's features resembled those of an Egyptian head depicted in James Cowles Prichard's *The Natural History of Man* (1845), a text that had argued for connections between Egyptians and blacks. (Douglass offers similar comments on his mother and Prichard in the opening chapter of the 1881 and 1892 editions of *Life and Times*.)[83] From this perspective, and in light of his visiting Egypt approximately thirty years after having asserted this familial connection, Douglass can be seen as having reached a kind of spiritual homeland in a nation that, although literally in Africa, is figured as a border zone between Western Europe and the southern reaches of an even "blacker" Africa.

But it is a "homeland" that ultimately makes Douglass uneasy. In his diary he describes how he "saw various forms of squalor, disease, and deformity—all manner of importunate beggary. It was truly pitiful to see a people thus grovelling by filth and utter wretchedness" (19 February 1887). As a champion of women's rights since the 1840s, he was also troubled by the situation of Egyptian women. Less than a month before visiting Egypt, he wrote in his diary about the "very cheerful, happy—and successful" situation in Rome of the black artist Edmonia Lewis (26 January 1887). By way of contrast, Egyptian women, he states, are "kept in ignorance and degraded, having no existence except that of ministering to the pride and lusts of the men who *own* them as slaves are owned" (19 February 1887). In *Life and Times*, Douglass adopts a similarly critical perspective on Egypt, focusing on the country's lack of progress: "Egypt may have invented the plow, but it has not improved upon the invention."[84] Although his goal in visiting Egypt, as stated in letters and diary entries of 1887, was to adduce the evidence that would combat white racists' denigrations of blacks' place in Western history, by the time he wrote up the account for the 1892 edition of his autobiography, the road to Africa has led him back to Rome, where greater progress and racial mixing are on display. In describing his return to Rome in *Life and Times*, he evokes a sense of the progressive movement of history and race from east to west, as he talks of passing in "sight of Crete, looking from the deck of our steamer perhaps as it did when Paul saw it on the voyage to Rome eighteen hundred years ago."[85] Linking himself to an Egyptian Paul, he asserts his ties to the rise of Christianity and progress in the West and reaffirms his identity as an antiracist leader *and* a person of mixed blood.

Douglass's letters and diary entries of 1886 and 1887, then, suggest that he initially conceived of Rome as a stopping point on the road to Africa in his eastward journey from lighter-skinned to darker-skinned peoples and nations. But by the time he published the 1892 *Life and Times*, he had come to see Rome as the more rhetorically useful locale; he wants to place himself (and African Americans) more on the westward road to the American hemisphere than on the eastward road to Africa. One reason that Douglass wished to demonstrate a greater allegiance to Europe was that he sought to challenge the notion that he and other blacks had some "natural" connection to Africa; such a challenge was consistent with his career-long resistance to colonization and emigration programs that would transport African Americans to what he once termed "the pestilential shores of Africa." He was also concerned that the development of a chauvinistic race pride among African Americans would only further contribute to the (self-)segregationist practices that kept blacks in the anomalous position of being what he termed a "nation within a nation." And of course through his representation of his marriage and travels, he wanted to promote a racial mixing that would teach the large truth that

Douglass took from Acts 17:26, "that God has made of one blood all nations of men to dwell on all the face of the earth."[86]

There was also a specifically political reason for his desire to dissociate African Americans from Africa. In 1889 Douglass was appointed minister resident and consul general to the Republic of Haiti by president Benjamin Harrison, and in October of that year he arrived in Port au Prince with Helen to begin his work as a diplomat. Less than two years into the job, however, Douglass was criticized by a number of white politicians and journalists for having deliberately sabotaged U.S. efforts to obtain a naval base at Haiti. These critics believed that because Douglass was a black man, he must have been working secretly to forward the interests of a black nation. He resigned from the position in the summer of 1891 and around that time began writing up his account of his visit to Rome for the updated edition of *Life and Times*. A celebration of Africa at the expense of Rome would have given additional quarter to racists' arguments about Douglass's larger allegiance to a black nationality. That said, it is worth noting that in the introduction to the 1881 edition of *Life and Times*, George L. Ruffin (probably with Douglass's approval) had hailed the "worth and genius" of an autobiography that links Douglass to great traditions of black revolutionism and artistry. "To the names of Toussaint Louverture and Alexander Dumas," Ruffin proclaims, "is to be added that of Frederick Douglass."[87]

Ruffin's invocation of the celebrated Haitian revolutionary anticipates with a surprising prescience Douglass's sympathetic depiction of Haiti in the 1892 expanded version of *Life and Times*. In this edition, the chapters on Haiti follow the chapter on Rome, and the entire new section added to the 1881 version could be read as a coherent unit in which Douglass traverses the United States, Rome, and Haiti in a sometimes dizzying rhetorical effort to simultaneously locate and dislocate racial and national identities. If the Rome chapter, read in isolation, presents a geography of racial gradation that appears to place a high value on racial mixing, that same chapter, read in the larger context of the final section of *Life and Times*, suggests that what Douglass regarded as of primary importance in his visit to Rome was precisely the discovery of blackness in even a "white" like Saint Peter. The racial thinking that informs his account of Rome bears significantly on the subsequent chapters on Haiti (and may have been generated by his recent experiences in Haiti) and helps us to see some of the crucial connections between Douglass's nation thinking of 1857–61 and 1883–92.

During the late 1850s, Douglass's interest in Haiti was spurred in part by the *Dred Scott* decision of 1857. Crucially, in an early chapter added to the final section of the 1892 edition of *Life and Times*, Douglass presents a *Dred Scott* moment of 1883. In the despicable tradition of "the Dred Scott decision," he declares, the Supreme Court has placed "itself on the side of prejudice, proscription, and persecution" by ruling in 1883 that the 1875 Civil Rights Law, which was intended to enforce the provisions of the Fourteenth Amendment, was unconstitutional. Coming not too long after the end of Reconstruction, the decision to renege on enforcing laws intended to ensure blacks' rights to U.S. citizenship, he says, is "the most flagrant example . . . of national deterioration." Douglass's narrative of his European tour follows shortly after the invocation of *Dred Scott*, and the expanded *Life and Times* culminates and concludes with an account of his troubled stint as a U.S. diplomat in Haiti. One senses from these chapters that Douglass's decision to publish an expanded edition of his autobiography was motivated in large part by his desire to tell his side of his controversial tenure as a diplomat in the Caribbean, to the extent that his narrative of the Rome visit itself, where he finds "evidences of a common identity with the African,"[88] needs to be read in relation to the autobiography's closing chapters on Haiti. For the surprise of those chapters is that while they seem to have been written in an effort to vindicate his U.S. Americanness, they speak equally if not more powerfully to his renewed sense of alliance with the black republic of Haiti.

That alliance developed from Douglass's warm friendships with Haitian officials while doing his diplomatic work, and it intensified when he was vilified by U.S. officials and the national press for his failure to negotiate a deal with the Haitian government that would have allowed the United States to use Haiti's Môle–St. Nicolas as a naval base. Douglass's critics claimed that the black Douglass had a "natural" proclivity to side with the Haitians, though the fact is that Harrison had appointed Douglass to the diplomatic position in 1889 precisely because members of his cabinet thought that Douglass's blackness would make him the best possible negotiator for a base they believed was owed the U.S. Navy as payback for helping General Hyppolite take power in a recent coup.

Douglass tells his side of the story in the final three chapters of his 1892 autobiography. Twice alluding to his earlier support for Santo Domingo annexation, Douglass uses that now two-decades-old controversy to assert that in the past he has demonstrated a willingness to extend U.S. influence into the Caribbean when particular nations "wished to come to us," and also to make the point that Haitian leaders, who had been "strongly opposed" to the Santo Domingo plan, basically understood his position at the time and were now prepared to work with him as a diplomat. As Douglass describes his diplomatic labors in Haiti, he quickly developed amicable relations with Haitian government officials that would have allowed him to act effectively as a negotiator had he not been pressured by U.S. officials for instant results. Reprinting within the 1892 *Life and Times* an article that he had published about the affair in the *North American Review* in late 1891, Douglass describes how in addition to pressures from the U.S. government, there were demands from New York's William P. Clyde and Company for a favorable contract for a steamer route between New York and Haiti. Even with all of these pressures, marked by increasing displays of thuggery by the U.S. government and the Clyde Company, Douglass asserts in the strongest possible terms that he sought to remain true to his diplomatic mission: "I am charged with sympathy for Haiti. I am not ashamed of that charge, but no man can say with truth that my sympathy with Haiti stood between me and my honorable duty that I owed to the United States or to any citizen of the United States."[89]

Douglass's candid concession of sympathy for Haiti is telling here. Ifeoma Nwankwo remarks that Douglass in his diplomatic role was caught up in a struggle "[n]ot only . . . to be both American and Negro, but also to be a 'good' U.S. citizen and a good 'brother' to the Haitians." And yet his reflections on the affair in *Life and Times* (and the *North American Review* and elsewhere) for the most part convey less a struggle than his affinity for Haiti and contempt for the United States. He condemns the United States for its long history of racist paternalism toward the black republic, remarking on the nation's "peculiar and intense prejudice against the colored race"; he lashes out at officials in the White House for deciding in early 1891 to give the bullying Rear Admiral Gherardi authority over his own diplomatic efforts during the negotiations; and he excoriates Gherardi and the U.S. Navy for trying to intimidate Haiti by placing U.S. naval vessels in a cruising position off the Haitian port of Grand-Gosier: "What wisdom was there in confronting Haiti at such a moment with a squadron of large ships of war with a hundred cannon and two thousand men?" As for the Clyde firm's attempt to force a trade-route contract on the Haitians, he says that he has "nothing but disgust for the method by which this scheme was pressed upon Haiti."[90]

Douglass's private correspondence to Secretary of State James D. Blaine similarly reveals a negotiator who increasingly sided with the Haitians in

the face of U.S. mendacity. His honesty in these letters no doubt contributed to the administration's decision to relieve him of his diplomatic
duties. On the one hand, as he would in *Life and Times*, he wishes to
demonstrate to Blaine that as a black he is fully capable of representing
the United States; on the other, he is annoyed with U.S. bullying tactics
and increasingly sympathetic to the position of the Haitians. Angered by
Gherardi's attempted naval intimidation of Haiti, Douglass in June 1890
writes Blaine that in his latest meeting with Haiti's minister of foreign
affairs Anténor Firmin, he (Douglass) found "it prudent . . . to express my
disapproval of the presence as described of the two schooners at Grand
Gosier, and to say to him that I will endeavor to prevent the recurrence of
any incident of a similar character." Approximately one year later, when
Douglass asks for a leave of absence (and in effect resigns under pressure
from Blaine and others), he extols the peace and calm of a country "under
fully organized Government," and then rhetorically serves as President
Hyppolite's ambassador in conveying his hopes that Haiti will have "been
able to refuse the lease requested by the United States without affecting
our relations to that great country."[91]

Douglass concludes *Life and Times* with this remarkable sentence: "I
have been the recipient of many honors, among which my unsought
appointment by President Benjamin Harrison to the office of Minister
Resident and Consul General to represent the United States at the capital
of Haiti, and my equally unsought appointment by President Florvil
Hyppolite to represent Haiti among all the civilized nations of the globe
at the World's Columbian Exposition, are crowning honors to my long
career and a fitting and happy close to my whole public life."[92] This is
remarkable for the way Douglass puts his U.S. and Haitian honors in an
equivalent balance, and it is perhaps most remarkable for the way it
suggests an alternative history to Douglass's career. What happens to our
understanding of Douglass as an "American" nationalist if we take his last-
mentioned achievement in the final edition of his autobiography—the
honor of representing Haiti at Chicago's World's Columbian Exposition—
as his final achievement? Would it not seem that, for Douglass, all roads
lead not to Rome (or Washington, D.C.) but to Haiti? A brief look at an
alternative Douglass—a Douglass who reaches his endpoint, or *telos*, in
1893—will provide the endpoint of this chapter and will suggest the
somewhat subterranean connections between Rome and Haiti in Douglass's thinking about race and nation in his final decade.

The wildly popular 1893 World's Columbian Exposition in Chicago celebrated an Anglo-Saxonist vision of U.S. nationalism in an architectural setting featuring a White City (the utopian figuration of a racially pure U.S. extending into a racially pure global space) and a Midway Plaisance (an ethnological figuration of the more anarchic space of the nonwhite world in a honky-tonk boardwalk with a Ferris wheel and displays of third-world and "primitive" peoples, such as Eskimos). African Americans were systematically excluded from all U.S. exhibits, and the only representation given to blacks in the Chicago fair was a sideshow-like display of a Dahomeyan village on the Midway and the more respectfully situated Haitian Pavilion overseen by Douglass. Given the exclusion of blackness from the exposition, it is not clear how Haiti managed to be invited at all, though one might speculate that Douglass or some other U.S. governmental authority had made the invitation during the negotiations over the Môle–St. Nicolas in a canny effort to suggest to Haitian officials that the black republic really did share common cause with the United States. However the invitation came about, the fact is that the Haitian pavilion provided the only space in the exposition for African American writers and leaders. As Robert W. Rydell remarks: "Just when Chicago's exposition authorities thought they had effectively excluded African Americans from their fair, America's best-known African American found a port of entry under the auspices of a foreign country long remembered for the slave insurrection led by Toussaint Louverture."[93] This was more than a "port of entry"; in some respects, Douglass had his own pavilion at the exposition, for the Haitian authorities turned over many of the responsibilities for running the pavilion to Douglass, ranging from contributing to the initial architectural design to hiring staff and arranging displays.

Among Douglass's most noted contributions to the Haitian pavilion was to make it into a site for the display of recent African American writing. This was a highly significant intervention on Douglass's part, for central to the self-celebrations of virtually all of the national pavilions at the exposition were displays of the respective nation's literary "products." Such displays were in the great tradition of the literary nationalism that took hold across Europe during the eighteenth century, in which national literatures were regarded as signal expressions of ethnic and racial character. Making use of the Haitian pavilion for the purposes of promoting African American writers such as Paul Laurence Dunbar and Ida B. Wells, Douglass, at least during the exposition, could not help but frame African American literature as more diasporic, hemispheric, and accented by race than he ever did as an African American literary nationalist for his various United States–based African American newspapers. Housed within "Haiti," such literature does not quite fit the race-less or cosmopolitan model for which Douglass has been celebrated, and it is decidedly not Anglo-American.

Shortly after receiving his commission from Haiti, Douglass hired Dunbar to work as his assistant. Dunbar wrote several poems devoted to the exposition and also distributed his first volume of poems, *Oak and Ivy*, at the Haitian pavilion. William Dean Howells, who became Dunbar's great champion, discovered him during the exposition. Working with journalists Ida B. Wells, Irvine Garland Penn, and Ferdinand Barnett, all of whom made visits to the pavilion, Douglass, while continuing to serve as Haiti's representative, edited and introduced a pamphlet, *The Reason Why the Colored American Is Not in the World's Columbian Exposition: The Afro-American's Contribution to Columbia Literature,* which declaimed against the exclusion of African Americans from Chicago's world's fair. Distributed during the 25 August 1893 "Colored American Day" that the exposition's organizers begrudgingly set aside to honor African Americans, the pamphlet features, among other things, an essay by Ida B. Wells on "Lynch Law" and an essay by I. Garland Penn on African Americans' "progress in education, in the professions, in the accumulation of wealth and literature."[94] Douglass himself chose to spend Colored American Day, or Jubilee Day, as African Americans preferred to call it, in the Haitian Pavilion, where Dunbar gave a poetry reading.

And it was from within the Haitian Pavilion and at the exposition's nearby Quinn Chapel that Douglass gave two of the most searching and revelatory speeches of his late career, "Haiti among the Foremost Civilized Nations of the Earth" and "Haiti and the Haitian People," both of which were delivered on 2 January 1893 on the occasion of the opening of the Haitian Pavilion. The lectures were published later that year as pamphlets, and "Haiti among the Foremost Civilized Nations of the Earth," which had been delivered in the Haitian Pavilion, was also published in the Haitian newspaper *Courier des Etats-Unis*, where it received accolades from its readers, helping further to establish Douglass's reputation there as an honorary citizen of Haiti. In this relatively short speech, Douglass takes the January opening of the pavilion as an opportunity to celebrate the January 1804 anniversary of Haiti's achievement of becoming an independent black republic. That achievement, he says, "is one of the most remarkable and one of the most wonderful events in the history of

this eventful century, and I may almost say, in the history of mankind."
What makes Haitian independence infinitely more remarkable than the
American Revolution, he declares, is that the Haitian people were battling
not just the French but also what Douglass terms "the ruling race of the
world": whites both within and beyond the borders of Haiti. Although
"[t]he world was all against them," the black revolutionaries succeeded
because "from these men of the negro race, came brave men, men who
loved liberty more than life," and none braver, "more humane, more free
from the spirit of revenge, more disposed to protect his enemies, and less
disposed to practice retaliation among his enemies than General Toussaint L'Ouverture." Reveling in "the success of the blacks," Douglass here
sets aside notions of a "composite nationality" in order to embrace a
hemispheric black nationality.[95]

In the longer and more substantial "Haiti and the Haitian People,"
Douglass similarly speaks less as a U.S. American or African American
than as a black man who has come to understand his close ties to the
independent black republic. "My subject is Haiti, the Black Republic; the
only self-made Black Republic in the world," he proclaims at the outset.
"It is a land strikingly beautiful, diversified by mountains, valleys, lakes,
rivers and plains"; "NO OTHER LAND HAS BRIGHTER SKIES." Over the
course of the speech, Douglass defends Haiti's refusal to be pressured by
the United States into granting rights to Môle–St. Nicolas ("Haiti has the
same right to refuse that we had to ask"); and he provides an extensive
historical and cultural overview of the nation while insisting that the
reason U.S. Americans have failed to appreciate the accomplishments of
the island nation is because they "have not yet forgiven Haiti for being
black . . . or forgiven the Almighty for making her black." Presenting the
Haitian revolution as having a remarkable impact on "the destiny of the
African race in our own country and elsewhere," Douglass, in the tradition of his 1857 address on West Indies emancipation, underscores the
role of black agency in achieving freedom for blacks in the American
hemisphere, holding up Haiti as "the original pioneer emancipator of the
nineteenth century": "We should not forget that the freedom you and I
enjoy to-day; that the freedom that eight hundred thousand colored
people enjoy in the British West Indies; the freedom that has come to the
colored race the world over, is largely due to the brave stand taken by the
black sons of Haiti ninety years ago." There is nothing in this speech
about the white sons, or fathers, of 1776. Sounding very much like the
Pan-African Martin Delany, he praises the black republic for "her progress

in the line of civilization" and in this way aligns Haiti on the westward course of civilization that, during his European and African travels, he had traced from Egypt to Rome and which he is now suggesting can be traced additionally to both the United States and Haiti. Haiti may have made slower progress because of its long history of having to fight off white colonial powers, but Douglass concludes that in light of "her known progress within the last twenty years," Haiti has every hope of becoming "highly progressive, prosperous, and happy."[96]

In this great Haitian speech of 1893, Douglass presents an image of blackness very different from the racial indistinctiveness or hybridity or just plain dissolution that he images in his idealized notion of a "composite nationality." Within a composite nationality, there is a blending and ultimately the possibility of the disappearance of racial identities. But in this speech, race is given a heightened political, cultural, and even biological prominence. With his celebration of the Haitian revolution and the continued example of Haiti as "the black man's country, now and forever," Douglass links African Americans to their southern neighbor and uses that hemispheric nationalism to invoke a larger global diasporic conception of "the destiny of the African race." In what has to be taken as a rather startling turn in Douglass's thought, he declares to his auditors: "[T]he people of Haiti, by reason of ancestral identity, are more interesting to the colored people of the United States than to all others, for the Negro, like the Jew, can never part with his identity and race." There was a time during the 1880s when Douglass, William Wells Brown, and other African Americans were suggesting that a possible way of addressing the race problem in the United States was to rid the nation of race altogether through intermarriage and "miscegenation." Here, Douglass embraces race as fundamental to transnational affiliations among black people, central to black consciousness and pride, and (contra Emerson) imperishable. And let us not forget Saint Peter's black toe. In that image of the persistence of blackness in a "white" saint, Douglass had discovered an enduring blackness that signals the centrality of blackness to Western civilization. That toe reappears in "Haiti and the Haitian People." Scoffing at the notion that Haiti has a "primitive" love of superstition, Douglass provides an example of European superstition that makes the Haitians seem positively civilized: "Christians at Rome kiss the great toe of a black image called St. Peter, and go up stairs on their knees to gain divine favor."[97] Contemplating that black toe from the vantage point of Haiti but from within the United States, Douglass through his humorous imaging of whites paying homage to blackness has never sounded more like David Walker in the way that he makes an appeal to the colored citizens of the world, but most expressly those of the American hemisphere, to take pride in their racial identity.

Douglass died on 20 February 1895, shortly after delivering a speech on women's suffrage to the International Council of Women at Metzerott Hall in Washington, D.C. That speech has been taken as a worthy end point to Douglass's approximately fifty-year commitment to women's suffrage and women's rights. Douglass's last major speech is "The Lessons of the Hour" (1894), which assails the "fiendish" practice of lynching and asserts that blacks are of a "mixed race" of "white and black" U.S. ancestors and that it would therefore be difficult to imagine "their native land anywhere outside of the United States."[98] That speech has been taken as a worthy end point to Douglass's equally long commitment to racial justice in a multiracial United States and a final summing up of his antiemigrationism. But what kind of narrative would we be telling about Douglass's life had he died not in February 1895 but shortly after delivering his two Haitian speeches in January 1893? Though there is admittedly something morbid about the question, my intent here is to push against the fixed narratives generated by overly confident assumptions of what constitutes the beginning, middle, and end point of careers under study. Were we for a moment to take January 1893 as our "end point" for a narrative about the life and career of Frederick Douglass, we would suddenly have a "new" Douglass: a Douglass who, rather than insisting on an African American (literary) nationalism that would contribute to a "composite" American nationality, recurrently moved beyond such nation-based conceptions to embrace a hemispheric (literary) nationalism that would contribute to a black transnationality; a Douglass who, rather than persisting in idealizations of an American Revolutionary tradition, found his greatest inspiration in a black revolutionary tradition; a Douglass who, rather than being complicitous in schemes of U.S. Caribbean expansionism, helped to develop some of the terms whereby critics have come to critique such expansionism; a Douglass who, rather than desiring to move beyond race, aligned himself with a blackness that extends from Saint Peter's toe to the republic of Haiti. This is a Douglass who never rests comfortably in race or nation, a Douglass whose literary and political writings make it excruciatingly difficult to locate race and nation. In short, this is a Douglass who does not lead us to but rather helps us better understand the imperial year of 1898.

Epilogue

Undoings Redux

The Spanish-American War of 1898, which led to the U.S. military occupation of Cuba and the Philippines in 1899, brought the United States a
glimpse of a new bi-oceanic empire far beyond the imaginings of Ulysses
S. Grant or Frederick Douglass. Given that the occupation of the Philippines in particular was accomplished through deceit and against the
wishes of the Filipino people, one imagines that had Douglass been alive,
he would have been one of the most vociferous opponents of this new
imperialistic aggression on the part of the United States. Or was this
aggression truly new? A number of historians and cultural critics have
argued that 1898 was the "natural culmination" of a history of U.S. imperialism that can be traced back to the Louisiana Purchase and Monroe
Doctrine of the early decades of the nineteenth century and then forward
to the war with Mexico, diplomatic and filibustering efforts to gain Cuba
during the 1850s, and various other ventures in Caribbean and Asian
expansionism from the 1850s to the 1890s.[1] Although this imperialism
narrative continues to hold considerable sway, some historians have recently asked searching questions about whether history actually unfolded
so tidily and predictably. Louis A Pérez Jr., for instance, argues that there
is "a persistent historical elusiveness" about the war of 1898, and that the
longstanding interest of many U.S. leaders in taking possession of Cuba
was just one of a myriad of factors that led the nation to the war, including
widely held sympathies for Cuba's struggle for independence from Spain
and (with the sinking of the *Maine*) mere "accident." Eric T. L. Love is
similarly wary of seeing the war as a culminating expression of a national
consensus on white empire, pointing out that the December 1898 Treaty
of Paris, which authorized occupation, passed by only a single vote in the
Senate in February 1899.[2] What if one senator had voted otherwise?

Clearly, dissent and debate remained central to the war of 1898, as did thinking about race and nation. But the connections between white racial nationalism and the war remain unclear. The popularity of social Darwinism at a time of increased immigration may have led to what Anders Stephanson has termed "a kind of civilizational imperialism under Anglo-Saxon impress."[3] Or, as Love contends, the pronounced Anglo-Saxonism of the period may have contributed to a resistance to imperialism, grounded in long-standing concerns that expansion into "non-white" nations threatened to undermine the supposed purity of a white United States. Among the key anti-imperialists of the late 1890s, unsurprisingly, was Frederick Douglass's former nemesis Carl Schurz, whose racist desire for a white U.S. nation led him to join the Anti-Imperialist League of Mark Twain, William Dean Howells, and Thomas Wentworth Higginson, who had their own, nonracist reasons for opposing U.S. imperialism. Arguments that the war of 1898 was the inevitable expression of U.S. Anglo-Saxonist imperialism fail to note that some opponents of the war based their opposition on a privileging of whiteness. It was for this very reason, as Love observes, that supporters of the war "worked deliberately, and successfully enough, to *remove* race from the debates," so that the war was presented as an anticolonial intervention and revenge for the sinking of the *Maine* rather than as an effort to expand a white empire.[4] Indeed, the anti-imperialist Twain initially supported the war of 1898 on just such humanitarian and patriotic grounds. Though there were anti-imperialists of all sorts during the late 1890s, the time may have simply been ripe for imperialists like McKinley and Roosevelt to assert their collective will. Understood in this way, the war was at least partly the result of human decision making in the flux and confusions of the moment.

But perhaps it was also the result of an imperial literature that fueled the growing enthusiasm for war. According to some critics, Richard Harding Davis's popular novel *Soldiers of Fortune* (1897) helped to pave the way for foreign intervention through its presentation of "imperial masculinity" working on "behalf of political and economic freedoms." And yet contemporary reviews of *Soldiers* convey little sense that readers were making connections between the fictional South American country of Olancho, where Davis's hero Robert Clay works to develop U.S. economic empire, and a possible invasion of Cuba. Moreover, Clay himself is genealogically linked to the filibusterer William Walker, whose reputation was rather mixed in the late nineteenth century. This is not to say that the novel, along with other fictions of the period, did not contribute to a rising imperialistic temper, but it remains difficult to argue for a causal influence between literature of the 1890s and the war of 1898 (just as it remains difficult to argue for a causal influence between *Uncle Tom's Cabin* and the Civil War).[5]

It is worth emphasizing in this regard that some of the most noted "literary nationalists" of the period had become increasingly convinced of the limits of nation-based writing, and though they continued to argue for the value of U.S. literature, especially in relation to British literary traditions, their arguments generally focused on U.S. writers' larger connections to international trends in realism and naturalism. Howells, for example, who would join his friend Twain in adopting an anti-imperialistic politics, declared in the November 1891 *Harper's New Monthly Magazine*: "[W]e wish to ask our critics if they have not been looking for American literature in the wrong place; or, to use an American expression which is almost a literature in itself, whether they have not been barking up the wrong tree. It appears to us that at this stage of the proceedings there is no such thing as nationality in the highest literary expression; but there is a universality, a humanity, which is very much better."[6] With a commitment to such "universality" and "humanity," it is not surprising that Howells and other like-minded literary critics, such as Higginson, should have become ardent anti-imperialists, though appeals to the "universal" language of freedom were also deployed by the imperialists themselves— and even by Davis's fictional character Clay as he manipulates events in Olancho to serve the interests of a U.S. mining company. Still, for Howells, Higginson, Twain, and, from a somewhat different diasporic perspective, W. E. B. Du Bois, anti-imperialism was ultimately a moral response to what they feared were new and ominous developments in U.S. foreign policy.[7]

Howells's cosmopolitanism sets him apart from the tradition of American literary nationalism that I have been tracing in this study. But this is not to say that an Anglo-Saxonist literary nationalism in the spirit of John O. Sullivan and Evert Duyckinck's Young America was not an important part of the late nineteenth-century cultural scene. One finds such boosterish literary nationalism in the writings of the first great generation of professional critics of American literature, who published their popular literary histories during the closing decades of the nineteenth century. As Kermit Vanderbilt, David Shumway, and Claudia Stokes have made clear in their own institutional histories of the field, the influential critics Moses Coit Tyler, Charles Richardson, Brander Matthews, and Barrett Wendell shared a conviction that the American literary mind was grounded in an

Anglo-Saxonism that had its most profound expression in New England. In *A History of American Literature* (1878, 1880), for instance, Tyler identified 1640 as a moment of consolidation that helped give rise to a racially defined "American" literature: "Since the year 1640, the New England race has not received any notable additions to its original stock; and to-day their Anglican blood is as genuine and as unmixed as that of any county in England." For Tyler and then for Charles Richardson, it was the productive mix of Teutonic or Anglo-Saxon blood and the North American environment that led to the growth of a distinctively American literature. As Richardson declares in the opening chapter of *American Literature* (1887), titled "The Race-Element in American Literature": "Behind literature is race; behind race, climate and environment." For Richardson, the valued "race" is Anglo-Saxonism, which he says can be found in its purest form in New England; thus he proclaims in language that recalls the evolutionary metaphors ironized by Hawthorne in *The House of the Seven Gables*: "The seeds of American literature were most effectively sown in New England." After celebrating the "physical, mental, and spiritual characteristics of the Saxons," Richardson presents them as conquerors of sorts, capable of "assimilating such foreign elements as may come into their way." From this perspective, a "Saxon" American literature will always remain distinctively American because of what Richardson claims is the Anglo-Saxon ability to absorb (or conquer) competing influences: "[T]he American Irishman, or German, or Frenchman, notwithstanding his love for fatherland, soon loses somewhat of his former nature, under the potent influence of new conditions and of the dominant Saxon temper." Or as Richardson puts it elsewhere in his study: "[T]he foreign race elements in American literature . . . are merely subordinated influences." Similar views inform the popular histories of Barrett Wendell and Brander Matthews. Matthews, for example, announces in *An Introduction to the Study of American Literature* (1896) that American distinctiveness, or what he terms "Americanism," derives from "the greatly-gifted New Englanders," and, like Richardson, he locates that distinctiveness in the productive mixing of New England Anglo-Saxonism with the North American environment.[8]

These are the works that have helped to shape the field of U.S. literary study by linking, indeed soldering, race (Anglo-Saxonism, Teutonism, whiteness) and nation (the United States and its literary traditions). As such, these late nineteenth-century U.S. literary histories point to the ways in which literary canons can uphold or, perhaps more accurately, create fixed ideas of the nation. New England continues to remain of central importance to conceptions of American literary history, and there are reasons for this centrality that have a basis in literary influence and complexity as well. But for the authors of these foundational American literary histories, influence and complexity were only part of the story. Stokes remarks that the pioneering literary historians of the late nineteenth century sought to "defend the cultural fort from foreigners (and the literary traditions they brought with them)," convinced that a distinctively American literature emerged from factors connected to race and environment. Whether such beliefs can be tied to the imperialism of 1898 is a matter of debate, given that Anglo-Saxonism could be used both to justify and oppose the war. And yet Richardson's image of the conquering Anglo-Saxon surely spoke to the possibilities of regarding imperialism as a "natural" expression of U.S. white racial nationalism. Perhaps these literary historians did help to set the groundwork for 1898; we know, for example, that Roosevelt was friendly with Matthews and published an extensive positive review of his literary history in 1896.[9] In the literary histories of Richardson and his contemporaries, there are tight connections between race and nation, with respect to what they regarded as the valued status quo; in the revisionist literary histories of our own time, there remain tight connections between race and the nation with respect to what critics regard as the failures of the status quo (such as imperialism and racism). There are limits to both perspectives. As I suggested in the prologue to this study, dislocating race and nation may depend in part on interrogating our own disciplinary formations.

In this book, I have sought to complicate overarching assumptions that the idea of a national literature of necessity upholds fixed ideas of the nation. During the nineteenth century, there were numerous competing nationalisms and no sure sense of which (if any) would become *the* defining nationalism. Often there was a disconnect or dialectical tension between American literary nationalism (specifically, the calls for an "American" literature by various constituencies) and the literature that emerged in partial response. The writers considered in this study were not alone in "undoing" or challenging the connections among race, nation, and literature that nationalists of their own time attempted to forge.

It would be useful here to return to the notion of "undoing" that I discussed in the prologue. In her complex formulation of the value of counterfactuals for helping to promote an interventionist relation to the past, Catharine Gallagher argues that an enhanced sense of "plausible chronologies" can help to free us from fixed national histories in which there are clear beginnings, middles, and ends. Gallagher proposes the value of the "undoing plot," which she analogizes to the "back to the future" narrative of the popular 1985 film of the same name. In such a plot, Gallagher explains, a switch of the past, or the unmooring of a seemingly fixed narrative moment, activates "counterfactual possibility and throws the previously accomplished present into an unrealized state."[10] To extrapolate these thoughts onto 1898: a back-to-the-future "undoing plot" would achieve a certain measure of such "unrealizability" by taking full account of the conflicts of the period, the different choices that could have been made or unmade, and the many narratives that can be developed by resisting the temptation to regard 1898 as a culminating end point. As Pérez remarks in the evocative conclusion to his study of the war of 1898: "[T]he past is never really resolved: things do not simply happen and end."[11] Such open-endedness is lacking in the teleologically informed literary histories of the late nineteenth century, which are all about locating race and nation in New England.

One discerns far more open-ended perspectives in writings of the late nineteenth century that, contra the professional literary historians, attempted to dislocate race and nation, in part through a kind of "back to the future" time travel. We have already noted such strategies in earlier writers of the nineteenth century. Consider, for instance, the suggestive scenes in *Pierre* that imaginatively propel the eponymous hero back into the past and destabilize Glendinning white genealogies, and consider as well the retrospective account of the possible crib-switching of white and black babies in *The Bondwoman's Narrative*. Subsequent revelations or even hints of such past switches instantly make "whites" of the future into "blacks," or at the very least trouble the distinctions between white and black. It is significant that during the turn-of-the-century historical moment supposedly characterized by a heightened conviction among whites of the United States' Anglo-Saxonist identity, there was an upsurge of fictions by black and white writers depicting similar such switches, either in the cradle or through other forms of mistaken identity, which, when dramatically revealed, bring about abrupt redefinitions of racial identity. Howells's *An Imperative Duty* (1891), Frances Harper's *Iola Leroy* (1892), Kate Chopin's "Désirée's Baby" (1893), Twain's *Pudd'nhead Wilson* (1894), Charles Chesnutt's *The House behind the Cedars* (1900), Pauline Hopkins's *Hagar's Daughter* (1901–2), among others, all depict such racial turns in which white suddenly becomes black and black white.[12] As was true of *The House of the Seven Gables, Pierre,* and *The Bondwoman's Narrative,* we might regard these works less as oddities than as representative expressions of cultural knowledge—the knowledge that at this particular moment was repressed by the Supreme Court's 1896 decision in *Plessy v. Ferguson* and by the militant Anglo-Saxon masculine imperialism of a Theodore Roosevelt. Anxieties about whiteness rather than confident assertions of whiteness may have inspired both the emergence of the new U.S. literary histories and even the imperial moment itself. But implicit in back-to-the-future moments of racial discovery is the more humane vision of racial commonality, and thus of the new or revised genealogical histories that could emerge through imaginative acts of dislocation.

In *Dislocating Race and Nation,* I have attempted to keep past and present in a productive tension so that we might learn as much about racial genealogies, imperialism, and minority perspectives on U.S. nationalism from the past (in the writings of Brockden Brown, Walker, Hawthorne, Melville, Crafts, Douglass, and others) as we do from our differently theorized perspectives at our present critical moment. Twain's *A Connecticut Yankee in King Arthur's Court* (1889), arguably the great back-to-the-future novel of the nineteenth century, addresses head-on the value of such a reading practice. The Connecticut reformer and "imperialist" Hank Morgan conveys his respect for history by being engaged with history, remarking at a certain point about his imposition of nineteenth-century "Yankee" technology and ideologies on sixth-century Britain: "It was not fair to spring those nineteenth-century technicalities upon the untutored infant of the sixth and then rail at her because she couldn't get their drift."[13] At the same time, Morgan's inability to see Arthurian Britain as anything much other than an "untutored infant" leads to the cataclysmic ending in which he destroys the world that he tried to improve through his nineteenth-century techno-republicanism.

But even as *Connecticut Yankee* seems to anticipate the destructive force of the self-righteous nationalism that would engage Twain's anti-imperialistic political energies at the turn of the century, the novel does not leave us at an impasse. After all, we can learn from Hank's ultimate inability to see the past as anything other than a limited version of his former present, and the fact is that most readers find themselves at an ironic remove from Morgan (after all, the "Final P.S. by M.T." slyly suggests that all along we've been reading the tale of a madman). It is precisely our recognition of our distance from Morgan that prompts us to imagine different ways of reading and responding to sixth-century Britain and ultimately to want to "undo" the Yankee's plottings. Twain does not withhold his own skepticism about his protagonist until the closing P.S. From the very beginning, Twain's authorial persona encourages the reader to develop a different interpretive perspective from Morgan's when he describes the manuscript he is about to read as "a palimpsest." As his persona explains: "Under the old dim writing of the Yankee historian appeared traces of a penmanship which was older and dimmer still—Latin words and sentences."[14] A palimpsestic reading practice, one that attends to the resistant "traces" of the past, may be our best hope for creating possible futures that do not need to be undone, because they will always be open to revision.

Notes

Prologue

1. David Scott, *Conscripts of Modernity: The Tragedy of Colonial Enlightenment* (Durham: Duke University Press, 2004), 22.

2. Brook Thomas makes a similar point about the need to attend to "whether and how the literary can resist particular ideologies" (*The New Historicism and Other Old-Fashioned Topics* [Princeton: Princeton University Press, 1991], 167). Such an approach, he says, in terms that echo my own, may "[allow] us to use knowledge of the past to judge the very conditions of our own judgments" (18).

3. Eve Kornfeld, *Creating an American Culture, 1775–1800: A Brief History with Documents* (Boston and New York: Bedford/St. Martin's, 2001), 8.

4. For provocative efforts to enlarge the historical and national frame of American literary studies, see Wai Chee Dimock, *Through Other Continents: American Literature across Deep Time* (Princeton: Princeton University Press, 2006); and Laura Doyle, *Freedom's Empire: Race and the Rise of the Novel in Atlantic Modernity, 1640–1840* (Durham: Duke University Press, 2008). In a recent revisionary study, Leonard Tennenhouse argues not only that U.S. writers were in conversation with British writers but that they also sought to emphasize their Americanness through assertions of their diasporic connection to English literary traditions. As he remarks: "What makes our literature distinctly and indelibly American is our literature's insistence on reproducing those aspects of Englishness that do not require one to be in England so much as among English people" (*The Importance of Feeling English: American Literature and the British Diaspora, 1750–1850* [Princeton: Princeton University Press, 2007], 9). Scholars will no doubt be debating Tennenhouse's claims for years to come, but I would here point out two problems with his thesis: its reliance on consensus models of U.S. literary nationalism (exemplified by his recurrent use of the word "our") and its failure to take account of the place of ethnic and racial minorities in the emergence of various U.S. literary nationalisms.

5. Benjamin T. Spencer, *The Quest for Nationality: An American Literary Campaign* (Syracuse, N.Y.: Syracuse University Press, 1957), viii.

6. David Waldstreicher, *In the Midst of Perpetual Fetes: The Making of American*

Nationalism, 1776–1820 (Chapel Hill: University of North Carolina Press, 1997), 6. As the political theorist Gregory Jusdanis remarks: "Just because nationalist thought depicts identity as uniform does not mean it is or has ever been homogeneous. Identity is hybrid at all times, constantly changing due to movement of people, the exchange of ideas and products, and the passing of time" (*The Necessary Nation* [Princeton: Princeton University Press, 2001], 28).

7. For a good example of the multiculturalist turn in U.S. literary studies, see Timothy B. Powell, *Ruthless Democracy: A Multicultural Interpretation of the American Renaissance* (Princeton: Princeton University Press, 2000). Much excellent work has been done on connections between U.S. literary nationalism and the violent suppression of Native Americans; see, for example, Susan Scheckel, *The Insistence of the Indian: Race and Nationalism in Nineteenth-Century American Culture* (Princeton: Princeton University Press, 1998). My study has relatively little to say about the place of Indians in American literary nationalism, not because I don't regard this as an important topic but because my "episodic" method makes no pretense to comprehensiveness. It is my hope that the general method and perspective of the book will have broader applicability beyond what is covered in the four main chapters.

8. For an overview of critical developments in hemispheric studies, see Caroline F. Levander and Robert S. Levine, "Introduction: Essays beyond the Nation," in *Hemispheric American Studies*, ed. Caroline F. Levander and Robert S. Levine (New Brunswick: Rutgers University Press, 2008), 1–17.

9. Kwame Anthony Appiah, "Race," in *Critical Terms for Literary Study*, ed. Frank Lentricchia and Thomas McLaughlin (Chicago: University of Chicago Press, 1990), 282. See also Nicholas Hudson, "From 'Nation' to 'Race': The Origin of Racial Classification in Eighteenth-Century Thought," *Eighteenth-Century Studies* 29 (1996): 247–64. For a sampling of political writings on race and nation, see Ernest Gellner, *Nations and Nationalism* (Ithaca: Cornell University Press, 1983); Anthony D. Smith, *The Ethnic Origins of Nations* (Oxford: Basil Blackwell, 1986); Charles M. Mills, *The Racial Contract* (Ithaca: Cornell University Press, 1997); and David Theo Goldberg, *The Racial State* (New York: Blackwell, 2002). Benedict Anderson's *Imagined Communities: Reflections on the Origin and Spread of Nationalism* (London: Verso, 1983) remains essential to studies of nationalist theory; but for a critique of its relative failure to consider the importance of race to nation, see Arjun Appadurai, "The Heart of Whiteness," *Callaloo* 16 (1993): 796–807.

10. On citizenship and race, see Rogers M. Smith's magisterial *Civic Ideals: Conflicting Visions of Citizenship in U.S. History* (New Haven: Yale University Press, 1997).

11. Peter Kolchin, "Whiteness Studies: The New History of Race in America," *Journal of American History* 89 (2002): 172. Kolchin focuses on David R. Roediger's *The Wages of Whiteness: Race and the Making of the American Working Class* (London: Verso, 1991) and Matthew Frye Jacobson's *Whiteness of a Different Color:*

European Immigrants and the Alchemy of Race (Cambridge, Mass.: Harvard University Press, 1998). See also Robyn Wiegman, "Whiteness Studies and the Paradox of Particularity," *boundary 2* 26 (1999): 115–50.

12. Etienne Balibar, "Racism and Nationalism" and "The Nation Form: History and Ideology," in Etienne Balibar and Immanuel Wallerstein, *Race, Nation, Class: Ambiguous Identities* (London and New York: Verso, 1991), 49, 87.

13. See especially Reginald Horsman, *Race and Manifest Destiny: The Origins of American Racial Anglo-Saxonism* (Cambridge, Mass.: Harvard University Press, 1981).

14. Philip Freneau and Hugh Henry Brackenridge, "The Rising Glory of America," in *Poems of Freneau*, ed. Harry Hayden Clark (New York: Hafner Publishing Co., 1929), 3, 6–7, 14. (I am drawing on the text of the 1786 revision of the 1771 version.) My reading of the racializing of nationalism in this poem draws on the arguments of Jared Gardner, *Master Plots: Race and the Founding of an American Literature, 1787–1845* (Baltimore: Johns Hopkins Press, 1998), esp. chap. 1. I engage Gardner's book more critically in chapter 1 below. For a discussion of the poem in a hemispheric context, see Eric Wertheimer, *Imagined Empires: Incas, Aztecs, and the New World of American Literature, 1771–1876* (Cambridge: Cambridge University Press, 1999), 17–22. On the significance of the two versions of "The Rising Glory," see Tennenhouse, *The Importance of Feeling English*, 12–18.

15. Andy Doolen, *Fugitive Empire: Locating Early American Imperialism* (Minneapolis: University of Minnesota Press, 2005), xiii, xxvii, xiv. See also Richard Slotkin, *Regeneration through Violence: The Mythology of the American Frontier, 1600–1860* (1973; New York: HarperPerennial, 1996); and Norman Mailer, *Why Are We in Vietnam? A Novel* (New York: Putnam, 1967).

16. John Carlos Rowe, *Literary Culture and U.S. Imperialism: From the Revolution to World War II* (New York: Oxford University Press, 2000), ix–x, 11, x, 23. Amy Kaplan's "anarchic" view of imperialism as riddled with "internal contradictions, ambiguities, and frayed edges" is more consistent with my approach to the topic (*The Anarchy of Empire in the Making of U.S. Culture* [Cambridge, Mass.: Harvard University Press, 2002], 14). See also Sandra Gustafson, "Histories of Democracy and Empire," *American Quarterly* 59 (2007): 107–33.

17. In this respect, it is worth keeping in mind Thomas Bender's recent questioning of the value of such prenational narratives: "The beginnings of the United States . . . are the products—quite contingent and unpredictable—of many histories, several of them global in scope" (*A Nation among Nations: America's Place in World History* [New York: Hill and Wang, 2006], 60).

18. Jeremy Waldron, "Superseding Historic Injustice," *Ethics* 103 (1992): 5. For an entertaining collection of counterfactual historical narratives, see Niall Ferguson, ed., *Virtual History: Alternatives and Counterfactuals* (London: Papermac, 1997). Ferguson's introduction, "Virtual History: Towards a 'Chaotic' Theory of the Past," provides an excellent introduction to counterfactual historical modes.

See also David K. Lewis, *Counterfactuals* (Cambridge, Mass.: Harvard University Press, 1973); E. D. Hirsch Jr., "Counterfactuals in Interpretation," in *Interpreting Law and Literature: A Hermeneutic Reader*, ed. Sanford Levinson and Steven Mailloux (Evanston, Ill.: Northwestern University Press, 1988), 55–68; Geoffrey Hawthorne, "Counterfactuals, Explanation, and Understanding," in *Plausible Worlds: Possibility and Understanding in History and the Social Sciences* (Cambridge: Cambridge University Press, 1991), 1–37; and John Collins, Ned Hall, and L. A. Paul, eds., *Causation and Counterfactuals* (Cambridge: MIT Press, 2004).

19. Stephen Best, *The Fugitive's Properties: Law and the Poetics of Possession* (Chicago: University of Chicago Press, 2004), 214. And see Best's excellent discussion in chapter 3, "Counterfactuals, Causation, and the Tenses of 'Separate but Equal,'" 203–67, which elaborates the importance of counterfactuals for legal hermeneutics.

20. Catherine Gallagher, "Undoing," in *Time and the Literary*, ed. Karen Newman, Jay Clayton, and Marianne Hirsch (New York: Routledge, 2002), 12. Benedetto Croce influentially argued that counterfactual thinking is "useful for underlining the importance of certain decisive acts, and stimulating a new sense of responsibility" ("History as the History of Liberty," in *Philosophy, Poetry, History: An Anthology of Essays by Benedetto Croce*, ed. Cecil Sprigge [London: Oxford University Press, 1966], 557).

21. Hirsch, "Counterfactuals in Interpretation," 55.

Chapter 1

1. Charles Brockden Brown, *Edgar Huntly; or, Memoirs of a Sleep-Walker*, ed. Sydney J. Krause and S. W. Reid (Kent, Ohio: Kent State University Press, 1984), 3; [Charles Brockden Brown], "Preface," *Monthly Magazine and American Review* 3 (1800): iii; "On the State of American Literature," *Monthly Magazine and American Review* 1 (1799): 16; Charles Brockden Brown, "A Sketch of American Literature for 1806–7," *The American Register, or General Repository of History, Politics, and Science* 1 (1807): 185, 183. Given that Brown wrote much of what appeared in his journals (see notes 26 and 27 below), he is the probable author of the anonymous "On the State of American Literature."

2. For a contemporaneous discussion of American literary nationalism that brings together a number of sentiments expressed by Brown and other literary nationalists of the time, see the section on "Nations lately become Literary" in Samuel Miller, *A Brief Retrospect of the Eighteenth Century, Containing a Sketch of the Revolutions and Improvements in Science, Arts, and Literature during that Period*, 2 vols. (New York: T. and J. Swords, 1803), 2:406–11. Like Brown, Miller states that the emergence of a distinctive American literature has been hindered by the commercial spirit of the United States ("the *love of gain*" [2:407]) and the nation's "colonial dependence" (2:408) on England. Nevertheless, Miller, like Brown and

many other such commentators, predicts "that letters will flourish as much in America as in any part of the world" (2:410).

3. Benjamin T. Spencer, *The Quest for Nationality: An American Literary Campaign* (Syracuse, N.Y.: Syracuse University Press, 1957), 59, ix; Robert S. Spiller, ed., *The American Literary Revolution, 1783–1837* (New York: Anchor Books, 1967), viii; John P. McWilliams Jr., *The American Epic: Transforming a Genre, 1770–1860* (Cambridge: Cambridge University Press, 1989), 16; Gordon S. Wood, "Launching the 'Extended Republic': The Federalist Era," in *Launching the "Extended Republic": The Federalist Era*, ed. Ronald Hoffman and Peter J. Albert (Charlottesville: University of Virginia Press, 1996), 2. See also Richard Ruland, ed., *The Native Muse: Theories of American Literature from Bradford to Whitman* (1972; New York: Dutton, 1976); and Eve Kornfeld, ed., *Creating an American Culture, 1775–1800: A Brief History with Documents* (Boston and New York: Bedford/St. Martin's, 2001).

4. Jared Gardner, *Master Plots: Race and the Founding of an American Literature, 1787–1845* (Baltimore: Johns Hopkins University Press, 1998), xi; John Carlos Rowe, *Literary Culture and U.S. Imperialism: From the Revolution to World War II* (New York: Oxford University Press, 2000), 28, 43; David Kazanjian, *The Colonizing Trick: National Culture and Imperial Citizenship in Early America* (Minneapolis: University of Minnesota Press, 2003), 5.

5. Rowe, *Literary Culture and U.S. Imperialism*, 50; Nancy Ruttenburg, *Democratic Personality: Popular Voice and the Trial of American Authorship* (Stanford: Stanford University Press, 1998), 4.

6. David Waldstreicher, *In the Midst of Perpetual Fetes: The Making of American Nationalism, 1776–1820* (Chapel Hill: University of North Carolina Press, 1997), 14, 6.

7. Thomas Jefferson to Robert R. Livingston, letter of 18 April 1802, in *State Papers and Correspondence Bearing upon the Purchase of the Territory of Louisiana* (Washington, D.C.: Government Printing Office, 1903), 18. For a famous instance of Jefferson's invocation of an "empire of liberty," see Jefferson to James Madison, letter of 27 April 1809, in *The Writings of Thomas Jefferson*, ed. Andrew A. Lipscomb and Albert Ellery Bergh (Washington, D.C.: Thomas Jefferson Memorial Association, 1903–4), 12:277. For an early instance, see Jefferson to George Rogers Clark, letter of 25 December 1780, in *Papers of Thomas Jefferson*, ed. Julian P. Boyd (Princeton: Princeton University Press, 1951), 4:238.

8. Peter J. Kastor, *The Nation's Crucible: The Louisiana Purchase and the Creation of America* (New Haven: Yale University Press, 2004), 8.

9. Etienne Balibar, "Racism and Nationalism," in Etienne Balibar and Immanuel Wallerstein, *Race, Nation, Class: Ambiguous Identities* (London and New York: Verso, 1991), 91.

10. Sean X. Goudie, "On the Origin of American Specie(s): The West Indies, Classification, and the Emergence of Supremacist Consciousness in *Arthur Mer-*

vyn," in *Revising Charles Brockden Brown: Culture, Politics, and Sexuality in the Early Republic*, ed. Philip Barnard, Mark L. Kamrath, Stephen Shapiro (Knoxville: University of Tennessee Press, 2004), 87. For a similar reading of Brown's critical engagement and entanglement in early national culture, see Robert S. Levine, *Conspiracy and Romance: Studies in Brockden Brown, Cooper, Hawthorne, and Melville* (Cambridge: Cambridge University Press, 1989), chap. 1.

11. [Charles Brockden Brown], *An Address to the Government of the United States, on the Cession of Louisiana to the French; and on the Late Breach of Treaty by the Spaniards; Including the Translation of a Memorial, on the War of St. Domingo, and Cession of the Mississippi to France, Drawn up by a French Counsellor of State* (Philadelphia: 1803), 79, 74; [Charles Brockden Brown], *Monroe's Embassy, or, The Conduct of the Government, in Relation to Our Claims to the Navigation of the Mississippi, Considered by the Author of An Address to the Government of the United States on the Cession of Louisiana, &c. &c* (Philadelphia: John Conrad & Co., 1803), 54, 33; [Brown], *Address*, 92.

12. Gardner, *Master Plots*, 56, 60. On Brown and the alien, see also Shirley Samuels, *Romances of the Republic: Women, the Family, and Violence in the Literature of the Early American Nation* (New York: Oxford University Press, 1996), chap. 2.

13. On this point, see Julia Stern's reading of blackface masquerade in *Ormond* (1799) in *The Plight of Feeling: Sympathy and Dissent in the Early American Novel* (Chicago: University of Chicago Press, 1997), chap. 4.

14. Steven Watts, *The Romance of Real Life: Charles Brockden Brown and the Origins of American Culture* (Baltimore: Johns Hopkins University Press, 1994), 131, 130, 177; and see Jane Tompkins, *Sensational Designs: The Cultural Work of American Fiction, 1790–1860* (New York: Oxford University Press, 1985), chaps. 2 and 3.

15. Andy Doolen, for instance, uses the word "tragic" to describe Brown's Federalist inclinations, claiming that as an editor in particular he merely reproduced "the dominant and didactic voice of Federalist orthodoxy" (*Fugitive Empire: Locating Early American Imperialism* [Minneapolis: University of Minnesota Press, 2005], 72, 43). But as I will be arguing in this section, Brown's journals, like certain aspects of Federalism itself, were committed to a wide range of human rights.

16. Ira Berlin, *Many Thousands Gone: The First Two Centuries of Slavery in North America* (Cambridge, Mass.: Harvard University Press, 1998), esp. chap. 3. On the American Revolution and early national cultural in a global context, see also Thomas Bender, *A Nation among Nations: America's Place in World History* (New York: Hill and Wang, 2006), chap. 2; Lester D. Langley, *The Americas in the Age of Revolution* (New Haven: Yale University Press, 1996); and Peter Onuf and Nicholas Onuf, *Federal Union, Modern World: The Law of Nations in an Age of Revolutions, 1776–1815* (Madison, Wisc.: Madison House, 1993).

17. Hamilton's letter of 26 January to Otis is quoted in James Roger Sharp,

American Politics in the Early Republic: The New Nation in Crisis (New Haven: Yale University Press, 1993), 215.

18. "Thomas Jefferson to the president and legislative council, the speaker of the house of representatives of the territory of Indiana, 28 December 1805," quoted in Drew W. McCoy, *The Elusive Republic: Political Economy in Jeffersonian America* (Chapel Hill: University of North Carolina Press, 1980), 203. For good discussions of the Louisiana Purchase, see McCoy, *Elusive Republic*, 196–208; Gregory H. Nobles, *American Frontiers: Cultural Encounters and Continental Conquest* (New York: Hill and Wang, 1997), 116–19; Alexander deConde, *The Affair of Louisiana* (New York: Charles Scribner's Sons, 1976); Richard Kluger, *Seizing Destiny: How America Grew from Sea to Shining Sea* (New York: Alfred A. Knopf, 2007), chap. 7; and Joseph J. Ellis, *American Creation: Triumphs and Tragedies at the Founding of the Republic* (New York: Alfred A. Knopf, 2007), chap. 6. Two recent book-length studies take opposed views of the Louisiana Purchase. Roger G. Kennedy's *Mr. Jefferson's Lost Cause: Land, Farmers, Slavery, and the Louisiana Purchase* (New York: Oxford University Press, 2003) indicts a devious, untrustworthy Jefferson for using the Louisiana Purchase to expand the realm of slavery, while Jon Kukla's *A Wilderness So Immense: The Louisiana Purchase and the Destiny of America* (New York: Alfred A. Knopf, 2003) attacks the "nay saying Federalists" (290) for not jumping aboard the Jeffersonian expansionist bandwagon.

19. For an excellent discussion of Jefferson's concept of slavery diffusion, see Peter S. Onuf, *Jefferson's Empire: The Language of American Nationhood* (Charlottesville: University of Virginia Press, 2000), chap. 5. On Jefferson's complicity in spreading (and even advocating) slavery, see Paul Finkelman, "Jefferson and Slavery: 'Treason against the Hopes of the World,' " in *Jeffersonian Legacies*, ed. Peter S. Onuf (Charlottesville: University of Virginia Press, 1993), 181–222; and Reginald Horsman, "The Dimensions of an 'Empire for Liberty': Expansion and Republicanism, 1775–1825," *Journal of the Early Republic* 9 (1989): 1–20. On the contradictions at the heart of Jefferson's racism (his antiauthoritarianism, on the one hand, and his commitment to the "scientific" notions of polygenesis and black inferiority, on the other), see Alexander O. Boulton, "The American Paradox: Jeffersonian Equality and Racial Science," *American Quarterly* 47 (1995): 467–93. For a complex account of debates about whiteness among Jefferson and his (male) contemporaries, see Dana D. Nelson, *National Manhood: Capitalist Citizenship and the Imagined Fraternity of White Men* (Durham: Duke University Press, 1998), esp. chaps. 1 and 2.

20. Douglas R. Egerton, *Gabriel's Rebellion: The Virginia Slave Conspiracies of 1800–1802* (Chapel Hill: University of North Carolina Press, 1993), 47. On Jefferson's suspicion of the San Domingan rebels, who may well have been inspired by the Declaration of Independence, see also Douglas R. Egerton, *Rebels, Reformers, and Revolutionaries: Collected Essays and Second Thoughts* (New York: Routledge, 2002), 163–74.

21. Jefferson's instructions to Monroe are cited in Michael Zuckerman, "The Power of Blackness: Thomas Jefferson and the Revolution in St. Domingue," in *Almost Chosen People: Oblique Biographies in the American Grain* (Berkeley: University of California Press, 1993), 215. My reading of Jefferson and the geopolitical triangulation of Saint Domingue, the Louisiana Territory, and the United States draws on Zuckerman, *Almost Chosen People*, 175–217; Tim Matthewson, "Jefferson and the Nonrecognition of Haiti," *Proceedings of the American Philosophical Society* 140 (1996): 22–48; Robert L. Paquette, "Revolutionary Saint Domingue in the Making of Territorial Louisiana," in *A Turbulent Time: The French Revolution and the Greater Caribbean*, ed. David Barry Gaspar and David Patrick Geggus (Bloomington: Indiana University Press, 1997), 204–25; and Paul F. Lachance, "The Politics of Fear: French Louisianans and the Slave Trade, 1786–1809," *Plantation Society* 1 (1979): 162–97. On the important and, for Jefferson and other whites, threatening presence of blacks in Louisiana, see Caryn Cossé Bell, *Revolution, Romanticism, and the Afro-Creole Protest Tradition in Louisiana, 1718–1868* (Baton Rouge: Louisiana State University Press, 1997); and Gwendolyn Midlo Hall, *Africans in Colonial Louisiana: The Development of Afro-Creole Culture* (Baton Rouge: Louisiana State University Press, 1992). Also useful is Bender, *A Nation among Nations*, chap. 2.

22. Paul Finkelman, "The Problem of Slavery in the Age of Federalism," in *Federalists Reconsidered*, ed. Doron Ben-Atar and Barbara B. Obert (Charlottesville: University Press of Virginia, 1998), 149; Douglas R. Egerton, "The Empire of Liberty Reconsidered," in *The Revolution of 1800: Democracy, Race, and the New Republic*, ed. James Horn, Jan Ellen Lewis, and Peter S. Onuf (Charlottesville: University Press of Virginia, 2002), 314; Pickering's remarks on Toussaint L'Ouverture are quoted in Egerton, *Rebels, Reformers, and Revolutionaries*, 172; Zuckerman, *Almost Chosen People*, 185; Egerton, "The Empire of Liberty Reconsidered," 309. See also Gary B. Nash, *The Forgotten Fifth: African Americans in the Age of Revolution* (Cambridge, Mass.: Harvard University Press, 2006), 94–95, 123–24. On the Federalists' support of the rebellion in Saint Domingue "as a coherent movement mounted by black slaves in the supposedly restrained, rational style of the American Revolution," see Bruce Dain, *A Hideous Monster of the Mind: American Race Theory in the Early Republic* (Cambridge, Mass.: Harvard University Press, 2002), 85. On Adams's sympathetic response to the Haitian revolution, see also Bender, *A Nation among Nations*, 105–10. The Federalists are often portrayed as reactionaries, but a more complex picture emerges from David Hackett Fisher, *The Revolution of American Conservatism: The Federalist Party in the Era of Jeffersonian Democracy* (1965; New York: Harper Torchbooks, 1969), 163–72; and Linda K. Kerber, *Federalists in Dissent: Imagery and Ideology in Jeffersonian America* (Ithaca: Cornell University Press, 1970). Joyce Appleby's *Capitalism and the New Social Order* (New York: New York University Press, 1984) was influential in championing the Republicans as progressive democratic capitalists (even as she conceded that the

"Federalists . . . were not mindless conservatives" [59]), but for an argument that the Jeffersonians ruled as a benevolent gentry with an interest in maintaining social hierarchies, see John L. Brooke, "Ancient Lodges and Self-Created Societies: Voluntary Association and the Public Sphere in the Early Republic," in *Launching the "Extended Republic*," ed. Hoffman and Albert, 273–359. On the interest of some Federalists in championing the rights of workers, see Gary J. Kornblith, "Artisan Federalism: New England Mechanics and the Political Economy of the 1790s," in *Launching the "Extended Republic*," ed. Hoffman and Albert, 249–72. Sean Wilentz has posed a vigorous challenge to the recent recuperation of the Federalists, but as suggested by the title of his book, *The Rise of American Democracy: Jefferson to Lincoln* (New York: W. W. Norton & Company, 2005), he is committed to an unfolding teleological narrative in which a democratic Jefferson leads to an even more democratic Lincoln. He thus plays down Jefferson's white nationalist commitment to slavery and certain forms of social hierarchy, while presenting an almost cartoonish picture of "Federalist repression" (81, 83) and snobbery, beginning with his portrait of John Adams, whom he describes as "[g]arrulous, pudgy, short, and prone to anxious, self-absorbed outbursts" (76).

23. It is also worth noting that southerners, whether Federalist or Republican, were not monolithically committed to the spread of slavery into the West. In *Political, Commercial, and Moral Reflections on the Late Cession of Louisiana* (Lexington, Ky.: D. Bradford, 1803), the Kentucky poet and legislator Allan B. Magruder hoped that the Louisiana Purchase would help to destroy "A DESPOTISM THAT DOOMED TO SLAVERY, A MILLION AND A HALF HUMAN BEINGS!" (147). The Virginian St. George Tucker, in *Reflections on the Cession of Louisiana to the United States* (Washington City: Samuel Harrison Smith, 1803), similarly expressed his desire that the Louisiana Purchase would speed up "the great work of abolition" (25). Both Magruder and Tucker believed that abolition could be accomplished by colonizing the newly emancipated blacks to the Louisiana territories.

24. Timothy Dwight, *Greenfield Hill: A Poem, in Seven Parts* (New York: Childs and Swaine, 1794), 37, 38.

25. See James E. Cronin, ed., *The Diary of Elihu Hubbard Smith (1771–1798)* (Philadelphia: American Philosophical Society, 1973), 14 et passim. (Significantly, in *Edgar Huntly* we are told that the character Waldegrave had been teaching in a school for free blacks.) On the surprisingly radical politics of Smith and his circle, see W. M. Verhoeven, " 'The Blissful Period of Intellectual Liberty': Transatlantic Radicalism and Enlightened Conservatism in Brown's Early Writings," in *Revising Charles Brockden Brown*, ed. Barnard, Kamrath, and Shapiro, 7–40. As Bryan Waterman makes clear, Smith and Dunlap, despite their Federalist sympathies, "derided partisans generally and Federalist enthusiasms in particular" (*Republic of Intellect: The Friendly Club of New York City and the Making of American Literature* [Baltimore: Johns Hopkins University Press, 2007], 182).

26. In a letter of 4 July 1804 to J. B. Linn, Brown declared that he was "obliged

to spin out of my own brain" all of the unsigned essays in the "original depart-ment" of the June and July 1804 issues of the *Monthly Magazine* (William Dunlap, *The Life of Charles Brockden Brown: Together with Selections from the Rarest of His Printed Works, from His Original Letters, and from His Manuscripts before Un-published*, 2 vols. [Philadelphia: James P. Parke, 1815], 2:111). My thanks to Philip Barnard for calling this letter to my attention. Most Brown scholars agree that the unsigned essays in other issues were in all likelihood also authored by Brown.

27. "Selection from *Observations on the Conformation and Capacity of the Ne-groes* by Professor Blumenbach," *Monthly Magazine and American Review* 1 (1799): 454; "Poems by Robert Southey," *Monthly Magazine and American Review* 1 (1799): 136; "Thoughts on the Probable Termination of Negro Slavery in the United States," *Monthly Magazine and American Review* 2 (1800): 82, 81; "On the Conse-quences of Abolishing the Slave Trade in the West Indian Colonies," *Literary Magazine, and American Register* 4 (1805): 375, 378, 376, 379, 380. See also "Aboli-tion of Slavery in New Jersey," *Literary Magazine, and American Register* 1 (1804): 474; "Address of the American Convention to the People of the United States," *Literary Magazine, and American Register* 1 (1804): 472–74; "Horrors of West Indian Slavery," *Literary Magazine, and American Register* 5 (1806): 7–13; and "First Public Testimony of Friends against Slavery," *Literary Magazine, and American Register* 5 (1806): 218–19. Virtually all of the pieces in Brown's magazines, like *Address* and *Monroe's Embassy*, are unsigned, but as stated in note 26 above, the consensus among Brown scholars is that he wrote most of the material in *Monthly Magazine* and *Literary Magazine*. I share that assumption and see clear parallels in stylistic and thematic concerns between Brown's signed novels and unsigned magazine articles and columns.

28. Prince Hall, "A Charge, Delivered to the *African* Lodge, June 24, 1797, at Menotomy," in *"Face Zion Forward": First Writers of the Black Atlantic, 1785–1798*, ed. Joanna Brooks and John Saillant (Boston: Northeastern University Press, 2002), 204.

29. "Picture of St. Domingo," *Literary Magazine, and American Register* 1 (1804): 446, 448, 449; "St. Domingo," *Literary Magazine, and American Register* 2 (1804): 656, 657; "Annals of Europe and America," *American Register, or General Repository of History, Politics, and Science* 1 (1807): 75–76. For a useful discussion of Brown's depictions of Haitian revolutionaries as a model of national collectivity, see Mi-chael Drexler, "Brigands and Nuns: The Vernacular Sociology of Collectivity after the Haitian Revolution," in *Messy Beginnings: Postcoloniality and Early American Studies*, ed. Malini Johar Schueller and Edward Watts (New Brunswick: Rutgers University Press, 2003), 175–99. As Drexler notes, equally positive images of Hai-tian revolutionaries can be found in Leonara Sansay's *Secret History; or, The Horrors of St. Domingo* (1808); see Leonara Sansay, *Secret History: or, The Horrors of St. Domingo*, ed. Michael Drexler (Ontario, Canada: Broadview Press, 2007). On Brown, Sansay, and the revolution in Saint Domingue, see also Philip N.

Edmondson, "The St. Domingue Legacy in Black Activist and Antislavery Writings in the United States, 1791–1862" (Ph.D. diss., University of Maryland, 2003).

30. [Brown], *Address*, 1 (my emphasis). All future page references to *Address* will be supplied parenthetically in the body of the text.

31. Christopher Looby, *Voicing America: Language, Literary Form, and the Origins of the United States* (Chicago: University of Chicago Press, 1996), 194, 195; Peter S. Onuf, "The Expanding Union," in *Devising Liberty: Preserving and Creating Freedom in the New American Republic*, ed. David Thomas Konig (Stanford: Stanford University Press, 1995), 51. In a recent essay that wholly implicates Brown in Federalist countersubversion and hysteria, Luke Gibbons asserts that *Address* is "a notorious piece of black propaganda that took the form of a forged letter from a French minister of state" ("Ireland, America, and Gothic Memory: Transatlantic Terror in the Early Republic," *boundary 2* 31 [2004]: 36). Gibbons fails to note that the French minister's voice is one of two voices in the tract, and Gibbons's only citation from the tract itself comes from Gardner's *Master Plots*. My argument is that *Address* poses interpretive challenges, is anything but transparent, and has to be read in full as a complex literary and political document.

32. Hamilton's newspaper writings, along with the Jefferson and Livingston letters and other relevant documents, may be found in Peter J. Kastor, ed., *The Louisiana Purchase: Emergence of an American Nation* (Washington, D.C.: CQ Press, 2002), 168, 161, 165.

33. An important exception was the republican journalist William Duane, who published a series of letters in the *Aurora* attacking the "*war-whoop*" of Hamilton and perhaps even Brown (Duane scornfully refers to the "forged pamphlets, rescripts, and fictitious correspondence" that have been shaping public opinion). But ultimately Duane was naive on this issue, initially arguing that cession had not occurred and stating that even if it had, it would be a good thing for U.S. trade if France were to hold onto Saint Domingue and establish a colony in Louisiana; see Camillus [William Duane], *The Mississippi Question Fairly Stated, and the Views and Arguments of Those Who Clamor for War, Examined in Seven Letters, Originally Written for Publication in the Aurora, at Philadelphia* (Philadelphia: William Duane, 1803), 1 (and see also 46–47).

34. [Brown], *Monroe's Embassy*, 34.

35. On the "romance" elements of *Address*, see Alan Axelrod, *Charles Brockden Brown: An American Tale* (Austin: University of Texas Press, 1983), chap. 1. For an illuminating discussion of the place of secrecy in "Memoirs of Carwin" (1803–5) and Brown's political writings of the period, see Hsuan L. Hsu, "Democratic Expansionism in 'Memoirs of Carwin,'" *Early American Literature* 35 (2000): 137–56. Also useful on Brown's politics of secrecy is Paul Downes, "Constitutional Secrets: 'Memoirs of Carwin' and the Politics of Concealment," *Criticism* 39 (1997): 89–117; and Looby, *Voicing America*, 193–202.

It remains difficult to determine the actual influence of Brown's Louisiana pamphlets on the political debates of the time. *Address* was published in January 1803 and was republished a month later; notices of both printings appeared in the *Philadelphia Gazette and Daily Advertiser* (see issues of 4 January 1803 and 2 March 1803). Gardner argues that the pamphlet was effectively discredited by the Republicans in January and February 1803 issues of the *Aurora, and General Advertiser*. But in his unpublished biography of Brown, Daniel E. Kennedy suggests that the Pennsylvania senator James Ross, along with other of his Federalist colleagues, may well have read the pamphlet and drawn on it to make their own arguments for the acquisition of Louisiana during the late winter and spring debates in the Senate ("Charles Brockden Brown: His Life and Works," 1577A, 1577B, 1577C, Charles Brockden Brown Collection, Kent State University, Kent, Ohio).

36. See Gardner, *Master Plots*, 54–60. Gardner regards Brown's linkage of French and "savage" aliens as central to the national project of the time, but it is worth noting that Onuf discerns a very different project of nation making among the Jeffersonians circa 1800: "The Jeffersonian conception of American nationhood was predicated on the identification of Anglophile Federalists as foreigners" (*Jefferson's Empire*, 107).

37. Thomas Jefferson to James Monroe, letter of 24 November 1801, in *Writings of Thomas Jefferson*, ed. Lipscomb and Bergh, 11:296. For useful discussions of Native Americans and U.S. culture circa 1800, see Gregory Evans Dowd, "Spinning Wheel Revolution," in *The Revolution of 1800*, ed. Horn, Lewis, and Onuf, 267–87; Anthony F. C. Wallace, *Jefferson and the Indians: The Tragic Fate of the First Americans* (Cambridge, Mass.: Harvard University Press, 1999); Reginald Horsman, "The Indian Policy of an 'Empire for Liberty,'" in *Native Americans and the Early Republic*, ed. Frederick E. Hoxie, Ronald Hoffman, and Peter J. Albert (Charlottesville: University Press of Virginia, 1999), 37–61; and Bernard Sheehan, *The Seeds of Extinction: Jeffersonian Philanthropy and the American Indian* (Chapel Hill: University of North Carolina Press, 1973).

38. Doron Ben-Atar and Barbara B. Obert argue that the Federalists were "far more open to the rights of Indians . . . than their Jeffersonian opponents, who championed individual freedom and participatory politics" ("The Paradoxical Legacy of the Federalists," in *Federalists Reconsidered*, 10). Similarly, Rogers M. Smith writes that in their relative concern for the Indians, the Federalists "were on the more liberal but less popular side of most of the issues that mattered to the great majority of white American men" (*Civic Ideals: Conflicting Visions of Citizenship in U.S. History* [New Haven: Yale University Press, 1997], 164).

39. C. F. Volney, *A View of the Soil and Climate of the United States of America*, translated, with occasional remarks, by C. B. Brown (Philadelphia: J. Conrad & Co., 1804), 352, 379; "An Account of the Late Proceedings of the Society of Friends (or Quakers) for the Civilization of Indian Tribes," *Literary Magazine, and American Register* 4 (1805): 287. On the importance of Brown's family's Quakerism to his

overall career, see Peter Kafer, *Charles Brockden Brown's Revolution and the Birth of the American Gothic* (Philadelphia: University of Pennsylvania Press, 2004).

40. By presenting his readers with the French consul's letter, Brown makes use of narrative strategies typical not only of his earlier novels of the late 1790s but also of the epistolary novel in general; the challenge facing readers of *Address* is to interpret the letter in relation to the character of the writer. It is worth noting that the southerner William Wirt made similarly ironic use of first-person reports of a spy in his *The Letters of the British Spy*, published the same year as Brown's Louisiana pamphlets. Wirt's spy is British, not French, and in adopting the persona of a British spy who is critical of Virginia and the United States, Wirt expects his readers to see the limits of the British spy and thus patriotically to reject his critical narrative. As Richard Beale Davis points out in his introduction to a modern edition of the text, the use of an ironically limited narrator was a staple of literary culture and had important origins in Montesquieu's *Les Lettres Persanes* (1721). See William Wirt, *The Letters of the British Spy*, ed. Richard Beale Davis (1803; Chapel Hill: University of North Carolina Press, 1970).

41. Bill Christophersen, *The Apparition in the Glass: Charles Brockden Brown's American Gothic* (Athens: University of Georgia Press, 1993), 109.

42. "St. Domingo," *Literary Magazine, and American Register* 2 (1804): 657.

43. Watts, *The Romance of Real Life*, 177.

44. In 1804 Brown would celebrate the Purchase for precisely that reason, stating in an article in his *Literary Magazine*: "By the cession of Louisiana the Americans have gained a vast increase of territory; and the free navigation of the Mississippi, which is thereby secured to them, will increase the population of the western parts, and form a complete barrier on that side" ("Thoughts on the Probable Duration of the American Republic," *Literary Magazine, and American Register* 2 [1804]: 218).

45. [Brown], *Monroe's Embassy*, 54, 34, 33, 34–35. On Brown's critique of nationalist exceptionalism, particularly in his magazine writings and pamphlets of the 1800s, see Mark L. Kamrath, *The "Novel" Historicism of Charles Brockden Brown: Radical History and the Early Republic* (Kent, Ohio: Kent State University Press, forthcoming), chap. 6.

46. Brown, "Thoughts on the Probable Duration of the American Republic," 216; "How Far Do Slaves Influence Political Representation in America," *Literary Magazine, and American Register* 4 (1805): 441.

47. [Brown], "Editors' [sic] Address to the Public," *Literary Magazine, and American Register* 1 (1803): 4, 5.

48. Arguably, Brown was both an American literary nationalist and a cosmopolitan. Jared Gardner emphasizes the literary nationalistic side of his editorship, stating that as editor of the *Literary Magazine*, Brown took it upon himself "to collect and reflect the productions of his nation" ("The Literary Museum and the

Unsettling of the Early American Novel," *ELH* 67 [2000]: 747). That may well have been one of his roles, but it is worth noting that as editor Brown published, reviewed, and discussed Robert Southey, Samuel Richardson, Oliver Goldsmith, Samuel Johnson, Virgil, Hume, Gibbon, Dryden, Horace, Longinus, Racine, Hafiz, Spenser, and Voltaire, among many others.

49. Charles Brockden Brown, *Clara Howard; in a Series of Letters* with *Jane Talbot, A Novel*, ed. Sydney J. Krause, S. W. Reid, and Donald A. Ringe (Kent, Ohio: Kent State University Press, 1986), 24, 94, 200, 116. *Clara Howard* and *Jane Talbot* have traditionally been regarded as relatively minor productions in the Brown canon, though there has been a resurgence of interest. See, for example, Bruce Burgett, *Sentimental Bodies: Sex, Gender, and Citizenship in the Early Republic* (Princeton: Princeton University Press, 1998), 112–33; and Michelle Burnham, "Epistolarity, Anticipation, and Revolution in *Clara Howard*," in *Revising Charles Brockden Brown*, ed. Barnard, Kamrath, and Shapiro, 260–80.

50. Gardner, "Literary Museum," 747, 766. Brown also edited a journal in the late 1790s, which begs the question of why focus on the early 1800s as a moment of transformation.

51. William Hill Brown, *The Power of Sympathy*, ed. William S. Kable (Columbus: Ohio State University Press, 1969), 103.

52. Questions about slavery are also central to Susanna Rowson's play *Slaves in Algiers* (1794) and to the widely disseminated Barbary narratives of the period, which presented U.S. slavery in a larger global context. See Paul Baepler, *White Slaves, African Masters: An Anthology of American Barbary Captivity Narratives* (Chicago: University of Chicago Press, 1999), 1–58; Paul Baepler, "The Barbary Captivity Narrative in American Culture," *Early American Literature* 39 (2004): 217–46; Elizabeth Maddock Dillon, "*Slaves in Algiers*: Race, Republican Genealogies, and the Global Stage," *American Literary History* 16 (2004): 407–36; and Jacob Rama Berman, "The Barbarous Voice of Democracy: American Captivity in Barbary and the Multicultural Specter," *American Literature* 79 (2007): 1–27.

53. Tabitha Gilman Tenney, *Female Quixotism*, ed. Jean Nienkamp and Andrea Collins (New York: Oxford University Press, 1992), 55.

54. Looby, *Voicing America*, 214; Hugh Henry Brackenridge, *Modern Chivalry*, ed. Claude M. Newlin (1937; New York: Hafner Publishing Company, 1968), 329, 537. On the novel's interest in expanding democratic possibilities, see Dana D. Nelson, " 'Indications of the Public Will': *Modern Chivalry*'s Theory of Democratic Representation," *ANQ* 15 (2002): 23–39.

55. Hannah W. Foster, *The Coquette*, ed. Cathy N. Davidson (New York: Oxford University Press, 1986), 111.

56. For a sophisticated articulation of this argument in Brown and other writers of the period, see Samuels, *Romances of the Republic*, esp. chap. 1.

57. Michael T. Gilmore, *The Literature of the Revolutionary and Early National*

Periods, in *The Cambridge History of American Literature,* vol. 1, *1590–1820,* ed. Sacvan Bercovitch (Cambridge: Cambridge University Press, 1994), 645.

58. Charles Brockden Brown, *Wieland; or, The Transformation: An American Tale* and *Memoirs of Carwin the Biloquist,* ed. Sydney J. Krause, S. W. Reid, and Alexander Cowie (Kent, Ohio: Kent State University Press, 1977), 102.

59. J. G. A. Pocock, *The Machiavellian Moment: Florentine Political Thought and the Atlantic Republican Tradition* (Princeton: Princeton University Press, 1975), viii.

60. Brown, *Wieland,* 212, 179–80.

61. Charles Brockden Brown, *Arthur Mervyn; or, Memoirs of the Year 1793,* ed. Sydney J. Krause and S. W. Reid (Kent, Ohio: Kent State University Press, 1980), 370, 414. On slavery and race in *Arthur Mervyn,* see Carroll Smith-Rosenberg, "Black Gothic: The Shadowy Origins of the American Bourgeoisie," in *Possible Pasts: Becoming Colonial in Early America,* ed. Robert Blair St. George (Ithaca: Cornell University Press, 2000), 243–69; Philip Gould, *Barbaric Traffic: Commerce and Antislavery in the Eighteenth-Century Atlantic World* (Cambridge, Mass.: Harvard University Press, 2003), chap. 5; Teresa A. Goddu, *Gothic America: Narrative, History, and Nation* (New York: Columbia University Press, 1997), chap. 2; and Goudie, "On the Origin of American Specie(s)," 60–87. On slavery and race in *Ormond,* see Leonard Tennenhouse, "Caribbean Degeneracy and the Problem of Masculinity in Charles Brockden Brown's *Ormond,*" in *Finding Colonial Americas: Essays Honoring J. A. Leo Lamay,* ed. Carla Mulford and David S. Shields (Newark: University of Delaware Press, 2001), 104–21. In depicting blacks' generous labors during Philadelphia's yellow fever epidemic of 1793 in both *Ormond* and *Arthur Mervyn,* Brown was influenced by (and in dialogue with) Absalom Jones and Richard Allen's *A Narrative of the Proceedings of the Black People, During the Late Awful Calamity in Philadelphia* (1794); see Gould, *Barbaric Traffic,* chap. 5, and Joanna Brooks, *American Lazarus: Religion and the Rise of African American and Native American Literatures* (New York: Oxford University Press, 2003), 176–78.

62. Brown, *Edgar Huntly,* 6, 174, 91, 202, 212. Future page references to this edition will be supplied parenthetically in this section. For an excellent new edition with useful primary texts and historical discussions, see Charles Brockden Brown, *Edgar Huntly; or, Memoirs of a Sleepwalker, with Related Texts,* ed. Philip Barnard and Stephen Shapiro (Indianapolis: Hackett Publishing Company, Inc., 2006).

63. Geoffrey Hawthorne, *Plausible Worlds: Possibility and Understanding in History and the Social Sciences* (Cambridge: Cambridge University Press, 1991), 37.

64. Despite the clear connections between Edgar Huntly and Clithero Edny, Gibbons claims that Edgar's experiences in the novel suggest that "the fears expressed by proponents of the Alien and Sedition Acts—that the immigrant other, particularly of Irish or French origins, threatened to pollute the American body politic—were well founded, and among the most prominent pamphleteers against

alien influences was Charles Brockden Brown" ("Ireland, America, and Gothic Memory," 35). As it turns out, Clithero would appear to be innocent of the murder. Moreover, though Brown did write in support of taking the Louisiana Territory, he never wrote a pamphlet against the Irish and he did not participate as a pamphleteer during the debates on the Alien and Sedition Acts.

65. The specter of the Indian had been invoked earlier in the novel in the description of a panther lurking by the mouth of the cave, which the terrified Edgar describes as "the most ferocious and untamable of that detested race" (124). Edgar's racialist rhetoric here clearly aims to link Indian to beast, even as he assumes the superiority of the racial classifier. But how superior or different is he? Carrying "the tom-hawk" and prepared to use it on the "savage" panther, Edgar vows: "Henceforth I resolved never to traverse the wilderness unfurnished with my tom-hawk" (129). This is one of several indications, including his knowledge of the Norwalk wilderness, that the distance between Edgar and the Indian is not as large as he would want to imagine. For a lively and influential reading of Edgar Huntly's "savagery," see Leslie Fiedler, *Love and Death in the American Novel* (New York: Criterion Books, 1960), 73–80, 129–49.

66. Brown, *Wieland*, 221.

67. Sheehan, *Seeds of Extinction*, 187, 201.

68. Myra Jehlen, *The Literature of Colonization*, in *The Cambridge History of American Literature*, vol. 1, *1590–1820*, ed. Bercovitch, 164. For similar arguments, see Robert D. Newman, "Indians and Indian-Hating in *Edgar Huntly* and *The Confidence-Man*," *MELUS* 15 (1988): 65–74; and Eve Kornfeld, "Encountering the 'Other': American Intellectuals and Indians in the 1790s," *William and Mary Quarterly*, 3rd ser., 52 (1995): 287–314. Taking a very different perspective, Kafer argues strenuously that Brown's Quaker upbringing led him to reject the notion that the Indians were savages; in Kafar's view, an egalitarian vision informs *Edgar Huntly* (*Charles Brockden Brown's Revolution*, esp. 178–81).

69. Janie Hinds, "Animals, Indians, and Postcolonial Desire in Charles Brockden Brown's *Edgar Huntly*," *Early American Literature* 39 (2004): 345; Rowe, *Literary Culture and U.S. Imperialism*, 44.

70. Hinds, "Animals, Indians, and Postcolonial Desire," 342. For a useful postcolonial reading of Brown, see also Edward Watts, *Writing and Postcolonialism in the Early Republic* (Charlottesville: University Press of Virginia, 1998), 95–121.

71. As Gibbons points out, the Irish and Indians share a "history of dispossession and rebellion," and thus it may be significant that Clithero, after leaving the Lorimer estate, first goes to Belfast, "the center of revolutionary ferment in Ireland," before taking a ship to Philadelphia; see "Ireland, America, and Gothic Memory," 30, 32.

72. Sydney J. Krause links the fictional dispossession of Deb's people to "the infamous Walking Purchase Treaty of 1737," in which Thomas Penn used fraudu-

lent tactics to take 750,000 acres of the Indians' land ("Penn's Elm and *Edgar Huntly*: Dark 'Instructions to the Heart,'" *American Literature* 66 [1994]: 467–68).

73. My reading of Deb has been influenced by Hinds, "Animals, Indians, and Postcolonial Desire." See also Matthew Wyn Sivils, "Native American Sovereignty and Old Deb in Charles Brockden Brown's *Edgar Huntly*," *ATQ* 15 (2001): 293–304. I am departing from Carroll Smith-Rosenberg's "Surrogate Americans: Masculinity, Masquerade, and the Formation of a National Identity," *PMLA* 119 (2004): 1325–35, which argues rather coercively that performative "surrogacy *must* be seen as a form of colonization *as exploitative* [my emphases] as the seizure of Native American lands" (1331). Eric Lott's focus on the possibilities of both "love and theft" in minstrelsy has helped to inform my reading of Edgar as Indian; see *Love and Theft: Blackface Minstrelsy and the American Working Class* (New York: Oxford University Press, 1993).

74. Krause persuasively argues that Brown, through his use of the elm as the site of Waldegrave's murder, deliberately invokes the myth of William Penn's Elm, the place where Penn negotiated an amicable treaty with the Lenni Lanape in 1682. According to Krause, Brown over the course of his novel charts the white colonists' betrayal of Penn's ideals of interracial friendship (see "Penn's Elm and *Edgar Huntly*," 463–84).

75. Kazanjian, *The Colonizing Trick*, 170, 171.

76. In English folklore, Queen Mab is a whimsical, playful fairy, but Shakespeare presents her as having a darker side in the way she prompts dark, frightening dreams. Shelley's unpublished "Queen Mab," composed in 1812–13, also develops Mab's darker side, in the manner of Brown, by presenting her as intent on vengeance, and a similar image is central to the "Queen Mab" chapter of Melville's *Moby-Dick* (1851).

77. Gardner contends that "the project of the second half of the novel [is] to bring Edgar back to his rightful place in society and to demonstrate how and why he can make this journey of return while Clithero cannot." With respect to the Louisiana tracts, he maintains that *Edgar Huntly* enacts a relatively simple allegory of nation making through its depiction of Huntly's "proclivity for the hunt," which is the way that he "proves himself an American" (*Master Plots*, 72, 75, 80).

78. Gardner, "The Literary Museum," 744; Ed White, "Early American Nations as Imagined Communities," *American Quarterly* 56 (2004): 77.

79. Even in frontier fiction of more "knowing," ideological authors—one thinks of James Fenimore Cooper's *Last of the Mohicans* (1826) and William Gilmore Simms's *The Yemassee* (1835)—one senses the perpetual threats to fixed knowledge posed by racial binaries that threaten to become dualisms. See, for example, Wayne Franklin's splendid study of the anarchic tendencies of Cooper's fiction, *The New World of James Fenimore Cooper* (Chicago: University of Chicago Press, 1982).

80. "Thoughts on the Origin of the Claims of Europeans to North-America," *Monthly Magazine and American Review* 3 (1800): 16, 17.

81. David Ramsay, *An Oration on the Cession of Louisiana, to the United States* (Charleston, S.C.: W. P. Young, 1804), 4, 21, 11, 12.

82. Watts, *The Romance of Real Life*, 180.

83. Mark L. Kamrath, "American Exceptionalism and Radicalism in the 'Annals of Europe and America,'" in *Revising Charles Brockden Brown*, ed. Barnard, Kamrath, and Shapiro, 367. See also Philip Barnard, "Culture and Authority in Brown's Historical Sketches," in *Revising Charles Brockden Brown*, 310–31. Kamrath and Barnard develop compelling analyses of Brown's radical energies during the final years of his life, though at times they fall into the anachronistic trap of seeing his radicalism as anti-Federalist. As I have noted in this chapter, it was the Federalists who argued against slavery and against the terms of Jefferson's ever-expanding empire.

84. Kazanjian, *The Colonizing Trick*, 140, 141.

85. See the useful historical note in Brown, *Wieland; or, The Transformation: An American Tale* and *Memoirs of Carwin the Biloquist*, ed. Krause, Reid, and Cowie, 335–340.

86. Brown, *Memoirs of Carwin the Biloquist*, 249, 250, 251.

87. Ibid., 251, 252.

88. Ibid., 277.

89. Hsu, "Democratic Expansionism in 'Memoirs of Carwin,'" 137.

90. [Charles Brockden Brown], *The British Treaty. With an Appendix of State Papers* (London: Joseph Stockdale, 1808), 39. The tract was first published in Philadelphia in 1807.

91. Brown, *Memoirs of Carwin the Biloquist*, 310.

92. Brown, *Address*, 80.

93. On Jefferson's nonintercourse policy towards Haiti, see Kerber, *Federalists in Dissent*, 48–50.

94. Charles Brockden Brown, preface to C. F. Volney, *A View of the Soil*, xii; Brown, "How Far Do Slaves Influence Political Representation in America," 441.

95. "Politics," *Port Folio* 3 (1803): 293. The essay appeared in the issue of 10 September 1803. Though primarily a literary newspaper, *Port Folio* regularly had critical things to say about southern slavery. "There is a spirit of domination engrafted in the character of the southern people," the anonymous author of the "Politics" column wrote in the 31 January 1801 issue of the first volume, and in the issue of 11 April 1801, in the same "Politics" column, the writer lamented that the Declaration of Independence had no validity in the South: "[S]laves there are in America (particularly in Virginia;) and where there are slaves, there liberty is alienated" (*Port Folio* 1 [1801]: 24, 114).

96. Jefferson to Dr. Priestly, letter of 29 January 1804, in *State Papers and Correspondence Bearing upon the Purchase of the Territory of Louisiana*, 274; Jeffer-

son to Mr. Breckenridge, letter of 12 August 1803, in *State Papers and Correspondence Bearing upon the Purchase of the Territory of Louisiana*, 235.

97. Peter S. Onuf, "Thomas Jefferson, Missouri, and the 'Empire for Liberty,'" in *Thomas Jefferson and the Changing West*, ed. James P. Ronda (Albuquerque: University of New Mexico Press, 1997), 133.

98. Charles Brockden Brown, "Annals of Europe and America," *American Register, or General Repository of History, Politics, Science* 2 (1808): 85, 93, 97. Brown's relative calm is surprising given that, as Kastor notes, the Burr Conspiracy was "the source of no end of concern to Americans during 1806 and 1807" (*The Nation's Crucible*, 2).

99. [Charles Brockden Brown], review of William Robertson, D.D., *The History of America, Book IX and X. Containing the History of Virginia in the Year 1688, and of Connecticut in the Year 1652*, in *Monthly Magazine and American Review* 1 (1799): 131.

100. On sectionalism during this period, see Peter S. Onuf, "Federalism, Republicanism, and the Origins of American Sectionalism," in *All over the Map: Rethinking American Regions*, ed. Edward L. Ayers et al. (Baltimore: Johns Hopkins University Press, 1996), 11–37.

101. Joel Barlow, *The Columbiad. A Poem, with the Last Corrections of the Author* (Washington City: Joseph Milligan, 1825), 155, 153, 271, 275, 44, 279, 329, 353, 337, 335. For Barlow's note on the Louisiana Purchase, see 404–5. On Barlow, see McWilliams, *The American Epic*, chap. 2; William C. Dowling, *Poetry and Ideology in Revolutionary Connecticut* (Athens: University of Georgia Press, 1990); Eric Wertheimer, *Imagining Empires: Incas, Aztecs, and the New World of American Literature, 1771–1876* (Cambridge: Cambridge University Press, 1999), chap. 2; and Gould, *Barbaric Traffic*, 78–83.

102. [C. B. Brown], *An Address to the Congress of the United States, on the Utility and Justice of Restrictions upon Foreign Countries. With Reflections on Foreign Trade, in General, and the Future Prospects of America* (Philadelphia: C. & A. Conrad and Co., 1809), v, 87. (Brown credits his Quaker background for his desires for peace [vi].) In this final publication, Brown's vision of the regenerative force of U.S. economic empire bears some resemblance to Alexander Hamilton's; see Sean X. Goudie, *Creole America: The West Indies and the Formation of Literature and Culture in the New Republic* (Philadelphia: University of Pennsylvania Press, 2006), chap. 2.

Chapter 2

1. Jonathan Arac, *The Emergence of American Literary Narrative, 1820–1860* (1995; Cambridge, Mass.: Harvard University Press, 2005), 30. Arac defines the "national narrative" as that which "told the story of the nation's colonial beginnings and looked forward to its future as a model for the world" (2–3). As will be discussed in the final section of this chapter, such a teleological narrative is most characteristic of New England–based writing. Arac does allow that during the

1820s, "Space remained for local narratives that offered alternative emphases" (30). Such alternative emphases arguably make their way into most writing of the period, which could be described en masse as "local."

2. Robert E. Spiller, *The American Literary Revolution, 1783–1837* (Garden City, N.Y.: Anchor Books, 1967), x; Walter Channing, "Reflections on the Literary Delinquency of America," *North American Review and Miscellaneous Journal* 2 (1815): 35. The standard account of literary nationalism during this period is Benjamin Spencer, *The Quest for Nationality: An American Literary Campaign* (Syracuse, N.Y.: Syracuse University Press, 1957). For recent accounts of U.S. literary "emergence" in relation to England, see Susan S. Williams, "Publishing an Emergent 'American' Literature," in *Perspectives on Book History: Artifacts and Commentary*, ed. Scott E. Casper, Joanne D. Chaison, and Jeffrey D. Groves (Amherst: University of Massachusetts Press, 2002), 165–94; and Leonard Tennenhouse, *The Importance of Feeling English: American Literature and the British Diaspora, 1750–1850* (Princeton: Princeton University Press, 2007). Working with consensual notions of American writers and American literature, Williams sees conflict in U.S. writers' relation to English literary traditions, whereas Tennenhouse sees affiliation and appropriation.

3. Sean Wilentz, *The Rise of American Democracy: Jefferson to Lincoln* (New York: W. W. Norton and Company, 2005), 182.

4. David Waldstreicher, *In the Midst of Perpetual Fetes: The Making of American Nationalism, 1770–1820* (Chapel Hill: University of North Carolina Press, 1997), 142.

5. Donald E. Pease, "National Identities, Postmodern Artifacts, and Postnational Narratives," in *National Identities and Post-American Narratives*, ed. Donald E. Pease (Durham: Duke University Press, 1994), 3.

6. Xiomara Santamarina, "Thinkable Alternatives in African American Studies," *American Quarterly* 58 (2006): 251.

7. *David Walker's Appeal, in Four Articles; Together with a Preamble, to the Coloured Citizens of the World, but in Particular, and Very Expressly, to Those of the United States of America*, ed. Sean Wilentz (New York: Hill and Wang, 1995), 25. Wilentz reprints the third and final edition of the *Appeal*, published in June 1830.

8. Sterling Stuckey, *Slave Culture: Nationalist Theory and the Foundations of Black America* (New York: Oxford University Press, 1987), 120.

9. *David Walker's Appeal*, 12–13. On the importance of print to nationalism, see Benedict Anderson, *Imagined Communities: Reflections on the Origin and Spread of Nationalism* (London and New York: Verso, 1991).

10. Peter P. Hinks, *To Awaken My Afflicted Brethren: David Walker and the Problem of Antebellum Slave Resistance* (University Park: Pennsylvania State University Press, 1997), 173. Though I depart from Hinks's reading of the *Appeal*, I am indebted to his excellent study for much of my knowledge of Walker and his times.

11. Carol Sue Humphrey, *The Press of the Young Republic, 1783–1833* (Westport, Conn.: Greenwood Press, 1994), 102; David Paul Nord, "Newspapers and American Nationhood, 1776–1826," in *Three Hundred Years of the American Newspaper*, ed. John B. Hency (Worcester, Mass.: American Antiquarian Society, 1991), 404. Nord estimates that approximately 400 newspapers were founded between 1810 and 1825.

12. Michael P. Johnson, "Denmark Vesey and His Co-Conspirators," *William and Mary Quarterly*, 3rd ser., 58 (2001): 915–75.

13. Robert Pierce Forbes, *The Missouri Compromise and Its Aftermath: Slavery and the Meaning of America* (Chapel Hill: University of North Carolina Press, 2007), 36. In addition to Forbes's important study, see Glover Moore, *The Missouri Controversy, 1819–1821* (Lexington: University of Kentucky Press, 1953); Don E. Fehrenbacher, *The South and Three Sectional Crises* (Baton Rouge: Louisiana State University Press, 1980), 9–23; William W. Freehling, *The Road to Disunion: Secessionists at Bay, 1776–1854* (New York: Oxford University Press, 1990), chap. 8; Charles Sellers, *The Market Revolution: Jacksonian America, 1815–1846* (New York: Oxford University Press, 1991), chap. 4; Forrest McDonald, *States' Rights and the Union: Imperium in Imperio, 1776–1876* (Lawrence: University Press of Kansas, 2000), chap. 4; and David Brion Davis, *Challenging the Boundaries of Slavery* (Cambridge, Mass.: Harvard University Press, 2003), chap. 2. On Jefferson's outrage and despair over the Missouri crisis, see Peter S. Onuf, *Jefferson's Empire: The Language of American Nationhood* (Charlottesville: University Press of Virginia, 2000), chap. 4.

14. Cited in William M. Wiecek, *The Sources of Antislavery Constitutionalism in America, 1760–1848* (Ithaca: Cornell University Press, 1977), 122–23.

15. For crucial backgrounds on the constitutional issues surrounding the debate on black citizenship, see Don E. Fehrenbacher, *The Dred Scott Case: Its Significance in American Law and Politics* (New York: Oxford University Press, 1978), chap. 2; Wiecek, *The Sources of Antislavery Constitutionalism*, chap. 3; and Rogers M. Smith, *Civic Ideals: Conflicting Visions of Citizenship in U.S. History* (New Haven: Yale University Press, 1997), chap. 7. Arguably, there was no settled notion of national citizenship until the passage of the Fourteenth Amendment, and even here key issues remained moot with respect to race and gender.

16. Moore, *The Missouri Controversy*, 91.

17. *Annals of Congress of the United States*, 16th Cong., 2nd sess., 108, 109, 111, 636, 637.

18. See Smith, *Civic Ideals*, 175–78. As Smith and other historians have pointed out, there were blacks at the time of the Constitutional Convention who were in fact regarded as citizens.

19. *Annals of Congress of the United States*, 16th Cong., 2nd sess., 57, 58, 556, 555, 84, 86.

20. *Annals of Congress of the United States*, 16th Cong., 2nd sess., 1134, 1136. For a similar reading of Pinckney's key role in this debate, see Forbes, *Missouri Compromise*, 112–15.

21. *Annals of Congress of the United States*, 16th Cong., 2nd sess., 1228; George Dangerfield, *The Awakening of American Nationalism, 1815–1828* (New York: Harper Torchbooks, 1965), 136. In 1847 Missouri's legislators, with little debate, unconditionally banned all free blacks from entering the state.

22. *Annals of Congress of the United States*, 16th Cong., 2nd sess., 989, 558, 556, 557. On Benjamin Rush's racial views, see Bruce Dain, *A Hideous Monster of the Mind: American Race Theory in the Early Republic* (Cambridge, Mass.: Harvard University Press, 2002), 24–26; and on fever and revolution, see William L. Hedges, "Benjamin Rush, Charles Brockden Brown, and the American Plague Year," *Early American Literature* 7 (1973): 295–311.

23. See Richard C. Wade, "The Vesey Plot: A Reconsideration," *Journal of Southern History* 30 (1964): 143–61; and Stuckey, *Slave Culture*, 43–53.

24. Johnson, "Denmark Vesey and His Co-Conspirators," 971, 916. Among the books that Johnson attacks are Douglas R. Egerton, *He Shall Go Free: The Lives of Denmark Vesey* (Madison, Wisc.: Madison House, 1999); and Edward A. Pearson, ed., *Designs against Charleston: The Trial Record of the Denmark Vesey Slave Conspiracy of 1822* (Chapel Hill: University of North Carolina Press, 1999). Johnson does demonstrate that Pearson's editing of the trial records is, as Pearson himself concedes, "deeply flawed" (Pearson, "Trials and Errors: Denmark Vesey and His Historians," *William and Mary Quarterly*, 3rd ser., 59 [2002]: 139). For excellent responses to Johnson, see Douglas R. Egerton, "Forgetting Denmark Vesey; or, Oliver Stone Meets Richard Wade," *William and Mary Quarterly*, 3rd ser., 49 (2002): 143–52; and Robert L. Paquette, "From Rebellion to Revisionism: The Continuing Debate about the Denmark Vesey Affair," *Journal of the Historical Society* 4 (2004): 291–334.

25. Lionel H. Kennedy and Thomas Parker, *An Official Report of the Trials of Sundry Negroes, Charged with an Attempt to Raise an Insurrection in the State of South Carolina* (Charleston, 1822), repr. in *The Trial Record of Denmark Vesey*, ed. John Oliver Killens (Boston: Beacon Press, 1970), 88.

26. On Walker's acquaintance with Vesey and possible involvement in his conspiracy, see Hinks, *To Awaken My Afflicted Brethren*, 30–37; and Egerton, *He Shall Go Free*, 115–20.

27. The selections from the *National Intelligencer* and the *South Carolina State Gazette* may be found in Robert S. Starobin, ed., *Denmark Vesey: The Slave Conspiracy of 1822* (Englewood Cliffs, N.J.: Prentice-Hall, 1970), 90. For important early discussions of the relationship of the Missouri debates to the Vesey conspiracy, see Moore, *Missouri Controversy*, 295; and William W. Freehling, *Prelude to Civil War: The Nullification Controversy in South Carolina, 1816–1836* (New York: Harper Torchbooks, 1968), 53–61.

28. Kennedy and Parker, *Official Report*, 12.

29. My thinking about the hybridized, or dialogic, nature of the Vesey trial transcript has been influenced by Eric J. Sundquist's brilliant reading of Thomas Gray's *The Confessions of Nat Turner* in *To Wake the Nations: Race in the Making of American Literature* (Cambridge, Mass.: Harvard University Press, 1993), 36–56. For a meticulous discussion of how the court records suggest that a conspiracy in fact was in place, see Douglas R. Egerton and Robert L. Paquette, "Of Facts and Fables: New Light on the Denmark Vesey Affair," *South Carolina Historical Magazine* 105 (2004): 8–35.

30. Kennedy and Parker, *Official Report*, 42, 43, 64, 94, 128. On the impact of the Missouri debates on Vesey and his accomplices, see Forbes, *Missouri Compromise*, 144–47.

31. On this point, see Michael A. Gomez, *Exchanging Our Country Marks: The Transformation of African Identities in the Colonial and Antebellum South* (Chapel Hill: University of North Carolina Press, 1998), 2–11. See also Stuckey, *Slave Culture*, 43–53.

32. See Chris Dixon, *African America and Haiti: Emigration and Black Nationalism in the Nineteenth Century* (Westport, Conn.: Greenwood Press, 2000), chap. 1.

33. Egerton, *He Shall Go Free*, 130–31.

34. Kennedy and Parker, *Official Report*, 88.

35. Egerton, *He Shall Go Free*, 131.

36. See "The Missouri Question. Mr. King's Speeches," *Niles Register*, 4 December 1819, repr. in *A Documented History of Gullah Jack Pritchard and the Denmark Vesey Slave Insurrection of 1822*, ed. Louis A. Walker and Susan R. Silverman (Lewiston, N.Y.: Edwin Mellen Press, 2000), 103, 109, 110, 116, 114.

37. James Hamilton's *An Account of the Late Intended Insurrection among a Portion of the Blacks of this City* (Charleston, 1822) is conveniently reprinted in its entirety in *A Documented History of Gullah Jack Pritchard and the Denmark Vesey Slave Insurrection of 1822*, ed. Walker and Silverman, 295–337. According to Michael Johnson, Hamilton was among those who conspired to create what Johnson regards as the false story about the Vesey conspiracy. But again it is worth noting that the dissemination of texts about the Vesey conspiracy only worked to stimulate the interest of free blacks in what they regarded as a black hero who had devised new strategies for challenging white supremacy. If there had not been a conspiracy, Hamilton and others had stupidly helped to create insurrectionary feelings among African Americans in the North and South. It is hard to believe that Hamilton and his associates would have been so naive about the possible consequences of publicizing a false conspiracy.

38. James Oliver Horton and Lois E. Horton, *In Hope of Liberty: Culture, Community, and Protest among Northern Free Blacks, 1700–1860* (New York: Oxford University Press, 1997), 102. Controls over black mobility became even more stringent in the years immediately following the Vesey conspiracy. At the same

time, black resistance to such monitoring was emboldened by the increasingly pervasive discourse, which had important sources in the Missouri debates, challenging such monitoring as an affront to U.S. national ideals. It was precisely black resistance to such monitoring and other forms of the "black codes" that led to the major riots in Cincinnati in 1829 and the subsequent emigration of hundreds of black Ohioans to Canada. On mobility as an issue in slave revolts, fugitive slave law, and slave narratives, see Mark Simpson, *Trafficking Subjects: The Politics of Mobility in Nineteenth-Century America* (Minneapolis: University of Minnesota Press, 2005), chaps. 1 and 3.

39. On Walker and Boston, see Hinks, *To Awaken My Afflicted Brethren*, chap. 3; and Donald M. Jacobs, "David Walker: Boston Race Leader, 1825–1830," *Essex Institute Historical Collections* 107 (1971): 94–107. For a lively discussion of Walker in the context of the emergent black literary societies of the period, see Elizabeth McHenry, *Forgotten Readers: Recovering the Lost History of African American Literary Societies* (Durham: Duke University Press, 2002), 25–42. On the complex evolution of black nationalism in the North, see Patrick Rael, *Black Identity and Black Protest in the Antebellum North* (Chapel Hill: University of North Carolina Press, 2002), esp. chap. 6.

40. *David Walker's Appeal*, 69.

41. "Colonization Society," *African Repository and Colonial Journal* 1 (1825): 161. For an example of the ACS's celebration of Africa, which they hoped would encourage black emigration, or removal, to the continent, see [T. R.], "Observations on the Early History of the Negro Race," *African Repository and Colonial Journal* 1 (1825), which argues that those who "were called *Ethiopians*" helped transform Egypt from "a state of barbarism" to the "mother of science" and ultimately "gave to Africa, and through her to Europe and America, all the wisdom of the Egyptians" (7, 8).

42. Benedict Anderson, *Imagined Communities: Reflections on the Origin and Spread of Nationalism*, rev. ed. (London and New York: Verso, 1991), 7.

43. "To Our Patrons," *Freedom's Journal*, 16 March 1827, 1; for a report on the "Meeting of the People of Colour of the City of Boston," see page 2 of the same issue. For useful discussions of *Freedom's Journal*, see Bella Gross, "Freedom's Journal and the Rights of All," *Journal of Negro History* 17 (1932): 241–86; Lionel C. Barrow Jr., "'Our Own Cause': *Freedom's Journal* and the Beginnings of the Black Press," *Journalism History* 4 (1977–78): 118–22; and especially Dickson D. Bruce Jr., *The Origins of African American Literature, 1680–1865* (Charlottesville: University of Virginia Press, 2001), 163–83. Good general accounts include Frankie Hutton, *The Early Black Press in America, 1827 to 1860* (Westport, Conn.: Greenwood Press, 1993); and Armisted S. Pride and Clint C. Wilson II, *A History of the Black Press* (Washington, D.C.: Howard University Press, 1997).

44. See Kenneth D. Nordin, "In Search of Black Unity: An Interpretation of the Content and Function of *Freedom's Journal*," *Journalism History* 4 (1977–78): 123–

28. Ironically, many of the articles printed in *Freedom's Journal* celebrating the achievements of African civilization were reprinted from the *African Repository and Colonial Journal*, the very paper that *Freedom's Journal* meant to contest. See, for example, the articles on Ethiopia and Africa in *Freedom's Journal* from the *African Repository*, reprinted in the "Original Communications" column on page 2 of the issues of 5 December 1828 and 21 March 1829. See also the celebration of black Egypt in the three-part series "Mutability of Human Affairs," which appeared in the 6, 13, and 20 April 1827 issues of the *Freedom's Journal*. On the importance of the *African Repository* to African American writers, see Bruce, *Origins of African American Literature*, 154.

45. John Browne Russwurm, "The Condition and Prospects of Haiti," in *The Voice of Black America: Major Speeches by Negroes in the United States, 1797–1971*, ed. Philip S. Foner (New York: Simon and Schuster, 1972), 37; untitled article on Haiti, *Freedom's Journal*, 16 March 1827, 2; "Haytian Revolution," *Freedom's Journal*, 6 April 1827, 2. In "Haiti and Egypt in Early Black Racial Discourse in the United States" (*Slavery and Abolition* 14 [1993]: 139–61), Bruce Dain argues that Egypt took priority over Haiti in African American writings of the 1820s as "the most impressive example of black achievement" (141), but there was clearly considerable interest in Haiti in *Freedom's Journal*. On the importance of Haiti during this period, see Dixon, *African America and Haiti*, chap. 1; and Bruce, *Origins of African American Literature*, 155–56, 166–68.

46. "Original Communications," *Freedom's Journal*, 23 March 1827, 6; "The Surprising Influence of Prejudice," *Freedom's Journal*, 18 May 1827, 37–38; "Freedom's Journal," *Freedom's Journal*, 25 April 1828, 38; "George M. Horton," *Freedom's Journal*, 8 August 1828, 154; "George M. Horton," *Freedom's Journal*, 3 October 1828, 218. Horton's poems, which had begun to circulate in newspapers, would be collected in *The Hope of Liberty. Containing a Number of Poetical Pieces*, published in Raleigh, North Carolina, in 1829. For a modern edition, see Joan R. Sherman, ed., *The Black Bard of North Carolina: George Moses Horton and His Poetry* (Chapel Hill: University of North Carolina Press, 1997).

47. "Original Communications," *Freedom's Journal*, 7 September 1827, 101.

48. Richard S. Newman, *The Transformation of American Abolitionism: Fighting Slavery in the Early Republic* (Chapel Hill: University of North Carolina Press, 2002), 95. See also Bruce, *Origins of African American Literature*, 95, 169.

49. *Freedom's Journal*, 22 February 1828, 160; *Freedom's Journal*, 29 February 1828, 2; *Freedom's Journal*, 7 March 1828, 2.

50. *Freedom's Journal*, 16 March 1827, 4.

51. On Cornish's departure, see "To the Patrons and Friends of 'Freedom's Journal,'" *Freedom's Journal*, 14 September 1827, 107.

52. "Colonization," *Freedom's Journal*, 14 March 1828, 394; "To Our Patrons," *Freedom's Journal*, 28 March 1829, 410. On tensions between Russwurm's Africanism and African Americanism, see James Sidbury, *Becoming African in America:*

Race and Nation in the Early Black Atlantic (New York: Oxford University Press, 2007), 197–201.

53. *The Rights of All*, 29 May 1829, 2, 8.

54. Ibid., 12 June 1829, 15; ibid., 18 September 1829, 34.

55. "Address, Delivered before the General Colored Association of Boston, by David Walker," *Freedom's Journal*, 19 December 1828, 296.

56. *David Walker's Appeal*, 1. All further page references to Walker's *Appeal* will be provided parenthetically in the main body of the text.

57. Hinks, *To Awaken My Afflicted Brethren*, 193.

58. On Walker and the American Jeremiad, see Carla L. Peterson, *"Doers of the Word": African-American Women Speakers and Writers in the North (1830–1880)* (New York: Oxford University Press, 1995), 64–66; and Eddie S. Glaude Jr., *Exodus! Religion, Race, and Nation in Early Nineteenth-Century Black America* (Chicago: University of Chicago Press, 2000), 34–43.

59. On Walker's recontextualization strategies, see also John Ernest, *Liberation Historiography: African American Writers and the Challenge of History, 1794–1861* (Chapel Hill: University of North Carolina Press, 2004), 85–86.

60. According to Frank Luther Mott, during this time "all papers based their news of the government on the reports of the *National Intelligencer*" (*American Journalism, A History: 1690–1960* [New York: Macmillan, 1962], 177).

61. Walker refers as well to an influential book by John Taylor of Caroline, "which was widely circulated and much confided in, in Virginia" (55), perhaps *Tyranny Unmasked* (1822), which likewise underscored the need to keep free blacks apart from the black slaves. For a provocative reading of Walker's critique of the colonization schemes of Jefferson and others, see David Kazanjian, *The Colonizing Trick: National Culture and Imperial Citizenship in Early America* (Minneapolis: University of Minnesota Press, 2003), chap. 2.

62. Jürgen Habermas, *The Structural Transformation of the Public Sphere: An Inquiry into a Category of Bourgeois Society* (Cambridge: MIT Press, 1992), 161; Houston A. Baker Jr., "Critical Memory and the Black Public Sphere," in *The Black Public Sphere: A Public Culture Book*, ed. The Black Public Sphere Collective (Chicago: University of Chicago Press, 1995), 13; Nancy Fraser, "Rethinking the Public Sphere: A Contribution to the Critique of Actually Existing Democracy," in *Habermas and the Public Sphere*, ed. Craig Calhoun (Cambridge: MIT Press, 1992), 124. On print circulation and the formation of alternative public cultures, see also Michael Warner, *Publics and Counterpublics* (New York: Zone Books, 2002), esp. 90–114.

63. Hinks, *To Awaken My Afflicted Brethren*, 249.

64. See Jeremy Waldron, "Superseding Historic Injustice," *Ethics* 103 (1992): 4–28. On "undoing" plots, see Catherine Gallagher, "Undoing," in *Time and the Literary*, ed. Karen Newman, Jay Clayton, and Marianne Hirsch (New York: Routledge, 2002), 11–29.

65. My reading attempts to find a more flexible and strategic middle ground between Hinks's U.S. integrationist Walker, as presented in *To Awaken My Afflicted Brethren*, and Stuckey's Pan-Africanist Walker, as presented in *Slave Culture* (see esp. 98–137). For Hinks's articulation of his differences with Stuckey, see *To Awaken My Afflicted Brethren*, 250. Stuckey does in fact allow that Walker offers some hope for reconciliation between the races, "provided America ceased being a 'white' country" (*Slave Culture*, 131).

66. For a complementary reading of Walker as a writer who "both appeals to and undermines the terms of historical understanding," see Ernest, *Liberation Historiography*, 49–50.

67. Here I depart from Mia Bay, who sees Walker as convinced of essentialized notions of race, and racial difference, when he suggests that blacks are better than whites (*The White Image in the Black Mind: African-American Ideas about White People, 1830–1925* [New York: Oxford University Press, 2000], 33–36).

68. On the newspaper context of the Declaration of Independence, see Pauline Maier, *American Scripture: Making the Declaration of Independence* (New York: Alfred A. Knopf, 1997), esp. chap. 4. As Kazanjian points out, Walker's decision to structure the *Appeal* in terms of a preamble and four articles mimics (and ironizes) such founding texts as the Declaration and Constitution; see *The Colonizing Trick*, 9.

69. Stuckey, *Slave Culture*, 135.

70. Hinks, *To Awaken My Afflicted Brethren*, 238. W. Jeffrey Bolster writes: "From the used-clothing store that he operated on Brattle Street, near the Boston wharves, Walker buttonholed sailors and asked them to spread his message. It was no coincidence that the *Appeal* circulated first in seaports" (*Black Jacks: African American Seamen in the Age of Sail* [Cambridge, Mass.: Harvard University Press, 1997], 197). On North Carolina and Walker, see John Hope Franklin, *The Free Negro in North Carolina, 1790–1860* (1943; repr. Chapel Hill: University of North Carolina Press, 1995), 64–70. For discussions of other southern states' efforts to block circulation of the *Appeal*, see Clement Eaton, "A Dangerous Pamphlet in the Old South," *Journal of Southern History* 2 (1936): 323–34; William H. and Jane H. Pease, "Walker's *Appeal* Comes to Charleston: A Note and Documents," *Journal of Negro History* 59 (1974): 287–92; and Hinks, *To Awaken My Afflicted Brethren*, chap. 5.

71. Moore, *Missouri Controversy*, 307.

72. Lee Rust Brown, *The Emerson Museum: Practical Romanticism and the Pursuit of the Whole* (Cambridge, Mass.: Harvard University Press, 1997), 42; Ralph Waldo Emerson, "The American Scholar," in *Emerson: Essays and Lectures*, ed. Joel Porte (New York: Library of America, 1983), 42; Christopher Newfield, *The Emerson Effect: Individualism and Submission in America* (Chicago: University of Chicago Press, 1996), 5; Emerson, "The Poet," in *Essays and Lectures*, ed. Porte, 465.

73. Joanne Pope Melish, *Disowning Slavery: Gradual Emancipation and "Race" in New England, 1780–1860* (Ithaca: Cornell University Press, 1998), 218.

74. Daniel Webster, "First Settlement of New England," in *The Writings and Speeches of Daniel Webster*, 18 vols. (Boston: Little, Brown, and Company, 1903), 1:209, 224; Catharine Maria Sedgwick, *The Linwoods; or, "Sixty Years Since" in America*, 2 vols. (New York: Harper & Brothers, 1835), 1:xi, 65, 42; 2:54, 284, 286. Key critical works on New England regional/sectional identity include Lawrence Buell, *New England Literary Culture: From Revolution through Renaissance* (Cambridge: Cambridge University Press, 1986); Nina Baym, *Feminism and American Literary History: Essays* (New Brunswick: Rutgers University Press, 1992), 167–82; Stephen Nissenbaum, "New England as Region and Nation," in *All Over the Map: Rethinking American Regions*, ed. Edward L. Ayers et al. (Baltimore: Johns Hopkins University Press, 1996), 38–61; Joseph A. Conforti, *Imagining New England: Explorations of Regional Identity from the Pilgrims to the Mid-Twentieth Century* (Chapel Hill: University of North Carolina Press, 2001); and John McWilliams, *New England's Crises and Cultural Memory: Literature, Politics, History, Religion, 1620–1860* (Cambridge: Cambridge University Press, 2004). On the influential historiography of the late nineteenth century that placed New England at the center of American literary traditions, see Claudia Stokes, *Writers in Retrospect: The Rise of American Literary History, 1875–1910* (Chapel Hill: University of North Carolina Press, 2006), chap. 5.

75. Hugh Holman reports that Tucker's "opposition to the Missouri Compromise was bitter, for he felt it was unconstitutional in that it denied the inalienable right of a people to form their own constitution and state government"; see Holman's introduction to Nathaniel Beverley Tucker, *The Partisan Leader: A Tale of the Future* (Chapel Hill: University of North Carolina Press, 1971), xi. On Tucker, see also Michael O'Brien, *Conjectures of Order: Intellectual Life and the American South, 1810–1860*, 2 vols. (Chapel Hill: University of North Carolina Press, 2004), 2:863–72. William Gilmore Simms, as John D. Keckering argues, regarded sectionalism as central to literary nationalism (*The Poetics of National and Racial Identity in Nineteenth-Century American Literature* [Cambridge: Cambridge University Press, 2003], esp. 78–80). On territorial issues in Simms and other southern writers, see Caroline F. Levander, *Cradle of Liberty: Race, the Child, and National Belonging from Thomas Jefferson to W. E. B. Du Bois* (Durham: Duke University Press, 2006), chap. 2. For a useful collection of primary documents, see John E. Bassett, *Defining Southern Literature: Perspectives and Assessments, 1831–1952* (Madison, N.J.: Fairleigh Dickinson University Press, 1997).

76. Edgar Allan Poe, "Beverly Tucker," in *Poe: Essays and Reviews*, ed. G. R. Thompson (New York: Library of America, 1984), 978. The question of Poe's relationship to southern literary nationalism remains a matter of debate. Richard Gray argues that Poe adopted a southern identity out of his "distrust of New England" (*Southern Aberrations: Writers of the American South and the Problems of*

Regionalism [Baton Rouge: Louisiana State University Press, 2000], 19), while J. Gerald Kennedy asserts that Poe "critiqued literary nationalism not from a narrowly sectional viewpoint but rather from an assumed cultural cosmopolitanism" ("'A Mania for Composition': Poe's Annus Mirabilis and the Violence of Nation-building," *American Literary History* 17 [2005]: 6). For complex discussions of Poe in relation to debates on literary nationalism and print during the period, see Terence Whalen, *Edgar Allan Poe and the Masses: The Political Economy of Literature in Antebellum America* (Princeton: Princeton University Press, 1999); and Meredith L. McGill, *American Literature and the Culture of Reprinting, 1834–1853* (Philadelphia: University of Pennsylvania Press, 2003), chap. 5.

77. Tucker, *The Partisan Leader*, 132, 40, 320, 170, 48, 201–2.

78. Connections between racial and geographical borders and the matter of citizenship were of course also central to Native American writings of the period, and it is no great coincidence that Indian "removal" proceeded apace during the debates on Missouri. In 1820, for example, in the midst of the Missouri controversy, Andrew Jackson led soldiers into the territories running from Georgia to Mississippi and forced the removal of Cherokees, Choctaws, and Chickasaws to beyond the Mississippi. The historian Charles Sellers has remarked that "Monrovians sought to create a 'great' nation by pushing relentlessly against the territories of Indians, Spanish, and British" (*The Market Revolution*, 90). A fuller study of the literary implications of the Missouri controversy would need to attend to the international, geopolitical dimension of expansionism in relation to such foreign policy developments as the 1819 Adams-Onís Treaty (which gave the United States possession of Florida), the Monroe Doctrine, revolutions in Latin America during the early 1820s, and the Panama Congress of 1826. On the implications of the Monroe Doctrine for American literature of the period, see Gretchen Murphy, *Hemispheric Imaginings: The Monroe Doctrine and Narratives of U.S. Empire* (Durham: Duke University Press, 2005), chap. 1. Also useful is Stephanie LeManager's *Manifest and Other Destinies: Territorial Fictions of the Nineteenth-Century United States* (Lincoln: University of Nebraska Press, 2004) and Ann Baker's *Heartless Immensity: Literature, Culture, and Geography in Antebellum Literature* (Ann Arbor: University of Michigan Press, 2006). On Native Americans' negotiations with nationalism in the post-Missouri moment, see Maureen Konkle, *Writing Indian Nations: Native Intellectuals and the Politics of Historiography, 1827–1863* (Chapel Hill: University of North Carolina Press, 2004), esp. chap. 2.

79. See Toni Morrison, *Playing in the Dark: Whiteness and the Literary Imagination* (Cambridge, Mass.: Harvard University Press, 1992).

80. *Productions of Mrs. Maria W. Stewart, Presented to the First African Baptist Church & Society, of the City of Boston* (Boston: Friends of Freedom and Virtue, 1835), 5, 20; Marilyn Richardson, ed., *Maria W. Stewart, America's First Black Woman Political Writer: Essays and Speeches* (Bloomington: Indiana University Press, 1987), 19; *Productions of Mrs. Maria W. Stewart*, 64. On Stewart and black

nationalism, see also Peterson, *"Doers of the Word,"* chap. 3; and Lora Romero, *Home Fronts: Domesticity and Its Critics in the Antebellum United States* (Durham: Duke University Press, 1997), chap. 3.

81. *Productions of Mrs. Maria W. Stewart,* 11, 65, 5, 70.

82. Hosea Easton, *A Treatise on the Intellectual Character, and Civil and Political Condition of the Colored People of the U. States; and the Prejudice Exercised towards Them: With a Sermon on the Duty of the Church to Them* (Boston, 1837), in *To Heal the Scourge of Prejudice: The Life and Writings of Hosea Easton,* ed. George R. Price and James Brewer Stewart (Amherst: University of Massachusetts Press, 1999), 81, 80, 113. (Price and Stewart discuss Easton's friendship with Walker on page 5 of their volume.) On Easton, see also Ernest, *Liberation Historiography,* 62–63, 73–74. Nathaniel Paul's "Address, Delivered on the Celebration of the Abolition of Slavery in the State of New-York," appeared in the 10 August 1827 issue of *Freedom's Journal,* 85; the 25 April 1828 issue of *Freedom's Journal* reported that "Mr Horsea [*sic*] Eastern [*sic*] was called to the Chair" of the meeting of Boston's blacks on *Freedom's Journal* (38). On the transnational dimension of Nathaniel Paul's abolitionist and antiracist work, see Robert S. Levine, "Fifth of July: Nathaniel Paul and the Construction of Black Nationalism," in *Genius in Bondage: Literature of the Early Black Atlantic,* ed. Vincent Carretta and Philip Gould (Lexington: University of Kentucky Press, 2001), 242–60.

83. See Frederick Douglass, "Haiti and the Haitian People: An Address Delivered in Chicago, Illinois, on 2 January 1893," and Douglass, "Our Destiny Is Largely in Our Own Hands: An Address Delivered in Washington, D.C., on 16 April 1883," in *The Frederick Douglass Papers,* ser. 1, *Speeches, Debates, and Interviews,* 5 vols., ed. John W. Blassingame et al. (New Haven: Yale University Press, 1979–92), 5:528, 69.

84. *Walker's Appeal, With a Brief Sketch of His Life. By Henry Highland Garnet. And Also Garnet's Address to the Slaves of the United States of America* (New York: J. H. Tobitt, 1848), iii, v, vi.

85. Garnet, "An Address to the Slaves of the United States of America. (Rejected by the National Convention, 1843)," in *Walker's Appeal,* 90, 94, 94–95. On Garnet's rhetorical distance from the slaves when compared to Walker, see Hinks, *To Awaken My Afflicted Brethren,* 234–35.

Chapter 3

1. Nathaniel Hawthorne, "A Select Party," *The United States Magazine, and Democratic Review* (hereafter cited as *Democratic Review*) 15 (1844): 33, 34, 36. "A Select Party" can be conveniently found in Nathaniel Hawthorne, *Tales and Sketches,* ed. Roy Harvey Pearce (New York: Library of America, 1982), 945–58.

2. Hawthorne, "A Select Party," 36.

3. Ralph Waldo Emerson, "The Poet," in *Selected Essays,* ed. Larzer Ziff (New York: Penguin Books, 1982), 281; Hawthorne, "A Select Party," 37.

4. "The Re-Annexation of Texas: In Its Influence on the Duration of Slavery," *Democratic Review* 15 (1844): 15, 16.

5. Lee Quinby, "Introduction," *Genealogy and Literature*, ed. Lee Quinby (Minneapolis: University of Minnesota Press, 1995), xviii.

6. Teresa A. Goddu, *Gothic America: Narrative, History, and Nation* (New York: Columbia University Press, 1997), 132; Nathaniel Hawthorne, *The House of the Seven Gables*, ed. Fredson Bowers et al. (Columbus: Ohio State University Press, 1965), 17; Goddu, *Gothic America*, 132. Recent work in what could be termed "genealogical fictions," or fictions of racial instability and hybridity, includes Carolyn Sorisio, *Fleshing Out America: Race, Gender, and the Politics of the Body in American Literature, 1833–1879* (Athens: University of Georgia Press, 2002); Cassandra Jackson, *Barriers between Us: Interracial Sex in Nineteenth-Century American Literature* (Bloomington: Indiana University Press, 2004); and Debra J. Rosenthal, *Race Mixture in Nineteenth-Century U.S. and Spanish American Fictions* (Chapel Hill: University of North Carolina Press, 2004).

7. Nathaniel Hawthorne, "Main-Street," in *Tales and Sketches*, ed. Pearce, 1030, 1031. See Michael J. Colacurcio, "'Red Man's Grave': Art and Destiny in Hawthorne's 'Main-Street,'" *Nathaniel Hawthorne Review* 31 (2005): 1–18.

8. Arthur Riss, "The Art of Discrimination," *ELH* 71 (2004): 252; Renée Bergland, *The National Uncanny: Indian Ghosts and American Subjects* (Hanover, N.H.: University Press of New England, 2000), 111; Jean Fagan Yellin, "Hawthorne and the Slavery Question," in *A Historical Guide to Nathaniel Hawthorne*, ed. Larry J. Reynolds (New York: Oxford University Press, 2001), 157; Timothy B. Powell, *Ruthless Democracy: A Multicultural Interpretation of the American Renaissance* (Princeton: Princeton University Press, 2000), 40; Gretchen Murphy, *Hemispheric Imaginings: The Monroe Doctrine and Narratives of U.S. Empire* (Durham: Duke University Press, 2005), 95.

9. In *The Life of Franklin Pierce* (1852), his campaign biography for his friend from Bowdoin College, Hawthorne declared that "Slavery [is] one of those evils, which Divine Providence does not leave to be remedied by human contrivances" (*Miscellaneous Prose and Verse*, ed. Thomas Woodson, Claude M., Simpson, and L. Neal Smith [Columbus: Ohio State University Press, 1994], 352). Hawthorne's failure to work actively against slavery has gained him the disdain of Yellin and other recent critics, and one can only wish he chose otherwise. Still, as discussed in more detail in section one of this chapter, Hawthorne's politics are more complicated than this passage from a campaign biography might suggest, and in choosing not to align himself with political abolitionism, he wasn't all that different from the seemingly more radical Melville.

10. Joel Pfister, "Hawthorne as Cultural Theorist," in *The Cambridge Companion to Nathaniel Hawthorne*, ed. Richard H. Millington (Cambridge: Cambridge University Press, 2004), 36.

11. Murphy, *Hemispheric Imaginings*, 95, 67.

12. In a letter to Hawthorne of April 1851, Melville remarked on *House*: "This book is like a fine old chamber, abundantly, but still judiciously, furnished with precisely that sort of furniture best fitted to furnish it" (*Correspondence: The Writings of Herman Melville*, ed. Lynn Horth [Evanston: Northwestern University Press, 1993], 185).

13. As historian Charles Sellers notes, "Young America preached that a democracy of state rights and limited federal powers could harmonize local differences and extend indefinitely the area of freedom" (*The Market Revolution: Jacksonian America, 1815–1846* [New York: Oxford University Press, 1991], 415).

14. Sean Wilentz remarks that, in retrospect, the writings of Young America "can look like the most arrogant form of imperial bullying." But he goes on to point out that "there was a deeply idealistic democratic side to Manifest Destiny, that, to be understood, requires an appreciation of the situation facing democrats around the world, and especially in Britain and Europe, in the early 1840s. That situation was terrible" (*The Rise of American Democracy: Jefferson to Lincoln* [New York: W. W. Norton & Company, 2005], 562).

15. [John O'Sullivan], "The Democratic Principle—The Importance of Its Assertion, and Application to Our Political System and Literature," *Democratic Review* 1 (1838): 2; Anders Stephanson, *Manifest Destiny: American Expansionism and the Empire of Right* (New York: Hill and Wang, 1995), 39. For an excellent discussion of Young America and the literary nationalism of the period, see Edward L. Widmer, *Young America: The Flowering of Democracy in New York City* (New York: Oxford University Press, 1999). Also useful are John Stafford, *The Literary Criticism of "Young America": A Study in the Relationship of Politics and Literature, 1837–1850* (Berkeley: University of California Press, 1952); and Perry Miller, *The Raven and the Whale: The War of Words and Wits in the Era of Poe and Melville* (New York: Harcourt, Brace & World, Inc., 1956).

16. [Anon.], "Democracy in Literature," *Democratic Review* 11 (1842): 196, 199, 197.

17. Reginald Horsman, *Race and Manifest Destiny: The Origins of American Racial Anglo-Saxonism* (Cambridge, Mass.: Harvard University Press, 1981), 1. My discussion of race and expansionism is indebted to Horsman's important study; see esp. chapter 12, "Race, Expansion, and the Mexican War," 229–48. Also useful is Richard Kluger, *Seizing Destiny: How America Grew from Sea to Shining Sea* (New York: Alfred A. Knopf, 2007), chap. 11. On connections between the debates on the Missouri Compromise and the expansionism of the 1840s and 1850s, see Robert E. May, "Epilogue to the Missouri Compromise: The South, the Balance of Power, and the Tropics in the 1850s," *Plantation Society* 1 (1979): 201–25.

18. Louis Agassiz, "The Diversity of the Origin of the Human Races," *Christian Examiner* 14 (1850): 142. As corresponding secretary for the Salem Lyceum, Hawthorne arranged for Agassiz to speak in Salem in December 1848. On Morton and the American School, see Thomas F. Gossett, *Race: The History of an Idea in*

America (1963; rev. ed., New York: Oxford University Press, 1997), chap. 4; Dana D. Nelson, *National Manhood: Capitalist Citizenship and the Imagined Fraternity of White Men* (Durham: Duke University Press, 1998), chap. 3; and Bruce Dain, *A Hideous Monster of the Mind: American Race Theory in the Early Republic* (Cambridge, Mass.: Harvard University Press, 2002), chap. 7.

19. [John O'Sullivan], "Annexation," *Democratic Review* 17 (1845): 5, 9, 8, 9; [Caleb Cushing], "Mexico," *Democratic Review* 18 (1846): 434.

20. [Anon.], "Do the Various Races of Man Constitute a Single Species?," *Democratic Review* 11 (1842): 113, 113–14; [Anon.], "Mexico—The Church, and Peace," *Democratic Review* 21 (1847): 101. Such fears of racial mixing are consistent with the declaration of William Wick at the outset of the Mexican War: "I do not want any mixed races in our Union, nor men of any color except white, unless they be slaves" (*Congressional Globe*, 29th Cong. [30 January 1846], quoted in Thomas R. Hietala, *Manifest Design: Anxious Aggrandizement in Late Jacksonian America* [Ithaca: Cornell University Press, 1985], 167). Horsman is not quite accurate when he writes: "While it was not uncommon for the Americans to be described as a unique and superior blend of Europeans rather than simply as Anglo-Saxons, it was extremely rare for anyone to think of the possibility of Americans ultimately becoming a blend of white and nonwhite races" (*Race and Manifest Destiny*, 256).

21. Henry Highland Garnet, *The Past and the Present Condition and the Destiny, of the Colored Race: A Discourse Delivered at the Fifteenth Anniversary of the Female Benevolent Society of Troy, N.Y., Feb. 14, 1848* (Troy, N.Y.: J. C. Kneeland, 1848), 26, 24, 23, 22, 25.

22. Hietala, *Manifest Design*, 133.

23. On this point, see George B. Forgie, *Patricide in the House Divided: A Psychological Interpretation of Lincoln and His Age* (New York: W. W. Norton & Company, 1979), 115–22. For historical backgrounds on the associations among bodies, houses, and the state, see Robert Blair St. George, "Witchcraft, Bodily Affliction, and Domestic Space in Seventeenth-Century New England," in *A Centre of Wonders: The Body in Early America*, ed. Janet Moore Lindman and Michele Lise Tarter (Ithaca: Cornell University Press, 2001), 13–27.

24. [Anon.], "The War," *Democratic Review* 20 (1847): 100; [Evert Duyckinck], "Nationality in Literature," *Democratic Review* 20 (1847): 265, 269, 267, 265.

25. The most damning critique of Hawthorne's politics with respect to slavery is Yellin, "Hawthorne and the Slavery Question," in *A Historical Guide to Nathaniel Hawthorne*, ed. Reynolds, 135–64. For a compelling historical defense, see Larry J. Reynolds, "The Challenge of Cultural Relativity: The Case of Hawthorne," *ESQ: A Journal of the American Renaissance* 49 (2003): 129–47. Reynolds writes that "all evidence suggests that Hawthorne was opposed to slavery" (138), even though he, Fuller, Thoreau, and many others in Concord and Boston "shared a disdain for reformers (especially the abolitionists), a prejudice against Negroes, [and] an

aversion to amalgamation of the races" (138–39). See also Reynolds's " 'Strangely Ajar with the Human Race': Hawthorne, Slavery, and the Question of Moral Responsibility," in *Hawthorne and the Real: Bicentennial Essays*, ed. Millicent Bell (Columbus: Ohio State University Press, 2005), 40–69.

26. Jonathan H. Earle, *Jacksonian Antislavery and the Politics of Free Soil, 1824–1854* (Chapel Hill: University of North Carolina Press, 2004), 15.

27. Hawthorne to E. A. Duyckinck, letter of 2 March 1845, in Nathaniel Hawthorne, *The Letters, 1843–1853*, ed. Thomas Woodson, L. Neal Smith, and Norman Holmes Pearson (Columbus: Ohio State University Press, 1985), 82; Horatio Bridge, *Journal of an African Cruiser: Comprising Sketches of the Canaries, the Cape de Verds, Liberia, Madeira, Sierra Leone, and Other Places of Interest on the West Coast of Africa*, ed. Nathaniel Hawthorne (1845; New York: George P. Putnam, 1853), 163–64. For a discussion of Hawthorne's editing of the Bridge text as a shrewd career move, see Teresa A. Goddu, "Letters Turned to Gold: Hawthorne, Authorship, and Slavery," *Studies in American Fiction* 29 (2001): 49–76.

28. Charles Sumner, "Union among Men of all Parties against the Slave Power and the Extension of Slavery," in *The Works of Charles Sumner* (Boston: Lee and Shepard, 1874), 2:77; Charles Sumner, "The Law of Human Progress," in *Works*, 2:125, 126, 119. Hawthorne wrote Sumner on 8 January 1848 to confirm that he would be speaking on the "Law of Progress" at the Salem Lyceum; see Hawthorne, *Letters, 1843–1853*, 258. Around the time of the publication of *House*, Hawthorne wrote to his publisher James Fields asking him to send copies to a "multitude of friends," including Sumner (Hawthorne to Fields, letter of 22 February 1851, *Letters, 1843–1853*, 398).

29. Hawthorne to Longfellow, letter of 8 May 1851, *Letters, 1843–1853*, 431; Hawthorne to Zachariah Burchmore, letter of 15 July 1851, *Letters, 1843–1853*, 456. In his 8 May 1851 letter to Longfellow, Hawthorne remarks on his disgust with the Fugitive Slave Law in a manner that captures his own sense of the contingency of the moment: "This Fugitive Law is the only thing that could have blown me into any respectable degree of warmth on this great subject of the day—if it really be the great subject—a point which another age can determine better than ours" (*Letters, 1843–1853*, 431). Though he can be condemned for not recognizing the momentous importance of the debate on slavery, there is something humbling about Hawthorne's lack of clarity about the meaning of his own historical moment.

It is worth noting that when Hawthorne eventually got around to writing Pierce's campaign biography, he was aware that he was writing in support of a limited politician—"a college-friend of mine," as he puts it in a letter of 17 June 1852 to James T. Fields—who, as he remarks in a letter of 13 October 1853 to Horatio Bridge, failed to rise to the occasion of "such extraordinary opportunities for eminent distinction, civil and military" (*Letters, 1843–1853*, 551, 604).

30. Hawthorne famously remarked that his wife, Sophia, was so moved by his reading of the conclusion to *The Scarlet Letter* that she went "to bed with a griev-

ous headache—which I regard as triumphant success!" (Hawthorne to Horatio Bridge, letter of 4 February 1850, *Letters, 1843–1853*, 311).

31. Hawthorne, *House*, 185.

32. Ibid., 2. All further references to *House* in this section of the chapter will be supplied parenthetically in the main body of the text.

33. Peter J. Bellis, *Writing Revolution: Aesthetics and Politics in Hawthorne, Whitman, and Thoreau* (Athens: University of Georgia Press, 2003), 33. As Patricia A. Turner shows in *I Heard It through the Grapevine: Rumor in African-American Culture* (Berkeley: University of California Press, 1993), rumor has always had a key place in African American history telling. A prime example of the role of such historical rumor sharing in the nineteenth century was the talk among many African Americans that Thomas Jefferson fathered children with his slave Sally Hemings; that rumor became the foundation of William Wells Brown's genealogical fiction *Clotel* (1853).

34. Etienne Balibar, "The Nation Form: History and Ideology," in Etienne Balibar and Immanuel Wallerstein, *Race, Nation, Class: Ambiguous Identities* (London: Verso, 1991), 102.

35. Roy R. Male, *Hawthorne's Tragic Vision* (1957; New York: W. W. Norton & Company, Inc., 1964), 122; Frank Kermode, *The Classic: Literary Images of Permanence and Change* (New York: Viking Press, 1975), 104.

36. Christopher Castiglia, "The Marvelous Queer Interiors of *The House of the Seven Gables*," in *The Cambridge Companion to Nathaniel Hawthorne*, ed. Millington, 198. Phoebe, like Hepzibah, contemplates that which was "hereditary" (119) in Jaffrey, concluding that he is the very incarnation of "the progenitor of the whole race of New England Pyncheons, the founder of the House of the Seven Gables" (120). Perhaps so, but the narrator also terms her insights a "fantasy" (120), while repeatedly reminding us of Jaffrey's genealogical distance from the Colonel. On the importance of portraiture and daguerreotypy to *House*, see also Susan S. Williams, *Confounding Images: Photography and Portraiture in Antebellum American Fiction* (Philadelphia: University of Pennsylvania Press, 1997), 96–119; Cathy N. Davidson, "Photographs of the Dead: Sherman, Daguerre, Hawthorne," *South Atlantic Review* 89 (1990): 667–701; and Alan Trachtenberg, "Seeing and Believing: Hawthorne's Reflections on the Daguerreotype in *The House of the Seven Gables*," *American Literary History* 9 (1997): 460–81.

37. Nathaniel Hawthorne, "Rappaccini's Daughter," in *Tales and Sketches*, ed. Pearce, 987; Anna C. Brickhouse, " 'I Do Abhor an Indian Story': Hawthorne and the Allegorization of Racial 'Commixture,' " *ESQ: A Journal of the American Renaissance* 42 (1996): 233, 245. For useful backgrounds on nineteenth-century evolutionary theory, see Robert M. Young, *Darwin's Metaphor* (Cambridge: Cambridge University Press, 1985); and Bentley Glass, Owsei Temkin, and William L. Straus Jr., eds., *Forerunners of Darwin: 1745–1859* (Baltimore: Johns Hopkins University Press, 1959).

38. The use of the word "breed" for race or family points to the Pyncheons' foundational project of breeding a "better" bloodline. As historian Bruce Dain usefully points out, it was in the fifteenth and sixteenth centuries, when "animal breeding terminology seems to have fused with ancient ideas about aristocratic familial legacy and 'blood,'" that whites began to conceive of notions of racial difference (*Hideous Monster of the Mind*, 7). But as Harriet Ritvo observes, even the best animal breeders of the nineteenth century conceded that "purity . . . could prove problematic," and that it "was impossible to demonstrate the historic genealogical purity of even the most distinguished animals" ("Barring the Cross: Miscegenation and Purity in Eighteenth- and Nineteenth-Century Britain," in *Human, All Too Human*, ed. Diana Fuss [New York: Routledge, 1996], 48, 49).

39. Shawn Michelle Smith, *American Archives: Gender, Race, and Class in Visual Culture* (Princeton: Princeton University Press, 1999), 29. Kermode notes that Comte de Buffon, in his thirty-six-volume *Histoire Naturelle*, published between 1749 and 1789, famously supported his thesis of New World degeneration through the example of chickens (*Classic*, 98–102).

40. Paul Gilmore, *The Genuine Article: Race, Mass Culture, and American Literary Manhood* (Durham: Duke University Press, 2001), 129, 133. See also Walter Benn Michaels, "Romance and Real Estate," in *The American Renaissance Reconsidered*, ed. Walter Benn Michaels and Donald E. Pease (Baltimore: Johns Hopkins University Press, 1985), 156–82; Gillian Brown, *Domestic Individualism: Imagining Self in Nineteenth-Century America* (Berkeley: University of California Press, 1990), 63–95; and David Anthony, "Class, Culture, and the Trouble with White Skin in Hawthorne's *The House of the Seven Gables*," *Yale Journal of Criticism* 12 (1999): 249–68. On the Gothic and slavery in the novel, see Robert K. Martin, "Haunted by Jim Crow: Gothic Fictions by Hawthorne and Faulkner," in *American Gothic: New Interventions in a National Narrative*, ed. Robert K. Martin and Eric Savoy (Iowa City: University of Iowa Press, 1998), 129–42.

41. Gilmore, *Genuine Article*, 135.

42. Russ Castronovo notes that Holgrave is linked to blackness through the implied connections that the novel makes between the Maules as mesmerical wizards and the practice of vodoun. In late 1830s New England, mesmerism was initially tied to vodoun through the popular demonstrations of Charles Poyen, whose mesmerical practices were developed in Haiti. See Russ Castronovo, *Necro Citizenship: Death, Eroticism, and the Public Sphere in the Nineteenth-Century United States* (Durham: Duke University Press, 2001), 161–65.

43. Anthony, "Class, Culture, and the Trouble with White Skin," 261.

44. Thus Arthur Riss, in a book that offers a sharp critique of Hawthorne's supposed inability to regard blacks as eligible for legal personhood, nonetheless remarks that "Hawthorne and Stowe need to be regarded as two of the most powerful anti-slavery liberals of the antebellum period" (*Race, Slavery, and Liberalism in Nineteenth-Century American Literature* [Cambridge: Cambridge University

Press, 2006], 19). For a revisionary reading of Holgrave's story that emphasizes issues of class and gender, see Keiko Arai, "'Phoebe is no Pyncheon': Class, Gender, and Nation in *The House of the Seven Gables*," *Nathaniel Hawthorne Review*, forthcoming.

45. Michaels compares Alice Pyncheon to the "quadroon girl" of Longfellow's poem of the same name; see "Romance and Real Estate," 173.

46. Anthony, "Class, Culture, and the Trouble with White Skin," 264.

47. Murphy, *Hemispheric Imaginings*, 95; Smith, *American Archives*, 50, 41. Gilmore similarly states that Hawthorne's ending attempts "to whitewash the nation." But even as he laments the whitewashing, Gilmore remarks on how Hawthorne "acknowledge[s] the way in which the shadows and lights define one another and bleed over into one another" (*Genuine Article*, 149–50).

48. Cindy Weinstein, *Family, Kinship, and Sympathy in Nineteenth-Century American Literature* (Cambridge: Cambridge University Press, 2004), 9.

49. On the Native American presence, or lack of presence, in *House*, see Powell, *Ruthless Democracy*, 30–48. For a broader consideration of legal issues and reform in the novel, see Brook Thomas, *Cross-Examinations of Law and Literature: Cooper, Hawthorne, Stowe, and Melville* (Cambridge: Cambridge University Press, 1987), 45–90.

50. As Bellis remarks, "Both Holgrave and the novel maintain their opposition to the old Pyncheon desire to 'plant and endow a family'" (*Writing Revolution*, 49). On motifs of historical change in the novel, see also Susan L. Mizruchi, *The Power of Historical Knowledge: Narrating the Past in Hawthorne, James, and Dreiser* (Princeton: Princeton University Press, 1988), 83–133.

51. *New York Morning News*, 7 February 1845, 3, quoted in Robert D. Sampson, *John L. O'Sullivan and His Times* (Kent, Ohio: Kent State University Press, 2003), 201.

52. Hietala, *Manifest Design*, 197; John L. O'Sullivan, *New York Morning News*, 9, July 1845, quoted in Hietala, *Manifest Design*, 197. Samuel F. B. Morse (1791–1872), who pioneered the telegraph during the 1830s, emerged by the 1850s as a proslavery advocate, convinced that slavery was part of God's divine plan. It is important to note, however, that technological change was embraced across the political spectrum. Frederick Douglass, for example, connected the new railroads to his ability to escape from slavery and then travel across the free states as an abolitionist.

53. Brenda Wineapple, "Hawthorne and Melville; or, The Ambiguities," *ESQ: A Journal of the American Renaissance* 46 (2000): 77. In an important reading of *Moby-Dick* as inspired in part by Melville's response to Hawthorne's "Ethan Brand," Michael Colacurcio provocatively remarks in passing that "*Pierre* . . . presents itself as a sort of Goodman Brown in the House of the Seven Gables"; see "Reading Melville (Re-)Reading Hawthorne," *Nathaniel Hawthorne Review* 33 (2007): 4. Brian Higgins and Hershel Parker acknowledge the importance of the Gothic tropes that Melville drew on from *House* but fail to link those tropes to

questions of race or genealogy (*Reading Melville's "Pierre; or, The Ambiguities"* [Baton Rouge: Louisiana State University Press, 2006], 17–18). For more on textual conversations between Hawthorne and Melville, see Jana L. Argersinger and Leland S. Person, eds., *Hawthorne and Melville: Writing a Relationship* (Athens: University of Georgia Press, 2008).

54. Herman Melville, *Pierre; or, The Ambiguities*, ed. Harrison Hayford, Hershel Parker, and G. Thomas Tanselle (Evanston and Chicago: Northwestern University Press and The Newberry Library, 1971), 100. All future page references to *Pierre* in this section will be provided parenthetically in the body of the text. (Hawthorne's reference to the sins of the fathers has its sources in the Old Testament; see Exodus 20:5 and Deuteronomy 5:9.)

55. Herman Melville to Gansevoort Melville, letter of 29 May 1846, in *Correspondence*, ed. Horth, 40–41; Herman Melville, "Authentic Anecdotes of 'Old Zack,'" in *The Piazza Tales and Other Prose Pieces, 1839–1860*, ed. Harrison Hayford et al. (Evanston and Chicago: Northwestern University Press and The Newberry Library, 1987), 224; Herman Melville, *Mardi: And a Voyage Thither*, ed. Harrison Hayford, Hershel Parker, and G. Thomas Tanselle (Evanston and Chicago: Northwestern University Press and The Newberry Library, 1970), 530, 529; Herman Melville, *White-Jacket; or, The World in a Man-of-War*, ed. Harrison Hayford, Hershel Parker, and G. Thomas Tanselle (Evanston and Chicago: Northwestern University Press and The Newberry Library, 1970), 151. For an excellent reading of Gansevoort as an exponent of Manifest Destiny, see Michael Paul Rogin, *Subversive Genealogy: The Politics and Art of Herman Melville* (New York: Alfred A. Knopf, 1983), 48–68.

56. Herman Melville, "Hawthorne and His Mosses: By a Virginian Spending July in Vermont," in *The Piazza Tales and Other Prose Pieces*, ed. Hayford et al., 243, 248. For a reading of "Mosses" as a possible parody of the literary nationalism of Young America, see Priscilla Wald, *Constituting Americans: Cultural Anxiety and Narrative Form* (Durham: Duke University Press, 1995), 122–26. Rogin argues that "Mosses" was Melville's "own Young American literary manifesto" (*Subversive Genealogy*, 74).

57. Hawthorne voiced his complaints to Duyckinck himself, writing him on 1 December 1851: "What a book Melville has written! It gives me an idea of much greater power than his preceding ones. It hardly seemed to me that the review of it, in the Literary World, did justice to its best points" (*Letters, 1843–1853*, 508).

58. Melville to Hawthorne, letter of 16 April 1851, in *Correspondence*, ed. Horth, 187.

59. On Melville and race, see Carolyn L. Karcher, *Shadow over the Promised Land: Slavery, Race, and Violence in Melville's America* (Baton Rouge: Louisiana State University Press, 1980); Toni Morrison, "Unspeakable Things Unspoken: The Afro-American Presence in American Literature," *Michigan Quarterly Review* 28 (1989): 1–34 passim; Arnold Rampersad, "Shadow and Veil: Melville and Mod-

ern Black Consciousness," in *Melville's Evermoving Dawn: Centennial Essays*, ed. John Bryant and Robert Milder (Kent, Ohio: Kent State University Press, 1997), 162–77; Samuel Otter, " 'Race' in *Typee* and *White-Jacket*," in *The Cambridge Companion to Herman Melville*, ed. Robert S. Levine (Cambridge: Cambridge University Press, 1998), 12–36; and Sterling Stuckey, "The Tambourine in Glory: African Culture and Melville's Art," in *The Cambridge Companion to Herman Melville*, ed. Levine, 37–64. See also *Frederick Douglass and Herman Melville: Essays in Relation*, ed. Robert S. Levine and Samuel Otter (Chapel Hill: University of North Carolina Press, 2008).

60. Hawthorne, *House*, 88, 151–52.

61. By setting this crucial scene at the Black Swan Inn, Melville works with the rather obvious irony that Pierre himself cannot claim the "white swan"–like status of Lucy. And because "Black Swan," as Melville's readers would have known, was also the stage name of the renowned black singer of the 1850s, Elizabeth T. Greenfield, the musical Isabel is linked to the evocative name of the inn. On Greenfield, see [Anon.], *The Black Swan at Home and Abroad: A Biographical Sketch of Miss Elizabeth Taylor Greenfield* (Philadelphia: W. S. Young, 1855); and Don Michael Randel, ed., *The Harvard Biographical Dictionary of Music* (Cambridge, Mass.: Harvard University Press, 1996), 331.

62. Samuel Otter notes in his excellent discussion of landscape in *Pierre* that the narrator shows how the Glendinnings' possession of the land "is asserted in the name of 'race,' evoking not only the legacy of Pierre's great-grandfather, the Dutch patroon ('race' in the older sense of a group of persons descended from a common ancestor), but also evoking Anglo-Saxon authority in the struggle over the American land ('race' as defining the natures and places of different human types, a meaning with particular force in the context of nineteenth-century justifications of racial slavery and displacement)" ("The Eden of Saddle Meadows: Landscape and Ideology in *Pierre*," *American Literature* 66 [1994]: 67). See also Samuel Otter, *Melville's Anatomies* (Berkeley: University of California Press, 1999), 193–207, 238–54. My reading of genealogy in the novel has also been influenced by Eric J. Sundquist, *Home as Found: Authority and Genealogy in Nineteenth-Century American Literature* (Baltimore: Johns Hopkins University Press, 1979), chap. 4; and Wald, *Constituting Americans*, chap. 2. On genealogy and publicity, see Jennifer DiLalla Toner, "The Accustomed Signs of the Family: Rereading Genealogy in Melville's *Pierre*," *American Literature* 70 (1998): 237–63; and for a reading of the novel in the context of contemporaneous debates on slavery, see Nicola Nixon, "Compromising Politics and Herman Melville's *Pierre*," *American Literature* 69 (1997): 719–41; and Nancy F. Sweet, "Abolition, Compromise, and 'The Everlasting Elusiveness of Truth' in Melville's *Pierre*," *Studies in American Fiction* 26 (1998): 3–28.

63. As part of the arch emphasis on the slaves' supposed love of Pierre's grandfather, the narrator describes a special instance of their love: their willingness to

risk their lives to help him put out "a fire in the old manorial mansion" (29). For those who may have known the Melville-Gansevoort family history, however, the account of slaves coming to the aid of their master to put out a house fire would have resonated with some irony, for the fact is that on Melville's maternal side, the Gansevoort family owned slaves, and in 1793 some of those slaves attempted to burn down the house of Melville's great-uncle Leonard Gansevoort. According to Sterling Stuckey, a "slave named Pomp [was] said to have been offered a gold watch to put the Gansevoort residence to flames" ("Tambourine in Glory," 41). That slave and two others were executed on Albany's Pinkster Hill. Melville most likely would have known this family history, and thus he would have known of his own rather close implication in the institution of slavery. For a discussion of the Gansevoorts' slave trading into the early nineteenth century, see Shane White, *Somewhat More Independent: The End of Slavery in New York City, 1770–1810* (Athens: University of Georgia Press, 1991), 108–9. General Glendinning is loosely modeled on Melville's maternal grandfather, Colonel Peter Gansevoort, a Revolutionary hero and slave owner; see Laurie Robertson-Lorant, *Melville: A Biography* (New York: Clarkson Potter, 1996), 3, 364.

64. Unlike General Glendinning, Colonel Lloyd, as described in Frederick Douglass's *Narrative* (1845), flogs his slaves. But there are also similarities between Lloyd and the General. Douglass writes: "[I]n nothing was Colonel Lloyd more particular than in the management of his horses. The slightest inattention to these was unpardonable.... Every thing depended upon the looks of the horses, and the state of Colonel Lloyd's own when his horses were brought to him for use" (*Narrative of the Life of Frederick Douglass, an American Slave*, ed. Houston A. Baker Jr. [New York: Penguin Books, 1982], 60).

65. Maurice S. Lee, "Absolute Poe: His System of Transcendental Racism," *American Literature* 75 (2003): 755. In his conception of the General and his horses, Melville may have been influenced not only by slave narratives and antislavery fiction but also by Jonathan Swift's *Gulliver's Travels*. For the General is not unlike the bestial Yahoos (humans) of part IV of Swift's narrative, who are represented, from the Houyhnhnms' horselike perspective, as defiling horses whenever they "dared to venture upon a Houyhnhnm's back" (*Gulliver's Travels and Other Writings*, ed. Louis A. Landa [Cambridge: Riverside Press, 1960], 194).

66. Joel Williamson, *New People: Miscegenation and Mulattoes in the United States* (New York: Free Press, 1980), 52.

67. Pierre's obsession with obtaining conclusive evidence of Isabel's paternity can ultimately distract the reader from the novel's larger perspective on the tangled skeins of racial genealogies. Similarly, a biographical emphasis on Allan Melvill's supposed early affair as a source of the novel's meditation on genealogy can distract attention from the novel's racial and genealogical thematics. Still, the possibility of Melvill's secret paternity has its fascinations; see, for example, Amy Puett Emmers, "New Crosslights on the Illegitimate Daughter in *Pierre*," in *Critical*

Essays on Herman Melville's "Pierre; or, The Ambiguities," ed. Brian Higgins and Hershel Parker (Boston: G. K. Hall & Co., 1983), 237–40. Hershel Parker remains skeptical about the affair; see *Herman Melville: A Biography*, vol. 1, *1819–1851* (Baltimore: Johns Hopkins University Press, 1996), 62–64.

68. Joan Dayan, "Amorous Bondage: Poe, Ladies, and Slaves," in *The American Face of Edgar Allan Poe*, ed. Shawn Rosenheim and Stephen Rachman (Baltimore: Johns Hopkins University Press, 1995), 201. For an early, influential reading of Isabel as Dark Lady, see Henry A. Murray's introduction to Herman Melville, *Pierre; or, The Ambiguities*, ed. Henry A. Murray (New York: Hendricks House, 1949). For a reading of Isabel as a Native American, see Yukiko Oshima, "Isabel as Native American Ghost in Saddle Meadows: The Background of Pierre's 'Race,'" *Leviathan: A Journal of Melville Studies* 5 (2003): 5–17. In an illuminating analysis, Cindy Weinstein argues that blood is more important than "race" in the novel, which she reads as an attack on consanguinity (*Family, Kinship, and Sympathy*, 159–84).

69. Anna Brickhouse, *Transamerican Literary Relations and the Nineteenth-Century Public Sphere* (Cambridge: Cambridge University Press, 2004), 244. Frederick Douglass writes in *My Bondage and My Freedom* (1855): "[G]enealogical trees do not flourish among the slaves. A person of some consequence here in the north, sometimes designated *father*, is literally abolished in slave law and practice" (*My Bondage and My Freedom*, ed. William L. Andrews [Urbana: University of Illinois Press, 1987], 28).

70. Nancy Bentley, "White Slaves: The Mulatto Hero in Antebellum Fiction," *American Literature* 65 (1993): 513. There are some resemblances between the actions Pierre chooses to take and the actions of the "white" hero of Richard Hildreth's *The White Slave* (1852). In that antislavery novel, the mixed-blood protagonist, Archy Moore, knows that his common-law wife, Cassy, a mulatta, is the daughter of his father, a slave master, but he chooses to "marry" her anyway. A shorter and somewhat different version of Richard Hildreth's *The White Slave*, titled *The Slave; or, Memoirs of Archy Moore*, was published in 1836.

71. In his depiction of Pierre's and Isabel's mute entanglement, the great illustrator Maurice Sendak displays them in a mostly nude embrace with their skin, even in the darkness, looking an unambiguous brown. This is the one such representation in Parker and Sendak's illustrated (and critically abridged) edition, which otherwise presents the characters as almost surreally hyperwhite. See Herman Melville, *Pierre; Or, the Ambiguities*, The Kraken Edition, ed. Hershel Parker, pictures by Maurice Sendak (New York: HarperCollins Publishers, 1995), 276.

72. Wyn Kelley, "*Pierre's* Domestic Ambiguities," in *The Cambridge Companion to Herman Melville*, ed. Levine, 103.

73. Priscilla Wald argues that Pierre's "white male body becomes the emblem—the governing body—of the nation, and expansion becomes an expression of its very essence" (*Constituting Americans*, 116).

74. On cigars and literary imperialism, see Lori Merish, *Sentimental Materialism: Gender, Commodity Culture, and Nineteenth-Century American Literature* (Durham: Duke University Press, 2000), chap. 6. On Pierre as New York literary celebrity, see Susan M. Ryan, "Douglass, Melville, and the Moral Economies of American Authorship," in *Frederick Douglass and Herman Melville: Essays in Relation*, ed. Robert S. Levine and Samuel Otter (Chapel Hill: University of North Carolina Press, 2008), 88–109.

75. Melville to Evert A. Duyckinck, letter of 3 March 1849, in *Correspondence*, ed. Horth, 121.

76. William Shakespeare, *Othello*, ed. David Bevington (New York: Bantam Books, 1988), 118 (5.2.135). On Shakespeare and nineteenth-century America, see Lawrence W. Levine, *Highbrow/Lowbrow: The Emergence of Cultural Hierarchy in America* (Cambridge, Mass.: Harvard University Press, 1988), chap. 1; and Tilden G. Edelstein's "*Othello* in America: The Drama of Racial Intermarriage," in *Region, Race, and Reconstruction: Essays in Honor of C. Vann Woodward*, ed. J. Morgan Kousser and James M. McPherson (New York: Oxford University Press, 1982), 179–97. For a very different, "camp" reading of the homoerotic dimension of Pierre's relationship with Cousin Glen, see James Creech, *Closet Writing/Gay Reading: The Case of Melville's Pierre* (Chicago: University of Chicago Press, 1993), esp. 122–27.

77. On the parallels between the genealogies of Pierre and Enceladus, see Mark Z. Slouka, "Demonic History: Geography and Genealogy in Melville's *Pierre*," *ESQ: A Journal of the American Renaissance* 35 (1989): 147–60.

78. Werner Sollors, " 'Never Was Born': The Mulatto, An American Tragedy?," *Massachusetts Review* 37 (1986): 305. For a comprehensive discussion of interracial themes in American writing, see Werner Sollors, *Neither Black Nor White Yet Both: Thematic Explorations of Interracial Literature* (New York: Oxford University Press, 1997).

79. Samuel George Morton, *Crania Ægyptiaca* (1844), cited in J. C. Nott and Geo. R. Gliddon, *Types of Mankind: or, Ethnological Researches, Based upon the Ancient Monuments, Paintings, Sculptures, and Crania of Races, and upon Their Natural, Geographical, Philological, and Biblical History* (Philadelphia: Lippincott, Grambo & Co., 1854), 214, 218; Frederick Douglass, "The Claims of the Negro Ethnologically Considered: An Address Delivered in Hudson, Ohio, on 12 July 1854," in *The Frederick Douglass Papers*, ser. 1, *Speeches, Debates, and Interviews*, 5 vols., ed. John W. Blassingame et al. (New Haven: Yale University Press, 1979–92), 2:517; Nathaniel Hawthorne, *The Marble Faun: Or, The Romance of Monte Beni*, ed. William Charvat et al. (Columbus: Ohio State University Press, 1968), 126. For an excellent account of the pervasive influence of Egyptology on nineteenth-century U.S. culture, see Scott Trafton, *Egypt Land: Race and Nineteenth-Century American Egyptomania* (Durham: Duke University Press, 2004).

80. Balibar, "The Nation Form," 100. For a rich discussion of *Pierre* and national

myths, see Sacvan Bercovitch, *The Rites of Assent: Transformations in the Symbolic Construction of America* (New York: Routledge, 1993), 246–306.

81. William Wells Brown, *Clotel; or, The President's Daughter*, ed. Robert S. Levine (Boston: Bedford/St. Martin's, 2000), 173, 149.

82. On the possible composition date of the novel, see Henry Louis Gates Jr., "Introduction" to Hannah Crafts, *The Bondwoman's Narrative: A Novel*, ed. Henry Louis Gates Jr. (New York: Warner Books, 2002), esp. xlvi–liv. On Crafts's reading of Dickens and other contemporaneous writers, see Henry Louis Gates Jr., "A Note on Crafts's Literary Influences," in *The Bondwoman's Narrative*, 331–32; and Hollis Robbins, "Blackening *Bleak House*: Hannah Crafts's *The Bondwoman's Narrative*," in *In Search of Hannah Crafts: Critical Essays on "The Bondwoman's Narrative*," ed. Henry Louis Gates Jr. and Hollis Robbins (New York: BasicCivitas Books, 2004), 71–86. *Bleak House* was also important to Frederick Douglass, who serialized it in *Frederick Douglass' Paper* from 15 April 1852 to 16 December 1853 (see Elizabeth McHenry, *Forgotten Readers: Recovering the Lost History of African American Literary Societies* [Durham: Duke University Press, 2002], 124–26).

83. In his 2002 edition of *The Bondwoman's Narrative*, Gates adds a subtitle, "A Novel," to the manuscript's title page. Though I agree with Gates that the narrative is best read as a novel, I would also suggest that we need to attend to generic instabilities in reading the work both in the tradition of the novel and the slave narrative.

84. On "Crafts" as Johnson, see Gates, "Introduction," *The Bondwoman's Narrative*, l–lxii; and Katherine E. Flynn, "Jane Johnson, Found! But Is She 'Hannah Crafts'? The Search for the Author of *The Bondwoman's Narrative*," in *In Search of Hannah Crafts*, ed. Gates and Robbins, 371–405. On "Crafts" as the free black Hannah Vincent, see Nina Baym, "The Case for Hannah Vincent," and Joe Nickell, "Searching for Hannah Crafts," in *In Search of Hannah Crafts*, ed. Gates and Robbins, 315–31, 406–16. And for provocative suggestions that "Crafts" may have been a white male British abolitionist, see Celeste-Marie Bernie and Judie Newman, "*The Bondwoman's Narrative*: Text, Paratext, Intertext, and Hypertext," *Journal of American Studies* 39 (2001): 147–65.

85. My remarks on Wheeler draw on Thomas C. Parramore's "The Bondwoman and the Bureaucrat," in *In Search of Hannah Crafts*, ed. Gates and Robbins, 354–70.

86. Crafts, *The Bondwoman's Narrative*, 197. All future page references to Gates's edition will be supplied parenthetically in the main body of the text.

87. Nathaniel Hawthorne, *The Scarlet Letter* (1850), in *The Scarlet Letter and Other Writings*, ed. Leland S. Person (New York: W. W. Norton & Company, 2005), 83.

88. For useful discussions of the importance of portraits to the novel, see the following essays in *In Search of Hannah Crafts*: John Stauffer, "The Problem of Freedom in *The Bondwoman's Narrative*," esp. 56–57; Christopher Castiglia, " 'I

found a life of freedom all my fancy had pictured it to be': Hannah Crafts's Visual Speculation and the Inner Life of Slavery," 231–53; and Russ Castronovo, "The Art of Ghost-Writing: Memory, Materiality, and Slave Aesthetics," esp. 198–202.

89. Hawthorne, *House*, 8.

90. Melville, *Pierre*, 68.

91. Earlier in the novel, Hannah had described the "wave and curl to my hair" and the "black" mistress's "wavy curly hair" (*The Bondwoman's Narrative*, 6, 27).

92. See Robert S. Levine, "Disturbing Boundaries: Temperance, Black Elevation, and Violence in Frank J. Webb's *The Garies and Their Friends*," *Prospects: An Annual of American Cultural Studies* 19 (1994): 349–74.

93. Hawthorne, *House*, 240.

94. As Karen Sánchez-Eppler remarks on the novel's recurrent "blackening" of its white characters: "Crafts takes revenge on the system that enslaves her. Her delight in this plot motif counters the surety that nearly all slaves must have some white ancestry with the suggestion that all southern whites may have hidden blackness too" ("Gothic Liberties and Fugitive Novels: *The Bondwoman's Narrative* and the Fiction of Race," in *In Search of Hannah Crafts*, ed. Gates and Robbins, 268).

95. See Adam Smith, *The Theory of Moral Sentiments* (1759), ed. D. D. Raphael and A. L. Macfie (London: Oxford University Press, 1976), esp. 9. For a thoughtful discussion of the egotistical and sometimes cruel implications of sympathy, see Marianne Noble, *The Masochistic Pleasures of Sentimental Literature* (Princeton: Princeton University Press, 2000). On the problematics of sympathy in Hawthorne, see Robert S. Levine, "Sympathy and Reform in *The Blithedale Romance*," in *The Cambridge Companion to Nathaniel Hawthorne*, ed. Millington, 207–29.

96. Gates, "Introduction," *The Bondwoman's Narrative*, lxix–lxx.

97. William Gleason argues that Crafts's interest in cottages has its sources in the cultural influence of the rural republican writings of Andrew Jackson Downing; see " 'I Dwell Now in a Neat Little Cottage': Architecture, Race, and Desire in *The Bondwoman's Narrative*," in *In Search of Hannah Crafts*, ed. Gates and Robbins, 145–74. Downing also was an important influence on Hawthorne's conception of rural architecture in *House*.

98. Frank J. Webb, *The Garies and Their Friends*, ed. Robert Reid-Pharr (1857; repr. Baltimore: Johns Hopkins University Press, 1997), 372. In "Hannah Crafts's Sense of an Ending," William Andrews observes that the ending is inconsistent with writings by fugitive slaves (*In Search of Hannah Crafts*, ed. Gates and Robbins, 30–42).

99. For useful discussions of the value of moving beyond fixed notions of race, see Gene Andrew Jarrett, ed., *African American Literature beyond Race: An Alternative Reader* (New York: New York University Press, 2006).

100. See Robert S. Levine, "Antebellum Feminists on Hawthorne: Reconsidering the Reception of *The Scarlet Letter*," in Hawthorne, *The Scarlet Letter and Other*

Writings, ed. Person, 274–90. Hawthorne has been vilified by some critics not only for his Pierce biography but also for his 1862 "Chiefly about War-Matters. By a Peaceable Man," published in the July 1862 *Atlantic Magazine*. See, for example, Eric Cheyfitz, "The Irresistibleness of Great Literature: Reconstructing Hawthorne's Politics," *American Literary History* 6 (1994): 556; and Riss, "The Art of Discrimination," 251–87. In an excellent recent reading of Hawthorne's *Atlantic* essay, Brenda Wineapple shows how Hawthorne, through his insertion of faux editorial footnotes written by "a dull-witted editor," imagines dull-witted readers who would literalize and misunderstand his intentions in the essay, which, as Wineapple argues, are "Swiftian, corrosive, and funny, and directed at the foibles both of humankind and, more precisely, the *Atlantic* readership" (*Hawthorne: A Life* [New York: Alfred A. Knopf, 2003], 351, 349). For a subtle reading of Hawthorne's racial politics in the essay, see also Caroline F. Levander, *Cradle of Liberty: Race, the Child, and National Belonging from Thomas Jefferson to W. E. B. Du Bois* (Durham: Duke University Press, 2006), 44–45.

101. Shelley Streeby, *American Sensations: Class, Empire, and the Production of Popular Culture* (Berkeley: University of California Press, 2002), 256. On whiteness and antebellum culture, see Alexander Saxton, *The Rise and Fall of the White Republic: Class Politics and Mass Culture in Nineteenth-Century America* (London: Verso, 1990); David Roediger, *The Wages of Whiteness: Race and the Making of the American Working Class* (London: Verso, 1991); and Noel Ignatiev, *How the Irish Became White* (New York: Routledge, 1995).

102. Garnet, *The Past and the Present Condition*, 25. The term "structure of feeling" is drawn from Raymond Williams, *Marxism and Literature* (Oxford: Oxford University Press, 1977), 128–35.

Chapter 4

1. "The Colored People and Hayti," *Douglass' Monthly* 3 (January 1861): 398.

2. Frederick Douglass, "Emigration to Hayti," *Douglass' Monthly* 3 (January 1861): 387. See also "Call for Emigration," *Douglass' Monthly* 3 (January 1861): 399.

3. Frederick Douglass, "The War with Mexico," *North Star*, 21 January 1848, 3; Frederick Douglass, "Cuba and the United States" (1851), in *The Life and Writings of Frederick Douglass*, 5 vols., ed. Philip S. Foner (New York: International Publishers, 1950), 2:159; Frederick Douglass, "Aggressions of the Slave Power: An Address Delivered in Rochester, New York, on 22 May 1856," in *The Frederick Douglass Papers*, ser. 1, *Speeches, Debates, and Interviews*, 5 vols., ed. John W. Blassingame et al. (New Haven: Yale University Press, 1979–92), 3:129. For an illuminating discussion of slavery, race, and revolution in the context of the global South, see Matthew Pratt Guterl, "An American Mediterranean: Haiti, Cuba, and the American South," in *Hemispheric American Studies*, ed. Caroline F. Levander and Robert S. Levine (New Brunswick: Rutgers University Press, 2008), 96–115.

4. Douglass, "Emigration to Hayti," 386–87.

5. Waldo E. Martin Jr., *The Mind of Frederick Douglass* (Chapel Hill: University of North Carolina Press, 1984), 219; Paul Giles, *Virtual Americas: Transnational Fictions and the Transatlantic Imaginary* (Durham: Duke University Press, 2002), 30; Ifeoma Nwankwo, *Black Cosmopolitanism: Racial Consciousness, National Identity, and Transnational Ideology in the Americas* (Philadelphia: University of Pennsylvania Press, 2005), 132, 133.

6. Frederick Douglass, "Haiti and Faustin First," *North Star*, 26 April 1850, 2; Frederick Douglass, "The Heroic Slave," in *The Oxford Frederick Douglass Reader*, ed. William L. Andrews (New York: Oxford University Press, 1996), 163; Ivy G. Wilson, "On Native Grounds: Frederick Douglass and 'The Heroic Slave,'" *PMLA* 121 (2006): 466. For Douglass's speeches on Madison Washington, see "American Prejudice against Color: An Address Delivered in Cork, Ireland, 23 October 1845," and "American and Scottish Prejudice against the Slave: An Address Delivered in Edinburgh, Scotland, on 1 May 1846," in *The Frederick Douglass Papers*, ser. 1, esp. 1:67–69, 244–46.

7. [Dion], "Our Literature," *Frederick Douglass' Paper*, 23 September 1853, 2; Frederick Douglass, "Our Paper and Its Prospects," *North Star*, 3 December 1847, 2.

8. Niall Ferguson, "Virtual History: Towards a 'Chaotic' Theory of the Past," in *Virtual History: Alternatives and Counterfactuals*, ed. Niall Ferguson (London: Papermac, 1997), 68, 66.

9. In the *North Star*, for example, Douglass had attacked the "American press and American people, slaveholders and slave traders and all," for being "particularly anxious to make Haiti appear before the world as feeble, indolent and falling to decay" ("Haiti and Faustin First," 2).

10. Frederick Douglass, "The Twelfth Volume of Frederick Douglass' Paper," *Douglass' Monthly* 1 (January 1859): 2; Frederick Douglass, "The Anglo-African Magazine," *Douglass' Monthly* 1 (February 1859): 20; Douglass, review of W. W. Brown's *The Black Man*, *Douglass' Monthly* 3 (January 1863): 771.

11. David W. Blight, *Frederick Douglass's Civil War: Keeping Faith in Jubilee* (Baton Rouge: Louisiana State University Press, 1989), 59. Waldo E. Martin Jr. similarly argues that Douglass's "vision of racial, or ethnic, nationalism remained subordinate to his vision of American nationalism," and that he therefore continued to resist the lure of a separatist black nationalism possibly involving emigration ("Frederick Douglass: Humanist as Race Leader," in *Black Leaders of the Nineteenth-Century*, ed. Leon Litwack and August Meier [Urbana: University of Illinois Press, 1988], 71).

12. Blight, *Frederick Douglass's Civil War*, 133. There is no mention of Douglass and Haiti, circa 1859–61, in the two most widely cited biographies: Benjamin Quarles, *Frederick Douglass* (Washington, D.C.: Associated Publishers, Inc., 1948),

and William S. McFeely, *Frederick Douglass* (New York: W. W. Norton & Company, 1991).

13. Frederick Douglass, *Life and Times of Frederick Douglass: Written by Himself*, ed. Rayford W. Logan (1892; New York: Collier Books, 1962), 305, 273, 319, 326. Douglass published *Life and Times* in 1881, and in 1892 he added a new section without revising the earlier chapters.

14. Douglass, *Life and Times*, 329.

15. *Report of the Decision of the Supreme Court of the United States, and the Opinions of the Judges thereof, in the case of Dred Scott versus John F. A. Sandford. December Term, 1856* (Washington, D.C.: Cornelius Wendell, Printer, 1857), 10, 13. The literature on the *Dred Scott* case is extensive. The essential work is Don Fehrenbacher's *The Dred Scott Case: Its Significance in American Law and Politics* (1978; New York: Oxford University Press, 2001), but see also Rogers M. Smith, *Civic Ideals: Conflicting Visions of Citizenship in U.S. History* (New Haven: Yale University Press, 1997), 243–85; and Paul Finkleman, *Dred Scott v. Sandford: A Brief History with Documents* (Boston and New York: Bedford/St. Martin's, 1997).

16. As Fehrenbacher emphatically puts it, the upshot of the *Dred Scott* ruling was this: "*American Negroes, free and slave, were the only people on the face of the earth who (saving a constitutional amendment) were forever ineligible for American citizenship*" (*Dred Scott*, 357).

17. "Speech by Robert Purvis, Delivered at the City Assembly Rooms, New York, New York, 12 May 1857," in *The Black Abolitionist Papers: The United States, 1847–1858*, ed. C. Peter Ripley et al. (Chapel Hill: University of North Carolina Press, 1985), 364; William Wells Brown, *The Black Man: His Antecedents, His Genius, and His Achievements* (Boston: James Redpath, Publisher, 1863), 282–83. See also "Speech by Charles L. Remond, Delivered at Mozard Hall, New York, New York, 13 May 1858," *Liberator*, 21 March 1858, 1.

18. Douglass, "The Dred Scott Decision: An Address Delivered, in Part, in New York, New York, in May 1857," in *The Frederick Douglass Papers*, ser. 1, 3:172, 167; "Is the Plan of the American Union under the Constitution, Anti-Slavery or Not?: A Debate between Frederick Douglass and Charles Lenox Remond in New York, New York, on 20, 23 May 1857," in *The Frederick Douglass Papers*, ser. 1, 3:160, 152; Douglass, "The Dred Scott Decision," 175, 183. For an illuminating critical debate on Douglass's views on the Constitution, see David E. Schrader, "Natural Law in the Constitutional Thought of Frederick Douglass," and Charles W. Mills, "Whose Fourth of July? Frederick Douglass and 'Original Intent,'" in *Frederick Douglass: A Critical Reader*, ed. Bill E. Lawson and Frank M. Kirkland (Oxford: Blackwell Publishers, 1999), 85–99, 100–142. Schrader presents a sympathetic account of Douglass's natural-rights reading of the Constitution, while Mills regards Douglass as naive for failing to see how the Constitution was a racist document that allowed for the perpetuation of slavery.

19. Gregg D. Crane, *Race, Citizenship, and Law in American Literature* (Cambridge: Cambridge University Press, 2002), 119.

20. For instance, there is no mention of the West Indies speech in Eric J. Sundquist's *To Wake the Nations: Race and the Making of American Literature* (Cambridge, Mass.: Harvard University Press, 1993), and Andrews's *The Oxford Frederick Douglass Reader* jumps from excerpts from the 1855 *My Bondage and My Freedom* to the 1863 "Men of Color, To Arms!"

21. Frederick Douglass, "The Significance of Emancipation in the West Indies: An Address Delivered in Canadaigua, New York, on 3 August 1857," in *The Frederick Douglass Papers*, ser. 1, 3:194, 207, 206–7; Frederick Douglass, "A Day, A Deed, An Event, Glorious in the Annals of Philanthropy: An Address Delivered in Rochester, New York, on 1 August 1848," in *The Frederick Douglass Papers*, ser. 1, 2:134, 133; Douglass, "Significance of Emancipation," 207–8, 206. In his 1848 "A Day, A Deed, An Event," Douglass pays special tribute to British reformers, specifically George Thompson: "If there be one living orator more than another to whom we are indebted, that man is GEORGE THOMPSON . . . [who] devote[d] himself to the cause of the West Indian Slave" (143). The West Indian slave remains relatively passive and grateful in this earlier August First speech.

22. *Frederick Douglass' Paper*, 17 September 1858, 2. (The untitled editorial responds to a letter from Benjamin Coates, a supporter of the African Colonization Society, printed on page 1.)

23. See Chris Dixon's excellent *African America and Haiti: Emigration and Black Nationalism in the Nineteenth Century* (Westport, Conn.: Greenwood Press, 2000), esp. chap. 4. Also useful is Alfred N. Hunt, *Haiti's Influence on Antebellum America* (Baton Rouge: Louisiana State University Press, 1988). Approximately 2,000 African Americans emigrated to Haiti between 1859 and 1862.

24. Frederick Douglass, "All Going to Hayti," *Douglass' Monthly* 1 (May 1859): 68; Frederick Douglass, "Haytian Emigration Again," *Douglass' Monthly* 1 (May 1859): 70.

25. Frederick Douglass, "To My American Friends and Readers," *Douglass' Monthly* 2 (November 1859): 162.

26. Douglass, "Emigration to Hayti," 387, 386.

27. Frederick Douglass, "Haytian Emigration," *Douglass' Monthly* 3 (March 1861): 420; Frederick Douglass, "The New President," *Douglass' Monthly* 3 (March 1861): 419; Frederick Douglass, "The Inaugural Address," *Douglass' Monthly* 3 (April 1861): 444. On Douglass and Lincoln, see James Oakes, *The Radical and the Republican: Frederick Douglass, Abraham Lincoln, and the Triumph of Antislavery Politics* (New York: W. W. Norton & Company, 2007). In his informative study, Oakes, to my mind, underestimates Douglass's initial hostility to Lincoln and the tensions that would remain in their interactions. It is significant, for example, that Lincoln chose Martin Delany and not Douglass to be the first black officer in the Union army. Delany is not mentioned in Oakes's book.

28. Frederick Douglass, "A Trip to Hayti," *Douglass' Monthly* 3 (May 1861): 449.

29. Maria Diedrich, *Love across Color Lines: Ottilie Assing and Frederick Douglass* (New York: Hill and Wang, 1999), 235; Douglass, "All Going to Hayti," 68.

30. Douglass, "All Going to Hayti," 68.

31. Douglass, "A Trip to Hayti," 449–50.

32. Ibid., 450.

33. Frederick Douglass, "Nemesis," *Douglass' Monthly* 3 (May 1861): 450; Frederick Douglass, "How to End the War," *Douglass' Monthly* 3 (May 1861): 451. See also James Redpath, "Emigration to Hayti," *Douglass' Monthly* 3 (May 1861): 463–64.

34. Douglass, *Life and Times*, 329.

35. Frederick Douglass, "The Progress of the War," *Douglass' Monthly* 4 (September 1861): 513; Frederick Douglass, "The Slaveholders Rebellion," *Douglass' Monthly* 5 (August 1862): 690, 691, 693; "Remarks of Frederick Douglass at Zion Church on Sunday 28 of Dec.," *Douglass' Monthly* 5 (January 1863): 770. During the 1861–63 period, Lincoln developed an interest in Haiti and worked to restore diplomatic ties with the black republic. He sent diplomatic representatives to Haiti as he was working on the Emancipation Proclamation, and Haiti reciprocated shortly after the issuing of the proclamation by sending a diplomat to Washington. For provocative discussions of Douglass and the Civil War, see Russ Castronovo and Dana D. Nelson, "Fahrenheit 1861: Cross Patriotism in Melville and Douglass"; Carolyn L. Karcher, "White Fratricide, Black Liberation: Melville, Douglass, and Civil War Memory"; and Maurice S. Lee, "Melville, Douglass, the Civil War, Pragmatism," all in *Frederick Douglass and Herman Melville: Essays in Relation*, ed. Robert S. Levine and Samuel Otter (Chapel Hill: University of North Carolina Press, 2008), 329–48, 349–68, 396–415.

36. Frederick Douglass, "The Present and Future of the Colored Race in America," *Douglass' Monthly* 5 (June 1863): 833; Frederick Douglass, "Valedictory," *Douglass' Monthly* 5 (June 1863): 850; Frederick Douglass, "Men of Color, to Arms!," *Douglass' Monthly* 5 (March 1863): 801.

37. Frederick Douglass, "Santo Domingo—No. 6," *New National Era*, 11 May 1871, 2.

38. Frederick Douglass, "I Speak to You as an American Citizen: An Address Delivered in Washington, D.C., on 15 October 1870," in *The Frederick Douglass Papers*, ser. 1, 4:275.

39. Martin, *The Mind of Frederick Douglass*, 87; Merline Pitre, "Frederick Douglass and American Diplomacy in the Caribbean," *Journal of Black Studies* 13 (1983): 467; Merline Pitre, "Frederick Douglass and the Annexation of Santo Domingo," *Journal of Negro History* 62 (1977): 399; McFeely, *Frederick Douglass*, 276–77.

40. Douglass, *Life and Times*, 399, 400, 409, 408.

41. Ibid., 409.

42. Frederick Douglass, "Prospectus of the New Era! A National Journal," *New*

Era, 18 August 1870, 2. The "Prospectus" had been distributed separately in January 1870; Douglass reprinted it in the August 1870 and subsequent issues.

43. Frederick Douglass, "Salutatory of the Corresponding Editor," *New Era*, 27 January 1870, 2; George Rice, "The Negro and American Literature," *New Era*, 3 March 1870, 3. See also George B. Vashon, "The Lasting Benefits of Poetry," *New Era*, 17 March 1870, 1; and George Downing, "Negro Genius," *New Era*, 24 March 1870, 3. Frank J. Webb's novellas were serialized in the *New Era* from January through April 1870.

44. Frederick Douglass, "Colored Newspapers," *New National Era*, 8 September 1870, 2. The *Atlantic* essay on Nathaniel Hawthorne appeared in the issue of 30 March 1871, 4.

45. For backgrounds, see Charles Callen Tansill, *The United States and Santo Domingo, 1798–1873: A Chapter in Caribbean Diplomacy* (Baltimore: Johns Hopkins University Press, 1938), esp. 338–464; Pitre, "Frederick Douglass and American Diplomacy in the Caribbean"; Daniel Brantley, "Black Diplomacy and Frederick Douglass's Caribbean Experiences, 1871 and 1889–1891: The Untold History," *Phylon* 45 (1984): 197–209; Eric Foner, *Reconstruction: America's Unfinished Revolution, 1863–1877* (New York: Harper and Row, 1988), 493–98; William Javier Nelson, *Almost a Territory: American's Attempt to Annex the Dominican Republic* (Newark: University of Delaware Press, 1990); and Eric T. L. Love, *Race over Empire: Racism and U.S. Imperialism, 1865–1900* (Chapel Hill: University of North Carolina Press, 2004), chap. 2.

46. *Report of the Commission of Inquiry to Santo Domingo, with the Introductory Message of the President, Special Reports Made to the Commission, State Papers Furnished by the Dominican Government, and the Statements of over Seventy Witnesses* (Washington, D.C.: Government Printing Office, 1871), 13, 1, 34.

47. Charles Sumner to William Lloyd Garrison, letter of 26 April 1871, in *The Selected Letters of Charles Sumner*, 2 vols., ed. Beverly Wilson Palmer et al. (Boston: Northeastern University Press, 1990), 2:552; Sumner, 21 December 1870, *Congressional Globe*, 41st Cong., 3rd sess., 229, 231.

48. Agassiz's letter to Howe of 11 August 1863 is quoted in Stephen Jay Gould, *The Mismeasure of Man* (New York: W. W. Norton and Company, 1981), 50; his 1867 letter to Sumner is quoted in Love, *Race over Empire*, 32. Agassiz's "The Diversity of the Origin of the Human Races" can be found in the July 1850 issue of the *Christian Examiner*, 110–45.

49. Carl Schurz, 11 January 1871, *Congressional Globe*, 41st Cong., 3rd sess., appendix, 26, 29, 30.

50. Sumner's remarks were made during a secret Senate session, which was reported in various newspapers of the time; see David Donald, *Charles Sumner and the Rights of Man* (New York: Alfred A. Knopf, 1970), 443; and Love, *Race over Empire*, 56.

51. "Memorandum," in *The Papers of Ulysses S. Grant*, 28 vols., ed. John Y. Simon et al. (Carbondale: Southern Illinois University Press, 1967–), 20:74–75.

52. As David Blight notes, by the 1870s "the forces of reconciliation overwhelmed the emancipationist vision in the national culture" (*Race and Reunion: The Civil War in American Memory* [Cambridge, Mass.: Harvard University Press, 2001], 2). See also Nina Silber, *The Romance of Reunion: Northerners and the South, 1865–1900* (Chapel Hill: University of North Carolina Press, 1993).

53. Frederick Douglass, "The Mission of the War: An Address Delivered in New York, New York, on 13 January 1864," in *The Frederick Douglass Papers*, ser. 1, 4:21; T. W. Higginson, "Americanization in Literature," *Atlantic Monthly: A Magazine of Literature, Science, Art, and Politics* 25 (January 1870): 59.

54. Frederick Douglass, "Annexation of San Domingo," *New National Era*, 12 January 1871, 2.

55. Ibid., 2.

56. Frederick Douglass, "Our Composite Nationality: An Address Delivered in Boston, Massachusetts, on 7 December 1869," in *The Frederick Douglass Papers*, ser. 1, 4:253, 256, 257.

57. Frederick Douglass, "Letter on Santo Domingo—No. 2," *New National Era*, 6 April 1871, 2; Frederick Douglass, "Santo Domingo—No. 3," *New National Era*, 20 April 1871, 2.

58. Frederick Douglass, "Santo Domingo—No. 4," *New National Era*, 27 April 1871, 2.

59. Frederick Douglass, "Santo Domingo—No. 7," *New National Era*, 18 May 1871, 2.

60. Frederick Douglass, "Santo Domingo—No. 5," *New National Era*, 4 May 1871, 2. On Haiti, see also Frederick Douglass, "Santo Domingo—No. 6," *New National Era*, 11 Mary 1871, 2.

61. Along these lines, it should be noted that following a March 1871 meeting with President Grant, Douglass, as reported in the 30 March 1871 *New York Times*, stated "that in his judgment the Dominicans are a far superior people to the Haytians; that there is no republicanism whatever in Hayti, and that the Government there is an absolute despotism of the most oppressive character" (*The Papers of Ulysses S. Grant*, 21:291). In an 1872 speech on the public schools, which was reprinted in the 16 May 1872 *New National Era*, Douglass declared that without common schools, "the United States would be little better than uneducated Hayti" ("Schools Are a Common Platform of Nationality: An Address Delivered in Washington, D.C., on 9 May 1872," in *The Frederick Douglass Papers*, ser. 1, 4:301).

62. Frederick Douglass, "Santo Domingo: An Address Delivered in St. Louis, Missouri, on 13 January 1873," in *The Frederick Douglass Papers*, ser. 1, 4:344, 346.

63. Ibid., 354, 355.

64. For excellent accounts of nineteenth-century Americans' conflicted re-

sponses to Rome, see William L. Vance's magisterial *America's Rome*, 2 vols. (New Haven: Yale University Press, 1989); and Jenny Franchot's *Roads to Rome: The Antebellum Protestant Encounter with Catholicism* (Berkeley: University of California Press, 1994). Also useful are David Brion Davis, "Some Themes of Counter-Subversion: An Analysis of Anti-Masonic, Anti-Catholic, and Anti-Mormon Literature," *Mississippi Valley Historical Review* 47 (1960): 205–24; Paul Baker, *The Fortunate Pilgrims: Americans in Italy: 1800–1860* (Cambridge, Mass.: Harvard University Press, 1964); Nathalia Wright, *American Novelists in Italy; The Discoverers: Allston to James* (Philadelphia: University of Pennsylvania Press, 1965); and Robert S. Levine, *Conspiracy and Romance: Studies in Brockden Brown, Cooper, Hawthorne, and Melville* (Cambridge: Cambridge University Press, 1989), chap. 3. In their popular travel narratives, James Jackson Jarves and Charles Eliot Norton advanced the connections among U.S. republicanism, Anglo-Saxonism, and white privilege that informed the ethnological accounts of the American School and the white supremacist politics of the pre- and post-Reconstruction period. On Anglo-Saxonism and aesthetic appreciation, particularly with reference to Charles Eliot Norton, see Jackson Lears, *No Place of Grace: Antimodernism and the Transformation of American Culture, 1880–1920* (New York: Pantheon Books, 1981), 243–47. Key nineteenth-century texts include James Jackson Jarves's *Italian Sights and Papal Principles, Seen through American Spectacles* (1856), Jarves's *Italian Rambles* (1883), and Charles Eliot Norton's *Notes of Travel and Study in Italy* (1859; repr. 1887). On Rome and nineteenth-century American literary nationalism, see *Roman Holidays: American Writers and Artists in Nineteenth-Century Italy*, ed. Robert K. Martin and Leland S. Person (Iowa City: University of Iowa Press, 2002).

65. Douglass, *Life and Times*, 572, 575, 576. On Hawthorne and Rome, see Robert S. Levine, "'Antebellum Rome' in *The Marble Faun*," *American Literary History* 2 (1990): 24–50.

66. "God Almighty Made But One Race: An Interview Given in Washington, D.C., on 25 January 1884," in *The Frederick Douglass Papers*, ser. 1, 5:146, 147. For an excellent discussion of how Douglass sought to display his interracial marriage as a mediatory symbol that spoke to the possibilities of overcoming racial hatreds, see Gregory Stephens, *On Racial Frontiers: The Biracial Culture of Frederick Douglass, Ralph Ellison, and Bob Marley* (Cambridge: Cambridge University Press, 1999), chap. 2.

67. Douglass, *Life and Times*, 513.

68. In a letter of 1 September 1887, Douglass remarked to Francis J. Grimké: "Egypt and Greece were not in our calculations when we left home—and Rome was definitely not so" (*Life and Writings of Frederick Douglass*, 4:448).

69. Douglass to Lewis Douglass, letter of 20 February 1887, quoted in McFeely, *Frederick Douglass*, 332.

70. Douglass, *Life and Times*, 579.

71. On Douglass in England, see McFeely, *Frederick Douglass*, 324–28; and on

the Garrisonians' invidious (and racist) efforts during the early 1850s to link Douglass and Julia Griffiths (Crofts) as lovers, see 162–66.

72. Douglass to Hayden and Watson, letter of 19 November 1886, in *Life and Writings of Frederick Douglass*, 5:446; Theodore Stanton, "Frederick Douglass in Paris," *The Open Court. A Fortnightly Journal, Devoted to the Work of Establishing Ethics and Religion Upon a Scientific Basis* 1 (1887): 151. For a useful discussion of Douglass in Paris, see Quarles, *Frederick Douglass*, 305–8.

73. Douglass, *Life and Times*, 562, 563.

74. Samuel Morton, *Crania Ægyptiaca* (1844), cited in J. C. Nott and Geo. R. Gliddon's highly influential *Types of Mankind: or, Ethnological Researches, Based upon the Ancient Monuments, Paintings, Sculptures, and Crania of Races, and upon Their Nature, Geographical, Philological, and Biblical History* (Philadelphia: Lippincott, Grambo & Co., 1854), 214; Frederick Douglass, "The Claims of the Negro Ethnologically Considered: An Address Delivered in Hudson, Ohio, on 12 July 1854," in *The Frederick Douglass Papers*, ser. 1, 2:508, 517, 506. For a fuller discussion of this speech, see Robert S. Levine, *Martin Delany, Frederick Douglass, and the Politics of Representative Identity* (Chapel Hill: University of North Carolina Press, 1997), 9–12. On Morton and the "American School" of anthropology, see Thomas F. Gossett, *Race: The History of an Idea in America* (1963; repr. New York: Oxford University Press, 1997), chap. 4; Martin, *The Mind of Frederick Douglass*, chap. 9; and Dana D. Nelson, *National Manhood: Capitalist Citizenship and the Imagined Fraternity of White Men* (Durham: Duke University Press, 1998), chap. 3. As Martin points out, Morton eventually modified his views on Egypt, though he continued to argue "that ancient Egypt's greatness derived from the Caucasian admixture" (*The Mind of Frederick Douglass*, 226).

75. Douglass, *Life and Times*, 554.

76. "Diary, 1886–1894," container no. 1, The Papers of Frederick Douglass, Library of Congress, Washington, D.C. Future references to Douglass's unpaginated diary will be made parenthetically, by date of entry, in the main body of the text. My thanks to the librarians in the Manuscript Division of the Library of Congress for allowing me to work with the actual diary, which is also available on reel no. 1 of the library's microfilm collection of the Papers of Frederick Douglass.

77. Ralph Waldo Emerson, *English Traits* (Boston and New York: Houghton, Mifflin, and Company, 1904), 44, 48, 49–50, 54.

78. On Douglass and Rome, see Quarles, *Frederick Douglass*, 309–11; and McFeely, *Frederick Douglass*, 328–29. Douglass was not alone in remarking on the darkness of the Romans. In *Italian Hours*, Henry James regularly refers to the "dusky" Italians. On race and "ethnography" in other travel writings of the period, see Sara Blair, *Henry James and the Writing of Race and Nation* (Cambridge: Cambridge University Press, 1996), 15–59.

79. Douglass, *Life and Times*, 573, 577.

80. Ibid., 577, 578.

81. Ibid., 579; Frederick Douglass, "Claims of the Negro," *The Frederick Douglass Papers*, ser. 1, 2:508. See also Douglass's remarks on the American School in a letter of 19 November 1886, in *Life and Writings of Frederick Douglass*, 4:446.

82. Douglass to Lewis Douglass, letter of 20 February 1887, quoted in McFeely, *Frederick Douglass*, 332; David Walker, *David Walker's Appeal, in Four Articles; Together with a Preamble, to the Coloured Citizens of the World, but in Particular, and Very Expressly, to Those of the United States of America* (1829; repr. New York: Hill and Wang, 1995), 8.

83. See Douglass, *Life and Times*, 28–36.

84. Ibid., 585. Martin criticizes Douglass's turn against Egypt and Africa (*The Mind of Frederick Douglass*, 207–10). For a more sympathetic account of Douglass's ultimate dissatisfaction with Egypt, see Wilson Jeremiah Moses, *Afrotopia: The Roots of African American Popular History* (Cambridge: Cambridge University Press, 1998), 80–81, 130. For an illuminating discussion of ancient Egypt in nineteenth-century U.S. culture, particularly with respect to questions of race and nation, see Scott Trafton's *Egypt Land: Race and Nineteenth-Century American Egyptomania* (Durham: Duke University Press, 2004). On the importance of notions of progress to Douglass's *Life and Times*, see Kenneth W. Warren, "Frederick Douglass's *Life and Times*: Progressive Rhetoric and the Problem of Constituency," in *Frederick Douglass: New Literary and Historical Essays*, ed. Eric J. Sundquist (Cambridge: Cambridge University Press, 1990), 253–70. For the essential (and still controversial) study of connections among Africa and ancient Rome and Greece, see Martin Bernal, *The Afroasiatic Roots of Classical Civilization*, 2 vols. (New Brunswick: Rutgers University Press, 1987).

85. Douglass, *Life and Times*, 587. Nwankwo argues that Douglass in his discussion of Rome and Egypt in *Life and Times* sought as an American tourist to "allow Americans to differentiate themselves from barbaric nations" (*Black Cosmopolitanism*, 138). I see more of a tension between identification and differentiation.

86. Frederick Douglass, "A Nation in the Midst of a Nation," in *The Frederick Douglass Papers*, ser. 1, 2:437; Frederick Douglass, "The Nation's Problem," *The Frederick Douglass Papers*, ser. 1, 5:413.

87. Ruffin's "Introduction" can be found in Douglass, *Life and Times of Frederick Douglass, Written by Himself* (1881; New York: Pathway Press, 1951), xxx. References to *Life and Times* in the notes will continue to be to the 1962 Collier Press reprinting of the 1892 edition.

88. Douglass, *Life and Times*, 539, 563.

89. Ibid., 602, 597, 602. For backgrounds on Douglass's diplomatic mission, see Pitre, "Frederick Douglass and American Diplomacy in the Caribbean," esp. 465–75; Brantley, "Black Diplomacy and Frederick Douglass' Caribbean Experiences," esp. 204–9; and Nwankwo, *Black Cosmopolitanism*, chap. 5.

90. Nwankwo, *Black Cosmopolitanism*, 140; Douglass, *Life and Times*, 613, 614, 618.

91. Douglass to James G. Blaine, letters of 13 June 1890, 31 May 1891, and 27 June 1891, in *A Black Diplomat in Haiti: The Diplomatic Correspondence of U.S. Minister Frederick Douglass from Haiti, 1889–1891*, 2 vols., ed. Norma Brown (Salisbury, N.C.: Documentary Publications, 1977), 1:266, 265; 2:244. For a surprising defense of Douglass, see Booker T. Washington, *Frederick Douglass* (1906; Honolulu: University Press of the Pacific, 2003), 297–301. Washington writes: "As an evidence of the mean spirit of Mr. Douglass's enemies, he was grossly misrepresented as being the cause of the failure of the United States to obtain the Môle" (299). For a very different and, I think, inaccurate account of Douglass as a diplomat in Haiti, see John Michael, *Identity and the Failure of America: From Thomas Jefferson to the War on Terror* (Minneapolis: University of Minnesota Press, 2008), chap. 6. Michael argues that Douglass was a dupe of the U.S. government who failed to condemn or recognize U.S. imperialist designs.

92. Douglass, *Life and Times*, 620.

93. Robert W. Rydell, "Editor's Introduction," in Ida B. Wells, Frederick Douglass, Irvine Garland Penn, and Ferdinand L. Barnett, *The Reason Why the Colored American Is Not in the World's Columbian Exposition: The Afro-American's Contribution to Columbia Literature*, ed. Robert W. Rydell (Urbana: University of Illinois Press, 1999), xxiii. For additional background on the Columbian Exposition, see Robert W. Rydell, *All the World's a Fair: Visions of Empire at American International Expositions, 1876–1916* (Chicago: University of Chicago Press, 1984), chap. 2; and James Gilbert, *Perfect Cities: Chicago's Utopias of 1893* (Chicago: University of Chicago Press, 1991). For an excellent account of Douglass at the exposition, see Barbara J. Ballard, "African-American Protest and the Role of the Haitian Pavilion at the 1893 Chicago World's Fair," in *Multiculturalism: Roots and Realities*, ed. C. James Trotman (Bloomington: Indiana University Press, 2002), 108–24. On white supremacy and Anglo-Saxonism at the turn of the century, see Matthew Frye Jacobson, *Whiteness of a Different Color: European Immigrants and the Alchemy of Race* (Cambridge, Mass.: Harvard University Press, 1998), chap. 5.

94. I. Garland Penn, "The Progress of the Afro-American since Emancipation," in *The Reason Why*, ed. Rydell, 44. According to Rydell's "Editor's Introduction," Douglass and his coauthors printed approximately 20,000 copies of the pamphlet. On Douglass, lynching, and Ida B. Wells, see Gregory Jay, "Douglass, Melville, and the Lynching of Billy Budd," in *Frederick Douglass and Herman Melville*, ed. Levine and Otter, 369–95.

95. Douglass, "Haiti among the Foremost Civilized Nations of the Earth: An Address Delivered in Chicago, Illinois, on 2 January 1893," in *The Frederick Douglass Papers*, ser. 1, 5:506, 507. On Douglass's Haitian sympathies in his speeches at the World's Columbian Exposition, see also Nwankwo, *Black Cosmopolitanism*, 146–52; and Jana Evans Braziel, "Haiti, Guantánamo, and the 'One Dispensable Nation': U.S. Imperialism, 'Apparent States,' and Postcolonial Problematics of Sovereignty," *Cultural Critique* 64 (2006): 127–60, esp. 131–35. The Frederick

Douglass Papers at the Library of Congress contain undated drafts of two very admiring speeches on Toussaint L'Ouverture that Douglass most likely was working on around this time; see folders 1 and 2 of the "Speech, Article, and Book File, 1846–1894 and Undated."

96. Frederick Douglass, "Haiti and the Haitian People: An Address Delivered in Chicago, Illinois, on 2 January 1893," in *The Frederick Douglass Papers*, ser. 1, 5:510, 512, 515, 511, 510, 528, 534, 532.

97. Ibid., 527, 522, 525.

98. Frederick Douglass, "Lessons of the Hour: An Address Delivered in Washington, D.C., on 9 January 1894," in *The Frederick Douglass Papers*, ser. 1, 5:578, 598.

Epilogue

1. On the "natural culmination" thesis, see especially Walter LaFeber's influential *The New Empire: An Interpretation of American Expansion, 1860–1898* (Ithaca: Cornell University Press, 1963), vii.

2. Louis A. Pérez Jr., *The War of 1898: The United States and Cuba in History and Historiography* (Chapel Hill: University of North Carolina Press, 1998), 131, 112; Eric T. L. Love, *Race over Empire: Racism and U.S. Imperialism, 1865–1900* (Chapel Hill: University of North Carolina Press, 2004), chap. 5.

3. Anders Stephanson, *Manifest Destiny: American Expansionism and the Empire of Right* (New York: Hill and Wang, 1995), 67.

4. Love, *Race over Empire*, 164.

5. Brady Harrison, "Introduction," *Soldiers of Fortune*, ed. Brady Harrison (Ontario, Canada: Broadview Editions, 2006), 22; Gretchen Murphy, *Hemispheric Imaginings: The Monroe Doctrine and Narratives of U.S. Empire* (Durham: Duke University Press, 2005), 135. Harrison's excellent edition of *Soldiers of Fortune* includes contemporary reviews, which talk of the novel's exciting plot but do not extrapolate from the novel to the contemporary political moment. For an interesting account of connections between historical fiction of the 1895–1902 period and contemporary debates on imperialism, see Amy Kaplan, *The Anarchy of Empire in the Making of U.S. Culture* (Cambridge, Mass.: Harvard University Press, 2002), chap. 3.

6. [William Dean Howells], "Editor's Study," *Harper's New Monthly Magazine* 83 (November 1891): 963.

7. On Du Bois's critique of U.S. imperialism, see John Carlos Rowe, *Literary Culture and U.S. Imperialism* (New York: Oxford University Press, 2000), chap. 9.

8. Moses Coit Tyler, *A History of American Literature*, vol. 1, *1607–1676* (1878; New York: G. P. Putnam's Sons, 1880), 94; Charles Richardson, *American Literature, 1607–1885*, vol. 1, *The Development of American Thought* (New York: G. P. Putnam's Sons, 1887), 1, 22, 9, 22, 34; Brander Matthews, *An Introduction to the Study of American Literature* (New York: American Book Company, 1896), 13, 229.

See Kermit Vanderbilt, *American Literature and the Academy: The Roots, Growth, and Maturity of a Profession* (Philadelphia: University of Pennsylvania Press, 1986), 110–40; David R. Shumway, *Creating American Civilization: A Genealogy of American Literature as an Academic Discipline* (Minneapolis: University of Minnesota Press, 1994), chap. 2; and Claudia Stokes, *Writers in Retrospect: The Rise of American Literary History, 1875–1910* (Chapel Hill: University of North Carolina Press, 2006). Also useful is Elizabeth Renker, *The Origins of American Literature Studies: An Institutional History* (Cambridge: Cambridge University Press, 2007).

9. Stokes, *Writers in Retrospect*, 34. Theodore Roosevelt's review of Matthews's *An Introduction to the Study of American Literature* appeared in *Bookman*, February 1896, 519–21; for a good discussion of the review, see Stokes, *Writers in Retrospect*, 44–47.

10. Catherine Gallagher, "Undoing," in *Time and the Literary*, ed. Karen Newman, Jay Clayton, and Marianne Hirsch (New York: Routledge, 2002), 11, 17, 19.

11. Pérez, *The War of 1898*, 133.

12. On racial indeterminancy in the fiction of the late nineteenth century, see, for example, Julie Cary Nerad, "Slippery Language and False Dilemmas: The Passing Novels of Child, Howells, and Harper," *American Literature* 75 (2003): 813–41; Susan Gillman, *Blood Talk: Racial Melodrama and the Culture of the Occult* (Chicago: University of Chicago Press, 2003); Debra Rosenthal, *Race Mixture in Nineteenth-Century U.S. and Spanish American Fiction* (Chapel Hill: University of North Carolina Press, 2004); Alys Eve Weinbaum, *Wayward Reproductions: Genealogies of Race and Nation in Transatlantic Modern Thought* (Durham: Duke University Press, 2004), chap. 1; and Caroline F. Levander, *Cradle of Liberty: Race, the Child, and National Belonging from Thomas Jefferson to W. E. B. Du Bois* (Durham: Duke University Press, 2006), chap. 4. For cultural backgrounds, see Matthew Frye Jackson, *Whiteness of a Different Color: European Immigrants and the Alchemy of Race* (Cambridge, Mass.: Harvard University Press, 1998), esp. chap. 4 on "The Instability of Race."

13. Mark Twain, *A Connecticut Yankee in King Arthur's Court*, ed. Bernard L. Stein (Berkeley: University of California Press, 1983), 212. Twain did his major anti-imperialistic writing post-1900 in such works as "To the Person Sitting in Darkness" (1901) and "King Leopold's Soliloquy" (1905), but John Carlos Rowe in his excellent chapter on *Connecticut Yankee* makes a persuasive case that "anticolonial and anti-imperialistic attitudes inflect virtually all of Twain's writings" (*Literary Culture and U.S. Imperialism: From the Revolution to World War II* [New York: Oxford University Press, 2000], 122). See also Jim Zwick, "Mark Twain and Imperialism," *A Historical Guide to Mark Twain*, ed. Shelley Fisher Fishkin (New York: Oxford University Press, 2002), 227–55; and Amanda Claybaugh, *The Novel of Purpose: Literature and Social Reform in the Anglo-American World* (Ithaca: Cornell University Press, 2007), 205–11.

14. Twain, *Connecticut Yankee*, 445, 7.

Index

Abolitionists, Abolition, 44, 116, 127, 164, 176, 177, 183, 193; black, 128, 183, 189; British and, 191; and *Dred Scott* decision, 189; feminist, 177. *See also* Antislavery

Adams, John, 29, 252 (n. 85), 253 (n. 22)

African American literary nationalism, 4, 69, 91, 96, 114, 201, 204; and American literary nationalism, 4, 5, 111, 167, 169–70, 201, 204–5; and circulation, 91; and Douglass, 183–84, 185, 203, 210–11, 214, 218, 232–33; and *Freedom's Journal*, 90; and journalism, 185; Missouri Compromise debates and, 67–73, 87–95; and Santo Domingo, 205; Walker and, 14, 67–73, 80–82, 87–88, 90–96, 110–17

African Americans, 31, 69, 76, 130, 176, 183, 189, 201, 211; and American literary nationalism, 4, 5, 67, 69–70, 111, 201, 204–5; communities of, 71; and Haiti, 85, 180; Hawthorne on, 121; lynching of, 219, 224; newspapers of, 67, 71, 89; and race/racism, 7, 227; and World's Columbian Exposition, 232. *See also* Blacks; Free blacks

African American writers, 122, 183, 185, 204–5, 232–33. *See also* African American literary nationalism; Black press; names of individual writers

African Methodist Episcopal (AME) Church, 81, 82, 98, 99

African Repository and Colonial Journal: and *Freedom's Journal*, 88–89, 90, 106

Africans, Africa, 68, 82, 84, 89, 114, 127, 150, 161, 179, 189, 192, 226; and African Americans, 106, 227, 228; and American Colonization Society, 88, 99; emigration to, 189; and Europe, 222. *See also* Egypt

Agassiz, Louis, 126, 207–8, 276 (n. 18)

Allen, Richard, 99–100

American Anti-Imperialist League, 238

American Colonization Society (ACS), 88–89, 93, 99–100, 268 (n. 41); opposition of Douglass to, 186, 192, 227

American Hemisphere, 82, 181, 197, 203, 206, 216, 218, 227, 234, 236. *See also* Hemispheric nationalism; Hemispheric perspective; Southern Americas

American literary nationalism, 1–9, 14, 15, 19, 68, 120, 123, 149, 150, 203, 219, 241, 248 (n. 2); and American Revolution, 18; and conflict, 1, 4, 5, 14, 124; consensus in, 4, 18; demystifying school of, 18, 19; exceptionalist assumptions of, 123; hemispheric dimensions of, 14; and man of genius, 120; and Missouri Compromise debates, 67; and race, 1, 5, 6–11, 15, 240; and regionalism, 5, 14; traditional narrative of, 3, 4–5, 6, 13, 15, 19, 22; and U.S. imperialism, 8–13; and Walker's *Appeal*, 110–17; whiteness of, 6, 44, 123, 140; and Young America, 3, 117, 123, 124, 140, 157. *See also* African American literary nationalism; American literary nationalists; American literature

American literary nationalists, 2–3, 4, 201, 239; Brockden Brown as, 17–18, 22, 42, 257–58 (n. 48); and Douglass, 218; Melville as, 149, 152; triumphalism of, 19, 68; of Young America, 3, 117, 123–24, 140, 157

American literature, 1, 4, 5, 68, 120, 125; African American literature, 204–5; canon of, 5, 11, 18, 123, 125, 183, 205; distinctiveness of, 3, 17–18, 68, 110; and man of genius, 120; and New England, 110–12

"American Renaissance," 3, 19

American Revolution, 4, 8, 21, 26, 45, 58, 72, 82, 92, 111, 153, 234; and American literary nationalism, 2, 18, 22; blacks in, 76, 192; in Brockden Brown's *Ormond*, 43; Bunker Hill, 192; and Saint Domingue uprising, 28; traditions of, 113, 187, 234, 236

Anderson, Benedict, 89, 107

Anglo-Saxons, Anglo-Saxonism, 8, 128, 133, 134, 209, 218, 232; exceptionalism and superiority of, 122, 126, 127, 134, 141, 144; and expansionism, 146, 149; and imperialism, 238, 243; and literary nationalism, 210, 239–40; and nationalism, 133, 211, 232; opposition to, 210–11; and whiteness, 6, 143, 296 (n. 64)

Anthony, David, 141, 143

Antislavery, 71, 72, 74, 87, 92, 110, 190,

194; of Brockden Brown, 30, 31, 40, 62, 65; of Crafts, 173; of Douglass, 87, 173, 190, 194, 198, 215; of Federalists, 26, 30; of Hawthorne, 123, 130–32, 142; and hidden paternity trope in Melville, 149, 155, 157; and Missouri debates, 71–72, 79, 82–85; northern rhetoric of, 73, 77, 79, 82–85; of Rufus King, 83, 85–87; of Sumner, 131–32, 203; of Wells Brown, 87, 162–63; writing, 155, 157, 160, 162, 163, 173, 284 (n. 65), 285 (n. 70). *See also* Abolitionists, Abolition

Appiah, Kwame Anthony, 6, 8

Arac, Jonathan, 67, 263–64 (n. 1)

Aristocrats, aristocracy, 134, 140, 142, 152–53, 155, 171

Assing, Ottilie: and Douglass, 196

Atlantic Monthly (*Atlantic Magazine*), 210, 218, 289 (n. 100)

Axelrod, Alan, 33

Baker, Houston A., Jr., 101

Bakhtin, Mikhail, 44

Balibar, Etienne, 7, 23, 135, 162

Banneker, Benjamin, 87, 90, 205

Barlow, Joel, 2; *Columbiad* (1807), 64–65, 263 (n. 101); *Vision of Columbus* (1782), 64

Beecher, Henry Ward, 221

Bentley, Nancy, 157

Berlin, Ira, 26

Best, Stephen M., 12, 13, 248 (n. 19)

Black nationalists, nationalism, 69–70, 72–73, 80, 87, 89, 104, 106, 189; and circulation, 95; diasporic, 82, 106, 115, 116; and Douglass, 181, 198, 228; and Haiti, 89, 95, 181, 189, 198, 200; hemispheric, 82, 87, 95, 181; and power of print, 82, 87–88

Black press, 73, 115, 189, 204; circulatory politics of, 91, 100–101; and Douglass, 183, 185, 204, 233; and Walker, 100–101, 108

Blacks, 6, 9–10, 30, 31, 47, 69, 71, 74, 114, 182, 234; and American hemisphere, 211, 216; in American Revolution, 76; in Brockden Brown's writings, 30–32, 34, 36–38, 40–41; churches of, 81, 82; circulation of, 79, 88, 91; citizenship of, 40, 72, 75, 76–79, 91, 92, 99, 100, 102, 106, 114, 115, 181, 188, 229; and Egypt, 162, 224, 226; emigration of, 77, 79, 88, 189, 192, 227; fear of, 28, 30, 31, 36, 37, 62, 80, 85, 216; as Freemasons, 88; and Haiti, 29, 73; "inferiority" of, 80, 104, 189, 222; literacy of, 88, 97; and Louisiana Purchase, 24, 27–32; lynching of, 183, 219, 224, 233; mobility of, 93, 96, 97, 267 (n. 38); and nationalist discourses, 69, 84; and nationality, 40, 84, 85; pride of, 89, 96, 105, 115; rebellion of, in Saint Domingue, 26, 28, 29, 31, 32, 34; revolutionism of, 30, 32, 36, 62, 73, 81, 83, 107, 113, 142, 189, 191, 228, 234; as seamen, 108–9; and Texas, 120–21; "tropical," 207, 212, 215–16; uplift of, 88, 90, 91, 104, 114, 176, 183, 185, 201–2, 204, 205; and voudon, 142, 145, 280 (n. 42); in Western history, 222, 235; writers, 90, 204. *See also* African Americans; Free blacks

Blaine, James D., 230–31

Blight, David, 186, 295 (n. 52)

Bolster, W. Jeffrey, 108

Boston, 88, 90, 114; Walker in, 73, 88, 89, 97

Brackenridge, Hugh Henry: *Modern Chivalry* (1792–1815), 45; "The Rising Glory of America" (1772), 8–9, 247 (n. 14)

Brickhouse, Anna, 139, 156

Bridge, Horatio, 130–31

British, 9, 10, 45, 68, 163, 239. *See also* English, England; Great Britain

Brown, Charles Brockden, 5, 14, 64, 66; *An Address to the Congress of the United States, on the Utility and Justice of Restrictions upon Foreign Countries. . . .* (1809), 24, 65–66, 263 (n. 102); *Alcuin* (1798), 25; as American literary nationalist, 17, 22, 42, 257 (n. 48); antiracism of, 30, 50–54, 55, 56, 57; antislavery of, 30–32, 36–38, 40, 62, 65; *Arthur Mervyn; or, Memoirs of the Year 1793* (1799–1800), 25, 47, 49, 259 (n. 61); on blacks, 30–32, 35–38, 40–41; *The British Treaty*, 61; and Brownian moment, 46; on Burr, 63–64; career of, 25, 43; change in politics and aesthetics of, 25–26, 41–42; *Clara Howard* (1801), 442, 258 (n. 49); death of, 25, 65; dislocating writings of, 23; epistolary fiction of, 25, 42, 43, 44; as Federalist, 25, 26, 250 (n. 15), 262 (n. 83); on Haitian revolution, 254 (n. 29); *Jane Talbot* (1801), 42, 43, 258 (n. 49); and Jefferson, 25, 61, 65; and Louisiana Purchase, 15, 17–66, 255–56 (n. 35), 257 (n. 44); as magazine editor and writer, 30–32, 35, 42, 43, 44, 65; and Manifest Destiny, 38; "Memoirs of Carwin the Biloquist" (1803–5), 33, 42, 58–61; *Monroe's Embassy; or, The Conduct of the Government, in Relation to Our Claims to the Navigation of the Mississippi* (1803), 23–25, 39; *Monthly Magazine and American Review*, 30, 57, 64, 253 (nn. 26, 27); on Native Americans, 35–36, 50–54, 55, 56, 57; novels of, 24, 25, 41, 44,

46; *Ormond* (1799), 43, 47; political pamphlets of, 22, 23–25, 32, 33, 40, 41, 42, 66; and Quakers 35–36; on Saint Domingue, 47, 54; unknowingness of, 66; and Volney's *A View of the Soil and Climate of the United States*, 35, 62; and white U.S. imperialism, 10, 13, 25

—*An Address to the Government of the United States, on the Cession of Louisiana to the French* (1803): anti-French message of, 32–34, 40, 257 (n. 40); comparison of, to earlier novels, 24–25, 33; Saint Domingue uprising in, 36–37; slave conspiracies in, 62; subversive and counter-subversive in, 46, 255 (n. 31); white imperialism of, 23–24

—*Edgar Huntly* (1799), 13, 23, 43, 47, 49, 50, 52, 57; as allegory of nation, 261 (n. 77); binaries collapsed in, 46–47, 53–54; Brownian moments in, 49–50; comparison of, to *Address*, 24, 33; ending of, 54–55, 56; frontier violence in, 50–54, 56; Indians in, 50–54, 55, 56, 260 (n. 65), 261 (n. 74); and "Memoirs of Carwin," 60; narrator of, 47–48; plot of, 48–50, 55; prefatory note to, 17, 18; race in, 17–19, 47–48, 51; unsettling of, 48, 55; and white imperialism, 19, 41

—*Literary Magazine, and American Register*, 41, 257–58 (n. 48); essays attributed to Brockden Brown in, 31–32, 35, 42, 254 (n. 27); "Memoirs of Carwin" in, 59

—*Wieland; or, The Transformation: An American Tale* (1798), 25, 40, 43, 46, 47, 50; and *Address*, 33; and "Memoirs of Carwin," 42, 61

Brown, John, 116, 187, 193, 194

Brown, Lee Rust, 110–11

Brown, William Hill, 44, 46

Brown, William Wells, 87, 191, 193, 205, 235; *The Black Man, His Antecedents, His Genius, and His Achievements* (1863), 185, 189; *Clotel; or, The President's Daughter* (1853), 99, 121, 122, 133, 155, 156, 162–63, 279 (n. 33); and emigration to Haiti, 193, 195, 197; genealogical fiction of, 124; and Haiti, 189, 192

Bryant, William Cullen, 205; *Poems* (1821), 68

Buchanan, James, 188, 207

Buffon, Comte de, 17–18, 280 (nn. 38, 39)

Burr, Aaron, 63–64, 263 (n. 98)

Canada, 94, 95, 164, 268 (n. 38); blacks in, 115; Douglass in, 194

Capitalism, 141, 145, 146, 252–23 (n. 22)

Caribbean, 10, 12, 22; American expansion into, 67, 157, 229–30, 236, 237; black revolutionism in, 30; blacks in, 179–80; Douglass in, 229, 236

Castiglia, Christopher, 138

Catholics, Catholicism, 217, 218–19, 235. *See also* Roman Catholic Church

Channing, Walter, 68, 125

Charleston, S.C., 80, 81, 85, 87, 98; Vesey conspiracy against, 73, 80, 82; Walker in, 73, 108

Chesnutt, Charles, 242

Child, Lydia Maria, 165

Chopin, Kate: *Désirée's Baby* (1893), 242

Christophersen, Bill, 36–37

Cinque, Joseph, 189, 191

Citizens, citizenship, 24, 42, 45, 72, 74, 76, 92, 229; black, 40, 72, 75–79, 91,

92, 99, 100, 102, 106, 114, 115, 181, 188, 229; and naturalization laws, 76, 77; white, 75, 115

Civil War, 183, 198, 201, 208; and Douglass, 185, 195, 197–200; and Louisiana Purchase, 21; as war to end slavery, 185, 195, 198, 199

Clay, Henry, 72, 75, 78, 88, 99

Cleveland, Grover, 219

Colonization of blacks. *See* American Colonization Society; Liberia

Commerce, and empire, 64, 65–66

Compromise of 1850, 189

Connecticut Wits, 5, 30

Consensus: and American culture, 10, 67–68; in American literary nationalism, 4, 18; in post–War of 1812 era, 67–68

Contingency, contingencies: of American literary nationalism, 1, 5; and better future, 11–12; in Brockden Brown's writings, 23, 40, 46, 66; and Douglass, 202; of empire, 15, 17–66; in Hawthorne's writings, 134; and Louisiana, 21, 22, 29; meanings of, 21–22; of race, 170; in U.S. imperialism, 11, 20; in Webb's *The Garies and Their Friends*, 170

Cooper, James Fenimore, 9, 10, 68, 261 (n. 79)

Cornish, Samuel, 93, 96, 183; anticolonization of, 100; as coeditor of *Freedom's Journal*, 71, 89, 92–93, 108; as editor of *The Rights of All*, 71; and Walker, 95–96

Counterfactual, counterfactuals, 12–15, 48, 124, 184, 248 (n. 20); and Brockden Brown's writings, 21–22; historical narratives, 247–48 (n. 18); and legal hermeneutics, 248 (n. 19); narration in Walker's *Appeal*, 103; and undoings, 241–42

Countermemory, countermemories, 121

Crafts, Hannah, 5, 15, 133; as escaped slave, 164; identity of, 163, 164, 175, 176–77; race of, 176–77; racial anxieties of, 174–75

—*The Bondwoman's Narrative* (ca. 1855), 163–78; Bill in, 173–75; blacks/blackness in, 164–66, 170, 176; blood/bloodlines in, 121, 163, 165, 167, 169, 172; Charlotte in, 172–73, 175; Sir Clifford De Vincent in, 167, 168–69, 171; Cosgroves in, 169, 170–71; death in, 166, 170–72; degradation of field hands in, 173–75; ending of, 171–76, 288 (n. 98); and expansionism, 164; family in, 165, 167, 168, 169, 171; as genealogical fiction, 124, 163, 165, 166, 172, 176; Hannah (narrator) in, 165, 166, 167–68, 169, 171, 172–75; and *The House of the Seven Gables*, 123–24, 133, 163, 171, 176; Lindendale Plantation in, 165, 167; linden tree in, 168–69, 171, 176; miscegenation in, 170, 171; mistresses in, 165, 166, 169, 173; New Jersey in, 175, 176; portraits in, 166, 167–68, 170, 171; publication of, 163; race and racial entanglement in, 165–66, 172, 168–69, 242–43; rumor in, 168; and *The Scarlet Letter*, 164, 165, 172; slaves/slavery in, 164, 168, 169, 170, 171, 172–75; social status in, 163; sympathy in, 173; Trappe in, 163, 165, 166, 169, 171–72, 177; violence in, 168–69, 173–74; Wheelers in, 164, 169–70, 173, 175; whites/whiteness in, 137, 165, 167–68, 169–70, 288 (n. 94)

Crane, Gregg D., 190

Creole, slave revolt on, 182

Crèvecoeur, Michel Guillaume Jean de, 40

Crofts, Julia Griffiths: and Douglass, 221

Cuba, 158, 164, 179, 189; and Douglass, 182; and U.S. imperialism, 180, 201, 237

Cultural nationalism, 3, 18–19, 121–22

Cummins, Maria: *The Lamplighter* (1854), 145

Dangerfield, George, 79

Davis, Jefferson, 199

Davis, Richard Harding: *Soldiers of Fortune* (1897), 238–39

Dayan, Joan, 155

Declaration of Independence, 68, 69, 74, 77; as black freedom document, 110, 114, 190; in Walker's *Appeal*, 106–7, 110

Delany, Martin, 116, 128, 186, 220, 234; and black emigration, 179, 189; "Political Destiny of the Colored Race on the American Continent" (1854), 181, 192; transnational black nationalism of, 191, 193

Democratic Review, 122, 208–9; and American literary nationalism, 120, 128; Hawthorne in, 119–20, 129; and Mexican War, 125–26, 128; and O'Sullivan, 125, 128; and race, 127–28, 131, 210; Texas in, 120–21; Young Americans of, 123, 149

Democrats, Democratic Party, 122, 125, 164, 188, 207, 219; creed of, 124–33; Hawthorne as, 117, 123, 129; and Melville, 148; and slavery, 129; and technology, 146

Dessalines, Jean-Jacques, 29, 189

Diaspora: and African American litera-ture, 232; and American literary nationalism, 68, 69; and black nationalism, 71, 72, 81–82, 190–91; and *Creole* slave revolt, 182; and race

and nation, 182, 186, 190–91; and Vesey conspiracy, 84, 267–68 (n. 38)

Dickens, Charles, 163, 205, 287 (n. 82)

Dislocating, dislocations, 14, 243; Brockden Brown and, 23, 46; in Crafts's *The Bondwoman's Narrative*, 163; of Douglass's nationalism, 182, 228; of *Dred Scott* ruling, 187, 190; in *The House of the Seven Gables*, 123, 147, 151, 163; in *Pierre*, 163; of race from geography, 212; of race and nation, 74, 182, 228, 241, 242; and Walker's *Appeal*, 70, 74, 103. *See also* Undoing, undoings; Counterfactual, counterfactuals

Dominican Republic, 180, 206. *See also* Santo Domingo

Doolen, Andy, 11, 9–10, 250 (n. 15)

Douglass, Anna, 219

Douglass, Frederick, 13, 196, 225, 234, 237; as African American nationalist, 181, 183–84, 186, 210–11, 231, 233, 236, 290 (n. 11); "Annexation of San Domingo" (1871), 202, 211–13; and annexation of Santo Domingo, 183, 197, 200–218, 229–30; antiracism of, 183, 227; antislavery of, 87, 173; in Canada, 194; as canonical writer, 5, 183; as champion of women's rights, 226–27, 236; children of, 195, 196, 217, 220, 226; and Civil War, 185, 195, 197, 198, 199, 210; "The Claims of the Negro Ethnologically Considered" (1854), 161, 222–23, 225–26; and composite nationality, 197, 213–18, 234, 235; death of, 236; diary of, 223, 224, 226, 227; *Douglass' Monthly*, 179, 180, 185, 186, 187, 189, 192–93, 194–95, 197, 199, 200; and Egypt, 221–22, 224, 225–27, 235; and Emer-son, 223–24, 225; "Emigration to Hayti" (1861), 180, 194–95; and emigration to Haiti, 179–81, 183, 184, 186, 192–95; in England, 194, 220, 221; and environmental determinism, 212–13, 216; in France, 221; *Frederick Douglass' Paper*, 180, 183, 185, 192, 193; and Freedman's Savings and Trust Company, 186; in Great Britain, 182, 194; and Haiti, 15, 184, 186–87, 192–200, 200–201, 202, 211, 217, 221, 229, 231–36, 290 (n. 9), 295 (n. 61), 299 (n. 91); "Haiti among the Foremost Civilized Nations of the Earth" (1893), 233–34; "Haiti and the Haitian People" (1893), 233, 234–36; and Harpers Ferry raid, 194; hemispheric nationalism of, 128, 178, 179–236; "The Heroic Slave" (1853), 182, 183, 190; as imperialist, 203, 213; "The Lessons of the Hour" (1894), 183, 236; and Lincoln, 187, 195, 199, 292 (n. 27); and lynching, 183, 219, 224, 233, 236; marriage of, 214, 296 (n. 66); mother of, 226; *My Bondage and My Freedom* (1855), 183, 196, 226, 285 (n. 69); *Narrative of the Life of Frederick Douglass, An American Slave* (1845), 168, 176, 183, 284 (n. 64); "Nemesis" (1861), 198; and *New Era*, 204, 205; as newspaper editor, 184, 185, 186, 201, 202, 205, 217; *North Star*, 116, 180, 182, 183, 290 (n. 9); "Our Composite Nationality" (1869), 213–14; purchase of, from slavery, 221; *The Reason Why the Colored American Is Not in the World's Columbian Exposition*, 233; as recorder of deeds for District of Columbia, 219; as Republican, 183, 184, 186, 187, 202, 203, 219; in Rome, 218–19, 224–25, 227; on Rome, 219, 221–22, 225–26, 229; "The San Domingan Commission"

(1871), 214; as secretary to Senate's commission on Santo Domingo, 206; "The Significance of Emancipation in the West Indies" (1857), 190–91, 197, 234; on South and slavery expansion, 180–81; speeches of, 182, 184, 189, 190, 191, 217, 233–35, 300 (n. 95); and Sumner, 203, 214–15; "A Trip to Hayti" (1861), 195–96, 197, 198; as U.S. minister to Haiti, 228, 229–31; and Vesey, 200; on Walker, 115–16; "What to the Slave Is the Fourth of July?" (1852), 18, 1913, 202; white father of, 218, 220; white wife of, 219–20, 223, 228; at World's Columbian Exposition, 231–33

—*Life and Times of Frederick Douglass* (1881; rev. ed. 1892), 183–84, 186, 191, 202, 220–21, 231, 291 (n. 13); absence of Haiti in, 192; Douglass as U.S. nationalist in, 186; Douglass's hemispheric nationalism in, 184; Douglass's mother in, 226; *Dred Scott* decision in, 187–88; 1892 expansion of, 184; Haiti in, 228, 230, 231; introduction to, 228; Lincoln in, 187, 199; Rome and Egypt in, 221–22, 225, 227, 228, 298 (n. 85); Santo Domingo in, 203; sectional conflict on slavery in, 187; trip to Rome in, 218–19; U.S. expansion in, 203; World's Columbian Exposition in, 231

—*New National Era*, 201, 202, 203, 205, 211, 214; African American literary nationalism in, 218; annexation of Santo Domingo in, 205–6, 211–18

Douglass, Helen Pitts, 219–20, 223, 228
Douglass, Lewis C., 217, 220, 226
Douglass, Rosetta, 195, 196
Dred Scott decision (1857), 184–86, 188–89, 197, 199, 217, 219, 229; as dis-

locating event, 187–90; Douglass on, 187–90, 195, 198, 200, 229; and emigration, 193, 217; and race and citizenship, 75, 291 (n. 16)

Dumas, Alexandre, 221, 228

Dunbar, Paul Laurence, 232–33

Dunlap, William, 30, 253 (n. 25), 254 (n. 26)

Duyckinck, Evert, 125, 130, 158; and Hawthorne and Melville, 149, 282 (n. 57); *Moby-Dick* reviewed by, 149–50; "Nationality in Literature," 128–29; and *Typee*, 149; and Young America, 239

Dwight, Timothy, 2, 3, 30, 253 (n. 24)

Earle, Jonathan, 130

Egerton, Douglas R., 28, 29, 81, 83, 85, 86

Egypt, 161, 220, 222, 226, 227; blackness in, 224, 226; and black pride, 96, 269 (n. 28); Caucasians in, 161, 297 (n. 74); and Douglass, 220, 225, 226–27; in Hawthorne, 162; in *Pierre*, 161, 162; racial mixture in, 224; slaves in, 104

Emancipation Proclamation, 199

Embargo, 62, 64, 65

Emerson, Ralph Waldo, 3, 5; "The American Scholar" (1837), 110–11; *English Traits* (1856), 223–24, 225; notions of self-reliance, 158; "The Poet" (1844), 110–11, 120; on race, 223–24, 128, 225, 235

Emigration, 75, 89, 92; to Africa, 90, 189; of blacks, 77, 79, 88, 189, 192, 227; to Haiti, 85, 179–81, 183, 189, 192–95, 197

English, England, 18, 42, 53, 93, 94, 125, 142, 148, 170, 223–24; and American literature, 68, 149, 245 (n. 4), 264 (n. 2); aristocratic lineage in, 152–

53, 155; blacks in, 115; Douglass in, 194, 220, 221; and Louisiana Purchase, 26; and United States, 2, 26. *See also* Great Britain

Enlightenment, 6, 35, 46

Ethnology, American school of, 126, 161, 222

Europe, 17, 57, 125, 222, 232; America vs., 18, 38–39, 58; and American literary nationalism, 19; Douglass in, 220, 221, 223, 234; mixed racial character of, 223, 224

Eustis, William, 76–77

Exceptionalism, 11, 58; Anglo-Saxonist, 122, 123, 134, 147; and Brockden Brown, 39, 257 (n. 45); and Grant, 209; Hawthorne on, 122–23, 144, 147; Melville on, 148, 149; national(ist), 26, 123, 125, 209, 257 (n. 45)

Expansionism, U.S., 26, 36, 66, 67, 148, 178; Anglo-Saxonist, 149; in Caribbean, 236; congressional debates on, 74; in Crafts, 164; and cultural nationalism, 121; and Douglass, 200, 201; hemispheric, 158; and *The House of the Seven Gables*, 136; and literary nationalism, 134; and Louisiana Purchase, 21, 61; and Manifest Destiny, 117; and *Pierre*, 157, 158; proslavery, 164, 182; and self-defense, 39; into Southwest, 125; and technology, 146; and whiteness, 124, 162. *See also* Imperialism, U.S.; Manifest Destiny

Federalists, Federalism, 27, 29, 30, 63, 64, 68, 74; antiracism of, 34–35; and antislavery, 26, 30, 31; Brockden Brown as, 25, 26, 62, 250 (n. 15), 262 (n. 83); and Haiti, 29, 35, 62, 252 (n. 22); vs. Jefferson's politics, 30, 35,

262 (n. 83); and Louisiana, 27, 63; and Native Americans, 35, 256 (n. 38); and *Port Folio*, 42, 63; and social control, 46

Ferguson, Niall, 184

Floridas, 21, 27, 117

Forten, James: *A Series of Letters by a Man of Color* (1813), 91–92

Foster, Hannah W.: *The Coquette* (1797), 45, 46

France, French, 6, 42, 43, 222; Douglass in, 221; and Federalists, 29; and Louisiana Purchase, 24, 26–27, 39; and Saint Domingue, 27–29, 31, 32, 33, 39, 62, 234; as U.S. enemy, 27, 32, 33–34, 38, 39

Franklin, Benjamin, 3, 209

Fraser, Nancy, 101

Free blacks, 20, 73, 75, 76, 77, 79, 80, 82, 91, 93, 99, 100, 109, 127, 176; disfranchisement of, 189; and emigration to Haiti, 85, 179–81, 183, 189, 192–95, 197; and Liberia, 192; of Northeast, 72, 193; rights of, 179, 198, 204; in territories, 188; as Union troops, 199–200

Freedom's Journal, 67, 90, 97, 99–100; African American literary nationalism of, 91; and *African Repository and Colonial Journal*, 269 (n. 28, 44); agents for, 92–94, 108, 115; anti-Missouri pieces in, 91; and circulation, 91, 92; editors of, 89; and emigration to Liberia, 90; Forten's *A Series of Letters by a Man of Color* in, 91–92; founding of, 89, 92–93; and Haiti, 93, 269 (n. 45); in South, 93, 94; Walker and, 73, 92–94, 95, 99–101

Free-Soil Party: and Hawthorne, 130–33

French Revolution, 22, 26, 28, 43, 156

Freneau, Philip, 2, 3; "The Rising Glory of America" (1786), 8–9, 247 (n. 14)

Fugitive Slave Law, 131–33, 163

Gallagher, Catherine, 13, 241–42

Gardner, Jared, 19, 24–25, 43–44, 247 (n. 14), 256 (nn. 35, 36), 257–58 (n. 48), 261 (n. 77)

Garnet, Henry Highland: *The Past and Present Condition, and the Destiny, of the Colored Race* (1848), 127–28, 178; *Walker's Appeal, with a Brief Sketch of His Life. . . .* (1848), 116–17

Garrison, William Lloyd, 116, 190, 191

Gates, Henry Louis, Jr.: and *The Bondwoman's Narrative*, 163, 164, 173–74, 287 (n. 83)

Geffrard, Fabre, 180, 193, 196, 197

Genealogical entanglements, 44, 122, 147

Genealogical fictions, 121–24, 135–40, 144, 147–48, 150–63, 165–72, 176–78, 275 (n. 6); and countermemory, 121, 135

Gherardi, Bancroft, 230, 231

Gibbons, Luke, 255 (n. 31), 259–60 (n. 64)

Giles, Paul, 181

Gilmore, Michael T., 46

Gilmore, Paul, 141

Gliddon, George, 222

Goddu, Teresa, 121–22

Goudie, Sean X., 23

Grant, Ulysses S., 200–203, 205–8, 211–12, 216–17, 237

Great Britain, 6, 17, 101; and American literary nationalism, 3, 6, 15, 19, 22, 68; and *Creole* slave revolt, 182; emancipation of slaves in West Indies by, 191, 234; U.S. relations with, 33. *See also* British; English, England

Habermas, Jürgen, 101

Haiti, 5–6, 93, 94, 206, 217, 230, 231, 233, 269 (n. 45); and black nationality/pride, 85, 87, 89, 96, 106, 196, 200; and Douglass, 15, 184, 186–87, 192–200, 200–201, 221, 229, 231–36; Douglass as minister to, 228, 229–31; Douglass on, 179–80, 217, 233–36; emigration to, 85, 179–81, 183, 189, 192–95, 197; and Federalists, 29, 62, 252 (n. 22); and Haitian Pavilion, 232, 233; as independent black republic, 29, 32, 62, 179–80, 192, 197, 202, 207, 216, 217, 229, 233–34; and Jefferson, 28, 29, 32, 62; mulattoes in, 194, 196; U.S. naval base in, 228, 229, 234; U.S. policy toward, 28, 29, 32, 62, 199, 229–31, 234; and Vesey's black conspiracy, 73, 82, 84; and World's Columbian Exposition, 231–33. See also Saint Domingue

Haitian Revolution, 22, 26, 28–33, 90, 232, 234, 235. See also Saint Domingue

Hamilton, Alexander, 27, 33, 74, 255 (n. 33)

Hamilton, James, An Account of the Late Intended Insurrection among a Portion of the Blacks of this City (1822), 88, 267 (n. 37)

Harper, Frances, 205; Iola Leroy (1892), 242

Harpers Ferry raid, 187. See also Brown, John

Harrison, Benjamin, 228, 229, 231

Hartford Convention (1814), 64

Hawthorne, Geoffrey, 48

Hawthorne, Nathaniel, 3, 13, 15, 122, 129, 134, 205; and Agassiz, 207; antislavery of, 123, 280 (n. 44); "The Birthmark," 122; and Bridge, 130–31; "Chiefly about War-Matters. By a Peaceable Man," 289 (n. 100); and

Free-Soil Party, 132, 148; as genealogical fictionalist, 177, 178; as incarnation of American genius, 149; as Jacksonian Democrat, 117, 123, 129, 131, 135, 147, 177; The Life of Franklin Pierce (1852), 129, 177, 275 (n. 9), 278 (n. 29); "Main Street" (1849), 122; The Marble Faun (1860), 162; and Melville, 120, 147–50, 281–82 (n. 53), 282 (n. 57); racism of, 123; O'Sullivan on, 125; "Rappaccini's Daughter," 122, 139; and Salem, Mass., 119–20, 131; "A Select Party" (1844), 119–20, 121, 122–23, 149, 166; on slavery, 132, 275 (n. 9), 277–78 (n. 25); and wife Sophia, 133; "Young Goodman Brown," 120

—The House of the Seven Gables (1851), 123, 133, 135, 137; Alice Pyncheon in, 139, 142, 159, 171; and Anglo-Saxonist exceptionalism, 122, 133–34, 144; as antislavery allegory, 142; blackness in, 140–41, 142, 151, 170; blood and bloodlines in, 121, 122, 123, 133, 135–41, 145, 155, 169, 280 (n. 38); Chanticleer in, 122, 139–40, 145, 150–51, 154; class in, 142, 143, 145; Clifford in, 136, 137, 138, 146; Colonel Pyncheon in, 122, 134, 135, 137, 138, 140, 141, 143, 145, 151, 166, 169, 177; deeds in, 140, 142, 145; dislocation of race and nation in, 123, 133–34, 140, 141–42, 151; ending of, 143–44, 147, 150; family in, 134, 136, 143, 145, 150, 151; garden and planting in, 139, 143; as genealogical fiction, 133, 134–35, 150; Gervayse Pyncheon in, 142–43; Hepzibah in, 136, 137, 138, 141, 146, 150, 171; Holgrave in, 142–43, 144, 145, 146, 150, 159, 172; house in, 137, 146, 171; Judge Jaffrey Pyncheon in, 122, 134, 136, 137, 138, 141, 143, 145–

47, 151, 163, 166, 170, 177; Maules in, 135, 137, 139, 142, 159, 168, 169; and Melville, 150, 276 (n. 12); and middle-class values, 132–33; narrator in, 135, 136, 137, 138, 143; passages in, 171; Phoebe Pyncheon in, 136, 137, 138, 142, 143, 144, 145, 146, 150, 166, 279 (n. 36); portraits in, 134, 137–38, 143, 145, 150, 151, 166; preface to, 134; race in, 133, 136–37, 140–43, 145, 150, 151, 243; railroad in, 146; Scipio in, 142, 159; sudden death in, 134, 135, 143; Uncle Venner in, 144–45, 146; white characters in, 121, 137, 143
—*The Scarlet Letter* (1850), 133, 278–79 (n. 30); Chillingworth in, 163, 165, 166, 172; Dimmesdale in, 165, 166
Hegel, Georg Wilhelm Friedrich, 142
Hemispheric nationalism: of Douglass, 128, 182, 183, 184, 202, 215–17, 221, 235, 236; and Haiti, 221, 235
Hemispheric perspective, 5, 26, 30, 216; of African American literature, 232; of American literary nationalism, 14, 68; of black nationalism, 81–82, 87, 95; of Louisiana Purchase, 26–27; of politics, 198, 215; of Walker, 108
Herder, Johann Gottfried, 6
Hietala, Thomas, 128
Higginson, Thomas Wentworth, 210, 238–39
Hildreth, Richard: *The White Slave*, 285 (n. 70)
Hinds, Janie, 52, 261 (n. 73)
Hinks, Peter P.: on Walker, 71, 102, 271 (n. 65); on Walker's *Appeal*, 81, 98, 109, 264 (n. 10)
Hirsch, E. D., Jr., 14
Hispaniola, 206
Historical narratives: contingency in, 12; and counterfactuals, 12, 184; fixed, 11; of historicist criticism, 1–2;

interpretive, 13; of nation, 69, 96; postnational, 69, 81–82; of "undo-ings," 13, 103
Historicism, 1–2, 10, 12
Holly, James, 193, 197
Holman, Hugh, 272 (n. 75)
Holmes, John, 77–78
Hopkins, Pauline, 242
Horsman, Reginald, 8, 126, 277 (n. 20)
Horton, George M., 90–91, 269 (n. 46)
Horton, James Oliver, 88
Horton, Louise E., 88
Howe, Samuel Gridley, 206, 208
Howells, William Dean, 233, 238–39; *An Imperative Duty* (1891), 242
Hsu, Hsuan L., 61
Humphrey, Carol Sue, 72
Hyppolite, Flovil, 229, 231

Ignatiev, Michael, 178
Imperialism, U.S., 8, 9–11, 13, 52, 177, 202; and American literary national-ism, 8–13, 15, 149; and Brockden Brown, 10, 13, 22, 23–24, 57; and Ca-ribbean, 157, 229–30; contingency in, 20, 57, 66; and Douglass, 217; and filibusterers, 164, 181; and Louisiana Purchase, 21, 22, 23–24, 237; and Mexico, 19, 121, 124–28, 148, 157; and Monroe Doctrine, 237; and race, 15, 238; and slave trade, 22. *See also* Ex-pansionism, U.S.; Manifest Destiny
Indians. *See* Native Americans
Irish, Ireland, 45, 48, 49, 55, 61, 259–60 (n. 64)
Irving, Washington, 3, 68
Italians, Italy, 143, 222, 297 (n. 78)

Jacksonian Democrats, 39, 135; anti-aristocracy of, 134; Hawthorne and, 117, 129, 142; nationalism of, 124; principles of, 130

Jacobs, Harriet, 176
James, William, 225
Jarves, James Jackson, 296 (n. 64)
Jim Crow, 141, 150, 219
Jefferson, Thomas, 28, 33, 35, 63, 74,
    106, 155, 162; and Brockden Brown,
    25, 61, 62, 65; and Declaration of
    Independence, 110; as democrat, 253
    (n. 22); Embargo of, 62, 64; "empire
    of liberty" of, 21, 27, 62; and Haiti,
    28, 29, 32, 62; hemispheric vision of,
    30, 61; and Louisiana Purchase, 20–
    21, 27–30, 251 (n. 18); *Notes on the
    State of Virginia* (1785), 30, 96, 97,
    104–5; racism of, 96, 104–5, 251
    (n. 19); and slavery, 27–30, 62
Jehlen, Myra, 51
Jews, 97, 104, 224
Johnson, Jane: as Hannah Crafts, 164
Johnson, Michael P.: on Vesey conspir-
    acy, 73, 80–81, 83, 266 (n. 24), 267
    (n. 37)

Kansas-Nebraska Act (1854), 186
Kaplan, Amy, 8, 247 (n. 16)
Kastor, Peter, 21, 263 (n. 98)
Kazanjian, David, 19, 53, 59, 271
    (n. 68)
Kelley, Wyn, 157
Kennedy, Lionel H., and Thomas
    Parker: *An Official Report of the
    Trials of Sundry Negroes, Charged
    with an Attempt to Raise an Insurrec-
    tion in the State of South Carolina*
    (1822), 83, 85–86, 88
Kermode, Frank, 137, 280 (n. 39)
King, Rufus, 83, 85–87
Knox, Robert, 223–24
Kolchin, Peter, 7, 246–47 (n. 11)
Kornfeld, Eve, 2–3
Krause, Sydney J., 260 (n. 72), 261
    (n. 74)

Lamarck, Jean Baptiste, 137–38
Lamartine, Alphonse Marie Louis de,
    221
Lee, Maurice S., 155
Lewis, Edmonia, 224, 227
Liberia, 90, 93, 100, 131, 192
Lincoln, Abraham, 187, 199, 221; and
    Civil War, 198, 199; and Douglass,
    187, 195, 199; and Haiti, 199, 293
    (n. 35)
Linn, John Blair, 31, 253–54 (n. 26)
Literary World, 149
Livingston, Robert R., 21, 27, 33
Looby, Christopher, 32, 45
Longfellow, Henry Wadsworth, 132,
    278 (n. 29)
Louisiana Purchase, 12, 13, 26–29, 58,
    64–65, 75; blacks in, 28, 252 (n. 21);
    and Brockden Brown, 15, 17–66;
    contingency and, 21–22, 29; debates
    on, 22, 251 (n. 18); historical impact
    of, 20, 21, 69, 237; and slavery, 29,
    62–63, 64–65, 253 (n. 23)
Love, Eric T. L., 207, 208, 237, 238
Lynching, 183, 219, 224, 233, 236

Madison, James, 21, 33, 62, 64
Maine, 75, 77
Male, Roy, 137
Manifest Destiny, 10, 127, 128, 177, 282
    (n. 55); and Brockden Brown, 25,
    38–40; democratic side to, 276
    (n. 14); and Douglass, 201, 217; and
    expansionism, 117; and Hawthorne,
    133, 177; and Jacksonians, 39; Mel-
    ville on, 148, 149; O'Sullivan on, 126;
    and race, 128, 133
Martin, J. Sella, 204, 205, 210, 217
Martin, Waldo E., Jr., 181, 201
Massachusetts, 76, 111, 126, 180, 203;
    Boston, 179, 193, 208; Douglass on,
    211, 212, 215; free blacks in, 77, 212;

proposed anti-immigration law in, 88; Salem, 119; Walker in, 88, 101, 108

Massachusetts General Colored Association (MGCA), 88, 95, 100

Matthews, Brander, 239–40

Matthiessen, F. O., *American Renaissance* (1941), 3, 19

McFeely, William S., 201

McWilliams, John P., 18

Melville, Gansevoort, 148, 149

Melville, Herman, 15, 147, 148; and American literary nationalism, 149, 152; antislavery of, 148, 149; "Authentic Anecdotes of 'Old Zack' " (1847), 148, 149; "Benito Cereno" (1855), 157; and Democrats, 149; and Hawthorne, 120, 133, 147–48, 149–50, 281–82 (n. 53); "Hawthorne and His Mosses" (1850), 120, 149, 150, 282 (n. 56); on *The House of the Seven Gables*, 150, 276 (n. 12); on Manifest Destiny, 148, 149; *Mardi* (1849), 148; as "Master Genius," 120; on Mexican War, 148; *Moby-Dick; or, The Whale* (1851), 149–50; *Typee* (1846), 148, 149; *White-Jacket* (1850), 148; and Young America, 148–50

—*Pierre* (1852): American literary nationalism in, 150; blacks/blackness in, 152, 155, 156, 157, 159, 160, 161–62, 170; blood/bloodlines in, 121, 136, 147, 152–55, 158, 159, 160, 285 (n. 68); and Egypt, 161; Enceladus in, 157, 159; as genealogical fiction, 124, 150, 155, 158, 284 (n. 67); General Glendinning in, 153, 284 (n. 65); Glendinning family in, 152, 153; Glendinning Stanly in, 158–59, 160; Greek mythology in, 159; hidden paternity in, 152, 155; horses in, 153–55; and *The House of the Seven Gables*, 123–24, 133, 136, 147, 150–57,

158; incest in, 159, 160; Indians in, 153; Isabel Banford in, 151–52, 155–60, 161, 285 (n. 71); Lucy Tartan in, 151, 152, 154, 159, 160; Mary Glendinning in, 151, 153, 156, 157; miscegenation in, 152–53, 155, 156, 159, 161–62; murder in, 160; narrator in, 152–53, 154, 157, 158; New York City in, 157, 158; Pierre in, 150, 151–52, 154, 155–60, 161, 283 (n. 61), 285 (n. 71); portraits and paintings in, 150, 152, 156, 159–60; race in, 147, 151–53, 155, 159, 161–62, 242–43, 284 (n. 67); Reverend Falsgrave in, 147, 157; rumor in, 150; sexual imagery in, 155; and Shakespeare, 158–59, 160, 161; slaves and slavery in, 153–55, 283–84 (n. 63); sonnets in, 157–58; suicide in, 160–61; unsettling racial identity in, 159–60; U.S. expansionism in, 157, 158; whites and whiteness in, 121, 152, 283 (n. 62), 285 (n. 73); Young America in, 157–60

Mexican War, 8, 21, 148, 182

Mexico, 63, 117, 124, 208; in *Democratic Review*, 121, 126–27; Douglass on, 180, 182; and expansion of slavery, 180; and U.S. imperialism, 19, 121, 124–28, 157, 178

Miller, Samuel, 248–49 (n. 2)

Mississippi River, 38, 39, 43, 59, 63; imperial conflict by, 22, 34; and Louisiana Purchase, 21, 24, 27

Missouri Compromise: debates on, 4, 69, 74–80, 92, 96, 112, 188, 272 (n. 75); and African American literary nationalism, 110; African American responses to, 71–72, 85; and American literary nationalism, 67; Kansas-Nebraska Act's repeal of, 186; and Louisiana Purchase, 21, 69; and Missouri state constitution, 72,

74–79, 91, 100, 109; in newspapers, 72, 73, 75–76, 91; and race, 105; and U.S. borders and boundaries, 68–69, 72; and Vesey conspiracy, 80, 82–85, 267 (n. 30); Walker and, 15, 67–117

Monroe, James, 27, 28, 35

Monroe Doctrine (1823), 39, 237

Moore, Glover, 75, 110

Morse, Samuel F. B., 281 (n. 52)

Morton, Samuel, 126, 138, 161, 297 (n. 74); Douglass vs., 222–23

Mulatto, mulattoes, 226; Douglass as, 196, 218, 226, 227; and Haiti, 194, 196; and Missouri Compromise, 72, 75, 76, 77, 78, 79; and racial mixing, 127

Murphy, Gretchen, 123, 144

Napoleon, 26, 28, 32, 33; in Brockden Brown's *Address*, 34, 36, 38, 62

Nation, 20, 44, 72; and abolition, 44–45; and black nationalism, 84, 87, 189; Brockden Brown and, 13, 15, 22, 23, 24–25, 34, 56; character of United States, 24, 54–55; dislocation of, 1, 14, 141–42, 177, 228, 241, 242; Douglass on, 214–15, 217–18, 231–36; and Haiti, 15, 196–97; and Hawthorne, 123, 177; incarnation of genius of, 120; and Louisiana Territory, 15, 28, 34; and Melville, 148–49, 161–62; and nation building, 2, 24, 29, 43; narratives of, 67, 69, 263 (n. 1); and race, 2, 6, 7, 8, 15, 22, 30, 72, 121, 124, 177, 211, 238; and Walker, 70, 73–74

National identity, 5, 26, 111, 144, 189; dislocation of, 228; fluidity of, 42; incoherent, 162; and *Pierre*, 152; white, 34, 77

National Intelligencer, 76, 83, 99–100, 270 (n. 60)

Nationalists, nationalism, U.S., 4, 6, 20, 22, 43, 68, 69, 87, 124, 217; and African American nationalism, 106, 114; and composite nationality, 197; conflicted and contingent nature of, 67, 72; dislocation of, 182; Douglass as, 181–82, 185, 186, 198; postnational, 218; racist, 7, 122; redemptive, 198; Revolutionary, 106, 198; southern, 113; white, 120, 126, 127, 149, 209, 218. *See also* American literary nationalism; Black nationalists, nationalism

Native Americans, 6, 9–10, 24, 58–59, 69, 153; and American literary nationalism, 2, 5, 246 (n. 7); in Brockden Brown, 17–19, 34–36, 50–57, 60–61, 260 (n. 65); and Federalists, 35, 256 (n. 38); and Indian removal, 26, 35, 59; and Quakers, 35–36; as "savages," 8–9, 35, 58; as writers, 10, 273 (n. 78)

New England, 64, 68; and American literature, 110–12, 240–42

New Era, 204–5, 210

Newfield, Christopher, 111

New Orleans, 27, 28, 33, 63, 94, 108

Newspapers, 70, 101, 107; African American, 67, 97, 115, 204; and Missouri crisis, 72, 73, 75–76, 79; sectionalization of, 72, 98; and Vesey conspiracy, 83, 84, 85. *See also* individual newspapers

New York, 74, 89, 111, 191

New York City, 9–10, 30, 28, 56, 91, 115, 157, 230; African American press in, 89, 185; Walker in, 97; Young America literary circle of, 3, 9, 117, 125, 157

New York Morning News, 128

Niles' Register, 76, 86–87

Nord, David Paul, 72, 265 (n. 11)

North, northerners: abolition in, 44; and American literary nationalism,

69; free blacks in, 72, 77, 78; and Jefferson, 30; and Louisiana Purchase, 29; and Missouri crisis, 74, 76, 78, 84; newspapers in, 70, 73; and sectional conflict, 4, 63, 111; and Vesey conspiracy, 82–85. *See also* Sections, sectionalism

North American Review, 68, 230

North Carolina, 73, 90–91, 93, 94, 109, 164, 173; Walker's *Appeal* in, 108

Nullifiers, Nullification, 67, 109

Nwankwo, Ifeoma, 181–82, 230

Onuf, Peter S., 33, 256 (n. 36)

O'Sullivan, John: "The Democratic Principle," 125; and *Democratic Review*, 125, 128, 131; and filibusterers, 164; and Hawthorne, 122; on Manifest Destiny, 126; on Mexican War, 128; "More! More! More!," 146; on national expansion, 125, 128; optative nationalism of, 124–25; on politics and art, 125; on technology, 146; as Young America literary nationalist, 123–25, 133, 146, 239

Pacific Ocean, 10, 61, 67, 10

Paquette, Robert L., 83

Parker, Thomas, and Lionel H. Kennedy: *An Official Report of the Trials of Sundry Negroes, Charged with an Attempt to Raise an Insurrection in the State of South Carolina* (1822), 83, 85–86, 88

Paul, Nathaniel, 115, 274 (n. 74)

Paul, Saint, 224, 227

Pease, Donald E., 8, 69

Pennsylvania, 52, 54, 59, 91

Pérez, Louis A., Jr., 237, 242

Peter, Saint, 224, 225, 228, 235, 236

Pfister, Joel, 123

Philadelphia, 49, 79, 91, 99, 126, 170, 176; antislavery newspapers in, 72; blacks in, 180; Brockden Brown in, 29; Federalists, 30; Saint Domingue emigrants in, 28; Walker in, 97; yellow fever in, 80

Philippines, 10, 19, 237

Pierce, Franklin, 129, 131, 164, 207

Pinckney, Charles, 78

Pitre, Merline, 201

Plessy v. Ferguson, 220

Pocock, J. G. A., 46

Poe, Edgar Allan, 112, 272–73 (n. 76); "The Fall of the House of Usher" (1839), 136

Polk, James K., 148

Port Folio, 42, 63, 262 (n. 95)

Prichard, James Cowles, 226

Prince Hall, 31, 88

Prince Saunders, 85

Print culture, 101; and black nationalism, 81–82, 87–88; and Vesey conspiracy, 84, 85; and Walker's *Appeal*, 96, 97

Puritans, 9, 11, 135–36, 240–41

Purvis, Robert, 189

Quakers, 35–36

Quinby, Lee, 121

Race, racism, 7, 9, 34, 57, 65, 102, 105, 114–18, 123, 125, 177, 199, 206, 212, 228; Agassiz on, 207–8; and American literary nationalism, 5, 6–11, 121; and antiracism, 30, 31; and biracial marriage, 45, 219–20, 235; in Brockden Brown, 17, 18–19, 44–45; and Caucasian, 126, 132, 161, 217, 220, 222, 297 (n. 74); and color, 105; destabilization of, 47, 141–42; distinctions of, 78, 127; Emerson on, 223–24; and environmentalism, 31, 208, 212–13; hybridity, 235; of Jeffer-

son, 27–28, 104, 251 (n. 19); and
Manifest Destiny, 127–28, 133; and
Missouri crisis, 75, 77, 78, 79; performance of, 142; and polygenesis, 126,
207–8, 210, 212, 222, 251 (n. 19); and
racial categories, 226; and racial
identity, 122, 162, 163, 176, 213, 228,
235; and racial inversion, 224–25;
and racial mixing and entanglement,
121, 127, 128, 133, 145, 223, 224, 227,
228, 277 (n. 20); and racial pride,
227, 236; and racial purity, 121, 122;
and racial stereotypes, 90; "science"
of, 30, 74, 104, 126, 132, 133, 186, 223;
and segregation, 208; and tropics,
209, 212–13; in United States, 209,
211, 216; and U.S. imperialism, 10,
216, 238; Walker on, 73–74. *See also*
Nation; Whiteness
Racial genealogy, 7–8, 44
Railroads, 146, 164
Ramsay, David, 58, 59
Randolph, John, 99
Reconstruction, 186, 202, 218, 219, 229
Redpath, James, 179, 193, 195, 198; "The
Colored People and Hayti," 179–80,
194
Regions, regionalism, 4, 37–38, 67
Remond, Charles Lenox, 189, 190, 224
Remond, Sarah, 224
Republic, republicanism, 2, 11, 33, 46,
68, 79
Republican Party: and Douglass, 183,
184, 186, 187, 194, 201
Republicans, Jeffersonian, 27, 31, 33,
64; Brockden Brown as, 25, 26; and
Haiti, 29, 32, 35; and Indian removal,
26, 35
Rice, George, 204
Richardson, Anna, 221
Richardson, Ellen, 221
Richardson, Charles, 239–41

Richardson, Marilyn, 114
Rights of All, The (newspaper), 97;
agents of, 94–95, 108; circulation of,
100; Walker and, 71, 94, 100
Riss, Arthur, 122–23
Robertson, William, 64
Roediger, David, 178
Roman Catholic Church, 218–19, 224,
225; Douglass on, 219, 224. *See also*
Catholics, Catholicism
Romans, Rome, 183, 218, 221, 223–26,
227, 228, 229, 231
Rowe, John Carlos, 10–11, 13, 19–20, 52,
301 (n. 13)
Rowson, Susanna, *Charlotte Temple*
(1791, 1794), 3, 45, 46; *Slaves in
Algiers* (1794), 258 (n. 52)
Ruffin, George L., 228
Russwurm, John, 96, 183; as coeditor of
Freedom's Journal, 71, 89, 92–93, 108;
on Haiti, 89–90; and Liberian colo-
nization, 90, 93–94, 100
Ruttenburg, Nancy, 20
Rydell, Robert W., 232

Saint Domingue, 179; Brockden Brown
on, 43, 52, 54; and France, 26, 27, 32,
33, 39; and Louisiana Purchase, 26,
65; rebellion in, 23, 26, 28, 29, 31, 36,
54, 65, 79, 82, 156, 197; and Vesey
conspiracy, 84, 85. *See also* Haiti
Santamarina, Xiomara, 69
Santo Domingo: annexation of, 128,
183, 200–201, 202–12, 214–18, 229–
30; Douglass and, 183, 200–218;
Senate opposition to annexation of,
206–7; Sumner and, 203, 207
Saxton, Alexander, 178
Schurz, Carl, 207–9, 212, 215–16, 238
Scott, David, 2, 11
Sections, sectionalism, 37–38, 64, 67,
72, 96, 112; debates on, 74; literary,

4, 69; and Louisiana Purchase, 21, 28–29, 61; and Missouri crisis, 69, 78; and slavery, 63. *See also* North, northerners; South, southerners; West, westerners

Sedgwick, Catharine Maria, 111–12, 113

Shakespeare, William, 120, 286 (n. 76); *Antony and Cleopatra*, 161; *Hamlet*, 158, 161; Hawthorne as, 120; *Othello*, 158–59, 160; romance of, 144; *Romeo and Juliet*, 54

Shumway, David, 239

Simms, William Gilmore, 67, 125, 272 (n. 75); "Americanism in Literature" (1844), 112; *The Yemassee* (1835), 261 (n. 79)

Slaves, slavery, 30, 74, 82, 87, 90–91, 96–97, 121, 153, 156, 164, 179, 181, 185, 191, 258 (n. 52); ancient, 97, 115; black responses to, 72–73; Brockden Brown on, 44–45, 62–63; and capitalism, 141; Democrats on, 129, 131; expansion of, 27–28, 178, 180–81; and Hawthorne, 131, 275 (n. 9); and Jefferson, 27–30, 62; and Louisiana Purchase, 20, 21, 27–32, 34, 58, 62; and Melville, 148; and Missouri crisis, 69, 71, 74; and national expansion, 117, 130, 164; as national sin, 198; and slave trade, 30, 31, 105, 111, 169; in South, 37, 62–63, 163; three-fifths compromise and, 62; uprisings of, 28, 31, 65, 73, 182; and U.S. imperialism, 10, 164, 216; and U.S. vulnerability, 62, 87; and Walker's *Appeal*, 70; white, 45, 163; and Wilmot Proviso, 130

Slotkin, Richard, 9, 11

Smith, Elihu Hubbard, 30, 253 (n. 25)

Smith, Shawn Michelle, 140, 143

Smith-Rosenberg, Carroll, 47

Smyth, Alexander, 77, 79–80

Social Darwinism, 238

Soulouque, Faustin, 196

South, southerners, 7, 28, 62, 77; and American literary nationalism, 5, 67, 69; literary nationalism of, 112–13, 272–73 (n. 76); and Louisiana Purchase, 21, 28, 62; and Missouri Compromise debates, 69; newspapers in, 70, 73; vs. North, 4, 78, 85, 111; and secession, 112, 113; and slavery expansion, 180–81, 253 (n. 23); slavery in, 37, 44–45, 62–63, 70, 163, 186; and slave uprisings, 28, 29, 82; views of, during Missouri crisis, 74, 76, 78; Walker's *Appeal* in, 108–9. *See also* Sections, sectionalism

South Carolina, 44, 78, 81, 98, 175, 180; newspapers in, 70, 72, 83; slaves in, 82, 98; Vesey conspiracy in, 73, 81, 83–84, 200; Walker in, 73; Walker's *Appeal* in, 108

Southern Americas, 62, 67, 68, 82, 85, 202, 209; abolition of slavery in, 209; black emigration to, 179; and Douglass, 180, 181, 182, 187, 191, 192, 198, 211, 212, 216, 218; and race and empire, 178, 179–80; revolutionary black nationalism of, 198, 217

Southey, Robert, 30

Spain, Spanish, 6, 24, 26–27, 29, 43, 61

Spanish-American War, 237

Spencer, Benjamin T., 4, 18

Spiller, Robert E., 18, 67–68

Stanton, Theodore, 221

Stephanson, Anders, 125, 238

Stewart, Maria W., 113–15

Stokes, Claudia, 239, 241

Stowe, Harriet Beecher, 87, 280 (n. 44); *Dred* (1856), 121; *Uncle Tom's Cabin* (1852), 3, 168

Streeby, Shelly, 178

Stuckey, Sterling, 70, 80, 107–8, 271 (n. 65), 284 (n. 63)

Sumner, Charles, 180; and annexation of Santo Domingo, 203, 207–9, 214–15; and Douglass, 218; and Hawthorne, 278 (n. 28); "The Law of Human Progress," 131–32

Taney, Roger, 188–89, 190
Taylor, Zachary, 148
Telegraph, 146
Tenney, Tabita Gilman, 45
Texas, 117, 120–21, 164
Thomas, Jesse B., 75
Tilton, Theodore, 221
Tompkins, Jane, 25
Toussaint L'Ouverture, 29, 228, 232; Douglass on, 234, 300 (n. 95)
Transcendentalism, 111
Tucker, Nathaniel Beverley: *The Partisan Leader* (1836), 112–13
Tucker, St. George, 253 (n. 23)
Turner, Nat, 82, 112, 113, 191
Twain, Mark, 238, 301 (n. 13); *A Connecticut Yankee in King Arthur's Court* (1889), 243–44; *Pudd'nhead Wilson* (1894), 165, 242
Tyler, Moses Coit, 110, 239–40
Tyler, Royall, 45

Undoing, undoings, 1, 13–15, 103, 104, 241–42. *See also* Counterfactuals
United States: boundaries and borders of, 5, 24, 58, 68–69, 72, 191; and Europe, 18, 38–39, 58; expansion of, 128, 213–14; hemispheric hegemony of, 123, 214; millennial destiny of, 122; as mixed-race nation, 127, 210, 213–18; national imaginary of, 191; as white republic, 124, 210, 242
U.S. Congress, 76, 180; antislavery petitions in, 110, 114; and Brockden

Brown, 24, 65–66; debates in, on Missouri, 71, 73, 74–80, 83; and Santo Domingo annexation, 206–8, 217; Senate committees, 206; and slavery, 86, 130, 188–89; and Vesey conspiracy, 83, 84, 85

U.S. Constitution: and constraints on mobility, 92; framers of, 78, 92; meaning of, 72; and Missouri Compromise debates, 75–78; post–Civil War amendments to, 203, 204, 229, 265 (n. 15); preamble to, 77; principles of, 68; privileges and immunities clause of, 75, 76, 78–79, 92; sectional interpretation of, 69; and slavery, 87, 190; and states' rights, 113; three-fifths compromise in, 62, 72, 74–75; violations of, 113

U.S. Supreme Court, 198; and Civil Rights Law (1875), 229; Douglass on, 190, 195, 229; *Dred Scott* decision of, 187–89, 195; *Plessy v. Ferguson*, 220

Unknowingness, 2, 48, 66

Van Buren, Martin, 112–13
Vanderbilt, Kermit, 239
Vesey, Denmark, 83, 91, 96, 113, 189; arrest and trial of, 82; coconspirators of, 84, 85–86; and Douglass, 200; as "fall guy," 80–81; and Haiti, 84; as heroic black revolutionary, 80, 81, 106; as martyr to freedom, 117; and Missouri Compromise debates, 74, 85; pan-Africanism of, 95, 108; and Walker, 73, 81
—conspiracy of, 73, 110; accounts of, 88; details of, 82; execution of leaders of, 80, 82; and Missouri Compromise debates, 80, 83, 85; and newspapers, 84, 85; southern reaction to, 109; trial transcript of, 80, 81,

83–84, 85–88, 106; and Walker, 81–82, 87

Virginia, 30, 64, 77, 112, 113, 149, 165; English planter families of, 153; *Freedom's Journal* in, 93; resolutions of 1799, 74; slave uprisings in, 28

Volney, C. F., 35, 62

Voudon, 142, 145, 217, 280 (n. 42)

Wade, Richard C., 80–81

Waldron, Jeremy, 12, 103

Waldstreicher, David, 4, 20, 69

Walker, David, 5, 71, 94, 116, 183, 186, 236, 271 (n. 65); and African American literary nationalism, 14, 67–117, 128; in Boston, 88, 89, 91; in Charleston, 81; circulation of, 70–71, 73; death of, 74, 113; and Douglass, 226; as freedom fighter, 116; and *Freedom's Journal*, 71, 73, 90, 94; militant reputation of, 70, 81; Missouri Compromise debates and, 67–117; self-declaration of Africanness of, 103; speeches of, 95, 100; travels of, 96, 97; and Vesey, 73, 81, 87

—*David Walker's Appeal, in Four Articles;* . . . (1829), 70, 71, 81, 106, 109, 113; anticolonization of, 99–100; black citizenship and mobility in, 73; black empowerment/uplift strategies in, 70, 96, 108; and circulation, 95–110, 116, 271 (n. 70); counterfactual narration in, 103; Declaration of Independence in, 106–7, 110, 271 (n. 68); diasporic consciousness in, 73; dislocation of race and nation in, 70, 103, 105–6; Egypt in, 226; goals of, 96; influence of, 70; militancy in, 70, 96, 107; oral dimension to, 98; preamble to, 96; readers of, 101–2; as refutation of Jefferson's *Notes on the State of Virginia*, 96, 97,

102, 105; and *The Rights of All*, 95–96; and white sectional nationalism, 113

Walker, William, 164, 238

Warner, Susan, 145

War of 1812, 64, 67–68, 76

Washington, D.C., 93, 94, 99, 114, 164; and Douglass, 231, 236

Washington, Madison, 182, 191–92

Watts, Steven, 25, 38

Webb, Frank J., 204; *The Garies and Their Friends* (1857), 121, 170, 176

Webster, Daniel, 111, 163

Weinstein, Cindy, 145

Wells, Ida B., 232, 233

Wendell, Barrett, 239–40

West, westerners: and American literary nationalism, 5; blacks in, 78; Brockden Brown on, 17, 38–39, 43; Jefferson and, 27; loyalty of, 33; slavery and, 62–63, 70. *See also* Westward expansion

West Indies, 179, 191–92, 234

Westward expansion, 8, 26, 27–28

Wheatley, Phillis, 90

Wheeler, John Hill, 164

White, Ed, 56–57

Whiteness studies, 6–7, 13, 178, 246–47 (n. 11)

Whites, whiteness, 7–9, 76, 121, 126, 132, 143, 161, 162, 165, 178, 217, 220, 222, 297 (n. 74); ambiguity of, 157; and black revolutionism, 30, 36; civilization and, 9, 222; enslavement of, 45, 163; and expansionism, 124, 180; in Hawthorne's "A Select Party," 120; identity of, 47; inferiority of, 131; and Manifest Destiny, 127; privileging of, 6, 220; racial prejudice of, 70, 105, 210; slave power, 84; of U.S. imperialism, 8, 104, 238; violence of, against Indians, 51–54; and White

City, 232; and white racial identity of nation, 6, 28, 40, 54, 56, 77, 88, 104, 106, 121, 241; and white supremacy and superiority, 7, 81, 84, 104, 122, 126, 170, 175, 178, 186, 196, 208, 213, 218, 224. *See also* Anglo-Saxons, Anglo-Saxonism
Whitman, Walt, 3, 5
Whittier, John Greenleaf, 205
Wilentz, Sean, 68, 264 (n. 7), 276 (n. 14)
Williamson, Joel, 155
Wilmot, David, 130
Wilson, Harriet, *Our Nig* (1859), 176
Wilson, Ivy G., 182
Wineapple, Brenda, 147
Women's rights, 45, 114, 226–27, 236

Wood, Gordon S., 18
Worcester Spy, 179–80
World's Columbian Exposition (Chicago, 1893): Douglass and, 116, 231–33

Yellow fever, 47
Young America, 3, 9; and Anglo-Saxon nationalism, 131, 133, 157, 178; and *Democratic Review*, 149; and expansionism, 162, 276 (n. 14); literary nationalists of, 117, 123, 124, 125, 140, 149; and Melville, 148–50; and New York City, 157; in *Pierre*, 157, 158; and technology, 146

Zuckerman, Michael, 29